ECONOMIC RELEVANCE
A Second Look

ROBERT L. HEILBRONER
New School for Social Research

and

ARTHUR M. FORD
Southern Illinois University

GOODYEAR PUBLISHING COMPANY, INC.
Pacific Palisades, California

Library of Congress Cataloging in Publication Data
Main entry under title:
Economic relevance.

   1. Economics—Addresses, essays, lectures.
I. Heilbroner, Robert L.   II. Ford, Arthur M.
HB71.E26   330   75-35004
ISBN 0-87620-262-8

Y-2628-9

Current printing (last digit):
10 9 8 7 6 5 4 3 2 1

Printed in the United States of America

CONTENTS

INTRODUCTION

ROBERT L. HEILBRONER

There is a word that makes professors of economics wince these days, as I can testify from personal experience. The word is, of course, *relevance*. There was a time, not so many years ago, when I could teach an introductory class the mysteries of diminishing marginal utility, explaining why the man in the Sahara desert would not be willing to pay as much for the third pint of water as for the second, confident that when the hands went up it would be because someone wasn't convinced that he shouldn't pay more, because his *total* utility was greater. Now when the hands go up, I know what the question is going to be: "That's clear enough, Professor Heilbroner, but we don't see how it's relevant."

Is it relevant? It is certainly easy enough to understand why it does not seem so. What has diminishing marginal utility to do with giant corporations, the military-industrial complex, imperialism, ghetto life? Isn't time spent on the study of marginal utility simply time diverted from the consideration of real issues, such as these? Worse, isn't the very act of taking seriously a figment like "diminishing marginal utility" apt to cultivate an ivory-tower frame of mind that will no longer wish to come to grips with the brute problems of the real world?

I think these are the kinds of misgivings that first come to the surface when economics students begin to ask questions about the discipline they are learning, rather than merely swallowing it down like so much medicine. Yet I do not think that these initial objections count for very much. As a rule, the aspect of economics that upsets those who begin to study it is its abstractness, its seeming removal from life, but any instructor worth his salt can reassure his students that this abstract quality is a strength and not a weakness if we are to study large-scale questions, and that the "unreality" of many economic conceptions conceals a sharp cutting edge.

Thus, for example, the rationale for progressive taxation hinges on nothing less than the belief that successive dollars of income, like successive pints of water in the Sahara, yield ever smaller increments of enjoyment to its recipients. In the same way, an ivory-tower idea such as pure competition, which every first-year student regards as utterly irrelevant, suddenly turns up as the indispensable starting point for an understanding of Marx's model of capitalism; or the rarified assumptions of Pareto Optimality (that imaginary condition in which no further efficiency or consumer satisfaction can be squeezed out of a given economic system by rearranging its inputs or outputs) take on an unexpected political and social relevance in discussing the problems of socialist planning.

Indeed, by the time an overly zealous instructor is through, the danger is that the shoe will be on the other foot, and that the class will have been persuaded that the charge of "irrelevance" is nothing but the ill-considered objections of those who have not yet mastered the subject. But if he proceeds this far, it is now the instructor who risks becoming irrelevant. For if the initial objections to the abstractions of economics tend to be wide of the mark, this is very far from saying that the feelings of unease aroused by the study of economics have no validity. What the freshman student wants from economics—and hopefully what he will continue to want when he has become an instructor—is a heightened ability to understand, and if possible to control, important aspects of the social system in which he lives. Long after he has accepted the need for the abstract character of economic thought, the student (and his instructor, too) may still feel that economics ignores the most pressing issues of society, or that it gives unsatisfactory answers to them. At that point, the charge of "irrelevance" is no longer an objection that can be easily overcome, but a serious challenge to the validity of the discipline itself.

Is economics a penetrative and reliable guide to the nature of society? The purpose of this book of readings is to demonstrate that it *can* be—that it can ask piercing questions, give cogent advice, and offer deep perspectives on history and on social evolution. To that extent, of course, economics is as relevant as any study of society can be. But in a sense, a book of readings that emphasizes the relevance of economics fails to explain the other side of the coin—the reasons why economics is often not relevant. It would hardly do to fill the pages of this book with examples of economics at its worst. Hence, in this initial essay I shall try to point out why and to what extent economics does not succeed in being useful; that is, why economics frequently does not ask the kinds of questions that would most clearly illumine society, or why it gets unsatisfactory answers to some of the questions it does ask, or why it often fails to offer us the historic or philosophic guidance we seek from it.

The Irrelevance of Economists

Let me begin this analysis of the failures of economics by taking up a touchy issue, but one that cannot be sidestepped. This is the fact that the "irrelevance" that most disturbs many students is the unwillingness of academic economists to ask disturbing or unpleasant questions with regard to the social order, and in particular to avoid social criticism that is radical in intent. Economics thus appears to many students not as a genuinely objective science that sheds its illumination on the good and bad aspects of society alike, but as a kind of high-level apologetics that tends to illumine only those issues for which economics has an "answer," and to overlook those for which it has none.

I think one should admit that, on the whole, this criticism is fairly taken. Most textbooks are bland in tone and pussyfoot around thorny questions. How many, for example, ever mention the issues of imperialism, or present the facts with regard to the concentration of wealth in the United States, or examine very deeply the behavior of the corporate sector? Moreover, students who have gone beyond the textbooks into the professional journals know that this blandness is by no means confined to the delicate atmosphere of the classroom, but extends into the dialogue that the profession holds with itself. With exceptions to which we will return, it is simply a fact that most of the things that economists write about are not matters of burning social importance, and that the prevailing tone in which they do write about social questions tends to be one of a sympathetic conservatism rather than of indignant radicalism.

Why are most economists so conservative in their outlook? Professor Stigler, one of the best-known exponents of the conservative economic philosophy, has contended that it is the result of the training that economists undergo, a training that disabuses them of heady notions with respect to the changes that socialism (or some other form of institutional rearrangement) could bring and that persuades them of the propriety of the market system.[1]

It is probably true that a study of economics does tend to make one wary of sweeping statements and unconsidered jumps, as does the study of almost anything; but I am not wholly convinced by Stigler's argument that conservatism is somehow more *intelligent* than radicalism. I would rather raise another, less elegant, possibility as to why economists are predominantly conservative in their outlooks. This is because economists tend to be located in the upper echelons of the pyramid of incomes and thus tend to share,

[1]Stigler's essay, "The Politics of Political Economists" first appeared in the *Quarterly Journal of Economics* (November 1959) and has been reprinted in his *Essays in the History of Economic Thought*. His actual words read: "It becomes impossible for the trained economist to believe that a small group of selfish capitalists dictates the main outlines of the allocation of resources. . . . He cannot unblushingly repeat such slogans as 'production for use rather than for profit.' He cannot believe that a change in the *form* of social organization will eliminate basic economic problems." (*Essays*, pp. 59-60.)

consciously or otherwise, the conserving attitude that is characteristic of top echelons in all societies. I do not mean that economists are the spineless servants of the very rich. But in 1967 the average income of associate professors of economics (the middle group of academic rankings) was $14,000 and the average income of a "superior" full professor was $21,000. That was sufficient to place associate professors in the top 10 percent of income receivers in the country, and superior full professors in the top 2 percent. I do not see why it should be doubted that economists, like all groups, take on the values and standards of the socioeconomic milieu in which they live.

Yet, what is generally true of the group as a whole is certainly not true of each and every member of it. If, as both Professor Stigler and I believe, the economics profession is marked by a general conservatism of views, there are still economists enough, including some very eminent ones, who do not share the prevailing attitude. What the essays in Part I of this reader will show is that economics can be a formidable vehicle of social criticism and a powerful agent of social change. Hence, it is not the discipline of economics, diminishing marginal utility and all, that can be held responsible for its lack of relevance, if we mean by this its frequently observed failure to direct its attention to important social issues. The fault lies rather with the reluctance of many of its practitioners to use their economic skills for purposes that may be intellectually uncomfortable, or politically risky, or simply out-of-step with their colleagues. To that extent, the irrelevance of which students complain lies not within the discipline of economics but within that of sociology, and the cure for the problem lies in the determination of these students to put their own skills to good use when they take the places of their former instructors.

The Limitations of Economics

But there is a second, and perhaps deeper, meaning to the charge that economics is "irrelevant." It is that the results produced by the application of conventional economics too often have no usefulness—that the answers that economics gives to the problems to which it does address itself are frequently untrustworthy as guides to social policy.

This is a charge that, as we shall shortly see, contains what I believe to be an important core of truth. Yet, before we examine the limits beyond which economic reasoning cannot be relied upon, it is important to establish the things that economics can do and the extent to which it can be put to practical use.

The dividing line, as I see it, that separates what economics can do from what it cannot, lies between the usefulness of economics in explaining the structural characteristics of a market economy, and its relative uselessness in predicting how a market economy will behave in a given instance. To put it differently, economics is extremely relevant when we want to know how the economy is constructed, so that we can trace the numerous possible connections between one part and another, but usually "irrelevant" (by which I mean unreliable) if we want to know exactly which of these connections will be triggered off by a particular economic stimulus.

We shall consider in a moment the reasons for this predictive failing of economics. But at this juncture, while we are still concerned with the positive, relevant aspects of conventional economic thought, it is important to emphasize the enormous contribution that the structural insights of economics offer us. Perhaps only someone who can remember the intellectual confusion of the Great Depression, or the sense of heretical shock that greeted President Kennedy's proposal to spur economic growth by deliberately incurring a federal budgetary deficit, can fully appreciate the gain that has been won by the gradual clarification of the macrostructure of the economy. For the first time in the history of industrial society, we have finally grasped the nature of the mechanism by which the critical aggregates of employment and income are determined. Even if we still cannot manipulate that mechanism very well, the gain in intellectual clarity in itself constitutes the strongest single claim that conventional economics has for its own relevance, and it is a powerful claim indeed.

Microeconomics is not far behind, moreover, in claiming for itself a similar relevance. As with macroeconomics, microeconomics is also a poor guide for prediction. But without its general structural concepts—its ideas of demand and supply, of short and long run, of elasticity and inelasticity, of marginal and average costs and revenues and products—the operations of a market system would be virtually impossible to conceive, much less to control. Because all economic systems, socialism included, depend to some extent on the operation of a market mechanism, the linkages revealed by microeconomic analysis are indispensable for the understanding of all modern industrial systems. Whether it is to determine the best way to alleviate poverty, or to curb pollution, or to distribute scarce resources, or to judge the incidence of a tax, or to gauge the effects of raising the price in a nationalized industry, it is to the apparatus of microeconomics with its criss-crossed lines and its bowl-shaped curves that we must turn if we are to think clearly about the consequences of our actions.

The articles in the second section of this reader are selected to display the power of economic reasoning in action, and I doubt that anyone can read through these selections and not be impressed with the clarification that economic analysis can bring to tangled social problems. Yet I do not want to leave the impression that economics, in its conventional use, is therefore always relevant, in the sense of giving us clear answers and reliable solutions. Rather, as I have already stated, I believe that there are very important limits on the extent of the reasoning power of economics, and it is to these limits that I will now turn.

I have already indicated one of the limits—the poor capabilities of economics as a predictive science. One reason for this, with which we are all familiar, is the inability of the discipline to handle more than a limited number of variables at one time. Economics is forced to approach the complexity of real-life situations exactly as we do in the classroom, on a *ceteris paribus*—other things being equal—basis. But the one-thing-at-a-time approach often breaks down hopelessly when we try to apply it to the world. Economics caluculates its predictions as if the disturbance it studies were the only stone dropped in a pond; whereas in fact, of course, the surface of the pond is covered with the expanding concentric waves of a hundred disturbances. It is hardly surprising that the patterns of the disturbance in which we are interested become confused with or indistinguishable from those of other disturbances, and that our predictions lose their sharpness accordingly.

There is, however, a deeper reason for the unreliability of economic prediction than this. It is that the entire predictive capability of macro- and micro-theory rests on a highly simplified set of assumptions with regard to economic activity itself. These assumptions tell us that human beings constantly try to maximize their receipts (or to minimize their expenditures) as the paramount "behavior directives" in the course of their daily lives. To the extent that firms or factors or consumers do not obey these assumptions—that is, to the extent that they do not constantly strive to move to the frontiers of their production possibilities or their indifference maps— economics loses virtually all of its ability to predict the effects of stimuli on the economic system. In that case, for example, we can no longer state with certainty that a rise in price will result in a fall in the quantity demanded and an increase in the quantity supplied, for both of these classical behavior patterns are nothing but maximization in action.

Do we actually maximize? The concept itself is full of ambiguities. Maximize what, over what period of time? If we define *maximization* to mean "psychic income" or "satisfactions," then the concept loses its predictive power because *any* course of action may be said to lead to maximum "well-being" because we have no objective measure of whether that well-being is really maximized or not. On the other hand, if we define maximization to mean something specific, such as cash income, then we encounter a problem with regard to predictions over any period of time but the shortest run. A giant corporation, consciously trying to maximize its income over a period of ten years, may rationally decide to undertake any number of actions—raising prices, lowering them, increasing or decreasing its current investment—depending on how it interprets the future. In this case, maximization may accurately enough describe the state of mind of the management, but it is of little use in foretelling exactly what management will do.

It is because of these difficulties that economics is much better at describing the *consequences* of various paths that corporations or consumers may follow, than in predicting exactly which they will in fact elect to take. But there is a still more troublesome limit to its power of prediction. For even if we could define maximization in such a clear-cut way that we knew precisely what course of action it would enjoin, economic theory still finds itself stymied before the awkward fact that maximization can lead to different—indeed, contradictory—behavior in different expectational settings.

Ordinarily, as we have just said, a factor or a firm will try to maximize its income by selling more of a commodity when its price goes up and less when its price goes down. But what if the rise in price leads us to believe that prices will continue to rise in the future? In that case, the road to maximization lies in a different direction, namely in holding back on our offerings today so that they can be sold at a better price tomorrow, or in buying more today before the price goes up further. In a word, when expectations tell us that an observed change in price will continue in the same direction, then the rational pursuit of maximum income bids us to behave in exactly the contrary fashion to that which we do "normally."

If this abnormal kind of economic behavior were limited to occasional periods of extreme crisis, we might relegate it to a footnote. But unfortunately, precisely this kind of behavior is all too normal, whenever the economy is moving from one prevailing psychology, whether boom or bust, to another. Then, typically, markets become unstable just because expectations change, and the predictive capabilities of economics diminish accordingly.[2] That is why even the most sophisticated econometric models of the economy do well only as long as the basic direction of economic movement remains the same, but fail badly in telling us the one thing we want to know; that is, when that basic direction itself will change.

Thus, one endemic shortcoming of economic reasoning is its inability to alert us to the timing of economic events. But there is a second quite different limitation to economic theory that interferes with its predictive capability from another angle. It is that economic reasoning is unable to connect changes in the economic variables with changes in the political and social spheres of social activity. As a result, economics makes its predictions as if the stimuli and constraints of the market were the only forces impinging on the activities of men, ignoring entirely the social and political and psychological consequences of economic action. To put the matter differently, conventional economics deals with the economy as if it were only a mechanism for allocating goods and services, and overlooks the fact that the economy is also a mechanism for allocating privilege and power.

As a result, economic predictions often fail because they do not anticipate the "feedbacks" of noneconomic activity. Typically, for instance, economic theory will project a growth path by calculating the effects of labor

---

[2]The most searching critique of the shortcomings of the conventional economics can be found in Adolph Lowe, *On Economic Knowledge* (New York: Harper & Row, 1965, paperback, 1970).

and capital inputs, capital-output ratios, and so forth, in this way arriving at a course of economic output in the future. But the trouble with these projections is that economic theory does not take into account the noneconomic changes that the growth process itself may initiate. Economics does not, for example, connect the trajectory of growth with social frictions to which the growth process may give rise, or with political resistances that may be encountered if growth brings a shift in income as between regions or social groups. Nor does it ask whether a growing level of income may alter our lifestyles or our working habits in such a way as to change our labor inputs. In a word, economic theory gives us a picture of change from which the political or sociological elements have been rigorously excluded, although it is just these factors that are often all-important in determining the ultimate results of economic change itself.

This restricted scope of economic vision serves to limit the relevance of economic theorizing even more severely than its inability to handle the vagaries of economic behavior. Indeed, here is where the freshman's unease about the "abstractness" of economics comes home with a vengeance. But at this level of analysis the student's objections are not so easily brushed aside. No one denies that abstraction is an essential precondition for a social science if it is to reduce the complexity of the real world to manageable proportions. But we can now see that the sharper and clearer the abstract model we create, the less "interdisciplinary" that model tends to be. Thus we learn how to handle the idea of a "firm," but only by blotting out the political and sociological attributes of real corporations; or we invent the very convenient fiction of a "factor of production," but only at the cost of losing sight of the existence of individuals who are also voters and members of social classes.

The fault, however, is not just that of a failure of nerve on the part of economists. *The essential problem is that we do not know the nature of these subtle linkages between the economic mechanism and the political and social spheres of activity.* What we lack, in a word, is a unifying theory of social change in which the distinctions of "economics" and "sociology" and "political science" would yield to a new "holistic" science of society. As we shall see in our next section, there was a time when economics seemed to be close to such a holistic science. It is not today. Instead we stand impotent before the problem of understanding how to integrate our knowledge of the economic structure and of economic behavior (unpredictable though the latter often is), with a corresponding knowledge of political or sociological structures or of political or social behavior. The discovery of such a new integrating model or paradigm would be the greatest triumph of social science in our time, but at the moment no such paradigm exists. As a result, we must admit to a profound limitation to economic analysis for which no solution is now in sight.

The Relevance of Economic Philosophy

These considerations bring us to the last meaning that we can attach to the word *relevance*—the possibility of using economics as a guide for social philosophy, in the sense of helping us to understand the direction in which our social system is headed, or still more important, the direction in which it should head.

In the light of the severe limitations that we have put upon the predictive power of economics, can we really look to economics as a reliable guide for the future? The answer is necessarily disconcerting. We cannot. At best, an economist who postulates a rationale for the historic setting of our time or who projects the shape of society into the future is engaged in no more than a kind of controlled speculation. That these speculations can be both eloquent and plausible we shall leave for the reader to discover for himself in Part III of this book. But it would be wrong to pretend that even at their most convincing these speculations attain the status of genuine scientific effort, at least in the meaning that economics usually arrogates to that word.

This is an important matter to which we shall revert at the very conclusion of this essay. But meanwhile, for students who have read the works of Smith, Ricardo, Mill, or Marx, this must seem like a serious retreat for economics. For surely the great classical writers did not regard their large-scale economic philosophies as mere "controlled speculations." In their hands economics seemed capable of presenting a perspective on the present and the future in full accord with the scientific canons of their day. Why, then were they able to create economic philosophies of greater power than we can?

From the vantage point of contemporary history, we can discern two attributes of classical economic thought from which this extraordinary self-assurance emanates. One of these, which is frequently overlooked, is the strong feeling of social destination that infuses all the classical writers. Smith, Ricardo, Malthus, Mill, and above all Marx, firmly believed that they knew the direction in which society was heading, and moreover they strongly approved of that destination as being in the best interests of mankind. Thus, economics became for them not alone an objective explanation of the "laws of motion" of their respective economic societies, but also an instrument to assist the evolution of those societies in the various directions in which they wished them to hurry.

A second common attribute of their thought was their frank willingness to discuss their societies from the point of view of class composition and conflict. In place of the neutral "factors of production" with which modern theory deals, the classical writers spoke openly of a contest of landlords, workers, and capitalists, so that their theories of distribution (which were intimately intertwined with their theories of growth) were also guides to major political and social tensions within their societies. And whereas the outcome of the struggle among the classes was differently diagnosed by each writer, according to his differing assessments and assumptions regarding resources, demographic behavior, technology, and the psychology of the social classes, in every instance his pursuit of the logic of economic interaction led him directly to an associated drama of political and social change.

In our own day, both these underlying premises of classical reasoning have lost much of their erstwhile force. The blows of 20th-century history, devastating for the prospects of liberal capitalism and orthodox socialism alike, have largely obscured the vista of welcome historic destination that unified and fortified so much of classical thought. Today the great majority of social scientists, economists included, stand before the realities of 20th-century technology, bureaucracy, nationalism, and militarism with a sense of genuine perplexity, or even despair, that blurs the vision of even the boldest of them.

Then, too, the increased complexity and growing modest affluence of Western society have equally undermined the second of the premises of classical analysis—that the dynamics of social change could be directly predicted from the clash of social classes. In our day, the once decisive clash of classes has given way to the cohesion of a "mass society" in which the sources of social conflict take on wholly new forms, such as the conflict between generations. As a result, even the most fully worked-out philosophy of historic change and social evolution—the imposing structure of Marxism— finds itself in need of rethinking its traditional views in the light of present-day realities.[3]

Against these vast historic changes, it is hardly surprising that economics has lost the self-assurance of a former age. The problem of constructing a plausible model of social change is much more difficult in our day than in a simpler age, for all the reasons we have discussed in the previous section as well as in this one. Yet it is one thing to take cognizance of the difficulties of a task, and another to abandon it. Rarely has there been a period of history as much in need of illumination as our own, and however partial or uncertain, the controlled speculations of economic thought, meshed as best they can be with political and sociological analysis, still constitute the best response that we can make to our human situation.

Perhaps in the end, the answer to this impasse of the social sciences lies in a new appraisal of the relevance of *science* itself. When we said before that economics could offer no foresight that could be given the name "scientific," we may have inadvertently opened the direction in which to seek the new paradigm of social unity that we need. The word "scientific," as we commonly use it, refers today to a rigorous model of a mathematical

[3]The evolution of Marxist thought can be followed in such books as Ernest Mandel's *Marxian Economic Theory* (see the last essay in this collection), Ralph Milliband's *The State in Capitalist Society,* or in the various contributions to Erich Fromm's *Socialist Humanism.*

kind from which all considerations of social values have been carefully excluded. In the great question of human destination, however, values must surely occupy a central place: the future is meaningful because it offers us choice. Perhaps, then, the very aim of economic philosophy as a "scientific" guide to the future must give way to economic philosophy as a consciously value-laden guide—a guide that uses the enormous powers of scientific analysis, not to predict the future, but to assist society in reaching the goals that it has elected to pursue. In such a basic reorientation of the discipline, economics would become the handmaiden of politics, advising us of the institutional and behavioral and technical conditions necessary to achieve a destination that society has chosen through its political processes. Such a far-reaching suggestion takes us well beyond the confines of this essay, although not, I am glad to say, beyond the confines of what may ultimately be most relevant for economic thought.[4]

---

[4]See R. Heilbroner, "On the Possibility of a Political Economics," *Journal of Economic Issues* (December 1970), and "On the Limited Relevance of Economics," *The Public Interest* (Fall 1970).

To our wives

PART I

ECONOMIC CRITIQUES

As one of the authors in this collection of essays points out, "economics long has suffered from a superiority complex." This occurred for a number of reasons. First, among the social sciences, economists have the most rigorous, highly developed, mathematically oriented, theoretical structure. Second, this theoretical structure has produced a set of propositions with seemingly wide application. Consequently, economists have been called to counsel kings and presidents and, as a general rule, being admitted to court almost always raises one's self esteem. Finally, economists have received a significant degree of popular acclaim with their opinions being sought by labor, management, state governments, and so on. Respectability has gone so far as to allow some economists to provide "Ann Landers" type services for readers in several news media. Still, for all the acceptance and acclaim, there has been concern in some quarters of the profession about the way the discipline has been developing.

1. Has economics, in the quest for rigor, developed models based on theoretical assumptions that have no basis in the social system in question?
2. Has the profession been uncritical about its philosophical foundations?
3. Has there been a tendency for the profession to confuse increased proficiency in mathematics with increased economic knowledge?
4. Has the profession been dominated by one particular paradigm?
5. Why are there some questions that the profession either tends not to ask or about which it has very little to say?

In short, has economics become too abstract in theory and too narrow in its methodology to come to grips with the basic social issues of our time? Does the poor record in economic forecasting of late lie in the fact that established theory has no adequate explanation of unemployment-inflation?

It is our feeling that the issues raised here are so basic and fundamental to the economic profession that they must be faced. Consequently, to get at this question the first part of our reader presents a sampling of economists who maintain, frequently for quite different reasons, that the major thrust of economics in the postwar era has been misdirected.

A.F.

Economists Are Asking: "What Went Wrong?"

KAREN J. WINKLER

The following criticisms of Harvard's economic program reflect the critical issues facing the economic profession as a whole.

Spiraling inflation coupled with a crippling recession took professional economists by surprise in 1974. With the economic crisis continuing to worsen in the past year, they have been asking:

1. "Where did our predictions go wrong?"
2. "How useful are our analytic tools?"

Slowly, some economists have begun to re-evaluate their discipline.

The self-criticism came to an explosive head at Harvard University this year when Nobel prize-winning economist Wassily W. Leontief publicly denounced his department as too narrow. He resigned a year before retirement after 44 years as a faculty member.

Mr. Leontief's attack had been preceded by another indictment of the economics department by an outside visiting committee of eminent economists. They called it aloof and over-specialized.

The controversy at Harvard represents not simply the specific problems of one faculty. It reflects deeper concerns troubling the economics profession as a whole.

In many respects, the way in which the Harvard department has grown in the last 30 years mirrors the direction in which the discipline has developed generally.

From Karen J. Winkler, "Economists Are Asking: What Went Wrong?" *The Chronicle of Higher Education* (May 5, 1975), pp. 1, 8. Reprinted with the permission of the publisher.

According to tradition it was a diverse, mostly policy-oriented department, interested in the 1940s with applying John Maynard Keynes's theories of governmental manipulation of the economy.

In the early 1960s, most of its present members agree, the faculty believed it would lose prestige unless it brought in some of the new econometricians—persons who use complex statistical methods to test economic hypotheses and who were considered the new leaders in research. Such scholars have tended to be more theoretically oriented, concerned as much with mathematical models that explain the economy as with specific matters of economic policy.

Now there is "somewhat less diversity" in outlook, says James S. Duesenberry, chairman of the economics department, plus "a swing away from more direct interest in politics" as some of the older, more policy-minded faculty members retire.

The profession also underwent, first, the Keynesian revolution in theory in the 1930s and 1940s and then the mathematical shift in the 1950s and 1960s.

"The new model was the physical sciences," says the dean of the Harvard faculty, Henry Rosovsky, who is also an economist. It seemed that basic laws governing the economy could be discovered and verified.

"Eventually we became too one-sided in the emphasis on mathematical theory," he says, "and more and more divorced from some of the crucial questions facing the world." He adds:

"It will change. I look forward in the next 20 years to a new political economy, informed and enriched by scientific advances."

Such change will come, however, only as some key questions begin to be answered. They include:

1. Has economic theory become too abstract?
2. Has one school of theory become too dominant?
3. Have economists failed to criticize their own assumptions?
4. Has economics become too specialized?

One of the commonest charges against academic economists is that their studies have little relation to the real world. "A lot of economists do elegant analyses, using lots of statistics about the world," William M. Capron, associate dean of the Kennedy School of Government and Public Administration at Harvard, says, "without ever spending time to understand the actual context of the problem they're studying."

People Treated 'as Numbers'

Part of the context that some mathematical theories tend to miss are "some of the nuances of human behavior," Mr. Duesenberry believes. "Models treat people as numbers."

To do aggregate analyses, they make the assumption that people "maximize," or produce and consume as much as they possibly can, Marc J. Roberts, professor of economics, says.

Some theorists have also lost contact "with the political and legislative background" of economic problems, Mr. Dusenberry says. People like John Dunlop [former dean of the Harvard faculty and now Secretary of Labor] were directly involved in the politics of labor economics, and when it came to policy, they knew the people, the laws."

There is also concern that on one hand the questions economists emphasize are too often determined by the availability of the data they need while, on the other hand, some of their new theories are so complex that the finely detailed information needed to test them is not obtainable.

'Facts Are Just Facts'

If an economic theorist becomes too concerned with solving questions of policy, however, he runs the danger of considering only what is practically feasible at the moment, points out another Harvard Nobel laureate, Kenneth J. Arrow.

"He has to have the freedom to speculate, to come up with alternative policies no one has thought of or is likely to accept for 10 or 12 years."

Moreover, "without some kinds of models, facts are just facts, with no intellectual framework to talk about them," economist Richard E. Caves says.

Most theorists are constantly refining their models by testing them against reality, he adds. Many econometricians move easily back and forth between the realms of theory and practice.

The problem, others point out, is that only the most brilliant stars in the economics firmament are capable of both sophisticated mathematical analysis and concrete practical applications of it. "There are too many second-rate theorists," Mr. Capron says.

For students most interested in applying economic theory in policy roles, the Kennedy School at Harvard is building up M.A. and Ph.D. programs in public administration.

Faculty members in both areas agree that a complete separation of applied studies in the Kennedy School and theoretical pursuits in the economics department is undesirable. "There just isn't a neat split between applied and theoretical work as in some of the sciences—like, say, engineering," Mr. Duesenberry says.

Appointments 'Conditioned'

Crucial to keeping diversity in a discipline is "how a succession of younger people is made," says Nobel-winner Leontief. "When you have a certain attitude pervading economics as the fancy mathematics does, it conditions the tenure appointments that departments make."

"We've started breeding ourselves," he charges.

"I wanted to see a wider scope of interpretations," he said in an interview, "but the Harvard economics department didn't listen. So I'm leaving."

Other senior professors, including John Kenneth Galbraith, have also been concerned that Harvard may be becoming one-sided. They have urged the establishment of a new "experimental program and committee" within the economics department that would explore alternative curricula.

For several years, part of the friction between students and faculty members has focused on the department's refusal to give tenure to radical teachers using Marxist analyses of capitalism. While many students want specifically Marxist courses, "there has also been a basic concern that they're getting one kind of economic approach and that is being passed off as *the* approach," says Stephen A. Marglin, who was granted tenure before he became a Marxist.

"The issue is not just political discrimination. The department ought to offer different approaches on an equal footing. Marxism is just one of them," he says.

It appeared to some members of the visiting committee that evaluated the department last year that the radical cause was serving primarily as a focus for a much wider student discontent with aloofness and methodological bias in the department.

On the other side, some tenured faculty members charge that the radical students will be satisfied only if theirs is the dominant methodology. While the department has not offered tenure to any of its own Marxist assistant professors, they point out, it is bringing in a radical from outside next year with tenure.

The debate over Marxism in economics is not unique to Harvard. At its annual meeting this year the American Economics Association voted to investigate charges that seven radicals had been fired at two universities because of their politics.

Nevertheless, there is a danger that the increasingly tight academic job market may force students into the dominant mathematical mode because "that's the best way to get a job," Mr. Roberts says. The economic crisis in higher education will raise the question, "What price dissent?" he predicts.

Marxists are not the only ones who feel squeezed out of economics departments. "Policy-oriented people have been siphoned out of the profession," says Lawrence E. Lynn, Jr., an economist with the Kennedy School. They are being offered jobs in government, in business, in schools of public administration, law or business, he says, but not in traditional economics departments.

Mr. Duesenberry agrees that today's students and faculty members seem less diverse than 20 years ago, but then "if you can't find young people like the old, maybe the older ones weren't so eclectic when they were young, either."

"Looking for junior sages isn't too profitable," he says.

Suppositions Not Questioned

Many Marxists contend that their profession failed to predict the current economic crisis because economists did not question the basic laws assumed to govern the economy.

"They didn't see themselves as apologists for capitalism, but that's what happened," Mr. Marglin says. "They didn't spend enough time exploring different ways the economy works."

There are many more economists of different persuasions who also believe that too often they have avoided questioning the presuppositions that condition the economic models they develop.

"There's no real alternative structure" to the mathematical theories being built, no alternative that can cope with the increasing complexity of the economy as well as the statistical techniques can, Mr. Arrow believes.

"But we should recognize that we make some assumptions we can't verify, that a half-baked loaf is better than none but it is still half-baked," he says.

"When I teach I'm generally critical of myself. I tell my students, 'These are my assumptions. They may be wrong.' "

Many of his colleagues simply lay out the theory they teach as a "given," he maintains. They tend to be the most popular, he says wryly, perhaps because it confuses students to ask them to criticize their teachers.

The complexity of courses in theory also tends to make students passive, other economists contend. Mathematical techniques have become so sophisticated, they say, that students spend much of their time trying to master them and never ask, "What use are they?"

"There is a tendency, not altogether healthful, for any science to get a little too technical and abstract because the better students find that most interesting or intellectually challenging," says Thomas C. Schelling, who holds a joint appointment in both the Kennedy School and the economics department at Harvard.

"But it often means they lose their general critical ability to cope with any new or different problem."

When he sits on Ph.D. orals, Mr. Schelling says, he asks candidates how they would go about solving some problem unfamiliar to them. Usually they don't even know how to start grappling with it, he says, unless they have covered it in their theory courses.

Students Are Inhibited

"They're remarkable inept and shamefully unable to say anything to show that two years of study have helped them think critically," he says.

The fact that most rewards, in terms of job offers and opportunities to be published and read, go today to the mathematical experts also inhibits students from making their own judgments, others say.

"We praise them so much for abstract reasoning and making imaginative uses of analytic tools," Mr. Lynn suggests, that they are afraid to try anything different.

Generally, the students in the Kennedy school's program are less passive than those pursuing a traditional Ph.D., says the school's associate dean, Mr. Capron. "Their orientation is to question policies, to think of alternatives. But even we have a problem with students being intimidated by high-powered theoreticians."

Teachers Are Specialists

A major complaint of graduate students at universities like Harvard has been that their individual courses are becoming more and more specialized, while nothing in the curriculum helps them link the different classes together.

Part of the problem is that their teachers have become specialists—not always interested in anything but their own fields. Within the country's prestigious economics departments, many observers note, faculty members tend to be big-name stars who run their own fiefdoms of courses and graduate students and brook no interference.

Aside from questions of ego, the increasing isolation of many economists may also stem from the very broadening of their discipline.

New subjects have been developed in recent years—e.g., in the economics of urban life, of education, of health care. Each has its own questions, its own applications, and both researchers and policy analysts admit they find it difficult to master most of them and become the generalists of an earlier era.

At the same time economics has been "about 30 years behind" in developing some special fields, Mr. Duesenberry says. "We haven't structured the discipline in terms of the great social problems" facing society, he says.

The literature on economic development, for example, Mr. Rosovsky points out, "has left out more and more that is crucial to understanding the growth of underdeveloped nations."

Nor have departmental curricula, and to some extent the economics profession as a whole, been structured to grapple with a major problem like inflation.

No Synthesis

"Inflation has not been given nearly the attention one would expect in our curriculum," Mr. Duesenberry says, "because it cuts across lines of specialization."

Since it involves theories of labor-management relations, of industrial organization, of money and banking policy, no one has really yet synthesized all the facets of the problem.

Economists dealing with large questions such as inflation must take the theories developed in the different specialties and try to put them together to gain some overall insight.

"Unfortunately," says Mr. Duesenberry, "the different theories don't always fit neatly together."

Nevertheless, economics students and practitioners are going to "have to know something about everything," Mr. Arrow says, "because the whole economy is interrelated."

If the profession is imposing more and more rigorous demands on its members, those who cannot meet them should drop out, he says. "After all, do you want to have people monkeying around in your economy who can't think in complicated terms?" he asks.

In the final analysis, too abstract a theory, too narrow a focus on one methodology, too uncritical an acceptance of economic laws, or too specialized a structure of the discipline may all have contributed to the failure of economists to predict the present strange combination of inflation and recession.

'A New Phenomenon'

But most economists believe their lack of foresight was inevitable. "It was a new phenomenon that no one in any discipline really predicted," Mr. Lynn says.

The greatest problem for the economics profession has probably been that legislators, the public, and probably even the economists themselves have expected too much.

In the 1940s, John Maynard Keynes's theories of pump-priming and government regulation of the economy were presented to the American public as a panacea for tempering the cycles of inflation and depression of the 1920s and 1930s. Some economists may argue that World War II did more to stimulate the American economy than any Keynesian policy, but the influence of Keynes raised the economists to a new level of admiration.

It gave the economics profession a prestige it will have to live down.

What's Wrong with American Economics?

LEON H. KEYSERLING

A former chairman of the Council of Economic Advisers argues that economic policy has worked poorly, due in part to the poverty of formal economics.

During the early New Deal, I worked as legislative assistant to the great U.S. Senator from New York, Robert F. Wagner. He introduced numerous measures of lasting significance, including the National Industrial Recovery Act, the Social Security Act, the National Labor Relations Act, and the U.S. Housing Act. Whenever the Senator was asked whether these laws would be sustained by the Supreme Court, his answer invariably was: "If it works, it's constitutional." This turned out to be correct forecasting, and not entirely without merit as a commentary upon the nature of the judicial process.

Clearly, the best judgments about national economic policies are not to be discerned in the mist of ratiocination, but in the light of actual experience. For about 20 years to date, there must have been a lot wrong with these policies, in that they have worked poorly most of the time, and not nearly well enough at any time.

The First Requirement: Optimum Economic Growth

The first requirement imposed upon our economic system (or any other, for that matter) is to sustain an optimum rate of real economic growth,

Excerpted from Leon H. Keyserling, "What's Wrong With American Economics," *Challenge* (May–June 1973), pp. 18–25. Copyright © 1973 by International Arts and Sciences Press, Inc. Reprinted with the permission of International Arts and Sciences Press, Inc.

i.e., that sufficient to assure reasonably full but not excessive use of growing production capabilities. Large idleness means large waste, plus arrant discontent; and no nation can afford that. At least since 1953, our average annual growth performance has fallen lamentably short of the optimum. We have experienced what might be called a "roller-coaster" prosperity, with aborted periods of upturn being followed by periods of stagnation and then recession. This cycle is now on the way to repeating itself for the fifth time within two decades. Moreover, each successive upturn, at its peak, has tended to leave us with more unused manpower and plant than the peak of the previous upturn. Nobody knows how close we are to the peak of the current upturn, but there are few now who dare to forecast that this peak will bring unemployment even nearly as low as it was in 1969 (3.5 percent).

The upturn from 1961 to around the middle of 1970 was claimed by the proponents of "The New Economics" to augur a significant break in the unsatisfactory pattern, through application of superior national policies. There was much prideful talk about the "longest peacetime advance on record" (viewing the Vietnam engagement as minor in an economic sense). But the highly unsatisfactory upturn from 1961 to 1964 was a largely "autonomous" reaction to the preceding recession; there were no new and large injections of stimulative national policy. And even after the massive tax reductions of 1964 (erroneous, for reasons soon to be discussed), there was general agreement by early 1966 that an absolute downturn was in prospect, which was postponed mainly by the vast and unexpected acceleration of spending for the South-Asian war. Even with this, a pronounced slowdown in the rate of real economic growth took effect from 1966 onward, although few identified it or proposed remedial action until the recession began in 1970.

During the period 1953–72 as a whole, our average annual rate of real economic growth was only 3.5 percent. Meanwhile, conservatively estimated on the basis of the historical record and other relevant analysis, a real growth rate averaging annually in the neighborhood of 4.3 percent was needed during this period to maintain reasonably full resource use. The costs of this long-term retreat from reasonably full resource use have been staggering. During 1953–72 as a whole, the difference between the actual and the optimum growth rate involved the forfeiture of almost $1.8 *trillion* of total national production, measured in 1970 dollars, and about 45 million man-years of employment opportunity. And if we were to do no better in future—which seems the prospect without a veritable revolution in national economic policies—we would forfeit during 1973–80 another $1.7 *trillion* of total national production, again measured in 1970 dollars, and 16.5 million man-years of employment opportunity, the very much lower employment loss being due to trends in productivity, patterns of employment, and pay. The employment deficiency is based upon the true level of unemployment, taking into account full-time unemployment as officially measured, the full-time equivalent of part-time unemployment, and the concealed unemployment of those not officially counted as unemployed because shortage of job opportunity dissuades them from "participation" in the civilian labor force.

It has been argued in various quarters that our recent or current national output would be adequate in the future if income distribution were improved and allocations to the public sector were enlarged. Granted the need for these changes, this argument is frivolous. For the changes themselves are much easier to obtain, both economically and politically, when growth is high than when it is low. And although we may use unwisely much of what we produce, we cannot put to wiser use what we do not produce; and our pressing needs, both domestic and international, extend even beyond our optimum growth capabilities in the foreseeable future. Most important, low growth means high unemployment, the evil of evils.

The environmentalists advance the further argument that economic growth brings in its wake a host of ills, including pollution of the air and water. But the additional resources required to build factories and other facilities which do not pollute, and to build automobiles which do not emit noxious fumes, will be unavailable without optimum growth—or they would be available without such growth only at the price of creating an irreconcilable conflict between those who want to abolish pollution and those who want better schools, improved health services, the restoration of our deteriorating urban areas, and the like.

The Second Requirement:
Meeting Priority Needs

The failure to deal even tolerably with the great priorities of our domestic needs—too enduring to be fairly attributable to the Vietnam war—is inseparably associated with the unsatisfactory rate of economic growth. At existing tax rates, the $1.8 *trillion* shortfall in economic growth since 1953 has brought about a loss of at least $450 billion in tax revenues at all levels of government. And if the low average growth rate were to persist through 1980, we would forfeit more than another $400 billion in tax revenues, again measured in 1970 dollars.

The amplitude of common knowledge on the subject makes it unnecessary to detail the quantitative and qualitative shortages of facilities and services in our public schools; in available medical care at tolerable costs; in decent housing and urban renewal efforts; in modern transportation systems; in antipollution programs; in treatment of our senior citizens and disabled people; in the care of disadvantaged children; in programs to restore reasonable "parity" of income and public services to farm families and others in rural areas; and in other efforts to liquidate poverty and reduce deprivation (above poverty, but below an acceptable American standard of living).

The Third Requirement: Social Justice

A perfect definition of justice is not available, but gross injustice is easy to define, and it is all around us. As late as 1971 (and available data indicate that there has been further maldistribution since then), 42 percent of the total money income flowing to all multiple-person families went to the highest income fifth, and 66 percent to the highest two-fifths, while only 6 percent went to the lowest fifth, and only 18 percent to the lowest two-fifths. Among unattached individuals or single-person families, 50 percent went to the highest fifth, and 74 percent to the highest two-fifths, while only 3 percent went to the lowest fifth, and only 11 percent to the lowest two-fifths. This is iniquitous in terms of social justice, and, for reasons soon to be disclosed, utterly incompatible with a satisfactory growth performance.

Misapplication of Lord Keynes:
The Allocations Problem

Several decades ago, Lord Keynes observed that the maldistribution of income was generating too low a level of consumption, relative to the growing ability to produce. He found that an excessive share of total income accruing to those higher up in the income structure, who spend smaller portions of their incomes for immediate consumption than those lower down in the structure, generated more saving for private investment than could enduringly be absorbed. Hence, overcapacity, and massive unemployment of manpower and plant. Keynes therefore proposed that public borrowing be used to tap off the excessive private saving and put it to work through investment in enlarged public goods and services, which he also deemed manifestly desirable per se. But this was not *all* of the thought of the great Englishman. He insisted that this "compensatory" program could not succeed unless many other measures were adopted to improve the distribution of private income.

When the New Economics, from 1961 onward, came to wrestle with the evil of inadequate economic growth, the diagnoses upon which Keynes focused was clearly applicable, although the situation was not nearly as acute as the one he confronted. In each period of upturn during 1953–64, during the "roller-coaster" performance, the rate of growth in the investment which adds to plant and equipment had far outrun the rate of growth in consumption, which on analytical grounds should include both private consumption and public demand for goods and services. Income maldistribution all along the line, abetted by public policies, contributed to these misallocations of resources and economic activity.

But the New Economics took the position that it made little difference *where* the effort to increase demand was injected into the economy. Ignoring the central concern of most of the great economists about allocation of resources and incomes, the new thinkers forgot that the injection of increased *power* to spend would not *pro tanto* increase *actual* spending or demand, if the injections were grossly misplaced. Thus there was repeated resort to massive tax reduction, especially in 1964, which greatly augmented the availability of funds to those who were already "oversaving" and/or relatively overinvesting. Meanwhile, the composition of the tax reductions did not sufficiently augment the spending power of consumers. Simultaneously, the reckless tax reduction prevented the needed increases in allocations to public demand. In practical results, the New Economics gave the economy a very temporary "shot in the arm," followed by all of the unfortunate developments since 1966, abetted, to be sure, by the mistakes of later public officials who said "We are all Keynesians now."

The prevalent policy of insufficient expansion of the money supply in the long run accompanied by a fantastic increase in interest rates is subject to the same criticism. It was designated ("successfully") to reduce the real economic growth rate far below the optimum rate; and all of the inevitable consequences followed. The policy stimulated what needed restraint and repressed what needed expansion, thus feeding the fat and starving the lean. And the policy has been grossly inflationary, because rising interest costs are pyramided throughout the price structure.

The policy of repressed public spending, in all its aspects, has had precisely the same misallocation effects.

The Spurious Dichotomy between "Economic" and "Social" Objectives

A former Chairman of the Council of Economic Advisers in a liberal Administration stated recently before the Joint Economic Committee that President Nixon's latest budget represents "an impeccable economic program, but an intolerable social program." This confusing statement is tragically typical of recent and current thought and action. For no one can gainsay the proposition that the dominant purpose of our economic endeavors is to serve the ultimate social needs and aspirations of our people, reflected in rising private incomes and enlarged public services, and improved distribution of benefits, through action both private and public. Even more surprising is the failure to recognize, on an empirical basis, that the very reason we have done so poorly in a narrow economic sense is that we have neglected adequate private and public allocations to what we loosely call social needs. In a grossly underdeveloped society such as India, the hard necessity of choice may be temporarily to repress social advance, despite indescribably low living standards, in order to accumulate enough funds and resources for industrial development. But in the United States, we have never suffered, within the memory of living man, from inadequate accrual of resources for investment and production purposes when ultimate demand in the form of both private and public consumption was sufficient to clear the market of the potential product. If I were to make a list on one sheet of paper of our purely economic needs, and on another sheet of paper a list of the range and scope of our social needs, the two lists would turn out to be virtually identical, or at least functionally inseparable in terms of practical action. Actually, I would not know on which of the two lists to put many items. Is investment in children or housing "economic" or "social"?

The Confusion between Means and Ends

The neglect of appropriate attention to the three great ends of growth, priorities, and justice (depending basically upon the allocation of resources and incomes) implies necessarily that the specific policies and programs are not properly developed and applied. For policies in such fields as taxation, money, social security, housing, agriculture, income supports and welfare, and the international economy—to mention some of the most important—are merely *means* toward the three great ends, and must fall short if these ends are not constantly defined and reviewed in highly quantitative terms. Practically every policy I define as a "means" affects the distribution of income and resources in one way or another; and how can these policies be satisfactory if we do not bear constantly in mind what allocations we need on economic and social grounds?

A striking example of the failure to move toward this equilibrium or balance is to be found in the recent and current "control" efforts with respect to prices, wages, and profits. For these, too, are merely means toward allocations of resources and incomes in accord with the three great ends. The controls program has been applied and judged as if the *sole* purposes were to restrain the rate of price inflation. But as least equally important is the role of wages in the expansion of consumption toward improved equilibrium and optimum economic growth. Regardless of whether wage trends are now running too high or too low, it is amazing that the role of wages in consumption never surfaces in the public evaluation of the controls. My own belief is that we have suffered under a controls program which, in the name of fighting inflation, is excessively repressive upon growth, priorities, and justice.

The Erroneous Campaign against Inflation

What I have said above emphasizes the point that a rising, stable, or falling price level is not good or bad per se. It all depends upon the impact of price trends upon the three great ends I have stressed—a matter almost completely disregarded in the prevalent approaches.

Too many have overlooked that, during 1922–29, aside from falling farm prices, we had a remarkably stable price level. (I refer here to consumer, wholesale, and industrial prices. Stock prices are not properly used to measure whether or not inflation is in process; also, favorable stock trends at times indicate resource and income imbalances which bode ill for the future—again witness 1929.) The unusually stable price level during the 1920s plus increasing productive gains yielded a growth in business profits and investments which far outran the trends in wages and farm income. And as Paul H. Douglas and John Kenneth Galbraith have pointed out, this was the fundamental cause of the Great Depression.

In addition, whether price increases are good or bad should be judged in terms of the causes and consequences of the particular type of inflation we are experiencing. To illustrate: Let us assume for a moment that the same amount of price inflation as we have had since 1966 had been generated (a result which I challenge for reasons to be stated) by successful programs to maintain optimum economic growth and minimum unemployment; launch a more effective war against poverty; clear the slums and build the homes our people need; renovate our cities; modernize social security; and bring rural income and living standards up to some tolerable level of parity with those of others. The inflation thus generated would have been a wonderful bargain or tradeoff. In contrast, this same amount of actual inflation, accompanied and aggravated by contrived neglect of these crucial tasks through policies and programs avowedly designed to fight inflation, has been a cruel, stupid, and indefensible inflation.

All empirical evidence since 1953 has made it increasingly plain, contrary to the trade-off theory, that *we have more inflation when idle resources increase, and less inflation when they are reduced.* Although this has been demonstrated many times, a few examples will suffice. During 1958–66, when the average annual rate of real economic growth was 4.9 percent and unemployment dropped from 6.8 percent to 3.8 percent, the average annual increase in consumer prices was only 1.5 percent. But during 1966–72, when the average rate of real economic growth was only 3.1 percent and when unemployment rose from 3.8 percent to 5.6 percent, the average annual rate of consumer price inflation was 4.3 percent. The performance record from 12 months before the freeze to date again illustrates clearly that substantial reduction in the rate of inflation commenced well before the freeze as the economy moved from recession to a much higher though inadequate rate of economic growth. Most recently, there have been disturbing signs of an intensification of the inflationary process; and I believe this to be due mainly to the still inadequate economic performance and the vast uncertainties about the near future and about current national economic policies.

The theoretical reasons in support of the overwhelming empirical evidence are clear. During periods of low or negative growth, those who administer their prices attempt to compensate for inadequate volume by lifting their prices faster; reduced productivity gains increase *per unit* cost and lead to price increases; shortages of such public services as medical care and housing, aggravated by repressed public programs, add to inflationary pressures; exorbitant interest rates, undertaken to fight inflation, are inflationary per se. In addition, sharp changes in business expectations prompt price changes, usually upward no matter in which direction the economy is moving. It by now seems axiomatic that, in the long run, a stable and optimum rate of economic growth generates less *net* price inflation than the roller-coaster performance. And even were this more questionable than I deem it to be, the advantages of optimum economic performance immensely outweigh any marginal benefits in the area of prices which anyone might claim (I believe mistakenly) to result from holding the economy back and starving social programs.

The Need for Planning Under Freedom

All the sins of omission and commission reviewed above result essentially from the extreme dearth of planning under freedom in the formulation and application of national economic and social policies. The Employment Act of 1946 was intended to close this gap. It mandated a long-range process, akin to my *U.S. Economic and Social Performance Budget,* of setting long-range goals for growth, priorities, and justice (which should accent the extirpation of poverty) and integrating the entire range of relevant policies or means toward their attainment. But the *Reports* under the Act make slight contact with this requirement; they stress forecasts more than goals; they usually concentrate mainly upon fiscal and monetary policies, and greatly neglect many other policies of comparable impact. The result is many discrete plans and programs, but no single coherent plan or program. The term "fine tuning" has served as a poor excuse for the repeated bad guesses which are the inevitable consequence of planlessness.

In addition to the examples stated earlier, I will cite only a few others. In brutal fashion, the goal of farm parity has been abandoned, and scores of millions of farm people driven into the cities, where it was claimed they would find a haven of jobs and security. Instead, during two decades, they have contributed almost half of the nationwide total of excessive unemployment and soaring welfare costs. A strategic war against poverty would have resorted to a few highly selective efforts, such as assuring useful employment to those who can and should work, and income supplements for those who cannot or should not. Instead, the "war" deteriorated into a hopeless medley of errant experimentalism at all levels, underfunded and conflicting, and resulted in a frustration which is now prompting abandonment of by far the most important effort we should be recasting and carrying forward. I foretold all this in 1965. Our efforts to cure our international balance of payments have not been founded upon careful analysis of what composition of trade and exchange would really be best for us and the rest of the world, and, like the spurious war against inflation, have done much damage to our domestic economy while aggravating the specific evil they were designed to cure.

The type of planning I suggest does not involve precommitment to any particular policies, or to any particular philosophy of the division between private and public responsibilities, but rather a mature *method of arriving at decisions*. In fact, the weeding out of conflict and cross-purposes should in some respects reduce the role of the federal government, and certainly enlarge its effectiveness—a very different thing from the current reckless annihilation of vital programs. Looking far ahead does not mean delayed action, but rather judging better how to act now by knowing where we want to go instead of moving in fits and starts. Far from excessive centralization, this type of planning would reduce the divisions among our people, and bring the watchful eye of an informed people to bear on all that is attempted, so that we might steer between the Scylla of monolithic fiat and the Charybdis of aimless neglect and cross-purposes.

The Poverty of Formal Economics

The Employment Act of 1946 has immensely enlarged the participation of economists in public policy. This in itself makes much more serious the cultural lag in formal economics, a fact noted by a few stout protestants within the profession. Even a cursory examination of formal teaching, the leading textbooks, and the academic journals reveals that empirical observation, policy orientation, looking at the economy as whole, and "social" considerations remain substantially relegated to the rear.

More refreshment from within the profession is long overdue. Superficially, the leading economists divide into schools and battle with each other, but these manifestations relate largely to outmoded or secondary issues. On many of the most crucial issues, there is far too little critical disagreement and far too much uncritical accord; and on some of the most crucial issues, the preponderant majority remains strangely silent.

In terms of public policy, the trouble is multiplied because the members and staff of the Council of Economic Advisers are selected practically entirely from among formal economists, drawn from an increasingly limited circle in the universities and a few other eminent institutions. This inbreeding tends to mute challenge from outside the government as well as reconsideration within. The needed remedies are many; among them, those long-trained in the practicalities of making the American economy work better, including some who are not formal economists, should certainly form a substantial portion of the CEA membership and staff.

   We should remain optimistic. During the past four decades, our country has probably made more economic, social, and civil progress than has ever been registered anywhere in so short a time, and with slight upheaval related to the achievement. But we are now caught in a vise of apathy, cessation, and retreat, and we still have a tremendous way to go. In view of our domestic and international burdens, "time's winged chariot is drawing near." As Justice Brandeis said, if we would guide by the light of reason, we must let our minds be bold.

Wanted: A More Human, Less Dismal Science

LEONARD SILK

Here is an analysis that holds that the current antiseptic state of economics stems from its failure to interact significantly with the other social sciences.

Two centuries ago Edmund Burke proclaimed "The age of chivalry is gone. That of the sophisters, economists, and calculators has succeeded; and the glory of Europe is extinguished for ever." But is the age of the economists already come to an end?

Certainly the economists' once exalted reputation for worldly wisdom has been tarnished of late. They generally failed to anticipate the deterioration of the environment stemming from rising production, population growth, and technological advance. Nor did they foresee the impact of rapid economic change on America's cities. They have been preoccupied with economic growth and full employment, but the worrisome lesson of the past decade is that growth and full employment are no answers to what ails the United States.

Still, the economists may survive, if they change their ways. And there are signs that they are doing so. Within their ranks, there is some considerable soul-searching under way over the very philosophical and methodological bases of modern, Western, free-enterprise economics. Most economists today would still maintain, no doubt, that economics is simply a set of analytical techniques, applicable to certain aspects of production, distribution, exchange, and consumption. They would assert that economics aims at increasing the efficient use of resources but cannot specify goals for society.

From Leonard Silk, "Wanted: A More Human, Less Dismal Science," *Saturday Review* (January 22, 1972), pp. 34–35. Reprinted with the permission of the publisher.

Theirs is an antiseptic and truly dismal science, but a movement is stirring in the field toward a more human, ultimately more realistic economics. A sizable group of "radical economists" now ardently rejects "efficiency economics." They contend that the professionally cool and neutral economists have, in aiming at efficiency and the growth of production, helped build institutions and shape individual preferences—to the ultimate benefit of private enterprise, not the public weal.

Among economists and social scientists in general, there is mounting concern about the basic methodology of what they call "conventional economics." Conventional economics is the science of choice; it is orderly, definite, and linear, like classical music. Here, says the professor of conventional economics, are the factors of production—land, labor, and capital; decision makers combine those elements to maximize something—efficiency or production or short- or long-term profits.

But what happens, the critics ask, when research, technological change, innovation, and new ideas become major economic factors in increasing production and productivity? The focus then shifts from the neat strings of factors of production to the complex and unique human personalities and—in a corporate world where the creative process is institutionalized—to the large-scale organizations involved.

Hence, argue the critics of conventional economics, the walls of economic theory must be broken down to let in the other social sciences. Instead of the old simplifying psychological assumption that man is a pleasure/pain, profit/loss calculating machine, economists must look more profoundly at the question of what really makes man tick, alone and in groups. They must find better ways of both improving human beings ("investing in human capital" is the cliché for this) and of improving human performance.

The need for a broader and deeper economic analysis in a number of economic realms is beginning to be recognized. Economists once thought, for instance, that to bring a backward economy into the modern age, the essential job was to transfer gobs of capital to it. This, many now agree, was a laughably inadequate answer. The range of social, psychological, educational, organizational, managerial, political, and even moral complexities involved in economic development has shattered the simplistic assumptions of conventional economists. Similarly the persistence of poverty and the worsening of many social and environmental problems in rich, highly developed societies has forced economists to question the adequacy of their tools for improving human welfare—the classic aim of economics.

In my view, economics unquestionably needs a more realistic conception of human welfare itself than is provided by data on income and output. "What constitutes the well-being of a man?" Carlyle asked in 1839. Wages and the amount of bread his wages will buy, Carlyle answered in part, acknowledging two major areas of economic concern. But these, said Carlyle, were only the preliminaries:

Can the labourer, by thrift and industry, hope to rise to mastership; or is such hope cut off from him? How is he related to his employer—by bonds of friendliness and mutual help, or by hostility, opposition, and chains of mutual necessity alone? In a word, what degree of contentment can a human creature be supposed to enjoy in this position?

With hunger preying on him, his contentment is likely to be small! But even with abundance, his discontent, his real misery may be great. The labourer's feelings, his notion of being justly dealt with or unjustly; his wholesome composure, frugality, prosperity in the one case, his acrid unrest, recklessness, gin-drinking, and gradual ruin in the other—how shall figures of arithmetic represent all this?

How indeed? Commodities such as justice and opportunity and friendship are hardly touched upon by the usual arid arithmetic of economics. But economists are beginning to recognize such factors as being as central to real well-being as those that are more readily fitted with price tags. In an effort to devise and set forth measurements in these areas, some scholars are seeking to develop indexes of social conditions to set beside the economic indicators, to serve both as measures of well-being and as guides to social policy. The overall result sought is a numerical scale or set of scales that will give a truer picture of well-being than, say, the gross national product. The problem of quantification, however, is incredibly difficult because well-being is a complex cultural bundle, not a series of discrete phenomena. Is well-being necessarily increased if people have longer vacations but the highways are choked and the beaches overcrowded? More may not be better, but less is not better either—if it means less health, less freedom of movement in the city, less land, less friendship.

Individuals want very different things. Many really want big, fast cars, electric appliances and gadgets, the pleasures of Las Vegas or the numbers rackets in Harlem, or to hunt animals. Is it possible to reconcile the existing range of subjective preferences with the well-being of all? What degree of freedom is optimal for mankind? Jefferson offers one view, Dostoevsky another, Sartre a third, Camus a fourth, Milton Friedman a fifth, John Kenneth Galbraith a sixth, Leonid Brezhnev a seventh, Mao Tse-tung an eighth, etc.

After a long spell of quiet and even smugness about the state of their art, economists are asking themselves such questions as part of the broader questions of what they should be doing and how. Their answers may turn out to be important for solving some of the perplexing and stubborn problems afflicting this nation and many others. They may ultimately have a great deal to do with how men and nations can be helped to behave more decently and sensibly, with less harm to one another.

Perhaps some danger exists that economics—a limited field, but one with some significant achievements behind it—will drown prematurely in a sea of related disciplines before it has adequately solved some of its own traditional problems, such as how simultaneously to achieve full employment and price stability and how to put together a stable, essentially free, and expanding world economy.

Yet it seems to me that efforts to solve even those traditional economic problems cannot be hampered, but only advanced by a deeper understanding of many matters that lie beyond the boundaries of conventional economics.

New Maths and Old Sterilities

ROBERT A. SOLO

Has there been a tendency for the economic profession to confuse increased proficiency in mathematics for increased economic knowledge?

It comes down to this: The Establishment economics that is taught in the universities, proliferated in the journals, regurgitated in the councils of government, with all its mountains of published outputs, has not advanced our capaicty to control our economy beyond what it was in the late 1930s.

That after the clear failure of Neoclassical and Keynesian concepts and techniques of monetary and fiscal control, the nation is left with no answer to the persistent and profound economic problems of inflation and unemployment save a wage-price freeze in the manner of World War I or World War II, attests to the sterility of economic thought and policy. So does antitrustism, cast in the mold of the 1890s and allowing no role for industrial policy except to preserve market competition. In fact, the attack on monopoly has foundered of its own ineptitude, although the ritual threats continue. And when faced with a truly dangerous phenomenon, such as the conglomerate mergers of the 1960s, produced by financial manipulators making grist for their security mills, the professional antitrust economists were silent. Like other realities of a modern enterprise, this phenomenon, which will probably subvert management effectiveness and organizational rationale for generations, is outside their conceptual framework.

What remains for economics? International trade? Endless arabesques on eighteenth- and nineteenth-century themes. Economic development? Hackneyed formulas for sound money and capital accumulation and Malthusian forewarnings coupled with blinders against the realities and morals of

From Robert A. Solo, "New Maths and Old Sterilities," *Saturday Review* (January 22, 1972), pp. 47–48. Reprinted with the permission of the publisher.

politics. Urban economics? When confronted with the profound problem of racism, racial conflict, segregation, and the black ghetto in the deteriorating city, the economic *tour de force* was to consider racism as a matter of market preferences of and for blacks and whites.

There has also been a failure to develop less costly, more effective tools of public choice and policy implementation. Thus the gold standard, deficit financing, rediscounting, open-market operations, and the whole apparatus of monetary control, all clumsy, costly, and hoary, remain unchallenged and unchanged as instruments of policy.

Meanwhile, public authority has been drawn helter-skelter into salvaging, subsidizing, organizing, and planning national systems of transportation, of housing, of energy, and of communications. Yet, in respect to these tasks and responsibilities, the cupboard of thought stocked by Establishment economics has been entirely bare.

The real complexities of real economies elude us. Establishment economics provides no conceptual approach to measure and comprehend industrial performance, nor to reform, restructure, or control industry. The multifaceted dynamics of technological advance and industrial transformation—the underpinnings of increased productivity—are almost wholly excluded from the normal purview of Establishment economics. Nor does it offer any guide to a control of price that reflects a rational policy for allocation of resources, for the distribution of income, or for incentives for efficiency and technological progress.

The notion that a competitive price-directed market is the underlying economic reality lingers on, a fixation even of those who proclaim the organizational revolution. A shallow conception of the individual psyche as a mechanism for balancing the pleasures of consumption against the displeasures of work, with a map of preferences etched by the Invisible Hand of the Great Etcher upon each particular brain, remains, despite its total incongruity with the experience of our time. The notion that the formation of corporate policy can be understood as the personal choice of a self-seeking individual is accepted, amazingly, even by those who themselves dwell in the niches and grope through the labyrinths of organizational power. Productivity and growth are still analyzed as the consequence of capital accumulation, in spite of all evidence produced by economic research to the contrary. Like the Holy of Holies, the core concepts and basic assumptions of Establishment economics remain outside the reach of evidence and experience.

Why has this been so? Why have economists been unable to look at new problems with fresh eyes? What has kept conceptualization and assumption invulnerable to any assault by the hard evidence or the setbacks of experience or the commonplace observations of day to day? In part this can be accounted for by a methodological reorientation of the 1930s that gathered its force and became dominant in the postwar decades. The ostensible objective of the movement was to make economics a true "science." In the minds of protagonists, this meant making economics more like physics.

The development had two aspects; each might be associated with a particular economist. Call them the Hicks Effect and the Samuelson Effect, granting that the named individuals—Sir John Hicks of Oxford and Paul Samuelson of MIT—are representative of, rather than responsible for, what occurred. Hicks demanded that economics become free of values and entirely neutral with respect to the comparative needs and wants, pains and pleasures, frustrations and opportunities of the different persons or groups or classes that compose the social universe. Consuming vast energies and lots of paper, the endeavor to establish a value-free economics of welfare yielded nothing. Yet, that the enterprise so long withstood the assault of common sense can be explained only by the fact that it was insulated from any queries concerning its relevance or meaning by a dense wall of esoteric symbolism—the Samuelson Effect.

When Paul Samuelson wrote *Foundations of Economic Analysis*, his declared intention was to recast economic theory into a set of mathematical propositions *in order that those propositions could be tentatively verified or definitely refuted through experimental test*, thus giving to economics the same empirical base that physics had. In one sense, Samuelson was enormously successful. He set the tone and direction for his generation. He became a man of great influence and affluence, a Nobel Prize winner and a millionaire. In another sense, he failed completely. He and those who followed him succeeded certainly in recasting the whole of economics in complex and esoteric mathematical symbolism, *but not a single one of the propositions of theory has, as a consequence, been exposed to refutation through experimental test*. The basis for the acceptance or rejection of the propositions of economics remains as much a matter for intuitive judgment as ever before.

The problem in trying to establish and disestablish statements concerning social phenomena is that there are no precisely quantifiable relationships that are universal and continuing. Individual behavior, group action, social policy—all are functions of ideas, images, imageries, and ideologies that may be created out of nothing and vanish into nothing. In the social realm, every entity, every relationship is unique. Any general statement can do no more than refer to phenomena or relationships that are merely analogous to one another. Very untidy all that; inconvenient no doubt, not *comme il faut* at all. Still, statements are and must be made concerning social phenomena, and those statements will be accepted or rejected. The real question under those circumstances is how best to establish or disestablish the credibility of such statements.

Ultimately, the mode of expression that will most conform to the scientific ideal will not be the image-free symbols of mathematics but rather the imagery of normal communication and intercourse with its reference base in the specifics of experience, for only if the general statement is so framed can it be continuously bridged into direct observations and contrasted with ongoing experiences. The mathematizing of economics was no doubt an heroic achievement but, by the values of science, profoundly retrograde. It did not subject the propositions of economics to the test of refutation by specific prediction, and it shielded them from challenge on the basis of direct observation and experience. Whatever suited the narrow scope and limited capabilities of mathematical expression was drawn in, and what could not be so encompassed was excluded from consideration. The energies of generations were consumed not in a search for truth but in displays of virtuosity. As styles changed, faculties scurried not at all to learn more of the infinite complexities of the social universe but to keep up with the newest modes of mathematical expression. Graduate students are admonished that if they don't master this or that symbolism, "they won't be able to read the journals" a few years hence. Who can wonder then that 30 years of intense activity by Establishment economics has produced little of substantive significance?

This criticism of economics should be kept in perspective. The other social sciences have been equally sterile. After three decades of unprecedented affluence and unequaled activity, physics too has produced no "scientific revolutions." If we in economics suffer the pangs of role confusion and identity crisis, so do corporation officials, members of Congress, generals and diplomats, and university presidents. Confusion and uncertainty about our role are not ours alone but also society's, not only in what we expect of ourselves but in what society expects of us. If the body of economic thought and theory is out of date, what handed-down set of ideas or ideology is not? Being out of date, economics is, after all, very much in tune with the times.

An Unsimple Matter of Choice

MARC J. ROBERTS

Here it is maintained that formal choice theory is based upon outmoded assumptions about man and his psychology.

Current economic theory is built upon a classic, simplified view of man and his psychology. Economic man, if anything, is even more simplified than Platonic man. Do people always know exactly what they "really" want, no matter how complex the options? Will people always choose what makes them "happiest" or "best off"? Are individual choices effectively immune from outside influence and manipulation? Economic theory's answer to all of these questions basically is yes. Some of economics' greatest—and most outmoded—simplifications, in fact, are centered on the assumption of rational, purposeful, and autonomous choice by individuals who make up an economic system.

Yet an analysis based on such an assumption is hard-pressed to make sense out of many modern situations. For example, suppose we consider improving the level of water quality in a river that runs through a large city. Some vexing technical complications aside, economic analysis essentially suggests that we compare the cost of making the improvement with what people would be willing to pay for the benefits it would bring, in order to decide whether or not to undertake the project. Suppose we were to take this counsel seriously and go and ask people what they would be willing to pay for a body of water near at hand that they could swim and boat in. Many would be at a loss to give a reasonable answer. How accurately can a man know how much he prizes an experience or opportunity he has not had?

From Marc J. Roberts, "An Unsimple Matter of Choice," *Saturday Review* (January 22, 1972), pp. 46, 60. Reprinted with the permission of the publisher.

If we asked someone to put a price on the value of a river after it had been cleaned up and he had enjoyed its purified waters, would it differ from the value he assigned when the river was running dirty? Probably. The evidence is that experiencing an opportunity changes the degree of people's preferences for that opportunity. Almost all studies of the adoption of new goods have shown that familiarity breeds attachment. In the beginning, new goods are accepted slowly. But their rate of diffusion gradually accelerates as information about them and social pressures to acquire them expands.

Many of the questions society now faces, in fact, involve policies that will alter the preferences of individuals. How much, for instance, would a man accustomed to having his automobile carry him nearly everywhere eventually value and use a fast, flexible public transit system if he had one? Who, including the automobilist himself, can say before the fact?

In an earlier, simpler time when a farmer had to decide whether to trade some of his corn for potatoes or for seeds, the notion of fixed and autonomous choice by individuals perhaps more literally reflected reality. But consider a modern, socially insecure adolescent debating about purchasing an underarm deodorant, a hairspray, a mouthwash, or some cologne—all of which have been heavily advertised as enhancers of sexual attractiveness. In terms of the meaning and significance of choice, is this case really indistinguishable from the farmer selecting his family's vegetables? I am afraid that only someone with graduate training in economics is likely to fail to see the differences.

The fact is that an individual's preferences and the sort of choice he is inclined to make in a given situation are affected by any number of unaccountable pushes and pulls, not the least of which are governmental and corporate policies. Ignoring the fact that choices are affected by such policies is not a "neutral" error. It has the conservative effect of giving ethical significance to existing preferences.

If economics is to cope with such complex interrelationships, it will require a more complex view of man and the choices he makes. Economics today views man not only as extraordinarily simple but as almost limitlessly powerful. Men always know their own minds with perfect clarity and consistency. The implication of every option for their level of "utility" is immediately obvious—and clearly defined. But how can we seriously defend this naïve view of harmonious, unitary choice and motive long after Freud and others have given us so much more powerful and subtle a perspective on individual behavior? Simple introspection alone tells us that our choices are complicated and often difficult, subject to conflicting pressure and self-doubt. We do not, for instance, balance the call of duty and the pull of immediate pleasure by an obvious and infallible comparison of the "utility" offered by each alternative.

No doubt economic simplifications concerning choice have much value. They do provide models that are transparent in structure, easy to manipulate, and useful for clarification of thinking. But from the standpoint of understanding real economic behavior, the basic structure of microeconomics that every graduate student struggles so to master is of surprisingly limited practical assistance. As Columbia economist Kelvin Lancaster has put it, the theory demonstrates how to extract "a minimum of results from a minimum of assumptions."

In the relationship of choice to human welfare, where economic analysis could be of some help, we don't even use it properly. Sloppy thinking has led us to the unjustified view that the relative capacity of individuals to make certain kinds of choice—that is, their purchasing power—is a generally valid measure of their well-being. Thus, we have come to accept a narrow definition of "income" as the basic index for the impact of public policy.

But the notion that income is a measure of well-being or welfare does not even follow from a careful reading of the relevant economic theory. Here is a case of economics not only being inadequate but not even taking seriously the insights it does provide.

Our economic statistics and their exceedingly narrow reference to the important choices in real life shed very little light on what has come to be known as the "quality of life." The sense of deprivation due to discrimination, the fear and unpleasantness of a decaying urban neighborhood, loneliness, alienation, self-doubt, and social disorganization—all of this has little or no place in the calculations of economics. Smog, dirt, pollution, noise, ugliness, a sense of opportunity or its lack, a sense of belonging, much of what contributes to, indeed, constitutes individual experience and well-being are simply ignored.

Why is it that economics usually does not take these aspects of social choice—or lack of choice—into account? The problem is largely that these are "outputs," which due to either historical accident or technical difficulties do not have "prices" attached to them. Because they are not bought and sold, we have difficulty determining what people would be or are willing to pay for them. And given the price-tag basis of our national income accounts—including the gross national product—such factors fail to be reflected in economic measurements of national well-being.

Why should economics today still be employing concepts of limited applicability for social choice purposes? This situation is not unrelated to the fact that modern economic analysis is largely expressed in formal mathematical terms. And rational behavior, perfectly consistent behavior, precisely adjusted, fully determined behavior—these notions are more easily stated in mathematical terms than are the wide variances from such ideals that occur in real life.

It sometimes appears that an instinct for, an orientation toward, reality is lacking in economics. Many of the great advances in natural science (as

well as much modern business-cycle theory in economics itself) were prompt-
ed by a desire to explain, understand, and control specific puzzling phenomena. Yet, in economics today, formulas linked to specific sorts of economic
behavior are often explored for their own sake, and the empirical puzzle
at which the enterprise is directed has become unclear. If the enterprise
does not have some ultimate empirical aim, what then is to distinguish the
discipline from mathematics—pure, applied, or recreational?

The root problem may well be that economics is so difficult. People
and organizations are much more complex than electrons or molecules. The
appropriate analogies to economics in the natural sciences are not physics
or chemistry but rather meteorology or engineering, and even these deal
with much more regularly behaved phenomena than does economics. Simple
models of individual choice and welfare will have to give way to more
complex concepts. How else are we to develop empirically plausible and
ethically attractive arguments about public and private choices and welfare?
And that does seem to be one of the major reasons for economics to begin
with.

Theoretical Assumptions and Nonobserved Facts

WASSILY LEONTIEF

Simplifying assumptions are necessary to theoretical analysis. Unfortunately, Professor Leontief argues, a major shortcoming in the development of economic theory has been the tendency to base models on assumptions that have no empirical validity.

Economics today rides the crest of intellectual respectability and popular acclaim. The serious attention with which our pronouncements are received by the general public, hard-bitten politicians, and even skeptical businessmen is second only to that which was given to physicists and space experts a few years ago when the round trip to the moon seemed to be our only truly national goal. The flow of learned articles, monographs, and textbooks is swelling like a tidal wave; *Econometrica*, the leading journal in the field of mathematical economics, has just stepped up its publication schedule from four to six issues per annum.

And yet an uneasy feeling about the present state of our discipline has been growing in some of us who have watched its unprecedented development over the last three decades. This concern seems to be shared even by those who are themselves contributing successfully to the present boom. They play the game with professional skill but have serious doubts about its rules.

Much of current academic teaching and research has been criticized for its lack of relevance, that is, of immediate practical impact. In a nearly instant response to this criticism, research projects, seminars, and under-

From Wassily Leontief, "Theoretical Assumptions and Nonobserved Facts," *American Economic Review* (March 1971), pp. 1–7. Reprinted with the permission of

graduate courses have been set up on poverty, on city and small town slums, on pure water and fresh air. In an almost Pavlovian reflex, whenever a new complaint is raised, President Nixon appoints a commission and the university announces a new course. Far be it from me to argue that the fire should not be shifted when the target moves. The trouble is caused, however, not by an inadequate selection of targets, but rather by our inability to hit square-ly any one of them. The uneasiness of which I spoke before is caused not by the *irrelevance* of the practical problems to which present day economists address their efforts, but rather by the palpable *inadequacy* of the scientific means with which they try to solve them.

If this simply were a sign of the overly high aspiration level of a fast developing discipline, such a discrepancy between ends and means should cause no worry. But I submit that the consistently indifferent performance in practical applications is in fact a symptom of a fundamental imbalance in the present state of our discipline. The weak and all too slowly growing empirical foundation clearly cannot support the proliferating superstructure of pure, or should I say, speculative economic theory.

Much is being made of the widespread, nearly mandatory use by modern economic theorists of mathematics. To the extent to which the economic phenomena possess observable quantitative dimensions, this is indisputably a major forward step. Unfortunately, any one capable of learning elementary, or preferably advanced calculus and algebra, and acquiring acquaintance with the specialized terminology of economics can set himself up as a theorist. Uncritical enthusiasm for mathematical formulation tends often to conceal the ephemeral substantive content of the argument behind the formidable front of algebraic signs.

Professional journals have opened wide their pages to papers written in mathematical language; colleges train aspiring young economists to use this language; graduate schools require its knowledge and reward its use. The mathematical model-building industry has grown into one of the most prestigious, possibly the most prestigious branch of economics. Construction of a typical theoretical model can be handled now as a routine assembly job. All principal components such as production functions, consumption, and utility functions come in several standard types; so does the optional equipment as, for example, "factor augmentation"—to take care of techno-logical change. This particular device is, incidentally, available in a simple exponential design or with a special automatic regulator known as the "Ken-nedy function." Any model can be modernized with the help of special attachments. One popular way to upgrade a simple one-sector model is to bring it out in a two-sector version or even in a still more impressive form of the "n-sector," that is, many-sector class.

In the presentation of a new model, attention nowadays is usually centered on a step-by-step derivation of its formal properties. But if the

author—or at least the referee who recommended the manuscript for publication—is technically competent, such mathematical manipulations, however
long and intricate, can even without further checking be accepted as correct.
Nevertheless, they are usually spelled out at great length. By the time it
comes to interpretation of the substantive *conclusions*, the assumptions on
which the model has been based are easily forgotten. But it is precisely
the empirical validity of these *assumptions* on which the usefulness of the
entire exercise depends.

What is really needed, in most cases, is a very difficult and seldom
very neat assessment and verification of these assumptions in terms of observed facts. Here mathematics cannot help and because of this, the interest
and enthusiasm of the model builder suddenly begins to flag: "If you do
not like my set of assumptions, give me another and I will gladly make
you another model; have your pick."

Policy oriented models, in contrast to purely descriptive ones, are gaining favor, however nonoperational they may be. This, I submit, is in part
because the choice of the final policy objectives—the selection and justification of the shape of the so-called objective function—is, and rightly so, considered based on normative judgment, not on factual analysis. Thus, the model
builder can secure at least some convenient assumptions without running
the risk of being asked to justify them on empirical grounds.

To sum up with the words of a recent president of the Econometric
Society, " . . . the achievements of economic theory in the last two decades
are both impressive and in many ways beautiful. But it cannot be denied
that there is something scandalous in the spectacle of so many people refining
the analysis of economic states which they give no reason to suppose will
ever, or have ever, come about. . . . It is an unsatisfactory and slightly dishon-
est state of affairs."

But shouldn't this harsh judgment be suspended in the face of the impressive volume of econometric work? The answer is decidedly no. This work
can be in general characterized as an attempt to compensate for the glaring
weakness of the data base available to us by the widest possible use of more
and more sophisticated statistical techniques. Alongside the mounting pile
of elaborate theoretical models we see a fast-growing stock of equally intricate statistical tools. These are intended to stretch to the limit the meager
supply of facts.

Since, as I said before, the publishers' referees do a competent job,
most model-testing kits described in professional journals are internally consistent. However, like the economic models they are supposed to implement,
the validity of these statistical tools depends on the acceptance of certain
convenient assumptions pertaining to stochastic properties of the phenomena
which the particular models are intended to explain; assumptions that can
be seldom verified.

In no other field of empirical inquiry has so massive and sophisticated a statistical machinery been used with such indifferent results. Nevertheless, theorists continue to turn out model after model and mathematical statisticians to devise complicated procedures one after another. Most of these are relegated to the stockpile without any practical application or after only a perfunctory demonstration exercise. Even those used for a while soon fall out of favor, not because the methods that supersede them perform better, but because they are new and different.

Continued preoccupation with imaginary, hypothetical, rather than with observable reality has gradually led to a distortion of the informal valuation scale used in our academic community to assess and to rank the scientific performance of its members. Empirical analysis, according to this scale, gets a lower rating than formal mathematical reasoning. Devising a new statistical procedure, however tenuous, that makes it possible to squeeze out one more unknown parameter from a given set of data, is judged a greater scientific achievement than the successful search for additional information that would permit us to measure the magnitude of the same parameter in a less ingenious, but more reliable way. This despite the fact that in all too many instances sophisticated statistical analysis is performed on a set of data whose exact meaning and validity are unknown to the author or rather so well known to him that at the very end he warns the reader not to take the material conclusions of the entire "exercise" seriously.

A natural Darwinian feedback operating through selection of academic personnel contributes greatly to the perpetuation of this state of affairs. The scoring system that governs the distribution of rewards must naturally affect the make-up of the competing teams. Thus, it is not surprising that the younger economists, particularly those engaged in teaching and in academic research, seem by now quite content with a situation in which they can demonstrate their prowess (and incidentally, advance their careers) by building more and more complicated mathematical models and devising more and more sophisticated methods of statistical inference without ever engaging in empirical research. Complaints about the lack of indispensable primary data are heard from time to time, but they don't sound very urgent. The feeling of dissatisfaction with the present state of our discipline which prompts me to speak out so bluntly seems, alas, to be shared by relatively few. Yet even those few who do share it feel they can do little to improve the situation. How could they?

In contrast to most physical sciences, we study a system that is not only exceedingly complex but is also in a state of constant flux. I have in mind not the obvious change in the variables, such as outputs, prices, or levels of employment, that our equations are supposed to explain, but the basic structural relationships described by the form and the parameters of these equations. In order to know what the shape of these structural relationships actually are at any given time, we have to keep them under continuous surveillance.

By sinking the foundations of our analytical system deeper and deeper, by reducing, for example, cost functions to production functions and the production functions to some still more basic relationships eventually capable of explaining the technological change itself, we should be able to reduce this drift. It would, nevertheless, be quite unrealistic to expect to reach, in this way, the bedrock of invariant structural relationships (measurable parameters) which, once having been observed and described, could be used year after year, decade after decade, without revisions based on repeated observation.

On the relatively shallow level where the empirically implemented economic analysis now operates even the more invariant of the structural relationships, in terms of which the system is described, change rapidly. Without a constant inflow of new data the existing stock of factual information becomes obsolete very soon. What a contrast with physics, biology, or even psychology where the magnitude of most parameters is practically constant and where critical experiments and measurements don't have to be repeated every year!

Just to keep up our very modest current capabilities we have to maintain a steady flow of new data. A progressive expansion of these capabilities would be out of the question without a continuous and rapid rise of this flow. Moreover, the new, additional data in many instances will have to be qualitatively different from those provided hitherto.

To deepen the foundation of our analytical system it will be necessary to reach unhesitatingly beyond the limits of the domain of economic phenomena as it has been staked out up to now. The pursuit of a more fundamental understanding of the process of production inevitably leads into the area of engineering sciences. To penetrate below the skin-thin surface of conventional consumption functions, it will be necessary to develop a systematic study of the structural characteristics and of the functioning of households, an area in which description and analysis of social, anthropological, and demographic factors must obviously occupy the center of the stage.

Establishment of systematic cooperative relationships across the traditional frontiers now separating economics from these adjoining fields is hampered by the sense of self-sufficiency resulting from what I have already characterized as undue reliance on indirect statistical inference as the principal method of empirical research. As theorists, we construct systems in which prices, outputs, rates of saving, and investment, etc., are explained in terms of production functions, consumption functions, and other structural relationships whose parameters are assumed, at least for argument's sake, to be known. As econometricians, engaged in what passes for empirical research, we do not try, however, to ascertain the actual shapes of these functions and to measure the magnitudes of these parameters by turning up new factual information. We make an about face and rely on indirect statistical inference to derive the unknown structural relationships from the observed magnitudes of prices, outputs and other variables that, in our role as theoreticians, we treated as unknowns.

Formally, nothing is, of course, wrong with such an apparently circular procedure. Moreover, the model builder in erecting his hypothetical structures is free to take into account all possible kinds of factual knowledge and the econometrician in principle, at least, can introduce in the estimating procedure any amount of what is usually referred to as "exogenous" information before he feeds his programmed tape into the computer. Such options are exercised rarely and when they are, usually in a casual way.

The same well-known sets of figures are used again and again in all possible combinations to pit different theoretical models against each other in formal statistical combat. For obvious reasons a decision is reached in most cases not by a knock-out but by a few points. The orderly and systematic nature of the entire procedure generates a feeling of comfortable self-sufficiency.

This complacent feeling, as I said before, discourages venturesome attempts to widen and to deepen the empirical foundations of economic analysis, particularly those attempts that would involve crossing the conventional lines separating ours from the adjoining fields.

True advance can be achieved only through an iterative process in which improved theoretical formulation raises new empirical questions and the answers to these questions, in their turn, lead to new theoretical insights. The "givens" of today become the "unknowns" that will have to be explained tomorrow. This, incidentally, makes untenable the admittedly convenient methodological position according to which a theorist does not need to verify directly the factual assumptions on which he chooses to base his deductive arguments, provided his empirical conclusions seem to be correct. The prevalence of such a point of view is, to a large extent, responsible for the state of splendid isolation in which our discipline nowadays finds itself.

An exceptional example of a healthy balance between theoretical and empirical analysis and of the readiness of professional economists to cooperate with experts in the neighboring disciplines is offered by Agricultural Economics as it developed in this country over the last fifty years. A unique combination of social and political forces has secured for this area unusually strong organizational and generous financial support. Official agricultural statistics are more complete, reliable, and systematic than those pertaining to any other major sector of our economy. Close collaboration with agronomists provides agricultural economists with direct access to information of a technological kind. When they speak of crop rotation, fertilizers, or alternative harvesting techniques, they usually know, sometimes from personal experience, what they are talking about. Preoccupation with the standard of living of the rural population has led agricultural economists into collaboration with home economists and sociologists, that is, with social scientists of the "softer" kind. While centering their interest on only one part of the economic system, agricultural economists demonstrated the effectiveness of a systematic combination of theoretical approach with detailed factual analysis. They also were the first among economists to make use of the advanced methods of mathematical statistics. However, in their hands, statistical inference became a complement to, not a substitute for, empirical research.

The shift from casual empiricism that dominates much of today's econometric work to systematic large-scale factual analysis will not be easy. To start with, it will require a sharp increase in the annual appropriation for Federal Statistical Agencies. The quality of government statistics has, of course, been steadily improving. The coverage, however, does not keep up with the growing complexity of our social and economic system and our capability of handling larger and larger data flows.

The spectacular advances in computer technology increased the economists' potential ability to make effective analytical use of large sets of detailed data. The time is past when the best that could be done with large sets of variables was to reduce their number by averaging them out or what is essentially the same, combining them into broad aggregates; now we can manipulate complicated analytical systems without suppressing the identity of their individual elements. There is a certain irony in the fact that, next to the fast-growing service industries, the areas whose coverage by the Census is particularly deficient are the operations of government agencies, both federal and local.

To place all or even the major responsibility for the collection of economic data in the hands of one central organization would be a mistake. The prevailing decentralized approach that permits and encourages a great number of government agencies, non-profit institutions, and private businesses engaged in data gathering activities acquitted itself very well. Better information means more detailed information and detailed specialized information can be best collected by those immediately concerned with a particular field. What is, however, urgently needed is the establishment, maintenance, and enforcement of coordinated uniform classification systems by all agencies, private as well as public, involved in this work. Incompatible data are useless data. How far from a tolerable, not to say, ideal state our present economic statistics are in this respect, can be judged by the fact that because of differences in classification, domestic output data cannot be compared, for many goods, with the corresponding export and import figures. Neither can the official employment statistics be related without laborious adjustments to output data, industry by industry. An unreasonably high proportion of material and intellectual resources devoted to statistical work is now spent not on the collection of primary information but on a frustrating and wasteful struggle with incongruous definitions and irreconcilable classifications.

Without invoking a misplaced methodological analogy, the task of se-curing a massive flow of primary economic data can be compared to that of providing the high energy physicists with a gigantic accelerator. The scientists have their machines while the economists are still waiting for their data. In our case not only must the society be willing to provide year after year the millions of dollars required for maintenance of a vast statistical machine, but a large number of citizens must be prepared to play, at least, a passive and occasionally even an active part in actual fact-finding opera-tions. It is as if the electrons and protons had to be persuaded to cooperate with the physicist.

The average American does not seem to object to being interviewed, polled, and surveyed. Curiosity, the desire to find out how the economic system (in which most of us are small gears, and some, big wheels) works might in many instances provide sufficient inducement for cooperation of this kind.

One runs up, of course, occasionally against the attitude that "what you don't know can't hurt you" and that knowledge might be dangerous: it may generate a desire to tinker with the system. The experience of these years seems, however, to have convinced not only most economists—with a few notable exceptions—but also the public at large that a lack of economic knowledge can hurt badly. Our free enterprise system has rightly been com-pared to a gigantic computing machine capable of solving its own problems automatically. But any one who has had some practical experience with large computers knows that they do break down and can't operate unattend-ed. To keep the automatic, or rather the semi-automatic, engine of our economy in good working order we must not only understand the general principles on which it operates, but also be acquainted with the details of its actual design.

A new element has entered the picture in recent years—the adoption of methods of modern economic analysis by private business. Corporate sup-port of economic research goes as far back as the early 1920s when Wesley Mitchell founded the National Bureau. However, it is not this concern for broad issues of public policies or even the general interest in economic growth and business fluctuations that I have in mind, but rather the fast-spreading use of advanced methods of Operations Research and of so-called Systems' Analysis. Some of the standard concepts and analytical devices of economic theory first found their way into the curricula of our business schools and soon after that, sophisticated management began to put them into practice. While academic theorists are content with the formulation of general princi-ples, corporate operations researchers and practical systems' analysts have to answer questions pertaining to specific real situations. Demand for econom-ic data to be used in practical business planning is growing at an accelerated pace. It is a high quality demand: business users in most instances possess first-hand technical knowledge of the area to which the data they ask for refer. Moreover, this demand is usually "effective." Profit-making business is willing and able to pay the costs of gathering the information it wants to have. This raises the thorny question of public access to privately collected data and of the proper division of labor and cooperation between government and business in that fast-expanding field. Under the inexorable pressure of rising practical demand, these problems will be solved in one way or another. Our economy will be surveyed and mapped in all its many dimensions on a larger and larger scale.

Economists should be prepared to take a leading role in shaping this major social enterprise not as someone else's spokesmen and advisers, but on their own behalf. They have failed to do this up to now. The Conference of Federal Statistics Users organized several years ago had business, labor, and many other groups represented among its members, but not economists as such. How can we expect our needs to be satisfied if our voices are not heard?

We, I mean the academic economists, are ready to expound, to any one ready to lend an ear, our views on problems of public policy: give advice on the best ways to maintain full employment, to fight inflation, to foster economic growth. We should be equally prepared to share with the wider public the hopes and disappointments which accompany the advance of our own often desperately difficult, but always exciting intellectual enterprise. This public has amply demonstrated its readiness to back the pursuit of knowledge. It will lend its generous support to our venture too, if we take the trouble to explain what it is all about.

Post-Post-Keynes:
The Shattered Synthesis

DANIEL R. FUSFELD

A major theoretical accomplishment in modern economics was the synthesis of Keynesian and Marshallian economics. Here is an analysis that suggests the synthesis has come unstuck, necessitating a reconstruction of economics.

Events of the past five years have shattered a synthesis of economic theory and policy that has dominated thinking about economic issues in the United States for a quarter of a century. This synthesis, referred to by many economists as "post-Keynesian," was based on the national-scale macroeconomics of John Maynard Keynes together with the revived, closeup microeconomics of Alfred Marshall and his followers. The systems of these two great economists were unified in a framework of theory and policy, the principal professional exponent of which has been Paul Samuelson of MIT. The theoretical elements were taught to two generations of college students in Samuelson's great introductory economics text, titled simply and conclusively *Economics*, and by its many imitators. The policy principles were developed through a series of national administrations and expressed in the annual reports of the President's Council of Economic Advisers.

And for years it all seemed to be working. The synthesis appeared to provide an efficient analytical framework for understanding and running modern, industrial economies. Policies derived from Keynesian theory seemed capable of sustaining high levels of employment and high rates of economic growth. Marshallian neoclassical economics seemed to explain adequately enough how resources were allocated and incomes distributed in a private,

From Daniel R. Fusfeld, "Post-Post-Keynes: The Shattered Synthesis," *Saturday Review* (January 22, 1972), pp. 36–39. Reprinted with the permission of the publisher.

market-oriented economy. In crude terms, producers were seen as responding to consumer demand to turn out the products and services that maximize consumer welfare. Rewards were proportionate to an individual's contribution to production. Economic growth was ensured by the savings and enterprise of a success-oriented private-enterprise economy.

Much of the system rested on the assumption that competition would prevail and concentrated economic power could not control markets for its own benefit. To ensure competition and prevent monopolies from building up, the post-Keynesian synthesis required strong antitrust legislation, and where "natural" monopolies existed, such as in utilities or railroads, vigorous regulation by government agencies was prescribed. But such government intervention in the economic system, it was felt, could be limited. In fact, a number of studies in the 1950s seemed to show that the extent of monopoly was not increasing and that competitive pressures tended to erode monopolistic positions.

The primary role of government was to ensure full employment and growth by the proper mix of spending, taxation, and monetary policy. Although economic problems of a variety of sorts were found, they could largely be resolved as long as full employment and growth were sustained. Even poverty might be ended by a growing economy, for it would bring higher material standards of living and spread them to the poor. The rich might get richer, but the poor would get richer, too. The paradigm sketched by the post-Keynesian synthesis was of a benign social order that would move mankind toward a better and more stable future.

Economic growth played a crucial role in the post-Keynesian synthesis, which postulated a smooth expansion of output through increases in productivity financed by savings. Imbalances and discontinuities in the inner workings of the economic machinery are foreclosed by substitution of one factor of production for another; for example, relatively abundant machinery would fill in for labor when manpower became scarce. Short-run imbalances may occur, according to this theory, but they will be overcome in the long run by the flexibility of the private-enterprise economy and its ability to adjust to changing circumstances.

The underlying political implications of this theory of economic growth should be obvious. The theory was developed at a time when planning was being used in the Soviet Union to achieve high rates of economic growth. Indeed, during the early and mid-1960s, when U.S. growth speeded up and Soviet growth slowed down, the U.S. growth rate at its *peak* reached only as high as the Soviet growth rate at its *trough*. Planning was also being used in many underdeveloped countries that were moving toward a variety of socialist types of development programs. Yet the leading Western economists were saying that the traditional forces of the free market in a private-enterprise economy would generate the optimal growth path.

Furthermore, they said, economic growth could provide the resources for a series of domestic reforms and improvements: ending poverty, expanding opportunity, solving urban problems, building houses and highways, even shooting at the moon, although that was mostly a Cold War enterprise. All this could be done, mind you, without rocking the boat by redistributing income or breaking up the great industrial and financial centers of power. The structure of wealth and power would remain untouched.

Economic growth could also provide the resources for aid to the Third World. Aid programs would help keep those nations on our side in the Cold War. Aid would help them take off into sustained economic growth, making their economies more like ours, eventually allowing the aid programs themselves to taper off and end—according to the scenario sketched by W. W. Rostow in his *Stages of Economic Growth*, which was appropriately subtitled "An Anti-Communist Manifesto."

Finally, the post-Keynesian synthesis played a part in the ideological foundations of American foreign policy. Containment of communism and the strategy of the Cold War were based on the belief that communism contained the seeds of its own downfall. Tensions and conflicts within the Soviet Union and the Communist bloc were expected to weaken and perhaps destroy communism as a threat to the free world and its predominantly capitalist economy. Meanwhile, private enterprise in the managed Western economies would move strongly ahead toward continually higher living standards, economic strength, and material resources. Containment would prevent war, while economic growth would lead the West to superiority and victory.

Within the theoretical and political framework of the post-Keynesian synthesis, solutions seemed to be present for all of the great economic problems of the postwar world. Liberals and reformers flocked to embrace it. Yet, underneath the surface it was the economics of the status quo, of anticommunism and the Cold War, of reform around the edges of the social and economic order.

The post-Keynesian synthesis, in fact, reflected and provided justification for the concentration of power in American society in the years after World War II. The locus of governmental power had shifted to the federal government, and within the federal government to the Executive branch. With world power came a further concentration within the Executive branch itself, into the hands of the national security managers. This growing concentration of political power was paralleled by an increasing concentration of economic power in the business community. A recent Federal Trade Commission study showed that in 1968 the 100 largest manufacturing corporations held a larger share of manufacturing assets than the 200 largest in 1950 and that the 200 largest in 1968 controlled a share equal to that of the 1,000 largest in 1941.

Big business and big government have been coming together in an increasingly symbiotic relationship. Big government needs big business because the giant corporation has become the key to effective functioning of the economy—witness the Penn Central and Lockheed rescue operations—and because big business is the source of the weaponry on which national power rests. Government, in turn, provides the environment of economic growth within which the large corporation flourishes, educates the managers and technicians that big enterprises need, maintains the framework for settlement of labor disputes, and seeks to maintain a system of world order conducive to the growth of international corporations. Concentrated economic and political power are allies.

Sustained full employment and economic growth, emphasized by the post-Keynesian synthesis, became the twin keystones of an understanding between those who held and exercised power and those who did not. The levers of power remained in the hands of those who managed big business and big government. In exchange for allowing them a relatively free rein, the great middle-income majority obtained the material benefits that accrued from a quarter century of economic expansion.

How smoothly indeed the post-Keynesian synthesis seemed to be working, both in theory and in practice. Then, in the 1960s, at the height of its influence, the synthesis began to be faced with a group of problems that it could not handle effectively.

Inflation was the first to appear. The monetary and fiscal policies designed to achieve full employment and economic growth seemed to generate rising prices when full employment neared. Even during substantially slack economic periods, price levels showed an upward creep.

An incomes policy—government control of wages and prices—was never envisaged in the post-Keynesian synthesis, for one of its chief points is the idea that management of the economy need not extend into the microeconomic domain of wages, prices, profits, and incomes generally. But, of course, an incomes policy has come to us full force with the phases of the Nixon controls—an acknowledgment by a Republican administration that the private sector alone cannot be relied on to achieve stabilizing results in these areas.

Closely related to the problem of domestic inflation is a second problem: the continuing crisis in the international monetary system. The U.S. deficit in its balance of international payments, sustained since 1950 with the exception of the Suez crisis years, 1957–58, finally wrecked the system established at Bretton Woods in 1944. The immediate cause of the problem was U.S. private investment and military expenditures abroad on a scale too great to be financed by a favorable balance of trade. When our favorable trade balance fell victim to domestic inflation at the same time that military spending was vastly increased, the end quickly came. A historic devaluation of the dollar has resulted.

A deeper issue lurks beneath these events. A nation's domestic economic policies influence its balance of international payments, and its balance of payments limits the freedom it has in pursuing domestic economic goals. Moreover, the balance of payments of the United States, as the dominant nation in world trade and finance, affects the balance of payments of other nations, which affects their domestic economic policies and limits the alternatives among which they can choose. In this way, our domestic economic policies ultimately weigh on those of other nations. These are worldwide economic relationships that the post-Keynesian synthesis had hardly considered and for which it has almost no policy prescriptions.

A third problem to emerge in the 1960s concerned the underdeveloped countries. Growth of the advanced economies was supposed to generate capital resources that could be channeled into the less-developed economies, getting them started on the path to self-sustained growth. It didn't work out that way. Economic growth was spotty, and, as Gunnar Myrdal and others pointed out, in many areas there was a reverse drain of capital and skilled manpower out of the underdeveloped areas and into the advanced international economy. Meanwhile, the public health technology of the advanced countries was imported into the backward nations, causing declining death rates and rapid population growth that literally ate up the gains from economic growth. The gap between the rich and poor nations tended to widen rather than narrow, which is just the opposite of the results suggested by economic orthodoxy.

These three issues—inflation, the international financial system, and underdeveloped nations—were serious problems, but they did not involve the implicit values and goals of the post-Keynesian synthesis. In recent years, however, a series of issues which do just that has come to the fore: economic growth, the environment, the racial problem, and militarism. The discussions of these issues did not center on the theoretical basis of the post-Keynesian synthesis. Rather, its implicit policy goals were questioned, along with the social and economic institutions it sought to explain.

The once sacrosanct goal of economic growth was the first to be criticized, with the onslaught being led in this country by John Kenneth Galbraith and in England by E. J. Mishan. Galbraith pointed out that an economy dominated by private decisions about consumption and production tends to starve its public sector. This is especially true when motivations center on individual gains in income and wealth. Private spending on luxuries and entertainment expands while such foundations of the future as education and basic science are slighted. Furthermore, modern marketing and advertising techniques are used by business firms to mold consumer spending to their needs as producers, instead of adjusting production to match a pristine pattern of consumer wants. The system as a whole operates for the benefit of producers rather than consumers, if Galbraith's analysis is reasonably correct, and its goal is the aggrandizement of business wealth instead of the individual's welfare.

Mishan went even further, arguing that a materialistic society interested primarily in piling up more and more material goods was destructive of humane values and pursued goals antithetical to human happiness. The important point about Mishan's argument is not its novelty—his views are even older than the science of economics itself—but in its popularity. It struck a note that many were eager to hear.

The views expressed by Galbraith and Mishan were echoed by a new generation of youth disenchanted with the materialism of middle-income America, by workers dissatisfied with the monotony of their jobs and the limited horizons of their lives, and by blacks and Latins condemned to low wages, poverty, and welfare. Disenchantment, hostility, and alienation became facts of life for the economist as well as the psychiatrist to consider.

The growing militarism of American life raised further questions about economic goals. In the 1950s and 1960s, the greatest industrial nation in the world was using between 10 and 15 per cent of its huge and increasing output for military and related purposes. The obvious question arose: What is the advantage of economic growth if a large portion of the gain is used for wasteful or destructive purposes? But underlying that was an even more basic question: What is it about the economic system that drives it (or allows it to be driven) to such ends? Had military expenditures created such strong vested interests in the "military-industrial complex" that there was no going back to a humane economy? If these questions generated breezes of doubt before 1965, after the war in Southeast Asia escalated to high levels, they brought storms of dissent.

An equally fundamental issue arose as many people became aware of the potential environmental crisis the industrial nations seemed to be heading for. A growing economy produces increasing amounts of waste, and one in which high consumption levels are a major feature contributes even more. Modern industrial technology, furthermore, was not developed with compatibility with the natural environment in mind. Would continued economic growth destroy the ecological base not only of the economy but of human life as well? The economics of the post-Keynesian synthesis had no answer to that question, and the ameliorative measures suggested were only partial responses to a huge problem.

Finally, the persistence of poverty and the emergence of the urban-racial crisis in the United States in the late 1960s pointed up the fact that a large portion of the American people was not participating adequately in the affluence achieved by many. A devastating social and economic conflict emerged in the midst of what should have been a society with reduced conflict —because of growing affluence. It became clear that the benefits of affluence were *not* being so widely diffused as to strengthen the social fabric.

By now, even the orthodox post-Keynesian economist has good reason to doubt that the private-enterprise, market-oriented economy can resolve its problems effectively. A high-pressure economy has brought new strains on the social fabric and exposed intractable problems. Growth is now seen as potentially unbalanced, misdirected, or destructive. Inflation, a succession of international financial crises, problems of the Third World, cities torn by conflict, an endangered natural environment, militarism, the persistence of poverty, and growing alienation—instead of increased well-being, there is a crisis of confidence.

The tacit agreement between the haves and the have-nots has broken up. The war in Southeast Asis laid bare the shift in the locus of power to a relatively small group whose control over the decision-making process is supplemented by careful manipulation of public opinion and political process. The gains from economic growth stopped as the costs of the war escalated. Many young people saw, perhaps more clearly than their elders, the essential polity compromise that traded affluence for power and refused to accept it. Blacks and other minority groups, segregated in their urban ghettos and developing a racial and political consciousness, refused to accept their continued status as second-class citizens. The whole system of polity broke down. Along with it went the orthodox post-Keynesian synthesis of theory and policy. The paradigm of a smoothly adjusting system of largely competitive markets that produces what consumers want, provides rewards appropriate to effort, and is assured of stable economic growth through Keynesian macroeconomics policies lost its credibility. A growing radical movement sees the economic and political systems as essentially malign rather than benign, antagonistic to humane values rather than supportive of them. Contemporary economics is in crisis because the social order is in crisis, unable to go back to the old and unwilling to strike boldly toward the new.

The problems of the present indicate the path to the future. A reconstruction of economics—a new synthesis and a new paradigm—will have to move toward greater concern for humane values, toward a humane economy on a worldwide scale.

A humane economy requires more than prosperity and economic growth, more than efficient allocation of resources. It demands changes in the framework of economic institutions to achieve greater equality and freedom. It requires dispersal of the economic power and governmental authority that support the present disposition of income, wealth, and power. It requires a social environment that brings a sense of community and fellowship into human relationships. It demands compatibility among man, his technology, and the natural environment. And all of these things must be done on a worldwide scale. These are the goals of the future, to which economists and everyone else will have to devote their energies.

What *Did* Keynes Really Mean?

ALAN CODDINGTON

Is American Keynesian economics truly Keynesian or is it some deviant mutation?

One could easily get the impression that controlling the economy is a dramatic pursuit. A distinguished economist has likened it to the problem of driving a car while looking in the rear-view mirror and using the accelerator but not the brake; and the prevalence of nautical imagery always leaves room for the revelation that, despite skilled helmsmanship, one has been "blown off course." If one still appreciates that what is actually involved in all these cases are decisions about taxation, government spending, and financial arrangements, that appreciation represents a decisive triumph of mind over metaphor.

The way economists have tackled the problems of controlling the economy is hardly as dramatic or colorful as the imagery might lead one to expect. They cannot be blamed for the comparative dullness of the problems in practice, but they have been continually accused and found guilty of dismalness, narrowness, or base materialism in their outlook. "The age of chivalry is gone," it was announced. "That of sophisters, economists, and calculators has succeeded." (This remark is not found in a *Times* leader, nor even in a Noel Coward play, but in Burke's thoughts on the French Revolution.) Similar sentiments have been widely expressed ever since Carlyle and the Romantics, and stem partly from the mistaken impression that economics is somehow a celebration of acquisitiveness and an intellectual underwriting of the existing order. But, of course, "economic man" stands or falls on his explanatory value for economic phenomena, not the attractiveness

Excerpted from Alan Coddington, "What *Did* Keynes Really Mean?" *Challenge* (November-December 1974), pp. 13–19. Copyright © 1974 by International Arts and Sciences Press, Inc. Reprinted with the permission of International Arts and Sciences Press, Inc.

of his alleged character. At a more down-to-earth level, economists have been criticized for their tendency to take a two-handed approach to policy questions: that is, to make liberal use of the construction "on the one hand . . . but on the other hand. . . ." But, to be charitable, such an approach can often be useful in analyzing and clarifying the issues—in simply mapping out the various possibilities.

Indeed, I believe charity is not entirely out of place in one's view of the economics profession, if not of its individual members. For, unlike almost any other profession, economics is widely expected both to maintain standards of scholarship and to produce national policies that are administratively workable and politically acceptable. It should be noted that this is the role expected of the *profession;* very few economists would seriously attempt to encompass, at any point in time, the whole spectrum of endeavor from pure theory to practical politics, although they might traverse the spectrum over their careers as they move from the universities to Whitehall, or even the reverse.

Undeserved Credit

It is an exaggeration, however, to talk of economists "producing" policies, for their role is, at best, limited to advising on policy. In other words, they are but one link in the chain that produces economic policy. Also involved are the statistics on which diagnoses and forecasts are based, the ministers who take responsibility for the decisions which are made, and the administrators who put the decisions into effect. One might like to think of the policy advice as being the crucial link in the chain, but if the chain analogy is sound, how can one link be more crucial than another? Accordingly, one cannot, on the face of it, give credit solely to the economic advisers when things go well nor, for that matter, make them the sole objects of blame when things go badly.

Despite these reservations, it is clear from reading the literature of the subject that the economics profession took credit for the postwar era of full employment and growth. Indeed, this was presented as a clear-cut case of the success of Keynesian macroeconomics, suitably refined, developed and formalized, most notably by Hicks, Kaldor, and Harrod in Britain and Hansen and Samuelson in the United States. It was also during the 1940s and 1950s that the subject enjoyed a technical great leap forward through the development of econometrics and the application of analytically powerful concepts from such newly developing mathematical fields as linear programming and the theory of games. In such a heady atmosphere the fallacy of *post hoc ergo propter hoc* was hardly at the forefront of professional consciousness. And with the benefit of rather more hindsight, this interpretation of postwar economic policy as a decisive triumph for the economics profession in general and Keynesian doctrine in particular seems much less clearly justified. This is so not only as a result of the march of events, but also as a result of progress in economic analysis itself, as I shall attempt to show.

Depression Economics

Let us take the march of events first. It is no secret that the past few years have been a period of increasing puzzlement and disillusion among orthodox economists. It was only a few years ago that spokesmen of neo-Keynesianism could continue to claim that the problem of unemployment had been solved for all time, thanks to the efforts of the economics profession. It would take a remarkable facility in the postulation of Special Circumstances and Counteracting Forces to maintain such a claim now. Keynesian ideas were conceived in a period of depression, when the problem was one of stimulating the level of economic activity; the thought was that this could be achieved by means of the employment-generating effects of government spending in excess of tax receipts. (The effects of the methods of financing this spending complicate the picture, of course.) Fiscal measures also include reduction in tax rates. This and increased government spending are instruments of what has come to be called "reflation," which is distinct from both deflation and inflation. (The distinction between reflation and inflation is a nice one, depending more on intentions than on effects; it also depends a good deal on where one happens to be standing at the time.) At any rate, quite irrespective of the detailed workings of the processes, the *potency* of such fiscal measures became an article of faith in Keynesian doctrine, especially in relation to monetary measures, which were accordingly shunned as meager devices, or even as only passive reflections of deeper causes. Whether Keynes himself took this view is another story—in fact, the record is pretty clear that he did not. But, of course, it is hard to hold anyone responsible for the excesses of his disciples.

Economic Policies in Reverse

Now, on the face of it, there is no reason why these fiscal measures, given their alleged potency, should not be put in reverse in inflationary periods, when the problem is one of reducing aggregate demand relative to output. Increases in government spending would be replaced by economies, and correspondingly for the other measures. What events have taught us rather clearly is that although fiscal measures may have an impact on employment, the rate of inflation is pretty nearly impervious to them. Again, Keynes himself would not, perhaps, have been in the least surprised that this should be so. The idea that there is a definite inverse relationship between unemployment and the rate of inflation is a post-Keynesian doctrine, having its origin in the work of A. W. Phillips of the London School of Economics in the 1950s.

Let us return to the main substance of Keynesian ideas rather than the developments and offshoots. Lest one get the impression that they captured the whole economics profession, it should be pointed out that it is more accurate to say that they became the dominant orthodoxy. There always remained a fringe of dissent—or, rather, two fringes of dissent, since criticisms came principally from either the political right or the political left.

Criticism from the Left and Right

From the political right, Keynesian ideas were seen as a license for unlimited intervention in the workings of the economy and as a prescription for uninhibited growth of the public sector, all of which was presented as a threat to liberty and the proper functioning of what was repeatedly referred to as a free enterprise system. From the left, Keynesian ideas were regarded as a desperate and artificial propping up of an economic system overripe for revolutionary transformation, and hence, within the great historical scheme of things, deeply regressive. Thus, as is the fate of anyone who actually asserts something unfamiliar in the political arena, Keynes was branded as both a dangerous radical and an arch-reactionary. As a radical he was supposedly opening the gates to Creeping Socialism, while as a reactionary he was cast as the savior of Western Capitalism.

I am concerned not so much with these political attacks, interesting though they may be, but rather with the intellectual substance of Keynesian ideas: the claims that are made about the way a capitalist economy works. (This distinction is not so clear-cut in practice, since political attacks were often presented as first and foremost a criticism of the intellectual substance of Keynesian thought.)

Reappraisal

The intellectual reappraisal of Keynesian ideas was, considering their importance, a long time in coming: the major work was not published until 1968. Its title, *On Keynesian Economics and the Economics of Keynes,* embodies the distinction hinted at previously between the views of Keynes and those of his followers. Indeed, its author—a Swede working in the United States, with the imposingly forbidding name of Axel B. Leijonhufvud—made such a distinction crucial to his discussion. The general theme of this book is that there was much that was original and important in the work of Keynes himself, but that in the course of its ostensible systematization and development by his disciples, all that was most original and important was lost or destroyed. This is a serious charge, and if Leijonhufvud's account is correct, it means that true Keynesian Keynesianism has never been applied (with the assumption that it was rearmament and World War II rather than economic policy which cured the depression of the 1930s). In this view the history of Keynesian ideas becomes a story of intellectual corruption and decay.

Leijonhufvud's arguments are abstract and technical, and I can hope only to hint at some of his major insights here. However, he uses an analogy which may be illuminating, comparing classical and modern physics, on the one hand, with Classical economics and the economics of Keynes himself, on the other. In classical physics information has no part. A system working according to the laws of Newtonian mechanics unfolds in the same way irrespective of how much we know about its working. With Heisenberg's principle, however, all this was to change, for at the subatomic level, the behavior of a system and the knowledge we can acquire about it are no longer independent of one another; it is the behavior of the system which transmits information, and one must interfere with its behavior in order to acquire the information. It is a similar information revolution, Leijonhufvud suggests, that is involved in Keynes's own ideas.

Information in the Classical System

In the Classical system of economics, information is no problem; it is not even visible, for it is "reflected" in the price system itself. If everyone acts in response to market prices, this is sufficient to guide and coordinate their activity, and there is nothing else they need to know. In Keynes's ideas, however, all this was to change. For there, not only is the price system not transmitting or reflecting all the information that traders need to know, it is actually transmitting *mis*information. There is, accordingly, no presumption that behavior based on such misinformation alone will produce the guidance or coordination which separate economic activities need. (The particular prices which are crucial in this respect, and whose maladjustment is at the root of things in Keynes's thought, are wage rates, interest rates, and the prices of capital goods.) The parallel with physics is, of course, far from exact, but it is an interesting one, especially in light of the later development of the science of cybernetics, centering on the role of information in systems of control and adaptation.

When Markets Just Clear

How does this dramatic difference between Keynes's ideas and those that preceded them come about? The assumption of the classical system which was subject to most derision by its critics and which appears to be the most blatantly unrealistic of its suppositions is that of perfect competition. This assumption is retained by Keynes, however, and it turns out not to be crucial. What is crucial in the Classical system is not the assumption of perfect competition (or its equivalent, that no individual has any perceptible control over market prices) but the much less widely noted assumption that all prices adjust instantaneously so that markets clear. That is to say, the classical system was not a *general* theory of trading in a market economy; it was addressed to the special case of equilibrium trading, where all markets just clear. In reality markets are characterized by either surpluses (or excess supply) or shortages (or excess demand) at the prevailing market prices. And there is nothing in the assumption of perfect competition that guarantees that adaptation is always so fast that no surplus or shortage ever actually materializes. Thus, once we get away from the special case of equilibrium trading, there is no longer any presumption that the workings of the price system will automatically lead to the coordination of the independent activities in the economy. Such coordination would require an auctioneer to call out market prices until everyone's trading intentions meshed; trading would be allowed to take place only after such a suitable set of prices had been arrived at. That is, it would require information other than that which is automatically generated by and reflected in the workings of the economy; in the actual economy, trading goes ahead whether everyone's intentions will mesh or not. There is a strong resemblance, as Leijonhufvud points out, between the Walrasian auctioneer in economics and Maxwell's demon in physics.

In the Classical system it is *prices* that do all the adjusting necessary for the coordination of the economy. They do *all* the adjusting because they are supposed to do it instantaneously. But if, in the real world, we have markets characterized by surpluses and shortages, some of the burden of adjustment may be thrown onto the quantities bought and sold. This does not mean that prices are not adjusting, but only that they are not adjusting instantaneously to market-clearing levels. And here comes the *coup de grace*. For Leijonhufvud, building on the work of Robert Clower, shows that once we have a system involving *quantity* adjustment in the short run, the way is open for a process of perverse adaptation, more familiarly known as "the multiplier." The process becomes, in modern terminology, "disturbance amplifying" rather than the reverse.

Money Is an Institution

What is the role of money in all this? Since Keynes claimed that he had integrated the theory of money with the general theory of the functioning of the price system, there ought to be some mention of it. And indeed, the ideas already sketched have decisive implications for the role of money in the economy.

The point is that the Classical system might just as well be a barter economy as one using money. For in the Classical system all markets clear—everything can be marketed with equal ease at existing prices. But if money is anything it is something which can be marketed with *greater* ease than other goods. It is much easier to exchange a pound note for something than it is to exchange a pound's worth of soft-boiled eggs. The Classical system simply leaves no room for money; in a system which functions that way there would be no conceivable need for it. Of course, this reflects not so much on the dispensability of money as on the extreme artificiality of the classical system. And, accordingly, when money is introduced into the theory of such a system, it can only be in an extremely artificial and unilluminating way. Money is seen as just another good rather than as what it undoubtedly is—an institution. And this artificiality is not confined to pre-Keynesian writing on monetary theory.

The role of money may be illustrated by examining the conditions of a depression. Here we have a surplus of unemployed labor and of unsold commodities at existing prices and wages. But, because we live in a money-using economy, it is not possible to exchange labor services for commodities directly. Despite the fact that workers supply their labor because they demand commodities, this demand remains ineffective when it is not backed by possession of money. Accordingly, in this state the economy is simply not reflecting the wants and intentions of the individuals composing it. For if the unemployed workers' demand for commodities could only be made effective in the market, it would generate the very expansion in production which is needed to reduce the number of unemployed.

Once we have a picture of the economy that includes a transactions structure, so that money plays a crucial role, the way is open to analyze the processes set in motion by the existence of unemployment. If there is unemployment of labor, we may analyze its impact on the demand for goods and services in terms of the effect which a constraint on purchasing by households to which the unemployed belong will have on the incomes of those who are employed. In this way, what for Keynes was introduced as an ad hoc "psychological law"—the dependence of consumer spending on current income—becomes perfectly intelligible in economic terms as an "income-constrained process." The point is that once we get away from equilibrium trading, the adjustment processes quite naturally involve incomes rather than relative prices alone.

These ideas are a far cry indeed from what has been taught as Keynesian economics. What has happened at the level of teaching is that the ideas have been forced into the straitjacket of equilibrium (Keynes himself was partially guilty there, but he lacked much of the analytical apparatus that we have today). Students were told, in effect, that the Keynesian theory is much like the classical one except that, due to certain frictions and rigidities in the workings of the system, its "equilibrium" may be at less than full employment.

My own experience with students is that, given the staple fare they are brought up on in economics, Leijonhufvud's ideas produce blank incomprehension in general, and overt confusion in the more conscientious. Indeed, there are few things more disastrous for the student's state of mind than an actual attempt to read Keynes's *General Theory* rather than the innumerable guides and cribs to it.

So all this sets one wondering, and reopens questions that were generally thought to be long since settled. The dictum "we are all Keynesians now" is seriously undermined. We are driven back to the source to ask just what manner of book Keynes's *General Theory* was.

A Diversity of "Central Themes"

The startling thing about the book is that it is badly written, despite the fact that Keynes moved in the milieu of the Bloomsbury group and obviously had great aspirations as a stylist, and in addition already had had several books published. But in fact his attempt at polemical writing had always been extravagant to the point of embarrassment ("The nations of Europe throbbed together," he wrote to describe healthy trade conditions). This is not to say that the *General Theory* is badly written by the standards of other economics books. But there is one basic difference that makes Keynes's style forgivable: he was writing at the very limits of our collective comprehension of the workings of the economy.

It is not surprising, then, that a diversity of central messages has been read into the *General Theory*, and that the issue of what its key ideas are can be seriously reopened today. The crucial question that we are left with, though, is whether one can read into it what Leijonhufvud advances as "the economics of Keynes." My experience is of being unable to do so, and therefore having to conclude that, in his most central claim, Leijonhufvud is wrong: the very ingenuity of his attempts to find something coherent in Keynes's thought has led him to ideas far more subtle and profound than anything Keynes appears to have had in mind. Of course, the issue could be argued back and forth interminably in the form of detailed exegesis of Keynes's writings.

There is in the *General Theory* no "model"—no single, specifiable set of assumptions about how the economy works. Such neatness was the work of the disciples, and it now appears that, along with the untidiness, they discarded that which was most theoretically powerful and original.

Keynes and the Policy Makers

What is to be learned from all this? Perhaps that, in the end, nothing fails like the appearance of success. It would seem that, in public affairs, we really learn something only when things go wrong; at other times we learn things that are not so, by interpreting what happens as the result of our efforts, rather than as something which, to one degree or another, would have happened anyway. The real problem is appreciating, and coming to terms with, the extent of our ignorance.

From what we have seen, it appears that a true Keynesianism would have been much messier and more intricate than the sort we have had. Much more important, although it may be that such a faithful variant could have sustained an orthodoxy in economics, it is extremely difficult to see it providing a clear-cut and widely acceptable policy in the way that "Keynesian economics" did. For a belief in the potency of fiscal measures is tailor-made for the political center—allowing intervention in the economy without actually planning it. Its advocacy is the perfect compromise between being a socialist and not being a socialist.

Bourgeois and Radical Paradigms
in Economics

MICHAEL ZWEIG

Here is an analysis of two different economic paradigms in which differing
conceptions of society, man, and institutions are contrasted.

I

The study and teaching of economic relations as it has been done in
this century is now under attack from at least two directions. We see "modern
theory" developed in rigorous and highly abstract mathematical ways in work
such as Debreu's *Theory of Value*. This trend appears to challenge the traditional "literary" economics, but it is in fact not a departure from basic
traditional views on the economy, however threatening it may appear to
the uninitiated, or how painful its introduction into the regular curriculum
in some colleges and universities. And we see the development of a modern
radical "political economics" which seeks to investigate the character of
advanced capitalism and the position of economic activity in the larger social,
political, cultural, and sexual context in which it occurs. This tendency does
indeed challenge the foundations of most contemporary economics, on
grounds quite unrelated to mathematics *per se*.

The set-theoretic approach is working into graduate and even undergraduate curricula, while political economy is taking hold in undergraduate
and now even some graduate programs. One approach is narrowly focused
on mechanical operations of production and exchange, the other on broader
social processes and implications. Ask a student to explore the characteristic
roots of American capitalism, and one will begin by writing down (or asking
for) an appropriate assembly of linearly independent equations, while the
other raps about private property, class division, and the bourgeois democratic state.

From Michael Zweig, "Bourgeois and Radical Paradigms in Economics," *Review of Radical
Political Economics* (July 1971), pp. 43–55. Reprinted with the permission of the publisher.

II

Setting aside for a moment the language problem presented by mathematics, it is convenient to identify two large "kinds" of contemporary economics: bourgeois Neoclassical work; and radical (possibly Marxist or neo-Marxist) political economy. These can be usefully distinguished following the spirit of Thomas Kuhn's work. Kuhn proposes that the development of science is characterized by succeeding "paradigms," basic conceptions of matter, the universe, light, or whatever general object of study. A paradigm serves as a framework by which to choose "relevant" or "interesting" experiments or theorems, and also serves as the basis for interpretation of raw data and sense perceptions. A paradigm, or basic conception, is important in that it regulates and systematizes particular investigations and survives so long as it guides investigators into new problems which can be answered within the framework. One's choice of a paradigm within a discipline is therefore a critical determinant of the kind of problems to be generated and the work to be accomplished.

Kuhn traces out the history of science in these terms, focusing on chemistry, physics, and astronomy. Similar work can and should be done about the development of economic doctrines but here we will look only at two current paradigms. This contemporary cross-section abstracts from Kuhn's own essentially dialectic conception of history, borrowing only the category "paradigm" for help.

The two most central and distinctive elements of the bourgeois paradigm of capitalist economies are harmony and equilibrium. It may seem odd to foreclose on competition and substitute harmony, about which economists seldom say a word explicitly. Yet economic actors, all of them rational economic men and women, are homogenous behavioral units, no matter what their ethnic or racial background, their sources or amount of wealth and income. These different people all may behave differently in competition, but they are all motivated by formally identical desires (the standard "postulates of rationality"), and in a given situation (including tests and factor endowments) each would do the same. In this deep and important sense, all men are brothers, each recognizes himself in all others, all men are "about" the same thing in the same way. This harmony exists irrespective of the degree of competition, and indeed helps "explain" why competitors (are expected to) cooperate with the outcome of the market place in which they compete. One of the first lessons of bourgeois economics is precisely that in market exchanges, both parties gain from trade, establishing a supposed harmony of interest among all in the perpetuation of exchange through markets organized on a private, capitalist basis. Each economic actor, whatever his position, is a cooperative and committed member of capitalist society, in which he does the best he can.

This harmonious framework extends to the core of microeconomic activity, the process of maximization subject to constraint. For the bourgeois analyst of capitalism, economic man takes constraints as given and finds the best action consistent with those constraints. This suggests a passivity, or at least a resigned peace, with respect to the typical constraints, budget, and factor endowment, and with respect to the larger institutional and legal or customary constraints on production and distribution within a capitalist society. Once again, competitive behavior of actors is built on a more fundamental harmony, each person with respect to his own situation.

There are two superficial exceptions to this characterization of constrained behavior. Bourgeois economists analyze problems of economic development in Third World countries in terms of the systematic removal of constraints, particularly with regard to capital accumulation and sometimes mobility of labor. These problems arise because "backward," "irrational," and "primitive" people have institutional arrangements and personal criteria and expectations of success which are said to be unsuited to the task of development. Tribal and other traditional economic forms, as well as more modern socialist arrangements contain constraints which must be overcome in the process of becoming "forward," "rational," and "civilized," i.e., capitalist.

The second systematic treatment of constraint-breaking arises within the context of capitalism, and has to do with technology and capital accumulation. In the short run capital is fixed and constrains both output and the level of profit. In the long run this constraint is completely relaxed. The entrepreneur is constantly seeking ways to expand his capital, alter his technology, increase his profit and output. This is, after all, what capitalism is about. The entrepreneur is the engine of social and economic progress, to recall Schumpeter, and knows no bound. Any constraint of technology will fall by the wayside but only in a manner consistent with capitalism. This treatment of constraint, as in the case of development, does not alter the underlying harmoniousness of the bourgeois economists' view of capitalism.

The proposition that people do the best they can subject to unchallenged constraint is suspect insofar as it precludes revolt, revolution, and other means of assault on the constraints themselves. To bourgeois economists, such nonmarginal, systemic attacks are irrational and uncomprehensible in economic terms. They have no intellectual or formal analytic tools to deal with such behavior. This is another, and striking, indication of the harmony which is the foundation of bourgeois economics.

The second central element of the bourgeois paradigm is equilibrium. Almost all of economics, whether static or dynamic, micro or macro, long run or short, is organized on the basis of equilibrium or a tendency to such a state. Much effort and sophistication has been expended to prove its existence and explore its properties under a number of particular assumptions. Explorations of disequilibrium situations are done in terms of tendencies toward equilibrium, and even where these tendencies cannot be found, equilibrium positions constitute the reference point of the analysis. As a paradigm, equilibrium has been successful in guiding research on a variety of particular problems spanning the whole discipline. It provides unique solutions to formal problems and allows convenient mathematical properties to be explored. These are some of the immediate reasons for its wide acceptance despite the generally acknowledged view that the world is not in equilibrium or perhaps not even tending towards equilibrium.

But focusing on equilibrium conditions has other implications for one's view of the world. For one thing, the only interesting, important or noteworthy microeconomic actors are those still in the market at equilibrium. It is elementary that a "want" is not an economic "demand," nor is a skill or desire to produce a supply. Those demanders and producers who are priced out or who fall become irrelevant and cease to hold our attention.

This takes on more significance in light of the ordinary interpretation of equilibrium. A general static equilibrium is a situation in which all actors in all markets are "satisfied," in the two-fold sense that all expectations of each actor are just met (intentions are realized), and, therefore, no further adjustments or alterations in behavior are called for. This is, of course, entirely consistent with the paradigm of harmony. Dynamic equilibrium is interpreted as the static case, but in terms of rates of change per unit of time. At equilibrium, those in the market will continue to be there, those who have failed or been priced out will continue to be irrelevant, and each person, no matter what his position, will be "satisfied" in the behavioral sense. The acceptance of price rationing founded on a given distribution of income is complete and embraced by all, win or lose. At the least there is a smugness in this foundation of bourgeois economics.

Such as optimistic view of equilibrium was attacked by Keynes and his followers, particularly on the aggregate level. Yet that challenge is itself an equilibrium analysis, within the large bourgeois paradigm. And as it has developed, the challenging view is also optimistic in much the same sense as classical analysis, but with the significant addition of the State as a conscious economic actor, as a sort of happy equilibrator of last resort. In this view, private actors may reach a traditional equilibrium at a level of income and employment with large numbers of individuals frozen out in the process. If this result is unacceptable the government can intervene and bring some of those people back into the picture, at a "higher" equilibrium.

Aside from the technical questions raised in the post-Keynesian analysis, a theory of the State is at least implicit in it. The State acts (1) on behalf of the people, and in particular the poor, the unemployed, the small entrepreneur; (2) when the harmony of the economic world posited by the bourgeois economists begins to wear thin. The State as economic actor is therefore part of the harmony of capitalism and its people, part of an equilibrium in which jobs exist for all who want them (at the going wage), opportunities for investment are taken by those who seek them (at the going structure of interest rates), and the capitalist can continue to be the engine of progress. The world of the bourgeois post-Keynesian economist is also one of harmony and equilibrium, but now with a little help from everyone's friend, the State.

Economists have long deliberated on the proper role of government in economic affairs. Sometimes the work has been focused on the technical impact of tax, tariff and other policies, sometimes on broader questions of equity, power, and the nature of the State. On the last item Classical nineteenth century liberal economists took the view that the State is the enemy of freedom, and should be extremely limited in function. Milton Friedman carries that tradition on today, and contemporary anarchist economists like Murray Rothbard take it to its logical end. Modern twentieth century liberal economists subscribe to a pluralistic conception of the State and of the economy, consistent with post-Keynesian bourgeois analysis of capitalism and its continued reliance on harmony. Marxist and other radical political economists believe that the bourgeois capitalist State arises to serve the needs and interests of the dominant economic class, capitalists, who are antagonistic to other classes in the society. Foremost among these needs is the preservation of fundamental elements of private property. Radicals (other than anarchists) do not believe *in principle* that the State can or should play a limited role, nor do they believe that the bourgeois State is pluralist.

These different views of the State are intimately associated with alternative paradigms and elaborations of the economy. To the nineteenth century liberal, market equilibrium processes and harmony are hampered by State intervention. To the twentieth century liberal, market processes do not always guarantee "acceptable" equilibria, so the State functions to ensure social harmony in those instances where the market fails. To do this, the State must itself be an harmonious amalgam of different groups of economic actors, in order to be consistent with and complementary to the harmony of the marketplace where it functions well. To the radical, the State, with its monopoly of sanctioned force and violence, is a party to the basic conflicts of economic relations. The State attempts to regulate those conflicts while using its force to preserve the hegemony of the dominant class in property relations and in the ordinal ranking of the distributions of power and resource control. These different views of the State, together with their respective paradigms, differentiate bourgeois political economy from its radical counterpart.

It is this part of economic studies, together with associated institutional and historical inquiry which is challenged by the systematic mathematization of "economics." Questions of political economy, whether nineteenth or twentieth bourgeois in orientation, or Marxist, or whatever, do not seem to lend themselves to the abstract categorization required for general mathematical results. It is conceivable that the construction of much more sophisticated mathematical tools in game theory and related areas will make possible an intelligent mathematization of the development and role of the State, but now such messy problems are being expelled from serious economic study, leaving for our attention the narrow, mechanical processes of production and exchange which can be abstractly represented. To the extent that mathematical convenience confers suitability on a problem for study, and to the extent that people attracted to abstract mathematical thinking are intellectually or temperamentally incapable of dealing with broad, messy social and political questions, the domination of economics by mathematical analysis profoundly changes the character of the discipline.

The elaboration of the bourgeois paradigm by mathematical techniques does not, however, alter the central place of harmony and equilibrium in it. Reliance on mathematics limits only the scope of permissible elaboration and makes more difficult, obscure, and seemingly unscientific the inspection of the paradigm itself in social science.

III

Radical political economy organizes data and analytic categories in a framework of conflict and dialectic altogether alien to bourgeois economics. A paradigm of conflict asserts that for each conflict there is a grouping of the members of society into a small number of classes. The class position of an individual is determined by some objectively verifiable relation to the issue of conflict, although the individual need not himself be aware, or conscious, of his class status. A society is characterized by the conflicts it contains, and consequently by the class structures associated with these conflicts. Further, in any society there are a very small number of central conflicts to whose terms other conflicts are ultimately reduceable.

The best known elaboration of a paradigm of conflict is Marxist thought, in which the basic conflicts involve property rights. Relations among people, among classes, in capitalism are antagonistic, not harmonious. The antagonism lies not in market competition, which Marx analyzed in much the same way as other contemporary economists, but in the relations between classes of people; for instance, owners and nonowners of means of production. Since competition in the market is a feature of capitalism with which both Neoclassical economists and Marxists deal, it is not a distinctive feature of either paradigm. The distinction arises in the different social and interpersonal context in which that competition proceeds.

In the radical paradigm, there is no equilibrium, or tendency to it, within capitalism. While it is true that Marxist analysis includes an ultimate social equilibrium in advanced communism, this equilibrium is radically different from that of bourgeois economists. First, it is not a feature of capitalism. More important still, it is an equilibrium of the historical development of broad economic modes of production and exchange, not of a particular market or of market exchanges in general. Because Marxist social equilibrium is considered with respect to analytic categories wholly different from those of bourgeois thought, and occurs in an economic epoch remote from capitalism, it is incorrect to see a similarity between Marxist and bourgeois intellect on this point.

In place of equilibrium, the radical paradigm of capitalism proposes dialectic processes by which conflicts develop. Economic systems, and associated social relations, change over time in response to the tensions generated by the conflicts, or contradictions, which characterize them. A central tenet of dialectics is that the prime energy for systemic change is *internal* to the developing system, not exogenously imposed. Furthermore, this internal pressure is always operating within capitalism, first to develop it and then to transform it utterly.

For example, early stages of capitalist development in Europe were marked by sharp conflicts with feudal relations and values, which became increasingly vestigial as private property, mobility, and production for market exchange became hegemonic. Yet capitalism generates within itself the contradictions which lead to its transformation. The structure of private property and individual (or private group) decision making about production is in conflict with the cooperative and social process of production itself. As capitalism develops, increasing numbers of workers cooperate in production and exchange, while larger groups of people from more diverse backgrounds and more widespread geographic locations are integrated into the production of most commodities. The scope of industrial pollution and the social funding of education and research and development are examples of the latter, while extended division of labor relates to the former. As capitalism develops, tensions increase between private property and the increasingly communal nature and impact of production. The resolution of these internally generated conflicts may lead to fascism or socialism, but in any case, the complex of capitalism and bourgeois democratic political forms are seen to be unstable in the long run. Rather than focusing on equilibrium in capitalism, the radical employs dialectic reasoning to understand the ever-changing character and ultimate metamorphosis of capitalism.

In allowing for externalities, bourgeois analysis does recognize a part of the social character of production, but only as an exception, an anomaly. In the radical paradigm it is a central component of the analysis of capitalism as a dynamic system, fully expected and treated in dialectic thinking. What is to the radical an important part of an analysis of the transformation of capitalism is, understandably, anomalous to the bourgeois theorist.

Radical political economy based on a paradigm of conflict need not be Marxist in its analysis of the source of conflict. For Marxists the conflict is ultimately rooted in a labor theory of value. Such a theory of value gives rise to concepts of exploitation, surplus value, and other substantial and irreconcilable (under capitalism) characteristics of antagonistic class relations fundamental to Marx. Those who reject the labor theory of value see other roots of conflict endemic to capitalism.

There is, for instance, the degradation of consumers (particularly of women) through advertisement in the constant quest by capitalists to create markets for investment and further accumulation. This consumerism is responsible for some limited extension of genuine comfort beyond adequate subsistence, but it leads also to neurosis and to the waste of resources of energy, intellect, and material. These resources are perhaps better left unused, yet their use is imperative for growth and the continued accumulation of capital. Conflicts arise in advanced capitalism between the needs of the capitalist and the humanity of the mass of consumers. While Marxists have paid attention to the waste and general degradation associated with capitalist advertising, other radicals have recently focused especially on the conflicts between women and capitalist advertisers. Such a distinction is not easily made in Marxist thought, because women do not stand in this conflict as a class with some uniform relation to property.

The requirements of expansion lead abroad, as well, for added product markets and raw materials. To the extent that these international operations are necessary, and not merely convenient, and to the extent that a particular pattern of relations is imposed on foreign countries, something different from ordinary comparative advantage is operating. The conflict between the United States and Third World countries arises from such requirements, and American imperialism is being confronted militarily by popular forces in Vietnam and elsewhere.

One does not need a labor theory of value to view the State as an agency of those with economic wealth and power. It is a thesis of the revisionist school of history now growing that the character and policies of the federal government (at least) have been shaped by the changing requirements and consciousness of powerful corporate leaders, that the State has been captured by the big corporate bourgeoisie. The actions of the State in the overall task of preserving private property, and in the more specialized tasks of licensing and other "regulatory" functions, military protection of overseas interests, strike breaking, etc., suggest that the State is highly responsive to the needs of a small segment of the population with huge economic and political power. In radical political economy, the deep conflict between this group and the masses of people is a reflection of the very uneven distribution of resource control. Whether this distribution is itself due to exploitation in the Marxist sense, or to accumulation over generations through marginal productivity, or some other mechanism is a question of considerable importance. But disagreement among radicals over the source of conflict is on another level than the difference between the radical and bourgeois paradigm. The question cannot arise in a serious way within bourgeois analysis.

There are a number of phenomena treated differently by bourgeois and radical analysts, as well as other problems treated by one group but not the other. For instance, consider a person who spends 10 percent of her income on a given commodity or service, regardless of her income or the price of any other item. A clever bourgeois economist would characterize this behavior with the use of a logarithmic utility function. A clever radical would inspect the behavior to see if it is a tithing to the church, the State, a political party, etc., better to understand the concrete social relations reflected in exchange and underlying the abstract utility function concept.

Technology provides another example. Bourgeois analysis of technological change relates to productivity, profitability, and optimum investment policies. While radicals may also be interested in these relationships, they also explore broader economic and social implications of technology. Most important among these is the impact of technology on the socialization of the productive process. This development is further analyzed dialectically in relation to the private ownership and control of productive forces. Marx developed a general analysis of capitalism along these lines, as did such an anti-Marxist as Schumpeter. A radical analysis of technology also explores the relation of technological change to changing tastes, consumption needs, and educational forms.

Radical treatment of technology also must take into account the social implications of private criteria by which technological possibilities are implemented (or not) in actual practice. While ordinary notions of externalities are a part of the analysis, it is important to trace how social relations, alienation, and environmental transformations develop out of private decision making. Such considerations are different from the nonpecuniary externalities occasionally mentioned in bourgeois literature. This approach makes it possible to see that the kind of technology created, and the consequent social arrangements, are intimately bound up with the persons and interests controlling the creation.

Different views of technology relate to different analyses of "the long run" behavior of the firm. To the bourgeois, long-run problems refer to optimum plant size and output. The problem is messier with changing technology, but definite results obtain if future profitable technologies are known at the present, but not profitable until some definite time. If technology changes in unpredictable ways, nothing definite can be said, and one does best to reflect with Keynes on the mortal nature of man. Yet all of this (except the reflection) is folly to the radical. For in the long run technology does change, and new technologies cannot be analyzed separately from concommitant changes in tastes, which cannot be systematically integrated into abstract bourgeois microeconomics. And in the long run not only are we all dead, but so are the disembodied corporate person and capitalism itself.

IV

One of the claims made for bourgeois economics is that it is value-free. Milton Friedman's *Essays on Positive Economics* tries to make this case, and Professor Stigler has written that "economics as a positive science is ethically—and therefore politically—neutral." The tendency is to contrast this neutrality with the "polemical," "ideology-laden," or "biased" economics of Marx and other radicals. The strict computational techniques of marginalism may well be nonnormative, but computational techniques do not constitute a science. Rather the paradigm or world view which gives importance to one computation, skill, or problem over another is the central matter. In the case of economics, that choice has important ideological content and implications.

Acceptance of the bourgeois paradigm necessarily involves one in the position that efforts to break constraints without first "maximizing" within them are irrational acts. That is a political statement. One is led to focus on equilibrating processes, with a relegation to anomaly or irrelevance those dialectic interactions which continue throughout the capitalist epoch. That is an ideological statement. One has the view that economic actors are identically motivated, essentially interchangeable, and that each can do the best for himself through the institutions of private property and capitalism. That is a political and ideological statement.

It is of course true that Marxist and other radical political economy is also ideologically charged. That is a necessary component of any social science. The choice of problems, the choice of appropriate methodology, and the paradigmatic context in which limits and order are placed on inquiry must involve political and ideological components, no matter what the choice. For if it is ideological to structure an analysis around class struggle, it is equally so to deny that struggle, explicitly or by concentrating on harmonious relations. Professor Stigler's self-confident conclusion that political economists are conservative and duly appreciative of the beauties of capitalism, that they "cannot believe that a change in the *form* of social organization will eliminate basic economic problems," has been true. And this he correctly attributes to "the effect of the scientific training the economist receives." That is the power of education and an empirical validation of the ideological and political roots of bourgeois economics.

V

I have sketched out and tried to explain two competing paradigms: the bourgeois, based on harmony and equilibrium; and the radical, based on conflict and dialectic. Each is a way of organizing perception, each suggests problems and areas of research which are to a large extent nonoverlapping. As Kuhn points out, "To the extent, as significant as it is incomplete, that two scientific schools disagree about what is a problem and what a solution, they will inevitably talk through each other when debating the relative merits of their respective paradigms . . . paradigm debates always involve the question: Which problems is it more significant to have solved? Like the issue of competing standards, that question of values can be answered only in terms of criteria that lie outside normal science altogether, and it is that recourse to external criteria that most obviously makes paradigm debates revolutionary."

The current growth in attractiveness and power of the radical paradigm among faculty and students in economics originates in external criteria and demands on our analysis. The events of the past decade have involved us in a world best characterized by conflict, contradiction, and dialectic, at home and internationally. To understand those events, we have studied history and found it best characterized similarly. Yet bourgeois economics is based on an entirely different perception, one which is contradicted in our daily experience and therefore counterproductive in understanding social reality.

Bourgeois analysis explains the outcome of economic processes and even education in terms of fixed tastes. Yet we know that tastes are themselves the object of deliberate manipulation to suit the needs of profit seekers, whether through advertising or the socialization involved in education, even of economists. The distributions of income, wealth, and resource-control are central determinants of production and distribution, yet even bourgeois economists generally agree that they have no adequate theory of these distributions, which are among the most important constraints on people's activity and life. The legal requirements of private property reflect not only very particular standards and criteria of success, but limit substantially the permissible scope of economic reform. The State, with its monopoly of sanctioned violence, is the ultimate enforcer and guarantor of the domestic and international institutional and power relations without which American capitalism could not continue.

A central feature of the turmoil experienced in the past 10 or 15 years has been the systematic identification, questioning, rejection, and ultimate breaking of constraints by people seeking freedom from oppression. Whether in protracted wars of national liberation, the militant black movement in America, among fighters for women's liberation, the Yippies, and even within the relatively trivial movements for student power and curricular reform, the process is essentially the same. People are determined to control their own country, resources, intellect, body, culture, and energy. Externally imposed constraints which keep people from those goals become the target of assault, but only after they are sorted out from among all the feelings and attitudes at first unthinkingly internalized in the course of normal education and socialization, organized by existing powers. In the process, every major constraint in bourgeois economics has been challenged: tastes; distributions of income, wealth, and resource control; private property; the criteria of success. And in response to the State violence called down upon the challengers, the bourgeois State itself has become a target, and sometimes the State in any form.

These conflicts are deep and at the heart of life-and-death struggles. They cannot be analyzed in a context of harmony and equilibrium. They cannot be understood if their very essence is assumed, much less assumed in a manner consistent with the interests of one party to the struggle. However powerful bourgeois economics may be in answering questions generated by its paradigm, it cannot deal with the economic aspects of the major events of recent times and the likely future. It holds fixed what is changing. It takes for granted what is at issue.

Recognizing this analytic vacuum, and in response to the real struggles going on in the world, economics students and faculty are seeking to elaborate the radical paradigm outlined in this paper. Some are working in intellectual isolation, others have formed the Union for Radical Political Economics. Some are Marxists, others are working on alternate variants of the paradigm. All are seeking ways to resist the pressures of professional socialization in the bourgeois intellectual mold, and in that we find support and example among the people whose struggles, like our own, form the core of the radical paradigm.

The Image of Man in Economics

WALTER A. WEISSKOPF

A basic question in economic theory concerns itself with the theory of man on which economic theory in general is based. Here is an analysis that traces the evolution of economic theory in terms of the different view of man commonly employed.

Economists have never developed a philosophical framework for their implicit assumptions about human nature. When economics became an autonomous discipline, it separated itself from philosophy. During the ascendancy of economics, theology and philosophy declined in importance. Assumptions about human nature in economics were and are incidental byproducts of what was supposed to be empirical and logical truth. The very question of what is human nature cannot be and is not answered by any segmental discipline such as economics but only by a philosophy which encompasses the totality of experience. Such a philosophy existed before the scientific and industrial revolutions but has been gradually destroyed by modern thought.

Nevertheless, the history of economic thought abounds with statements and implicit assumptions which, put together, present an image of man. It was and is an image of how man should be in order to function in the economy. The economic image of man, although referring to actual economic behavior, has almost always a normative connotation: Man *should* be such and such in order to be an effective subject of the economy. Assumptions in economics about the nature of man, then, are rarely ever factual statements but value judgments—judgments how man ought to be, how the economy wants man to be, what he should want, will, think, and do so that the aims

Excerpted from Walter A. Weisskopf, "The Image of Man in Economics," *Social Research* (Autumn 1973), pp. 547–63. Reprinted with the permission of the publisher.

of the economy become his own aims. In analyzing the image of man in economics, one has to deal with hidden normative statements couched in factual language. Thus, most of what follows will deal with a sometimes explicit but more often hidden normative approach to human nature. Economists have implicitly shown how human nature *should be* to make the economic system work.

These normative assumptions about the kind of human nature required by the economy performed a twofold function. As far as they were presented in the form of factual statements, they supposedly served as explanations of reality. However, by presenting what should be in the form of statements about what is, they served the purpose of justification and legitimation of existing economic institutions such as the free market and private property. Identifying a desideratum as a fact is a way of justifying an ideal in a culture in which empiricism and naturalism of a narrowly defined science reign supreme. If theology and philosophy are abandoned, science remains the only source of cognitive *and* normative truth. By stating that an ideal is a fact, is rooted in the nature of man, in his reason or his drives and instincts, that ideal is vindicated. The continuing fight about the nature of economics—whether it is a "positive" or a "normative" discipline—overlooks the ambiguity of human existence and the dialectical nature of thought. Economics belongs to the social disciplines that deal with human beings and the human condition. As such, economics is a mixture of science and ethics; and it matters little whether one considers it as a science with normative implications or as an ethos with scientific foundations. Obiter dicta of economists about human nature have—consciously or unconsciously—a normative character; and they are presented in such a way as to justify and legitimize existing economic institutions in the light of an ideal norm presented as a fact.

The Classical Economists' View of Man

Against mercantilistic restrictions Adam Smith used critical reason; but his main ideas on how the wealth of nations is produced represent an exercise in confirming reason. He uses reason to justify and legitimize the free market by trying to prove that its governing principles are rooted in human nature and that they lead to a just and beneficial result. His concept of human nature still underlies the mainstream of economic thought; it performs a legitimizing function. This was clearly recognized two centuries later by F. S. Mason:

> . . . it seems to be a fact that the institutional stability . . . of an economic system is heavily dependent on the existence of a philosophy or ideology justifying a system in a manner generally acceptable to the leaders of thought in the community. Classical economics in the form of a philosophy of natural liberty performed that function admirably for the nineteenth century capitalism.

And still more recently a highly regarded market research survey discovered a general uneasiness among the buying public which it explains as follows:

> In making psychological and attitude studies over a period of many years, we have been continuously impressed with the need people have to find moral justifications for their own actions and even more important for what is done in their name by their own country. And the events of the past few years . . . have created a terrible uneasiness about the moral directions our institutions are taking.[1]

Economics, in its academic as well as in its popular formulations, has tried to fulfill this need for moral justification of the economic system and of the behavior it requires from its participants. The growing use of mathematics, econometrics, and abstract model building has obscured this function and tended to repress the moral philosophy which is implied in economics. However, its concepts of human nature were chosen, consciously or unconsciously, to serve the purpose of moral justification.

The normative elements in Adam Smith's thought are related to the natural-law tradition of the seventeenth and eighteenth centuries. Growing out of Christian theology, the idea of natural law represented a peculiar symbiosis of normative and "scientific" principles. It contains the scientific idea of a "natural law" that works with "necessity beyond all resistance," implying a deterministic scientism. But it also retained the idea of a just order. Natural-law thinking was always a combination of science, ethics, and politics, a normative discipline of an order of justice. The ambiguity of the term *law*—a scientific law on the one hand, and a part of the legal order on the other hand—shows the Janus character of natural-law thinking. In a society in which the universe was considered a creation of God, these two aspects of natural law ran together: Nature and society could be interpreted as a lawful order created by God. In the seventeenth and eighteenth centuries, nature and reason replaced God as a source of such an order. In the natural-law philosophy, "normative" law and the "positive" scientific law were not yet sharply separated. This is also the case in the economic teachings of the Physiocrats and the Classical economists. They derived their principles of political economy from nature and reason and implied that these principles would lead to a just order, a philosophy of natural law.

In *The Wealth of Nations* Adam Smith emphasizes again and again the acquisitive aspect of human behavior. What is important, however, is that he considers acquisitive action as rooted in human nature. Thus, he has laid the foundation to an approach that has become generally accepted in the Western world. The bar-stool philosopher who defends the venality of people by the statement "you can't change human nature" harks back to *The Wealth of Nations:*

[1]Daniel Yankelovich, "Business in the 70's: The Decade of Crisis," *Michigan Business Review* (November 1972), 27 ff.

> The desire of bettering our condition comes with us from the womb
> and never leaves us until we go to the grave. . . . Every individual
> is continuously exerting himself to find out the most advantageous em-
> ployment for whatever capital he can command. . . . There is a certain
> propensity in human nature . . . the propensity to truck, barter, and
> exchange one thing for another.

Adam Smith leaves open the question "whether this propensity be one of
those original principles in human nature of which no further account can
be given; or whether, as seems more probable, it be the necessary consequence
of the faculties of reason and speech. . . . It is common to all men." In
any case, the propensity to exchange is an innate trait of human nature.
It also rests on individual self-interest and self-love, which again are interpreted as basic traits of human nature.

Thus, the foundation was laid for a basic tradition of economic thought:
A historically relative, time- and culture-bound value attitude, the acquisitive orientation, was derived from human nature and human reason. The
striving for more and more money, wealth, possessions, and riches has developed against fierce resistance because it ran counter to the entire Occidental
tradition. Moneymaking for its own sake, the taking of interest, buying cheap
and selling dear, exploiting the fluctuations of supply and demand for one's
own advantage—all these and other activities which form the daily routine
of economic life in the modern economy were considered morally reprehen-
sible throughout Western civilization until the advent of capitalism.

In order to become socially acceptable against the resistance of tradi-
tionalism, acquisitiveness had to be morally justified. To accomplish this,
it had to be demonstrated that the acquisitive orientation was part and parcel
of the central belief system of the period, a natural-law philosophy which
unified cognitive and normative beliefs. If the acquisitive attitude could be
interpreted as part of a comprehensible and meaningful whole, it would
thus be justified in spite of the tradition which rejected it. The value orientation—acquisitiveness—had to be derived from a cognitive belief system. Religious justification, tracing acquisitiveness back to God and revelation, was
unacceptable to the eighteenth century. Nature and reason had replaced
them. Thus, by deriving acquisitiveness from nature and reason, Adam Smith
made it morally acceptable and legitimate.

That Adam Smith aimed—consciously or unconsciously—at a justification of acquisitiveness becomes quite clear from his definition of economic
liberty and from his theory of the natural harmony of interests. The idea
of the natural identity or harmony of interests is the cornerstone of the
philosophy of economic liberty and of the free market. It is obviously a
justification of economic liberty by trying to demonstrate that it leads to
social harmony. It rejects the Calvinistic and Hobbesian tradition of general
human depravity, and aligns itself with the Lockean tradition: Man is natural-

ly good; his natural instincts and his reason do not inspire vicious behavior. In *The Wealth of Nations,* the pursuit of economic self-interest is not a vice (as it still is in Mandeville's *Fable of the Bees,* whose subtitle is *Private Vices—Public Benefits*); the pursuit of economic self-interest is natural and reasonable because it promotes the *public* good, that is, the wealth of the nation. This is still the cornerstone of the popular belief in the free-enterprise system as far as it is still alive and the philosophical ground for statements such as: "What is good for General Motors is good for the country." It implies a *natural* harmony of interests: Individual economic interests are not in conflict with each other and with the common good. This comes about "naturally," through economic liberty, and not through governmental coordination. That this line of reasoning is clearly apologetic can hardly be denied.

The implicit intention to justify the goal of the free-market economy through economic reasoning about human nature and society is even more obvious in the way in which the harmony of interest is made plausible by defining individual and common economic interests in an identical way. The reasoning proceeds in these steps: (1) Nature and reason have instilled in people the drive toward economic self-interest consisting of monetary gain. (2) Monetary gain is accomplished by the individual working harder, producing more products, and selling them to others. (3) The common economic interest consists in an increase of the national "produce," the volume of goods produced and supplied for sale. Thus, by defining individual and social economic goals in the same way the natural identity of all interests is demonstrated.

The labor theory of value is another construct which serves to justify the moral legitimacy of the market and price system. Its morality rests on the presupposition that reward should increase in proportion to effort. To see this, it is not necessary to go into the intricacies of the labor theory of value. Labor was still the main factor of production in the time of Adam Smith. Also, John Locke had justified individual private property as the result of personal labor ("the labor of his body and the work of his hands . . . are properly his"). Hard work, together with thrift, became the foremost virtues of the bourgeosie in contrast to the idleness and profligacy of the aristocracy. If it could be demonstrated that price differentials conform to differences in effort and that those who work harder (and longer) will receive a higher reward in the form of a higher price, differences in prices and incomes are morally justified. This is what the labor theory of value tried to prove.

This moral principle is assumed to be rooted in human nature insofar as it relates merit and reward. In a way, the labor theory of value as presented by Adam Smith and Ricardo interpreted the free market and price system as a meritocracy where merit is defined as labor effort (measured by labor-time). The underlying feeling is still alive in the slogan "equal pay for equal

work." It relates to the antinomy of equality and inequality. The feeling
that human beings are equals and should be treated as such is qualified by
the recognition that there can be differences justified by an accepted scale
of values. In the Western political system, equality before the law is a basic
principle. In the Western free-market system, however, this principle is qualified by the principle of achievement leading to differences in income and
wealth. In order to coordinate political equality with the differences created
by economic competition, the idea of equality of opportunity, which com-
bines initial equality with the inequality resulting from competition, has been
introduced.

In present-day economics, these inequalities are justified mainly on
functional grounds: They are necessary as incentives for increased effort and
production. Classical economics, however, supplemented this functional argument by a moral defense of price and income differentials through the
labor theory of value. The producer is justified in charging a higher price
and thus receiving a higher reward if he has invested more labor in the
production of the product. Hence the desperate attempts of Ricardo to explain profits, the rewards of capital, as accumulated labor. If there were
no labor involved, profits would lack a moral basis. He could not detect
such a moral basis for the rent paid to the landlord. Therefore Ricardo could
not explain rent in the same way as he did other prices and incomes (in
terms of labor invested); rent had to be declared the result of the price
of corn, and not a constituent; a residue without a moral basis: "the landlords
. . . love to reap where they never sowed." Ricardo tried and failed to explain profits in terms of labor. Thus important types of incomes could
not be morally justified on the basis of merit. They were felt to be "unearned
increments."

Marx, using the same implicit moral principle of the interdependence
of effort and reward, carried Ricardo's analysis to its logical conclusion. If
actual prices and incomes are not commensurate to effort, the economic
system is morally wrong and should be changed. Income differentials *should*
be determined by merit—that is, by labor effort—and those who are not
putting in this effort should be expropriated. The surplus value is value
unearned by labor and therefore immoral.

To summarize: The main ideas of the classical economists on acquisitive
self-interest, the natural harmony of these interests, and the principle that
man has a natural property right in the fruits of his labor form a syndrome
of assumptions about men and their economic interrelations which aimed
at the moral justification of the free market and price system as they saw
it. These ideas about human nature and social relations were dictated by
the need of the period to find a ground for the legitimacy of the economic
system.

These fundamental ideas have never been completely abandoned in
the mainstream of orthodox economic thought. However, a gradual disin-

tegration of the philosophy of natural law took place. In the following, this development will be illustrated by describing some of the images of man in postclassical economic thought.

The Prudent Victorian Economic Man of Alfred Marshall

The intellectual framework erected by Alfred Marshall, the "father" of economic Neoclassicism, and retained by economics up to the present, rested on two pillars: economic rationality on the one hand and a subjective interpretation of human wants on the other hand. Whereas the Classicists had founded economic value on objective factors (labor–time, costs of production), the Neoclassicists explain economic value of a good by its utility. In a way, utility is the denatured offspring of Bentham's pleasure principle. According to the Utilitarians, man strives for pleasure (utility) and avoids pain (disutility). *Utility* was defined as the benefit derived from the satisfaction of *entirely subjective* drives, wants, desires, and tastes, originating with the individual as the last, indivisible entity of the economic system. This subjectivism is, however, thoroughly blended with an attitude already present in Classical thought, namely, economic rationality. The turn toward subjective needs—utility, happiness, and individual desires—brought to the fore a hidden problem of our economic civilization: the existence of human inclinations incompatible with the type of conduct which the economic system required, such as the disinclination to work, the resistance to activism, the desire for passivity, contemplation, enjoyment of nature, art and the senses, the unwillingness to pursue long-run goals in a systematic, consistent fashion, to act deliberately and calculatedly, to repress capricious, impulsive behavior. If satisfaction of subjective desires is the ultimate goal, much of economic activity is endangered by the fact that the exchange economy permits only the fulfillment of those needs which can be satisfied by the acquisition of money and wealth and through exchange in the market; and only in a way which often conflicts with many "noneconomic" human propensities. Also, no social order is conceivable in which the satisfaction of purely individual aims is the supreme goal; such a system must end in anarchy.

Alfred Marshall provided a counterweight against purely relativistic and anarchic subjectivity through his emphasis on economic rationality. He represents economic rationalism as an ideal and, at the same time, as the ultimate result of the working of economic laws. He shows that the behavior of consumers and producers can be understood with the help of models of rational economic action and that this type of conduct will have long-run beneficial results.

> . . . It is deliberateness not selfishness that is the characteristic of the modern age. . . . Now the side of life with which economics is especially concerned is that in which he most often reckons up the advantages and disadvantages of any particular action before he enters in it.

The value symbol of rational economic man becomes the focal point of economic thought. Through this emphasis on rationality, directed toward the goal of higher activities, the danger was avoided that nonrational, impulsive, emotional elements would enter through the door of subjectivism and destroy not only the regularity of the economic law, but also the discipline required for the working of the economic system. Therefore, it had to be demonstrated that rationality dominates all types of economic activity. The consumer, housewife, entrepreneur, firm, saver, etc., are all represented as people who consciously *balance* opposing forces, values, interests in such a fashion that they *maximize* the total of their advantages, utility, profits, etc. In all cases the existence of inner conflicts between goals, values, and impulses, and between what man wants to do and what the economic system permits him to do, is ignored. Human action is represented as directed toward a consciously calculable maximization point at which full satisfaction under given conditions can be reached. Conflicting drives and inclinations of a qualitatively different nature are reduced to a common quantitative denominator, so that conscious comparison of relative quantities of gain and loss can show the way to a clear-cut decision maximizing benefits and equilibrating opposing forces. Rational economic conducts, maximization of gains and equilibrium, became essential characteristics of human nature.

This well-known image of rational economic man is derived from the behavior required of a business manager. As David Riesman has formulated it: Man is supposed to act like a firm and like the firm's auditor. Thus, economics, ever since the Neoclassicists, developed a rationalistic concept of human nature.

The "Irrational" Consumer of Advertising Psychology

In Neoclassical and later economic thought, this maximizing rationality still had a relatively substantial content. Marshall and the Victorians knew how a prudent economic person is supposed to behave. Marshall counsels "wholesome enjoyment," "subordination of the desire for transient luxuries to the attainment of more solid and lasting resources which will assist industry in its future work, and will . . . tend to make life larger." He roundly condemns "superfluous" luxuries, and he advises the worker that only $1/40$ of the expense for green peas in March are productive; the other $39/40$ are superfluities.

All this shows that the Victorians filled the rational maximizing framework with the substance of their values. The goals of the individual were not yet considered as purely arbitrary and subjective. The individual was not really supposed to act as he pleases but should conform to the Victorian ideals of what a solid citizen should do and was doing.

In the course of history, economics became more and more value-empty. It abandoned the Victorian ideals of character formation. The rational framework disintegrated from within through the "liberation" of subjective impulses, drives, and desires. This was partly the effect of growing affluence and partly the reflection of the general disintegration of restraints and inner controls in Western civilization. This unchaining of subjective individual impulses and desires took place mainly in the field of consumption. This decontrol fulfilled not only a psychological but an economic need because the affluent growth economy required a continuous spurring of desires for more and new goods and services.

Thus in the twentieth century the prudent Victorian economic man became the "irrational" consumer directed by advertising and salesmanship. Pure subjective experiences, sensations, "kicks" were admitted into the economic image of man. The present-day orgies of spending caused by advertising receive their intellectual justification from this purely subjectivistic interpretation of consumers' desires. By eliminating all restraints from the formation of these desires, even the sale of the most wasteful, senseless, harmful goods and services is economically justified if they satisfy consumers' whims and demands.

The history of economic thought shows how this result was brought gradually about. Economic thought always retained the idea that subjective "utility" should be pursued in a deliberate fashion and the consumer should not give in to "blind forces of external stimuli and uncoordinated impulse at every moment" (Lionel Robbins). But if the consumer is completely free and sovereign to decide about his wishes, why should he not give in to sudden stimuli and impulses? Economic theory preached rational restraint; but modern advertising, indeed the modern style of art, leisure, and consumption, actually discarded all restraints. The stress on spontaneity, immediacy, and direct, momentary experience is the consequence of subjectivistic economic utilitarianism.

The image of man implied in advertising and in modern sales methods is one of a passive person, open and vulnerable to external and internal stimuli leading to spending. The unconscious mind becomes a vehicle for directing economic behavior. The prototype is the dissatisfied, restless housewife who, after husband and children have left for the day, visits the department store, lets herself be titillated by the exhibited goods, and spontaneously, without clear-cut wants and purpose, succumbs to the lure of salesmanship and buys something she does not "really" need and will later regret having bought. This is "man" or "woman" completely under the sway of the id in its commercial manifestations. What is bought is not a good but a momentarily pleasant, tickling experience.

The emerging image of human nature is partly derived from Bentham's "pleasure" principle, but its dialectic structure was brought to light by Freud. His image of human nature rests on the antinomic conflict between the id and the ego, between the pleasure and the reality principle. The id pursues libidinal pleasure without restraint. It has to be controlled by the ego (consciousness and conscience), which is ruled by the reality principle and thus preserves the id from pain through collision with the obstacles which the real world puts in the way of the libido. Similarly, economics, ever since its Neoclassical formulation, presents the "economic man" whose pursuit of subjective pleasure is restrained by conscious deliberate maximization. In the course of development, the Western mass-consumption society has to a large extent destroyed the shackles of rational restraint and instituted uncontrolled impulsive buying and consumption as the cornerstone of its continuous expansion. Still, rationality is required in production, in technology and organization. The dialectical conflicts of the economic and psychoanalytic images of man reflect Western man's economic contradictions.

The Revival of Political Economy

In the philosophy of economic liberty the market was supposed to be the beneficial regulator of the economy. If the Invisible Hand of the free market guides all economic activity in the right direction, no question of morality, no conflict between right and wrong economic action, arises. In the free market the individual person or firm has only one task: to pursue economic self-interest. The Invisible Hand will transform these egotistic actions into the common good. Thus questions of morality, of conflict between individual and public interests, cannot arise. This is why Milton Friedman and his school reject any demand for the social responsibility of the corporation; concern for the common good is left entirely to the free market. It supposedly performs like a cybernetic self-correcting system. Interfering with it would be like stoking up the furnace in an automatic heating system. This is again a case in which the "scientific" interpretation serves as a legitimizing and justifying device.

This device became obsolete when the belief in the beneficiality of the free market broke down. This happened in a slow process during the first half of the twentieth century. The growth of big business, monopolies, and market power, the countervailing growth of governmental interference and control, the disruption of the Western economies by World War I and the Great Depression of the 1930s, undermined the belief in the self-regenerating powers and beneficiality of the free market. In traditional economic thought, as presented in textbooks, this idea was never explicitly abandoned; but it was modified in the 1930s by admitting degrees and qualifications of market freedom, by distinguishing between perfect, pure, imperfect, monopolistic competition and market power. However, it was recognized that corporations with large shares of the market and governments and their agencies were not any more subject to the steamroller of the competitive market. They exercise power of their own; the Invisible Hand of the market was replaced by the visible hand of corporations and governments (Edward Mason). This opened the door for a revival of a normatively oriented political economy.

The recognition of market power led to the admission of choice between various economic goals and policies. Large firms can protect themselves against competition; they do not have to accept the market price but can administer their own prices within certain limits; they can create their own demand through advertising. And last but not least, they can assume the burden of social responsibility by modifying the relentless search for higher profits through welfare measures for their employees, through considering the social effects of their business, etc. Managers are now often considered as quasipublic officials who should try to balance the conflicting interests of stockholders, suppliers, customers, the labor force, and the general public.

All this implies a new image of man. Man in the free market is man without choices—at least man as a producer and seller. He can sell at the market price or go bankrupt. He has to produce as cheaply as the competition. He cannot engage in the luxury of noneconomic motivations (friendship, compassion, social responsibility) if it increases costs and prices him out of the market.

The large corporations with market power and government agencies *can* exercise choices; and this raises the question of norms, goals, ideals to guide these choices. The normative element was thus resurrected and reinstated. This changed the image of man in the modern economy.

Galbraith's *Affluent Society* is an example and symptom of this change. This book represents a renaissance of moral reasoning in economics. Galbraith subjects the result of the present economic system to a scrutiny from the point of view of moral and political standards. He denies the beneficiality of more and more production and applies standards of right and wrong to the present method of allocation. He raises the question of the individual and social good and condemns the overabundance of private production and the paucity of public services. Economics became again political economy and a branch of moral philosophy.

Thus, the image of man has changed: from an egotistic pursuer of profit and gain (although only through hard work and thrift), to a "rational" maximizing robot serving the competitive market mechanism; to emerge, at least in some economic thought, as a person confronted with moral choices. Only a small minority of economists today would approve of the last image; but under the impact of the ecological dangers and of growing alienation among intellectuals, blue-collar workers, academic youth, and disadvantaged groups, a real critical political economy, concerned with the choices between senseless cancerous growth and a more balanced existence, may emerge. Economists may once again become more interested in wisdom than in quantitative analysis. Their image of man may then change from a mathematical skeleton to a real human person with finite freedom guided by moral sense and the firmament of moral standards.

Economics as a "Value-Free" Science

ROBERT L. HEILBRONER

In the following analysis Professor Heilbroner argues that the fact that economics is not and should not be value-free does not invalidate the need to retain objective methods of science.

Is economics a science? Partly that depends on how we choose to define the word. Does science mean a search for "repeatable patterns of dependence" among variables, the definition suggested by Ernest Nagel? This nicely fits the current fashion for functional models in economics, but omits large areas of economic scrutiny, including economic history or economic taxonomy (comparative economic systems). Do we mean by science a reliance on the experimental method? This throws into limbo certain central ideas of economics, such as value or utility, for which no experiments seem to be possible. Do we mean only the acceptance of a common paradigm, as suggested by Kuhn? This then presents us with the problem of which economic paradigm to choose among a number of competing claimants: Neoclassicism, institutionalism, Marxism.

I do not propose to explore here the question of which definition of science best applies to economics. Rather, my concern will be the relevance for economics of an idea that runs through *all* the ideas of science—the conviction that science must be "value-free." By this I mean that all scientists agree that their work should be carried on in a manner quite independent of the biases and hopes, not to mention the willful interference, of the scientist. In a word, science exists to explain or clarify things that exist indepen-

Excerpted from Robert L. Heilbroner, "Economics as a Value-Free Science," *Social Research* (Spring 1973), pp. 129–43. Reprinted with the permission of the publisher.

dently of the values of the observer. It is the study of what "is," not of what "ought to be."

We shall have occasion later to glance at the purity with which science keeps its vows. But I think it fair to state that the vow itself constitutes an ideal to which almost all economists gladly and wholeheartedly subscribe. However they may define their task, nearly all would include "value-neutrality" as a necessary condition for the performance of those tasks in a "scientific" manner.

It is this central contention that I wish to challenge here. I will deny that the vital element of economic analysis can ever be wholly devoid of considerations of a normative or judgmental kind. To put it more strongly, I will try to show that the economic investigator is in a fundamentally different relationship *vis-à-vis* his subject from that of the natural scientist, so that advocacy or value-laden interpretation becomes an inescapable part of social inquiry—indeed, a desirable part.

That, however, is not all I wish to argue. For having sought to demonstrate that economics is not and should not be value-free, I will then turn around and insist that it should nonetheless retain as an objective the methods of science. The resolution of this seeming conflict will constitute the second objective of my paper.

Let me begin with the simpler part of my task, which is to argue that the work of the economist is laden with value judgments. Perhaps the best way to do so is to observe an economist at work. Let us say that he is collecting certain data—say the size distribution of corporations or the movement of prices. This is assuredly a procedure as objective and value-free as that of the natural scientist collecting data on the sizes of natural objects or the movements of the planets. Our economist may then relate his first set of data to a second set—say the profit rates of corporations ranked by size, or the quantities of goods exchanged at various prices. Here, too, he breaches no rules of value-neutrality, assuming of course that he does not winnow his facts or doctor his observations, and that he avoids falsely imputing causal relationships to his resulting correlations.

Is not such work quite as value-free as that of the natural scientist who performs similar observations or correlations on the objects of the physical universe? Indeed it is. Furthermore, these findings of the economist may be of the utmost importance. But what he has performed up to this point is not yet economic *analysis,* or at least not that "vital element" of analysis to which I earlier called attention. Thus far he has only performed the task of an economic statistician. If economic analysis stopped at this point, the basic contention of my paper would be false.

But an *economist*—not an economic statistician—does not stop here. Indeed, his task now begins—the task of ascribing meaning to the data and the relationships that he has so painstakingly acquired. This meaning takes the form of efforts to "explain," postdictively or predictively, how and why the social organism displays the objective characteristics he has unearthed. And here is where value judgments inevitably insinuate themselves into his work.

Consider a very simple case. In every elementary textbook on economics (including my own), we find a standard example of economic analysis in the discussion of the social result of imposing a price ceiling below the "equilibrium" price for a commodity, say, a rent ceiling on apartments. At the below-equilibrium price, we are told, there will be more would-be buyers (renters) "in the market" than before the ceiling was imposed. The result is the classic instance of a "shortage"—that is, a situation in which the quantity of a commodity demanded at a given price exceeds that which is offered at that price.

Now, is this not also a "value-free" finding, as removed from the wishes or biases of the economist as the finding of a natural scientist that a compass needle swings when a magnet is placed near it? Has not the unduly depressed price of the commodity "attracted" buyers in the first case, in the same way that the force field of the magnet has "attracted" the needle in the second? The question brings us to the critical parting of the ways between value-free natural science and value-laden social science. But the answer is not as simple as it might first appear, so I shall take some pains to spell it out carefully.

As perhaps you have anticipated, there is one very easy mode of demonstrating the value-laden content of economic analysis as contrasted with that of the natural scientist. It is that economists do not remain content with a simple observation (presumably derived by empirical techniques) that there co-exist a rent ceiling and a large number of disgruntled apartment-seekers. Invariably they go on to *prescribe* social remedies for this situation, usually remedies that fall back on the workings of the market system. "Thus," writes Paul Samuelson, "France had practically no residential construction from 1914 to 1948 because of rent controls. If new construction had been subject to such controls after World War II, the vigorous boom in French residential building since 1950 would never have taken place. . . ." He concludes: "To protect the poor from being gouged by landlords, maximal rentals are often fixed by law. These fiats may do short-run good, but they also do long-run harm."

It is not difficult to spot the value judgments latent in this example of economic analysis. There is a silent acquiescence in the propriety of the market as the mechanism for allocating apartments to would-be renters, rather than government allocations, or other means. There is also the assumption that the "long-run harm" cannot be overcome by non-market means, e.g., the provision of additional dwelling space by state construction. Now, Samuelson may have sound philosophical grounds for preferring the market means of allocation to nonmarket means, and he may be correct in his contention that the market will ultimately provide more housing than will a program of government construction. But it is quite clear that neither his preference nor his policy judgment follow as "value-free" conclusions from the raw data of ceiling prices and disgruntled apartment-seekers.

Since I have already declared that I do not believe that economists should aim at value-free analysis, it is not my intent to chastise Samuelson for introducing what are clearly value-laden statements into his text. (I *am* concerned about his failure to alert his readers to his value assumptions, but that is another matter—to which I will return later.) Therefore I will not further pursue the easy course of calling to attention other such institutional biases that affect the manner in which economists consciously or unconsciously move from initially neutral facts to ultimately loaded conclusions. Instead I shall set forth a more intricate and abstract, but I think more fundamental, argument. This is the argument that the inherent and inescapable value-content of economic analysis lies in the fact that the "behavior" of objects of social analysis is *not* like the behavior of the needle of the compass. In the difference between the two meanings of the word "behavior" lie the roots of the value problem for social science.

Of course we all know that human beings do not behave like so many iron filings or compass needles. Yet, when we inquire into the reasons for, or the nature of, the difference, the answer is not immediately apparent. Take the scientist who has observed the effect of a magnet on a compass a hundred times, and the economist who has observed the effects of lower prices on expenditures a hundred times. Assume that all the treacherous problems of extraneous influences are eliminated—that *ceteris paribus* truly prevails. In what way is the economist prevented from describing the behavior of his social universe by "laws" that are just as objective as those of the natural scientist?

The answer is obvious, but its implications may not be. The difference is that the objects observed by the social scientist all possess an attribute that is lacking in the objects of the natural universe. This is the attribute of consciousness—of cognition, of "calculation," of volition. Individuals and social organizations *do* often behave in ways that are as regular as those of the objects of physics and chemistry—if they did not, society would have long ago disintegrated. Yet, even in the most routine human actions there resides an element of latent willfulness that is lacking from even the most spectacular processes of nature. Indeed, one of the decisive attributes that distinguishes the social world from the physical is that social events are not merely interactions of forces, but contests of wills.

Thus behavior has both a purposiveness and a capriciousness that makes prediction infinitely more difficult than for the natural scientist. It is for these reasons that our efforts to predict economic behavior—however accurate in the "normal" case—suddenly become inaccurate when behavior changes its purpose or displays its caprices. The record of prediction with regard to stock market fluctuations, foreign exchange rates, price levels, or even the growth rate of vast aggregates like GNP, is all evidence of this "distressing" unreliability of behavioral regularity.

But what is the relevance of this unreliability to the problem of the value judgments concealed in economic analysis? The relevance lies in the central role played by behavior (and by the prediction of behavior) in the progress from value-free facts to value-laden conclusions. *Without assumptions about behavior, no conclusions whatsoever can be drawn from any set of social facts.* The problem, then, becomes one of discovering the value-component which is intrinsically part of our behavioral assumptions.

But why "intrinsically?" The answer is a curious one. If the economist hews to a strictly empirical description of behavior, given its latent unpredictability, he retains his value-neutrality, *but at the cost of any usable theory.* To put it differently, if the economist wishes to move from economic statistics to economic analysis, he must go beyond "observations" into "assumptions" with regard to behavior, and it is at this juncture that value judgment enters the picture. For when we examine the analytical work of economists, we do not find that their behavioral propositions are carefully framed to reflect the fundamental uncertainty that beclouds all behavioral "laws." Instead, we discover that economic behavior is almost universally described in precisely the "magnetic" fashion of the needle and the compass. The ruling "law" of behavior which is assumed to apply to consumers, workers, and businessmen alike is that they seek to "maximize"—consumers maximize their "utilities," workers their incomes, businessmen their profits.

Do they? The question is embarrassing on at least two counts. The first is that we have a great deal of difficulty in specifying exactly what kind of behavior we mean by "maximizing." For example, how shall we specify the behavior of a corporation which seeks to "maximize" its profits, presumably for a very long period of time, with respect to its price policies, its labor policies, its governmental relations, etc.?

Second, there is the awkward probability that whatever behavior presumably "maximizes" utility or profits in one period is not likely to be that which maximizes in another. Lowered rents will not attract renters, as a magnet attracts a needle, if the renters expect the rent ceilings to be still *lower* in the future. So, too, we must take into account changes in the state of mind of the economic actors over history. However consumers may have behaved in the days of the Industrial Revolution when they sought to maximize their utilities, it is surely not the way they behave in the days of the Advertising Age; nor do the entrepreneurs of the New Industrial State, wrestling with the difficulties of maximization of which I just spoke, resemble the entrepreneurs of Dickensian England, counting up each day's receipts.

Thus the claim to a knowledge of economic "laws" requires a degree of "insight" wholly different from that required to enunciate natural laws. The natural scientist does not care about how his needle feels about magnetism, but the social scientist *has to know* how his buyers and sellers feel about the "attraction" of prices if his analysis is to be grounded on anything other than guesswork or blind faith.

This crucial aspect in the meaning of social behavior infuses economic analysis with values in two ways. The first has to do with the fact that economists arbitrarily apply to economic reasoning "laws" that they know to be at best partial descriptions of reality and at worst outright misdescriptions of it. This is surely an attitude at variance with the willingness of the scientist to abandon a hypothesis when it no longer conforms with observations.

Why do economists persist in their *mumpsimus*—a term Joan Robinson has unearthed that means "persistence in a belief one knows to be mistaken?" The answer is, I believe, embarrassingly simple. It is that economists must have *some* kind of behavioral assumptions to make their theories "work." Lacking any better generalization, economists have retained the convenient assumption of maximization because it serves this purpose—even if the resulting theory often works very badly as a predictive instrument.

A second reason for the retention of the assumption of maximization introduces the problem of value-judgment from a different perspective. It is that maximization, for all its vagueness and error, generally accords with the prevailing orientation of most economists that "more is better." The idea of maximization thereby gives a certain "scientific" authority to textbook statements that the consumer who climbs to the peak of his indifference map is more "satisfied" than one who camps out, like a vagabond, on some lower contour, or that an economy with a high growth rate is "better off" than one with a lower rate. In a word, maximization becomes a prescription for conduct. Since we are all now acutely aware that more is not necessarily better, I will not belabor the value implications of this belief, other than to equate it with a latter-day version of Benthamism, in which push-pin, poetry, and pollution are all the same, so long as they get counted in the gross national product.

The charge that economics is deeply immersed in value orientations is not a new one, and I shall not spend more time in seeking to prove the point. Indeed, many readers may have wondered why I did not make a much more immediate attack. This is to point out that the value-judgments of economics can be discerned at a simpler level than the one to which I have paid attention—to wit, the ideological biases exemplified in my discussion of rent ceilings. There is an obvious political bias observable in the choice of research tasks arrogated to itself by the profession—the doubter may wish to compare the contents of *The American Economic Review* with that of the *Review of Radical Political Economics*. There is the general failure on the part of economists to recognize that the essential terms of their vocabulary—labor, capital, interest, even wealth—are all historical concepts fraught with sociopolitical implications.

If I have not chosen this road, it is not because it is not relevant to the topic but because it has been well covered by others. My purpose, therefore, was to call attention to a less well-explored aspect of the problem lodged in the interstices of economic analysis itself, rather than in the underlying premises of economic thought.

But all this is, in a sense, preamble to the more difficult task that I set myself at the outset. This is to question the legitimacy of the idea of "value neutrality" as an ideal for economics, and at the same time to defend the idea of "science" as an appropriate ideal for economics. The task sounds like a contradiction in terms, so I shall proceed with care, trying to specify with precision what I believe are the elements at stake.

The first problem with "value freedom" concerns the psychological or sociological relationship between the observer and the thing observed. Presumably the scientist approaches his research object in a frame of mind that is without conscious prejudice—fearlessly open to an acceptance of results, however unexpected or unwelcome these may be.

This attribute of scientific inquiry has come under sharp attack in the natural sciences. The work of both Polanyi and Kuhn has made it abundantly clear that scientists do not in fact behave with indifference to their observed results, but struggle desperately to fit "anomalies" into preconceived patterns or paradigms, explaining away or simply ignoring results that fly in the face of prevailing expectations. If this is the case with the natural sciences, it is far more so with the social sciences. Within the field of economics many instances can be cited to demonstrate the absence of that scientific detachment that supposedly characterizes the scientist at work. Let me only mention in passing the long intellectual struggle against Keynesianism and in more recent days the equal unwillingness to abandon the Keynesian notion that inflation was incompatible with substantial unemployment. Or I might call attention to the unwillingness of economists to admit the phenomenon of imperialism as a proper subject for economic investigation, or their dogged adherence to a benign theory of international trade in the face of disquieting evidence that trade has failed to benefit the poorer lands.

As in my previous discussion involving Paul Samuelson's unwitting use of value criteria, my purpose is not to scold economists for their lack of objectivity. It is rather to point to the cause for this universally observed state of affairs. This cause lies in the fact that the process of social investigation inescapably embroils the investigator in his subject in a way that is different from that of the natural scientist. For the latter, the discovery of an anomaly may constitute a blow to his intellectual "security," perhaps even to his psychological "integrity." *But it does not threaten his moral position as a member of a social order.*

On the contrary, the discovery of unexpected results in the social universe almost invariably threatens or confirms the legitimacy of the social system of which the social investigator is unavoidably a part. Indeed, at the risk of making an assertion that verges on a confession, I would venture the statement that every social scientist approaches his task with a wish, conscious or unconscious, to demonstrate the workability or unworkability of the social order he is investigating. It is not a matter of indifference to the Neoclassicist or to the Marxist whether his data fit the hypothesis he is testing, and each struggles mightily to explain away, to minimize, or to reject results that go counter to his initial beliefs.

Moreover, this extreme vulnerability to value judgments is not a sign of deficiency in the social investigator. On the contrary, he belongs to a certain order, has a place in it, benefits or loses from it, and sees his future bound up with its success or failure. In the face of this inescapable existential fact, an attitude of total "impartiality" to the universe of social events is psychologically unnatural, and more likely than not leads to a position of moral hypocrisy. It is not one of their flaws, but one of their claims to greatness as economists that Smith, Ricardo, Mill, Marx, Marshall, and Keynes were explicit in their use of facts and theories as instruments of advocacy. Smith's great model of the economic system was written not merely to "analyze" late eighteenth-century England, but to plead for a policy of "perfect liberty" and to assail the policies of mercantilism. Ricardo used his theory as the underpinnings of his attack against the Corn Laws. Mill's *Principles* advocated a stationary state and income redistribution. Marx espoused social revolution, based on his economic model of the "immanent" tendencies of capitalism. Marshall was a partisan of cautious and careful social change, the rationale for which was spelled out in his *Principles*. Keynes sought the social control over investment, for reasons that the *General Theory* made clear.

These "policy" prescriptions were not afterthoughts. On the contrary, they were an inextricable part of the great contributions of these economists to social understanding. Yet in every case, they rested on value-laden assumptions. The most obvious of these, to which I have referred in passing but have purposely not discussed in this paper, lay in their beliefs in the propriety or impropriety of the *class relations* of the societies they analyzed. Take away the sociological or institutional parameters from the thought of the classical economists (or from Marshall and Keynes) and there is nothing in their systems that could not have led them to conclusions similar to those of Marx. But—and this is the element I have chosen to highlight—there is also in every instance the assumption that maximization is the behavioral force that makes the social universe move. Take away maximization, and the conclusions of Marx can be rather easily made to conform with the mild policy prescriptions for the stationary state proposed by John Stuart Mill.

Thus value judgments, partly of a sociological kind, partly with respect to behavior, have infused economics from its earliest statements to its latest and most sophisticated representations. And indeed, insofar as economic analysis is concerned with social change, in which the fortunes of men (including the analyst) must be affected, how could it be otherwise?

But this leads me to my final contention—that despite its immersion in values, norms and advocacy, economics should nonetheless attempt to embrace "scientific" canons of procedure. How is it possible to reconcile such seemingly contradictory positions?

The reconciliation involves as its first step a return to our earlier dichotomy between economic statistics and economic analysis. So far as the former is concerned, there is little to trouble us. Precisely the same standards and precisely the same pitfalls confront the economic statistician as the biologist or the physicist. Both must struggle against the inhibitions imposed by the reigning paradigm, first in their choice of research objects, and second in their treatment of research results. Both confront, albeit in somewhat different ways, the problem of the interaction of the observer with the things he observes. It is not here that the problem lies.

The question is, rather, how the economic analyst, whose analysis *must* include normative elements, can aspire to the position of the scientist. Here, at this critical last juncture, I must first state with all the force at my command that I do not believe that the economist has the right, in the name of value-advocacy, to tamper with data, to promote or promulgate policy recommendations without supporting evidence, or to pass off his value-laden conclusions as possessing "scientific" validity. Indeed, one of my objections to much of contemporary economics is that it lends a gloss of such "objective" validity to conclusions that in fact only follow from arbitrary and value-laden assumptions—I refer, for example, to the use of Neoclassical economics to "disprove" the usefulness of minimum wage laws, etc. Of course minimum wage laws *may* bring consequences other than those desired by their sponsors. But I hope that my labors in analyzing the dubious nature of the usual assumptions about economic behavior now make it possible for me to state that no economic predictions or prescriptions that rest on these assumptions can lay claim to any "scientific" validity.

How then can the economist possibly aspire to the standards of a social *scientist*? The answer does not lie in efforts to produce behavioral "laws" that will be the counterpart of the laws of nature—that is a chimerical task. The answer lies rather in his efforts to duplicate the methods, not the models, of the natural sciences.

What are these methods? They are to be found, above all, in the openness of the procedures by which science goes about its task, exposing itself to informed criticism at every stage of its inquiry, engaging in painful self-scrutiny with regard to its premises, experiments, reasoning, conclusions. Revelation, "truths beyond question," unstated premises, missing links in the chain of deduction may all be found in "scientific" analysis, but they are by common consent its weakness to which criticism is rightly directed.

This element of science can be transposed in its entirety to economic analysis. Like the natural scientist, the economist (or for that matter, any social scientist) is expected to keep his journal, recording as best he can his starting points, his successive steps, his final conclusions. He records, with all the honesty and fidelity of which he is capable, not only his data and his processes of reasoning, but his initial commitments, hopes, and disappointments. Since economists perform few experiments that can be rerun in a laboratory, his results cannot be so easily falsified as those of the natural scientist, but they can be equally subject to scrutiny and criticism in the forum of expert opinion.

Thus when I urge the abandonment of the idea of a "value-free" economics, I do not thereby seek to abandon the idea of an economics committed to scientific standards. Rather, I want economics to make a virtue of necessity, exposing for all the world to see the indispensable and fructifying value grounds from which it begins its inquiries so that these inquiries may be fully exposed to—and not falsely shielded from—the public examination that is the true strength of science.

PART II

ECONOMIC REASONING AT WORK

There is a tendency among some students of social issues to view theoretical controversies as interesting for those who like to play intellectual chess, but regard such matters as having no relevance to the solution of socioeconomic problems. One frequently heard expression of such sentiment is the statement that something "may be true in theory but not in practice." This is an unfortunate position to take because quite the contrary is true. Policy statements concerned with what we should do about unemployment, inflation, or the distribution of income are always based on some theoretical supposition as to cause, behavior of economic actors, and so on. More important is the fact that our very perception of an economic problem is affected by the particular methodology we employ in our analysis. In essence, the point we are urging here is that debates over economic matters are in part theoretical debates. Theoretical in the sense that the differing economic perspectives of the participants in the debate stem from a general disagreement over theory and methodology. In sum, theory and policy are interrelated and controversies in theory are important in matters of policy, since theory shapes the way we tend to think about economic problems. In Part II we want to pursue further the controversies in theory we set forth in Part I. To do this we have chosen a small set of economic problems that will be confronting us for the next several years (growth, inflation, recession, income distribution, job discrimination). Notice that the authors presented here have diverging views about the problem and what should be done about it. Now when one keeps in mind the arguments about the relevance of economic theory presented in Part I, notice how deeply the authors' analyses in this section are affected by their stand on this question. A second question to keep in mind when reading this section is what suggestions are being made for theoretical redirection.

A.F.

Is Economics Obsolete?
No, Underemployed

CHARLES L. SCHULTZE

Here is an analysis that is not sympathetic to the view that there are fundamental problems with established economic theory and its application to policy issues. For a different view, see the next article.

The current disenchantment, particularly among the young, with the optimistic, problem-solving approach to social issues that characterized the 1960s not surprisingly has rubbed off on economics. As a number of other articles in this symposium demonstrate, many members of the economics profession now question the relevance and meaning of the fundamental assumptions underlying the economics that is currently taught and practiced. Some of the critics have been saying these things for several years but have only lately found someone to listen. A few are recent converts from orthodoxy. And among the younger members of the profession, these critical views are becoming fairly widespread.

There is merit in some of the criticism, but little in the general notion that economics has grown obsolete or irrelevant. The indictment against it should read not that economics is irrelevant but that its very relevant tools have been too sparingly applied to the kinds of problems now confronting us. In some instances, economics is a victim of its own highly relevant successes.

One of the major counts in the indictment is that Keynesian economics is incapable of handling the central policy issue of the era: how to make full employment compatible with reasonable price stability. Yet, in the twenty-five years since the Second World War, a period during which Keynesian fiscal policy emerged from advanced theory courses to become the

From Charles L. Schultze, "Is Economics Obsolete? No, Underemployed," *Saturday Review* (January 22, 1972), pp. 50–52, 57. Reprinted with the permission of the publisher.

conventional wisdom of Presidents, unemployment in no year averaged more than 7 percent, compared with the 1930s, during which unemployment never fell below 14 percent. The major depressions and massive financial panics that sporadically afflicted industrial economies for the century-and-a-half before 1940 are no longer even a dim threat. And aside from the brief aftermath of World War II, the inflations that quite rightly gave Americans cause for worry have not exceeded 5 or 6 percent per year at their worst, a far cry from the persistent rates of 10 and 20 percent per year with which some nations of the world have been living for decades.

Modern economics can and has successfully prescribed the means of preventing large-scale unemployment without bringing on major inflation. It can devise, and has devised, ways of preventing major inflation without precipitating serious depressions. Although the prescriptions of economists are not solely responsible for the sharply improved postwar performance of the Western economies, they surely played a major role. What we now label a failure of theory and policy has been a roaring success by pre-Keynesian standards.

The puzzle economics has not yet solved, and which critics quite properly point to, is the worrisome, but far from catastrophic, inflation that appears when overall demand and supply come into balance during periods of high, but not excessive, prosperity. Yet this failure may stem not so much from shortcomings of the basic theoretical apparatus as from the difficulty of making precise measurements. Economics has little difficulty in prescribing counterbalances to large swings in prices and employment. But in recent years we have been dealing with variations in the employment rate between 3.5 and 6 percent and with differences of 2 to 3 percent in the rate of inflation. And within these ranges the analysis of how wages and prices interact and the prescribing of policy require more precise and complex measurements than we have yet devised. Still, a good carpenter can make a perfectly satisfactory joint with instruments that would be useless for calibrating the tolerances in an Apollo guidance mechanism. Which is by no means to say that the carpenter should throw away his tools as being irrelevant to modern society.

A better understanding of the inflation that accompanies high (even though not excessively high) employment may not ultimately rest on some radical new breakthrough in economic theory. Rather it may well result from gradual improvement in our knowledge about labor markets, about the role of people's expectations during inflation, and about how the market power of unions and business is translated into specific wage and price decisions. Policy instruments to deal with the problem may correspondingly be found in improvements in manpower training programs and antitrust policy, and in the gradual development of wage-price standards sufficiently flexible to avoid smothering the economy in regulation, yet tough enough to influence a key decision when it counts.

Whatever the outcome, any successful prescription for jointly achieving full employment and price stability will undoubtedly contain a large dose of what I may loosely call Keynesian economics—extended, modified, and supplemented, but not abandoned.

Another major indictment against contemporary economics runs approximately like this: Because economics ignores the substantial economic power now concentrated in large firms and unions, and because on a larger scale it accepts the fundamental status quo of current power relationships in society and ignores the relationship between the distribution of power and the distribution of income, it either has no policy prescriptions for pressing social problems or offers ameliorative remedies that only scratch the surface.

To some extent, the charge that modern economics has produced little in the way of remedies for the current siege of social problems is valid, but paradoxically this is so for reasons precisely opposite to those advanced by economics' critics. Economics may be faulted, not because it possesses a theoretical apparatus of no relevance to current social problems, but because in many cases it has failed to apply, or only recently begun to apply, an apparatus that is particularly well suited to dealing with a large segment of those problems.

Much of economics deals with the problem of how a decentralized decision-making system can be made to provide proper incentives so that individual decision-makers, apparently pursuing their own ends, nevertheless tend to act in a way consistent with the public good—the "Invisible Hand" of Adam Smith. Since time immemorial it has been too often assumed that the apparatus of analysis which dealt with this problem applied only to the private market and that the public sector of the economy must operate by a completely different set of rules. Yet, a little reflection will demonstrate that many of the major social problems with which government is now seized require solutions under which the decisions of thousands of communities and millions of individuals are somehow channeled toward nationally desired objectives.

Cleaning up environmental pollution, changing the delivery structure of an ineffective and inequitable medical-care system, providing compensatory educational programs, and offering training and labor market opportunities to the previously disadvantaged depend for their success or failure on day-to-day decisions made by particular communities, business firms, and individuals throughout the nation. No program that merely seeks to transfer these hundreds of thousands, indeed millions, of decisions to a few officials in Washington can hope to be effective. Nor, conversely, can any program that simply shovels federal revenues to state and local governments, and then hopes for the best. Somehow institutional frameworks and incentives that guide a multitude of particular decisions toward national ends have to be developed.

And here, traditional economics and its incentive-oriented apparatus suggest a number of approaches. The major problems of environmental pollution, for instance, stem from the fact that air and water are given free to all comers, and like any good that is given away these commodities will be overused; with no incentives to conserve them, neither individuals nor business firms will lend their talents toward developing and using new conservation technology. But old-fashioned economic analysis suggests that placing a stiff charge on the dumping of pollutants into the air or water will marvelously stimulate the discovery of production methods that reduce pollution, just as the rising cost of labor has promoted a steady growth in techniques to increase output per man-hour, at a rate that roughly doubles the efficiency of labor every 25 years. Economics also brings into question whether it makes any more sense to rely solely on detailed regulation and court decision for minimizing pollution than it would to use these devices for minimizing other industrial costs.

As for health care, conventional economics indicates that the nation can hardly hope to have an efficient use of scarce medical resources when the current health care system provides a powerful set of incentives to waste and misdirect those resources: insurance plans that cover hospitalization but not office visits, thereby encouraging excessive use of hospitals; private and governmental insurance that reimburses hospitals on a cost-plus basis, penalizing the efficient and rewarding the inefficient; financial rewards keyed to dramatic intervention (the cardiac surgeon) but quite niggardly for the practice of preventive medicine, etc.

In the area of public education, economic analysis points to the difficulty of getting superior performances from a monopoly with a captive market (the public school system of the inner city) and can help design means of introducing incentives for improvement and innovations. It also emphasizes the impossibility of designing and enforcing urban land-use plans in an economic environment where many aspects of the tax laws and land laws provide large positive incentives for urban sprawl. It provides insights into the problem of urban congestion by showing how most auto users are not now required to pay the real social costs that their ride imposes on other citizens and how this fact provides incentives for socially excessive use of crowded highways.

As these examples indicate, many of our social problems arise because the current system of markets, laws, and customs provides positive incentives for individuals, business firms, and local communities to engage in what can objectively be called antisocial conduct. Correspondingly, substantial improvement in these areas is most unlikely to come from governmental programs that rely principally on traditional, centralized decision making, but must rest in part on a restructuring of incentives and institutions—a task for which economics, far from being obsolete, has been too little used.

In terms of social problems, economic analysis also has a relevant role to play as a bearer of unpleasant truths—that in some areas of social policy the nation is seeking to pursue conflicting goals. It is literally impossible, for example, to design a welfare program that simultaneously meets four often-sought goals: providing a generous minimum income to the poor; preserving incentives for productive work by avoiding a rapid reduction in welfare benefits as recipients begin to earn outside money; instituting welfare reform in a way that does not reduce the income of any beneficiaries under the current system; and preventing such large budgetary costs that those not far above the poverty line have to be taxed heavily to support those just below it. No program can do all of these things simultaneously.

In the same vein, a public service job program must seek a compromise between two conflicting objectives: to provide wages and working conditions sufficiently attractive to appeal to the unemployed and the low-paid casual worker and to avoid drawing workers away from productive jobs elsewhere. A national medical program cannot at one and the same time guarantee virtually all the medical care private citizens can demand regardless of income, provide a financial mechanism and a set of incentives that hold down escalation of costs, and avoid comprehensive detailed regulation of medical care by Washington bureaucrats.

Pointing out relevant truths of this sort, however, appears to be one of the factors underlying the charges of irrelevancy leveled against economics. Such observations about conflicting objectives imply the need for compromise. But to those for whom compromise is inherently evil, and for whom most problems fundamentally trace back to the greed of the power structure, calling attention to the technical difficulties that would face even a liberated world seems to be irrelevant at best and obstructionist at worst.

A similar reaction, perhaps, will greet the assertion that there are many social issues in which economics should not be expected to play a central role. Economists can seek to ferret out the economic consequences of racial discrimination and help in devising means to expand opportunities for racial minorities. But the eradication of discrimination itself will necessarily depend heavily on a combination of legal steps, education, and political leadership. Economists can trace many of the causes of financial crisis now afflicting large central cities. But the job of rationalizing the archaic jumble of local government in metropolitan areas, thereby providing a viable economic base for large cities, is a task beyond what should be expected of economists. While many of our social ills have major economic consequences, there are some that will yield only to political solutions.

One area in which the economics profession has a decidedly mixed record is the field of income distribution. The problem is not so much a deficiency in economic theory as it relates to income distribution but rather a tendency on the part of the profession to exhibit an excessive concern for efficiency as compared with equity in dealing with situations where the two are in conflict.

An economic system can be very efficient in providing private and public goods to meet the demands generated by a very lopsided income distribution—fine mansions, good public protection, and rapid mass transit for affluent suburbanites while the poor live in hovels, are victimized by crime, and spend inordinate amounts of time getting to work. The formal structure of economics recognizes that its rules for an efficient allocation of resources are blind with respect to the distribution of income; that efficiency considerations alone cannot justify policies which have significant effects on that distribution; and, conversely, that policies which redistribute income in a direction society thinks more just may be warranted even when those policies reduce efficiency. Most economists working in the field of taxation have paid close attention to matters of distribution, and the large majority have raised their voices in favor of strengthening the redistributive features of the tax system. On the other hand, in many areas of public policy, economists as a body have had a bias toward letting efficiency considerations rule.

Higher efficiency, however, is often secured at the expense of particular groups of workers and individual communities. It is not so much that the remedies for these problems need be sought in protectionism, subsidies to dying industries, or rigid featherbedding work rules. Rather, an affluent society might well be expected to provide better income guarantees to workers than ours now does, particularly to older workers, whose skills have been rendered obsolete by economic change and growth. Economists have generally been much more active in pointing to the efficiency gains of unimpeded economic change than in devising means of minimizing its impact on particular workers and communities. In a similar vein, it is only recently that economists and statisticians have begun to look deeply into the often perverse income distribution consequences of many public programs—farm subsidies, low tuition at state universities, urban highway building, irrigation and flood control projects, and the like.

Paying more attention to the problems of income distribution, however, would not rescue conventional economics from attack. To the Western economist, income distribution problems can be approached through such pragmatic measures as reforming the tax system, restructuring welfare programs, and providing more equal educational opportunities. But to radical critics, these are Band-Aid measures. The basic cause of maldistribution of income, they say, is the maldistribution of power that inevitably accompanies a market-oriented free-enterprise system. Any pragmatic measures will eventually be perverted by the holders of economic power to their own ends. Only the demise of the market system itself will make it possible to provide a just distribution of the fruits of man's productive activity.

Here indeed is a fundamental difference in approach. An evaluation of the merits of the case would go far beyond the scope of this article, and, in any event, logical argument seldom makes converts in this controversy. I cannot resist pointing out, however, that in any complex society, whatever its original structure, there is a tendency for power, influence, and wealth to become concentrated in relatively few hands, and this is particularly true whenever societies seek to provide incentives for abundant production. Eternal vigilance is the price of an egalitarian distribution of income. Even in the "post-revolutionary state," the old pragmatic measures of progressive taxation, transfer payments such as welfare benefits, and equal educational opportunities would still be important tools for securing a just distribution of income.

There remain two major areas in which even the most sympathetic view of modern economics would have to concede that charges against the state of the art do strike home. One involves the behavior of producers, the other, that of consumers.

The panoply of tools with which economics seeks to explain how resources are allocated in the private market relies quite heavily on the premise of profit-maximizing firms, each responding to but not controlling the market in which it operates and making decisions subject to reasonably good knowledge about the future consequences of those decisions. For purposes of analyzing the long-run effects of economic policy actions, this "model" of the world is quite serviceable. In the long run, firms do seek to maximize profits; they cannot control basic changes in their economic environment; and there is sufficient feedback from their decisions to provide reasonably accurate information. But in the short run, the behavior of firms with respect to modest changes in prices, wages, and investment policy is much less predictable. They can insulate their own markets against moderate threats; their search for long-run profits is roughly consistent with a number of alternative short-term strategies; and before the feedback from their decisions reaches them, they are faced with great uncertainty.

The inability of economic theory to predict the short-run behavior of firms might not be so important except for the problem of inflation. The long-run allocation of resources, and the shift in price relationships that brings it about, probably does proceed much in the manner explained by economic theory. But it may take place around a generally rising price trend. And unlike market shares, inflation is generally irreversible. A series of short-term decisions on the part of many firms and unions can lead to continuing inflation. The weakness of current economics in predicting the short-run behavior of modern firms and unions thus turns into a serious deficiency in terms of the ability of economists to explain today's inflation *cum* unemployment.

The second charge hits home in the sensitive area of consumer preference theory. Traditional economics takes consumer tastes and preferences as given. It neither looks behind them nor seeks to weigh their relative merits. This approach has two consequences. First, the economist has little to say about the social implications of advertising practices that create and destroy preferences, nor about the social waste represented by the resources devoted to the satisfaction of manipulated tastes. Nor does he have anything to contribute to the deeper problem of the way in which basic preferences themselves respond to economic development, except to note that "yes, this does indeed happen, and the sociologists better get to work."

Second, and perhaps more important, the economist, by taking individual preferences as given and absolute, sharply limits the field of his analysis when it comes to many matters of public policy. The tools of economics are designed to show how resources can best be deployed to meet society's wants. By its assumption that the relevant social wants are based on the existing preferences of individuals, and that those preferences cannot be questioned, economics has erected a barrier against the use of its analysis in some of the most important matters of public policy. The economist can give advice on the efficiency of the policy instruments chosen to meet an objective. But when it comes to choosing among different objectives, the economist *qua* economist must be silent. Personal tax cuts that increase society's consumption of beer and whitewall tires hold equal status with increased public expenditures for education. Choice between the two is a "value judgment," which he must eschew.

One promising line of research has been suggested as a means of breaking this impasse. Individual tastes and preferences are themselves hierarchical. Many of our wants are means to a higher set of goals. The demand for the services of physicians and hospitals is itself a means of attaining a higher end, the maintenance of health. The demand for automobiles is (in part, at least) a demand for transportation. To the extent that preferences are considered means to an end, rather than ends themselves, they can be judged in terms of their efficiency—how well does the satisfaction of a particular "lower-order" preference contribute to the attainment of the "higher-order" goal. At least some preferences can be looked at critically and not accepted unquestionably. Once the question of efficiency is introduced, economics is back on familiar ground. It is peculiarly suited to analyze matters of efficiency.

No one has pursued this line of approach at any great length. Whether it will pay off, in terms of providing a more solid footing for economic theory than the shifting sands of "absolute preferences," cannot be foretold. Barring some progress in this area, economics must stand guilty on part of one count of the indictment against it.

Reflection on the nature of radical criticism of economics leads to one further comment. Economics is fundamentally a discipline that deals with man as he is. At its best, economics seeks to harness man's very human motivations to the public interest. Much of the New Left is interested in changing man, elevating his motives, reducing his greed, and intensifying his love for his fellow man. Economics is a social science, but love is a religion. They are both relevant, but they are not on the same plane of discourse. The economist, for example, generally thinks it naïve to hope that pollution will somehow be conquered by bringing public pressure on corporations to exercise "social responsibility." But he does advocate changes in the structure of incentives and the network of contract laws to create a situation in which it becomes a corporation's own self-interest to act "responsibly."

To the young radical, such technical solutions, which accept and play upon man's drive for material advancement, seem shabby and mean. The evangelism of love and understanding mingle curiously with an intolerant hate for institutions built on the search for money and wealth. But they mingle no more curiously than in the Epistles of St. Paul. There is need for both the pragmatist who would harness in the public service man's drive for worldly goods and the idealist who would lift man's drive to more lofty goals. Neither is irrelevant.

Economics: Allocation or Valuation?

PHILIP A. KLEIN

Institutional economics has long been critical of the major thrust of modern economics. Here is a critical analysis of the applicability of economic theory as a science of allocation as well as a suggestion for redirection.

Among the social sciences, economics long has suffered from a superiority complex. The economist's view of his field has been of a discipline that was rigorous and precise, with an advanced and pragmatic methodology leading to a highly developed theoretical structure. All this left far behind the imprecise and murky theoretical strivings of political scientists, sociologists, anthropologists, and historians.

The promised land which economic analysis made possible was known as equilibrium. What sociologist or political scientist or anthropologist could offer any piece of analytical apparatus which for sheer beauty, precision, and logic could equal it? True, psychologists kept insisting that the behavioral assumptions of conventional economic theory—maximizing behavior, hedonism, rationality—all the characteristics of "Economic Man" which economics always has relied on for convenience, were fatally oversimplified. But economists mostly have ignored the complaints of psychologists. Moreover, the psychologists were only too willing to follow the economist down the quantitative primrose path. Both disciplines once worried about their ancient roots in philosophy and could never quite rid themselves of the nagging suspicion that questions of subjective valuation could not be eliminated entirely so as to render each a 100 percent pure science. Both embraced mathematics as the true methodological Messiah come at last. Together economists and

Excerpted from Philip A. Klein, "Economics: Allocation or Valuation?" *Journal of Economic Issues* (December 1974), pp. 785–804. Reprinted with the permission of the publisher and the Association for Evolutionary Economics.

psychologists measured all visibly quantifiable variables, developed models for all problems, and achieved intellectual orgasm through the contemplation of the possibilities of the electronic computer. By enshrining quantification, they believed they had set a standard of scientific excellence sufficiently ahead of their laggardly sister social sciences to enable them to continue virtually indefinitely to play the role of superego to the lowly id of sociology or history.

Without in any way demeaning the very real accomplishments of quantitative procedures in advancing knowledge in critical areas, I should like to suggest that at least in the case of economics, schizophrenia always has been latent in the discipline and has been kept that way only by sweeping under the rug important problems which increasingly have crept out to disturb the neat world of economist and econometrician alike. We can cope with any number of variables in ever more elaborate models, but we cannot cope with underlying questions of direction and meaning, of goals and objectives for the system. The excessive preoccupation with tools with which to cope with problems at best comprising a small corner of economics, and the obsessive need to believe these tools coped with the heart of economics, long has characterized the discipline. Facing up to this obsession involves the fundamental question of whether economics is a science of allocation or a science of valuation. For most of its existence economics has managed to equate the two, and there is a long and bloody literary road devoted to establishing that economics as a "science of price" thereby was coping with all the value problems with which it need legitimately concern itself.

Economics as a Science of Allocation

The central core of economic theory—at least microeconomic theory—was spelled out by Adam Smith and elaborated upon by the well-known nineteenth-century mainstream economists. The culmination was its restatement by Alfred Marshall, who not insignificantly changed the name of the discipline from political economy to economics. The profound changes of the past 80 years have left remarkably untouched much of the field which Marshall defined as "a study of mankind in the ordinary business of life; it examines that part of individual and social action which is most closely connected with the attainment and with the use of the material requisites of wellbeing." Marshall added that economics "concerns itself chiefly with those motives which affect most powerfully and most steadily man's conduct in the business part of his life." The latter is a far narrower perspective and considerably closer to what in fact Marshall's *Principles* dealt with. It was a critical reinforcement to the continued confusion between economics as allocation and economics as valuation.

Marshall's emphasis on materialism subsequently was questioned, for example, by Lionel Robbins, who wondered how a science concerned exclusively with the material could determine the wage rates for opera stars or orchestra conductors whose productivity is not quite so easily viewed as the more concretely material output of ditchdiggers, carpenters, and others among the myriad toilers in the economic vineyards. Robbins concluded that Marshall's materialism was a "pseudo-materialism" and that what was really at the heart of economics was not materialism but allocation. Robbins then defined the field in the way which is customarily utilized to this day: "Economics is the science which studies human behavior as a relationship between ends and scarce means which have alternative uses." Such a formulation extricated economists from the materialism quagmire; by adding to this the deceptively simple assumption that the allocation process as carried out through the use of prices in the market disposed of all the ends and scarce means that the proper study of economics need embrace, economists thought they were home free. The pricing process was assumed to be the vehicle by which the economic system expressed *all* the allocating priorities of concern to the economist. Thus price became, if it had not always been, the *only* measure of value with which economics had to concern itself.

Robbins himself reached this conclusion unequivocably by saying that the significance of economic science lay in the fact that "when we are faced with a choice between ultimates, it enables us to choose with a full awareness of the implications of what we are choosing." But he was very careful to add that "it is incapable of deciding between the desirability of different ends. It is fundamentally distinct from Ethics." But even if the distinction between economics and ethics were accepted, the discipline must provide mechanisms by which such "full awareness" choice can be made. The market alone cannot fill that bill in a modern industrial economy. Allocation and valuation are indeed different, and a discipline concerned only with the former can never permit "fully aware" choices to be made.

Those who view economics as a science of allocation customarily have argued that all participants in the economic process get their "values" from wherever they get them, that in fact societal values are of no concern to the economist. Thus all the economist need do is pontificate: "If an individual chooses to allocate his income in Direction A he must forego Direction B." "To achieve certain objectives, here is the most efficient way for society to achieve them, and here is what must be foregone in the process." Consequently, generations of economics students were taught that economics is not concerned with questions of "ought" but only with questions of "is." Economics as a science was not normative but positive. Thus economics was viewed as the administrator of social options, in charge of calculating costs and predicting results, but without any normative participation in the process. The economist *qua* economist occupied a role in which normative judgments definitionally had no place. Only the economist *qua* citizen was permitted to be filled with the minimal requisite quantities of passion, prejudice, and "subjective valuation" that reside in the breast of other mere mortals.

This view of economics had some convenient side effects. For one, it enabled economic theory to blind itself to the implicit subjective valuations of what it did in the guise of pursuit of the scientific method, rigor, and precision. It therefore enabled economics to emulate the physical sciences and thus led to the coronation of equilibrium as normatively "good" in economics because in physics, from whence it came, it was "natural." If Keynes's notion of underemployment equilibrium represented a severe jolt to this notion, in microeconomics it survived because equilibrium prices led to market clearing, which was definitionally good. Finally, equilibrium could be viewed as an end in itself because the continued assumption that Adam Smith's Invisible Hand (developed for atomistic competition) could be appropriately if only approximately attached to emergent prices in actual markets rationalized away any lurking doubts about how economics disposed of the value problem. Individual selfishness was transmogrified into a process optimizing social welfare, and emergent prices did indeed express the values of society in the only way that need concern the economist.

Economics as a Science of Valuation

The simple world of the classical economist, familiar to all economists, was orderly and attractive, but unrelated to much of the economic reality even of its own time. The history of economics has shown a remarkable tendency to cling to that world, however, and to make emendations only when pushed by a variety of inexorable forces. Even in its own time, classical price theory developed with the Industrial Revolution in England, and so Smith projected his Invisible Hand on a world replete with, among other things, subhuman factory conditions, child labor, widespread poverty, great inequality in the distribution of both wealth and income, vast slums and urban ghettos, and a rigid and uncompromising class system which severely restricted labor mobility and economic opportunity. In short, it was a world with a whole host of problems with which society still copes and from all of which Smith's economics was structured to dissociate itself.

It is interesting to note that this view of economics, based on emulating the physical sciences, has in our own day seen the physical sciences come to question the rigid distinction between the normative and the positive. The dynamism of technology was such that by the 1940s the physicists had begun to realize that merely suggesting what constitutes the most efficient way to destroy the world as we know it might not thoroughly discharge the ultimate responsibility of the physicist *qua* physicist. So much for the model economics chose to emulate.

To the extent that economics subsequently faced up to its value problem (as opposed to its allocation problem) at all, it did so through the introduction of the familiar notion of the Pareto Optimum, which fit extremely well the notion of the Invisible Hand. Pareto Optimality (however stated) never has been more than a very carefully hedged statement: With given tastes, technology, and resources, no reallocation of resources could better satisfy any member of the community without someone else being less well satisfied. Such a view, even leaving aside the old controversies about measuring satisfaction, nonetheless fits well into the conventional perspective because it does not ask how the distribution of satisfactions came to be what it is, what the rules of the game are in which satisfaction-seeking is played, and so forth. As was the case with the Invisible Hand, the Pareto Optimum was an attempt to define the value problem in economics in sufficiently narrow terms to make it coterminous with resource allocation in the market via prices.

To the extent that conventional theory altered its focus to cope with imperfect as opposed to pure competition, the following conclusions seem germane to our central concern with how economics copes with its value problem. Institutionalism in the past attacked the use of "competition" in conventional theory, but failed to note that *whatever* equilibrium might mean in competitive markets, it means something different in imperfect markets. Institutionalists were thus vulnerable to the charge of beating an ill if not dead horse. However, the charge that conventional economics continues to overemphasize the competitive model because it is elegant, precise, and deterministic while imperfect models have none of these characteristics is probably a fair one. Economists cling to the competitive model, partly at least as a child to a security blanket, and rationalize its continued emphasis in academic curricula by a variety of means. These contain enough truth to avoid broadside attacks on the theory as irrelevant, but enough error to prevent economists from easily addressing the modern world in a realistic, direct, and straightforward fashion. . . .

The Frontiers of Economics: Valuation in the Market

If, as I believe, economics is and always has been primarily a science of valuation rather than merely allocation, it follows that price is not the only relevant measure of value, even in the areas where the price system still serves as the sole or primary allocative mechanism. There are many questions to which conventional economics should address itself in the areas where prices in fact do the allocating, but which many economists still prefer to ignore. For example, it is by now fairly clear that assuming that consumer wants are "given" assumes away many critical problems bearing on "the meaning of the price system." The normative implications of emergent prices in a system in which large corporate businesses produce whatever they choose to produce and then persuade consumers (through advertising, appeals to snobbery or class, or whatever) that this is also what they want are most assuredly *not* what they would be in a system in which prices reflected the efforts of business firms to adapt to the "sovereign" wishes of consumers. This would, of course, be true no matter where consumer wants came from provided only that they were not created by profit-seeking business firms themselves. This charge always has been levelled at price theory by institutionalists, beginning with Thorstein Veblen and including today J. K. Galbraith. He refers to demand manipulation as "the revised sequence" and comments: "The revised sequence sends to the museum of irrelevant ideas the notion of an equilibrium in consumer outlays which reflect the maximum of consumer satisfaction."

It may be that Galbraith has exaggerated the degree of demand manipulation, as some have charged, but it is unlikely that any would argue that consumers and business firms interact on terms approaching parity. The attention given to Ralph Nader in recent years is due to the fact that consumerism is still so new and immature in our economy. Its rise is recognition that manipulation of consumers by firms unmatched by organized and informed consumer manipulation of firms seriously alters the normative implications of emergent prices. Only in economics as allocation can one argue that "the work or value of a thing is determined simply by what a person is willing to pay for it." There is no need here to linger over this point except to note that what lies "beyond demand," to use John Gambs's phrase, is an integral part of economics as valuation and always has been.

A second inadequacy of the economist's analysis of how markets operate is closely related to the first and involves again the tremendous concentration of power in the modern business corporation. Economics as allocation has not been unduly concerned with economic power *per se*, but only with how "market imperfections affected the allocation of resources." Economics as valuation can make no such convenient division. There is by now a vast literature dealing with the rise of the modern corporation, its basis in great wealth, its *raison d'être* in its unique ability to exploit the fruits of ongoing technological development, and the concentration of power (economic but also political and social) to which these factors led. Certainly relatively little attention has been paid by mainstream economists to the impact of concentrated power on the meaning of the price system in operation. Adolf Berle and Gardiner Means warned in the 1930s of the implications of separating ownership and control. R. A. Brady some years later warned of the implications of concentrated corporate power to the fabric of the sociopolitical as well as the economic system in a view anticipating Dwight Eisenhower's celebrated warning of the dangers to democracy inherent in the military-industrial complex. Despite the effort to develop models of imperfect competition, economics as allocation has never escaped from the dilemma posed by the dynamism of technology which simultaneously destroyed the world of Smithian competition, with its convenient assumptions of the Invisible Hand, and enormously increased the efficiency and productivity (but also the dangers to "sovereignty") of the system in fact operating.

This call to incorporate the realities of corporate economic power into conventional economics thus has a very old if relatively futile history. It may even be a cliché to mention, but like many clichés it represents an obvious necessity since it is still unrealized in economic theory. It is currently being urged most conspicuously by Galbraith. Thus, if institutionalists erred in failing to recognize the impact of imperfect competition theory on the normative implications of "equilibrium," this error was small in the face of the problem they did perceive in the operation of prices to allocate resources in the market. The realities of concentrated power, the implications of an allocative mechanism based on "one dollar, one vote" operating amidst tremendous inequality in the distribution of both wealth and income, the degree to which concentration exercised a pervasive influence on both the flow of information and the "wants" assumed to be given—all these and related aspects of the economy were not so much unknown to economists as simply ignored definitionally by the profession in considering economic theory. The result was that even in its *terra cognita*, the domain of allocation in markets via prices, economists could not really deal with the value problem effectively. But the greatest inadequacies resulted from concentrating the attention of the economists unduly in this corner of their field, thereby ignoring the full implications of economics as valuation.

Institutional Economics and the Valuation Process

The meaning of the price system is only part of the strategy of economic progress, and it is the latter that lies at the heart of economics as valuation. It was this view, of course, that gave institutionalism its characteristic flavor, and Ayres in particular tried to pull the separate threads together to make a complete statement of economics as a science of valuation directed at developing a strategy of progress. From Veblen came his great sensitivity to the impact of institutional forces (economic and noneconomic) in shaping the development of priorities and the resultant futility of presuming wants to be given when in fact they are shaped by the economy. From the disputes in the physical sciences came his conviction that the Newtonian emphasis on equilibrium was far less significant for economics than was the Darwinian emphasis on conflict, process, and change. From John Dewey came the instrumental theory of value, which succeeded in producing a dynamic from which the valuation process in economics could be analyzed.

What Ayres saw better than anyone else, in my judgment, was that instead of concentrating on how resources are allocated in markets via prices, economists should subsume that problem in the larger and more compelling problem, namely: How does the economy shape as well as channel human choice, both during a given period and through time? What mechanisms does it provide both for the development and for the expression of values? When Kenneth Arrow considered welfare economics, he still viewed the economy as a transmission mechanism for expressing "values" exogenously determined—hence his title *Social Choice and Individual Values*. But a more meaningful title might well have been *Individual Choice and Social Values*. It is the latter which "the economy" represents. And I dare say that the fallacy of composition scarcely could be of greater critical importance than in the placid assumption of economists that the economy is an adequate and effective mechanism for summing individual values into social values. There is clearly a complex interaction between individual and social values, but the way in which the economy directs this interrelationship is far from clear, let alone necessarily satisfactory.

The major critical frontier in economics, therefore, cannot be restricted even to market valuation; it lies in a far broader perspective.

The Frontiers of Political Economy: Individual Choice and Valuation in Society

. . . Increasingly it seems clear that economics as valuation cannot avoid concern with nonprice phenomena. The evidence is piling up on all sides that the old view of economics (as primarily concerned with how the market allocates resources via price under rigidly given assumptions) increasingly is being pushed aside by the necessity for facing many critical valuation problems. . . .

Thus Gunnar Myrdal recently suggested: "Modern establishment economists have retained the welfare theory from the earliest neoclassical authors, but have done their best to conceal and forget its foundation upon a particular and now obsolete moral philosophy."

No better corroboration can be found for the thrust of the argument being advanced than to consider the history of the argicultural sector during the past several decades. Such perusal shows that price is by no means the same thing as value. It should suggest that welfare economics—even of the conventional type—cannot neatly separate allocative from distributive welfare problems, although it customarily tries to do so. It should support the notion that economics as valuation cannot easily isolate utility-based welfare economics, which is conventionally viewed as more manageable, from ethically-based welfare economics, considered too ambiguous to be capable of economic analysis, but clearly involved in fact in determining resource allocation and distribution in this sector. It underscores the bases of essential allocative mechanisms in *both* the decision unit of one dollar-one vote and of one man-one vote, and it illustrates the manipulation of both to reveal and shape essential societal values. Finally, in the critical area of interrelationship between the origin and transmission of individual values, on the one hand, and the origin and transmission of societal values, on the other, it reminds us how every beginning student learns to corroborate the fallacy of composition. It is with the recognition that economic analysis shows that the result of individual farmers trying to lower their prices to increase their income may lower the prices and incomes of all. That being true, why is it so difficult to persuade economists who are not beginning students that they cannot blithely assume that individual choice, let alone values, will necessarily be transformed through simple summation into harmonious societal choice, let alone values? Is it not possible that in modern market-oriented economies, so far from atomistic competition, the Invisible Hand could fall victim to the fallacy of composition? Should we not at least attempt to develop a suitable analytical framework, specifically a realistic theory of political economy, in which the question could be pursued?

In fact the necessity for such an attempt is in process of being thrust upon us. Political economy as valuation is being forced to realize by the gap between the central concerns of the conventional analytical apparatus of economics and the central concerns of the economy that they need to be fused. Welfare economics never has been comfortable with notions of Pareto Optimality, although it has elaborated them endlessly, because for one thing Pareto Optimality never could cope satisfactorily with the Pandora's box Marshall so innocuously called externalities. Nor could it cope with welfare in any except a highly restricted sense involving the allocation of resources by prices with all the determinants of value given. The whole of the public sector, to which attention is shortly directed, is a monument to the limitations of Pareto Optimality. Critical resource allocation decisions need to be—and in fact are—made constantly that cannot revolve easily about a market-price-measurable calculus. Pareto's maxim that the improvement in any member of the community improves social welfare if no one in consequence "feels himself worse off" is already inadequate if one must consider (as in all taxation questions, for example) the decrease in welfare of those whose taxes are increased and the increased welfare of those on whom the resultant revenues are spent.

Political economy as valuation then is ultimately as closely related to political science as economics always has been to psychology. Total allocation is made by both dollar votes and man votes. To the conventional concern with how to measure the choices of individuals must be added the problem of how individuals influence each others' choices. Even more crucial is the question of how individual and societal choices are interrelated. We lack a coherent developed theory here for static analysis, let alone for a dynamic theory capable of coping with the notion of economic progress. These problems can best be approached in turn. . . .

Conclusions

It is perhaps possible to summarize the essential argument in a few propositions.

1. Economics always has recognized that its distinctive emphasis has been on the need to make choices in a world where the energy crisis is only the most recent reminder that affluence has yet to replace scarcity as a basic conditioner of human existence.

2. While economics, therefore, indubitably revolves about allocation, it is preeminently a science of valuation. To say this is to say something more specific than the philosopher's more cosmic concern with the ultimate destiny of man, but less specific than, say, Lionel Robbins's definition of economics would imply. Economic theory, in which market imperfections are noted, but values are assumed given, even when termed only "benchmark theory," is inadequate theory to cope with the economic problem.

3. Ayres well may have erred in his view of the meaning of modern market equilibria, but he surely was supremely correct in arguing that the central concern of economics is not how markets allocate resources, but rather how the total allocative thrust of the economy is perceived, determined, reviewed, transmitted, and altered over time.

4. Economics long has given in to the tendency, therefore, to convert what is essentially a complex value problem into a relatively simple and often mechanistic allocative problem because of the advantages of the latter in developing precise and rigorous models. But this effort has produced schizophrenia which has become ever more pronounced. The disproportionate attention given to theoretical apparatus which concentrated on simplistic allocation while the economy itself wrestled with valuation increasingly is being recognized. Perusal of any basic text will underscore this discrepancy between the complexity of our apparatus to deal with "markets" and the paucity of our apparatus to deal with value (in static terms) or progress (in dynamic terms).

5. Only when economic theory concentrates on the meaning of the political economy—the problem of value—will we be able to assess the adequacy of our current allocation (outside as well as inside the market) to accomplish the evolving ends which the participants in the economy currently set for it. Only then can we criticize either the actual functioning of the economy or the expectations of its participants in effective fashion.

6. If we accept consumer sovereignty as the important factor in economic allocation that classical and neoclassical economists assumed, the challenge is to turn their assumption into reality by developing a theory of political economy as valuation in terms of which the evolving total allocational thrust of society (its emerging values) can

be expressed. In such terms economic performance can be judged by the only criteria that ultimately make sense: How effectively and accurately does the system reflect emergent choice?

7. The frontier of the political economy, therefore, is to be found in developing criteria by which economies can be judged in terms of their ability successfully to express the emergent values of society. In dynamic terms these criteria will provide an avenue for judging the economy through time as the embodiment of the evolving values of its participants, that is, economic progress. Only then can we comment meaningfully on whether the current structures in the economy constitute a road to serfdom, a road to utopia, or some halfway road, and whether, whatever the road may be, it is what (rightly or wrongly) its inhabitants choose.

Is the End of the
World at Hand?

ROBERT M. SOLOW

Here Professor Solow argues that continued economic growth is not only possible but necessary. For a different view, see the next article.

I was having a hard time figuring out how to begin when I came across an excerpt from an interview with my MIT colleague, Professor Jay Forrester, who is either the Christopher Columbus or the Dr. Strangelove of this business, depending on how you look at it. Forrester said he would like to see about 100 individuals, the most gifted and best qualified in the world, brought together in a team to make a psychosocial analysis of the problem of world equilibrium. He thought it would take about ten years. When he was asked to define the composition of his problem-solving group, Forrester said: "Above all it shouldn't be mostly made up of professors. One would include people who had been successful in their personal careers, whether in politics, business, or anywhere else. We should also need radical philosophers, but we should take care to keep out representatives of the social sciences. Such people always want to go to the bottom of a particular problem. What we want to look at are the problems caused by interactions."

I don't know what you call people who believe they can be wrong about everything in particular, but expect to be lucky enough somehow to get it right on the interactions. They may be descendants of the famous merchant Lapidus, who said he lost money on every item he sold, but made it up on the volume. Well, I suppose that as an economist I am a representative of the social sciences; and I'm prepared to play out the role by talking

Excerpted from Robert M. Solow, "Is the End of the World at Hand?" *Challenge* (March-April 1973), pp. 39–50. Copyright © 1974 by International Arts and Sciences Press, Inc. Reprinted with the permission of International Arts and Sciences Press, Inc.

about first principles and trying to say what the Growth vs. No-Growth business is really all about. This is going to involve me in the old academic ploy of saying over and over again what I'm not talking about before I ever actually say what I think I am talking about. But I'm afraid that some of those boring distinctions are part of the price you have to pay for getting it right.

First of all, there are (at least) two separate questions you can ask about the prospects for economic growth. You can ask: Is growth desirable? Or you can ask: Is growth possible? I suppose that if continued economic growth is not possible, it hardly matters whether or not it's desirable. But if it is possible, it's presumably not inevitable, so we can discuss whether we should want it. But they are separate questions, and an answer to one of them is not necessarily an answer to the other. My main business is with the question about the possibility of continued growth; I want to discuss the validity of the negative answer given by the "Doomsday Models" associated with the names of Forrester and Meadows (and MIT!) and, to a lesser extent, with the group of English scientists who published a manifesto called "Blueprint for Survival." The main concern of Dr. E. J. Mishan, on the other hand, was with the desirability of continued economic growth (and, at least by implication, with the desirability of past economic growth). If I spend a few minutes poaching on his territory, it is mainly because that seems like a good way to get some concepts straight, but also just to keep a discussion going.

Sorting Out the Issues

Arguments about the desirability of economic growth often turn quickly into arguments about the "quality" of modern life. One gets the notion that you favor growth if you are the sort of person whose idea of heaven is to drive at 90 miles an hour down a six-lane highway reading billboards, in order to pollute the air over some crowded lake with the exhaust from twin 100-horsepower outboards, and whose idea of food is Cocoa Krispies. On the other hand, to be against economic growth is to be a granola-eating, backpacking, transcendental-meditating canoe freak. That may even be a true statistical association, but I will argue that there is no necessary or logical connection between your answer to the growth question and your answer to the quality-of-life question. Suppose there were no issue about economic growth; suppose it were impossible; suppose each man or each woman were equipped to have only two children; suppose we were stuck with the technology we have now and had no concept of invention, or even of increased mechanization through capital investment. We could still argue about the relative merits of cutting timber for building houses or leaving it stand to be enjoyed as forest. Some people would still be willing to breathe carbon monoxide in big cities in return for the excitement of urban life, while others would prefer cleaner air and fewer TV channels. Macy's would still not tell Gimbel's. Admen would still try to tell you that all those beautiful women are actually just looking for somebody who smokes Winchesters, thus managing to insult both men and women at once. Some people would still bring transistor radios to the beach. All or nearly all of the arguments about the quality of life would be just as valid if the question of growth never arose.

I won't go so far as to say there is no connection. In particular, one can argue that if population density were low enough, people would interfere much less with each other, and everyone could find a part of the world and style of civilization that suited him. Then differences of opinion about the quality of life wouldn't matter so much. Even if I grant the truth of that observation, it is still the case that, from here on out, questions about the quality of life are separable from questions about the desirability of growth. If growth stopped, there would be just about as much to complain about; and, as I shall argue later on, one can imagine continued growth that is directed against pollution, against congestion, against sliced white bread.

I suppose it is only fair to admit that if you get very enthusiastic about economic growth you are likely to be attracted to easily quantifiable and measurable things as objects of study, to point at with pride or to view with alarm. You are likely to pay less attention to important, intangible aspects of the standard of living. Although you can't know whether people are happier than they used to be, you can at least determine that they drink more orange juice or take more aspirin. But that's mere weakness of imagination and has nothing to do in principle with the desirability of economic growth, let alone with its possibility.

There is another practical argument that is often made; and although it is important, it sometimes serves as a way of avoiding coming to grips with the real issues. This argument says that economic growth, increasing output per person, is the only way we are likely to achieve a more equitable distribution of income in society. There is a lot of home truth in that. It is inevitably less likely that a middle-class electorate will vote to redistribute part of its own income to the poor than that it will be willing to allocate a slightly larger share of a growing total. Even more pessimistically, I might suggest that even a given relative distribution of income, supposing it cannot be made more nearly equal, for political or other reasons, is less unattractive if the absolute standard of living at the bottom is fairly high than it is if the absolute standard at the bottom is very low. From this point of view, even if economic growth doesn't lead to more equity in distribution, it makes the inequity we've got more tolerable. I think it is one of the lessons of history as recent as the McGovern campaign that this is a realistic statement of the prospects.

It is even clearer if one looks, not at the distribution of income within a rich country like the U.S., but at the distribution of income between the developed countries of the world and the undeveloped ones. The rich Western nations have never been able to agree on the principle of allocating as much as one percent of their GNP to aid undeveloped countries. They are unlikely to be willing to share their wealth on any substantial scale with the poor countries. Even if they were, there are so many more poor people in the world that an equally shared income would be quite low. The *only* prospect of a decent life for Asia, Africa, and Latin America is in more total output.

But I point this out only to warn you that it is not the heart of the question. I think that those who oppose continued growth should in honesty face up to the implications of their position for distributional equity and the prospects of the world's poor. I think those who favor continued growth on the grounds that only thus can we achieve some real equality ought to be serious about that. If economic growth with equality is a good thing, it doesn't follow that economic growth with a lot of pious talk about equality is a good thing. In principle, we can have growth with or without equity; and we can have stagnation with or without equity. An argument about first principles should keep those things separate.

What Has Posterity Done for Us?

Well, then, what *is* the problem of economic growth all about? . . . Whenever there is a question about what to *do*, the desirability of economic growth turns on the claims of the future against the claims of the present. The pro-growth man is someone who is prepared to sacrifice something useful and desirable right now so that people should be better off in the future; the anti-growth man is someone who thinks that is unnecessary or undesirable. The nature of the sacrifice of present enjoyment for future enjoyment can be almost anything. The classic example is investment: We can use our labor and our resources to build very durable things like roads or subways or factories or blast furnaces or dams that will be used for a long time by people who were not even born when those things were created, and so will certainly have contributed nothing to their construction. That labor and those resources can just as well be used to produce shorter-run pleasures for us now.

Such a sacrifice of current consumption on behalf of the future may not strike you as much of a sacrifice. But that's because you live in a country that is already rich; if you had lived in Stalin's Russia, that need to sacrifice would be one of the reasons you would have been given to explain why you had to live without comfort and pleasures while the Ministry of Heavy Industry got all the play. If you lived in an underdeveloped country now you would face the same problem: What shall you do with the foreign currency earned by sales of cocoa or copper or crude oil—spend it on imports of consumer goods for those alive and working now, or spend it on imports of machinery to start building an industry that may help to raise the standard of living in 30 years' time?

There are other ways in which the same choice can be made, including, for instance, the direction of intellectual resources to the invention of things (like the generation of electricity from nuclear fusion) that will benefit future generations. Paradoxically, one of the ways in which the present can do something for the future is to conserve natural resources. If we get along with less lumber now so that there will be more forests standing for our grandchildren, or if we limit the present consumption of oil or zinc so that there will be some left for the twenty-first century, or if we worry about siltation behind dams that would otherwise be fun for fishermen and water-skiers, in all those cases we are promoting economic growth. I call that paradoxical because I think most people identify the conservation freak with the anti-growth party whereas, in this view of the matter, the conservationist is trading present satisfaction for future satisfaction, that is, he is promoting economic growth. I think the confusion comes from mixing up the quality-of-life problem with the growth problem. But it is nonetheless a confusion.

Why should we be concerned with the welfare of posterity, given the indubitable fact that posterity has never done a thing for us? I am not anthropologist enough to know how rare or common it is that our culture should teach us to care not only about our children but about their children, and their children. I suppose there are good Darwinian reasons why cultures without any future-orientation should fail to survive very long in the course of history. Moreover, we now enjoy the investments made by our ancestors, so there is a kind of equity in passing it on. Also, unless something terrible happens, there will be a lot more future than there has been past; and, for better or worse—probably worse—there will be more people at each future instant than there are now or have been. So all in all, the future will involve many more man-years of life than the present or the past, and a kind of intergenerational democracy suggests that all those man-years-to-be deserve some consideration out of sheer numbers.

On the other hand, *if* continued economic growth is possible—which is the question I'm coming to—then it is very likely that posterity will be richer than we are even if we make no special efforts on its behalf. If history offers any guide, then, in the developed part of the world at least, the accumulation of technological knowledge will probably make our great-grandchildren better off than we are, even if we make no great effort in that direction. Leaving aside the possibility of greater equality—I have already discussed that—there is hardly a crying need for posterity to be on average very much richer than we are. Why should we poor folk make any sacrifices for those who will in any case live in luxury in the future? Of course, if the end of the world is at hand, if continued economic growth is *not* possible, then we ought to care more about posterity, because they won't be so well off. Paradoxically, if continued growth is not possible, or less possible, then we probably ought to do more to promote it. Actually, there's no paradox in that, as every student of economics will realize, because it is a way of saying that the marginal return on investment is high.

Overshoot, Collapse, Doom

There is, as you know, a school of thought that claims that continued economic growth is in fact not possible anymore, or at least not for very long. This judgment has been expressed more or less casually by several observers in recent years. What distinguishes the "Doomsday Models" from their predecessors is that they claim to much more than a casual judgment: they deduce their beliefs about future prospects from mathematical models or systems analysis. They don't merely say that the end of the world is at hand—they can show you computer output that says the same thing.

Characteristically, the Doomsday Models do more than just say that continued economic growth is impossible. They tell us why: in brief, because (*a*) the earth's natural resources will soon be used up; (*b*) increased industrial production will soon strangle us in pollution; and (*c*) increasing population will eventually outrun the world's capacity to grow food, so that famine must eventually result. And, finally, the models tell us one more thing: the world will end with a bang, not a whimper. The natural evolution of the world economy is not at all toward some kind of smooth approach to its natural limits, wherever they are. Instead, it is inevitable—unless we make drastic changes in the way we live and organize ourselves—that the world will overshoot any level of population and production it can possibly sustain and will then collapse, probably by the middle of the next century.

I would like to say why I think that the Doomsday Models are bad science and therefore bad guides to public policy. I hope nobody will conclude that I believe the problems of population control, environmental degradation, and resource exhaustion to be unimportant, or that I am one of those people who believe that an adequate response to such problems is a vague confidence that some technological solution will turn up. On the contrary, it is precisely because these are important problems that public policy had better be based on sound and careful analysis. I want to explain some of my reasons for believing that the global models don't provide even the beginnings of a foundation of that kind.

The first thing to realize is that the characteristic conclusion of the Doomsday Models is very near the surface. It is, in fact, more nearly an assumption than a conclusion, in the sense that the chain of logic from the assumptions to the conclusion is very short and rather obvious.

The basic assumption is that stocks of things like the world's natural resources and the waste-disposal capacity of the environment are finite, that the world economy tends to consume the stock at an increasing rate (through the mining of minerals and the production of goods), and that there are no built-in mechanisms by which approaching exhaustion tends to turn off consumption gradually and in advance. You hardly need a giant computer to tell you that a system with those behavior rules is going to bounce off its ceiling and collapse to a low level. Then, in case anyone is inclined to relax into the optimistic belief that maybe things aren't that bad, we are told: Imagine that the stock of natural resources were actually twice as big as the best current evidence suggests, or imagine that the annual amount of pollution could be halved all at once and then set to growing again. All that would happen is that the date of collapse would be postponed by T years, where T is not a large number. But once you grasp the quite simple essence of the models, this should come as no surprise. It is important to realize where these powerful conclusions come from, because, if you ask yourself "Why didn't I realize earlier that the end of the world was at hand?" the answer is not that you weren't clever enough to figure it out for yourself. The answer is that the imminent end of the world is an immediate deduction from certain assumptions, and one must really ask if the assumptions are any good.

It is a commonplace that if you calculate the annual output of any production process, large or small, and divide it by the annual employment of labor, you get a ratio that is called the productivity of labor. At the most aggregative level, for example, we can say that the GNP in 1971 was $1,050 billion and that about 82 million people were employed in producing it, so that GNP per worker or the productivity of a year of labor was about $12,800. Symmetrically, though the usage is less common, one could just as well calculate the GNP per unit of some particular natural resource and call that the productivity of coal, or GNP per pound of vanadium. We usually think of the productivity of labor as rising more or less exponentially, say at 2 or 3 percent a year, because that is the way it has in fact behaved over the past century or so since the statistics began to be collected. The rate of increase in the productivity of labor is not a constant of nature. Sometimes it is faster, sometimes slower. For example, we know that labor productivity must have increased more slowly a long time ago, because if we extrapolate backward at 2 percent a year, we come to a much lower labor productivity in 1492 than can possibly have been the case. And the productivity of labor has risen faster in the past 25 years than in the 50 years before that. It also varies from place to place, being faster in Japan and Germany and slower in Great Britain, for reasons that are not at all certain. But it rises, and we expect it to keep rising.

Now, how about the productivity of natural resources? All the Doomsday Models will allow is a one-time hypothetical increase in the world supply of natural resources, which is the equivalent of a one-time increase in the productivity of natural resources. Why shouldn't the productivity of most natural resources rise more or less steadily through time, like the productivity of labor?

Of course it does for some resources, but not for others. Real GNP roughly doubled between 1950 and 1970. But the consumption of primary and scrap iron increased by about 20 percent, so the productivity of iron, GNP per ton of iron, increased by about 2.5 percent a year on the average during those 20 years. The U.S. consumption of manganese rose by 30 percent in the same period, so the productivity of manganese went up by some 70 percent in 20 years, a bit under 2.25 percent a year. Aggregate consumption of nickel just about doubled, like GNP, so the productivity of nickel didn't change. U.S. consumption of copper, both primary and secondary, went up by a third between 1951 and 1970, so GNP per pound of copper rose at 2 percent a year on the average. The story on lead and zinc is very similar, so their productivity increased at some 2 percent a year. The productivity of bituminous coal rose at 3 percent a year.

Naturally, there are important exceptions, and unimportant exceptions. GNP per barrel of oil was about the same in 1970 as in 1951: no productivity increase there. The consumption of natural gas tripled in the same period, so GNP per cubic foot of natural gas fell at about 2.5 percent a year. Our industrial demand for aluminum quadrupled in two decades, so the productivity of aluminum fell at a good 3.5 percent a year. And industrial demand for columbium was multiplied by a factor of 25: in 1951 we managed $2.25 million of GNP (in 1967 prices) per pound of columbium, whereas in 1970 we were down to $170 thousand of GNP per pound of columbium. On the other hand, it is a little hard to imagine civilization toppling because of a shortage of columbium.

Obviously many factors combine to govern the course of the productivity of any given mineral over time. When a rare natural resource is first available, it acquires new uses with a rush; and consumption goes up much faster than GNP. That's the columbium story, no doubt, and, to a lesser extent, the vanadium story. But once the novelty has worn off, the productivity of a resource tends to rise as better or worse substitutes for it appear, as new commodities replace old ones, and as manufacturing processes improve. One of the reasons the productivity of copper rises is because that of aluminum falls, as aluminum replaces copper in many uses. The same is true of coal and oil. A resource, like petroleum, which is versatile because of its role as a source of energy, is an interesting special case. It is hardly any wonder that the productivity of petroleum has stagnated, because the consumption of energy—both as electricity for domestic and industrial use and in the automobile—has recently increased even faster than GNP. But no one can doubt that we will run out of oil, that coal and nuclear fission will replace oil as the major sources of energy. It is already becoming probable that the high-value use of oil will soon be as feed stock for the petrochemical industries, rather than as a source of energy. Sooner or later, the productivity of oil will rise out of sight, because the production and consumption of oil will eventually dwindle toward zero, but real GNP will not.

So there really is no reason why we should not think of the productivity of natural resources as increasing more or less exponentially over time. But then overshoot and collapse are no longer the inevitable trajectory of the world system, and the typical assumption-conclusion of the Doomsday Models falls by the wayside. We are in a different sort of ball game. The system might still burn itself out and collapse in finite time, but one cannot say with any honesty that it must. It all depends on the particular, detailed facts of modern economic life as well as on the economic policies we and the rest of the world pursue. I don't want to argue for any particular counter-story; all I want to say now is that the overshoot-collapse pattern is built into the models very near the surface, by assumption, and by implausible assumption at that.

Scarcity—and High Prices

There is at least one reason for believing that the Doomsday story is almost certainly wrong. The most glaring defect of the Forrester-Meadows models is the absence of any sort of functioning price system. I am no believer that the market is always right, and I am certainly no advocate of laissez-faire where the environment is concerned. But the price system is, after all, the main social institution evolved by capitalist economies (and, to an increasing extent, socialist economies too) for registering and reacting to relative scarcity. There are several ways that the working of the price system will push our society into faster and more systematic increases in the productivity of natural resources.

First of all, let me go back to the analogy between natural resources and labor. We are not surprised to learn that industry quite consciously tries to make inventions that save labor, i.e., permit the same product to be made with fewer man-hours of work. After all, on the average, labor costs amount to almost three-fourths of all costs in our economy. An invention that reduces labor requirements per unit of GNP by 1 percent reduces all costs by about 0.75 percent. Natural resource costs are a much smaller proportion of total GNP, something nearer 5 percent. So industry and engineering have a much stronger motive to reduce labor requirements by 1 percent than to reduce resource requirements by 1 percent, assuming—which may or not be true— that it is about as hard to do one as to do the other. But then, as the earth's supply of particular natural resources nears exhaustion, and as natural resources become more and more valuable, the motive to economize those natural resources should become as strong as the motive to economize labor.

The productivity of resources should rise faster than now—it is hard to imagine otherwise.

There are other ways in which the market mechanism can be expected to push us all to economize on natural resources as they become scarcer. Higher and rising prices of exhaustible resources lead competing producers to substitute other materials that are more plentiful and therefore cheaper. To the extent that it is impossible to design around or find substitutes for expensive natural resources, the prices of commodities that contain a lot of them will rise relative to the prices of other goods and services that don't use up a lot of resources. Consumers will be driven to buy fewer resource-intensive goods and more of other things. All these effects work automatically to increase the productivity of natural resources, i.e., to reduce resource requirements per unit of GNP.

As I mentioned a moment ago, this is not an argument for laissez-faire. We may feel that the private decisions of buyers and sellers give inadequate representation to future generations. Or we may feel that private interests are in conflict with a distinct public interest—strip-mining of coal is an obvious case in point, and there are many others as soon as we begin to think about environmental effects. Private market responses may be too uncoordinated, too slow, based on insufficient and faulty information. In every case there will be actions that public agencies can take and should take; and it will be a major political struggle to see that they are taken. But I don't see how one can have the slightest confidence in the predictions of models that seem to make no room for the operation of everyday market forces. If the forecasts are wrong, then so are the policy implications, to the extent that there are any realistic policy implications.

Every analysis of resource scarcity has to come to terms with the fact that the prices of natural resources and resource products have not shown any tendency to rise over the past half-century, relative to the prices of other things. This must mean that there have so far been adequate offsets to any progressive impoverishment of deposits—like improvements in the technology of extraction, savings in end uses, or the availability of cheaper substitutes. The situation could, of course, change; and very likely some day it will. If the experienced and expert participants in the market now believed that resource prices would be sharply higher at some foreseeable time, prices would *already* be rising, as I will try to explain in a moment. The historical steadiness of resource prices suggests that buyers and sellers in the market have not been acting as if they foresaw exhaustion in the absence of substitutes, and therefore sharply higher future prices. They may turn out to be wrong; but the Doomsday Models give us absolutely no reason to expect that—in fact, they claim to get whatever meager empirical basis they have from such experts.

Why is it true that if the market saw higher prices in the future, prices would already be rising? It is a rather technical point, but I want to explain it because, in a way, it summarizes the important thing about natural resources: conserving a mineral deposit is just as much of an investment as building a factory, and it has to be analyzed that way. Any owner of a mineral deposit owns a valuable asset, whether the owner is a private capitalist or the government of an underdeveloped country. The asset is worth keeping only if at the margin it earns a return equal to that earned on other kinds of assets. A factory produces things each year of its life, but a mineral deposit just lies there: its owner can realize a return only if he either mines the deposit or if it *increases in value.* So if you are sitting on your little pile of X and confidently expect to be able to sell it for a very high price in the year 2000 because it will be very scarce by then, you must be earning your 5 percent a year, or 10 percent a year, or whatever the going rate of return is, each year between now and 2000. The only way this can happen is for the value of X to go up by 5 percent a year or 10 percent a year. And that means that anyone who wants to use any X any time between now and 2000 will have to pay a price for it that is rising at that same 5 percent or 10 percent a year. Well, it's not happening. Of course, we are exploiting our hoard of exhaustible resources; we have no choice about that. We are certainly exploiting it wastefully, in the sense that we allow each other to dump waste products into the environment without full accounting for costs. But there is very little evidence that we are exploiting it too fast.

Crowding on Planet Earth

I have less to say about the question of population growth, because it doesn't seem to involve any difficult conceptual problems. At any time, in any place, there is presumably an optimal size of population—with the property that the average person would be somewhat worse off if the population were a bit larger, and also worse off if the population were a bit smaller. In any real case it must be very difficult to know what the optimum population is, especially because it will change over time as technology changes, and also because it is probably more like a band or zone than a sharply defined number. I mean that if you could somehow plot a graph of economic welfare per person against population size, there would be a very gentle dome or plateau at the top, rather than a sharp peak.

I don't intend to guess what the optimal population for the United States may be. But I am prepared to hazard the guess that there is no point in opting for a perceptibly larger population than we now have, and we might well be content with a slightly smaller one. (I want to emphasize the likelihood that a 15 percent larger or 15 percent smaller population would make very little difference in our standard of well-being. I also want to emphasize that I am talking only about our own country. The underdeveloped world offers very special problems.) My general reason for believing that we should not want a substantially larger population is this. We all know the bad consequences of too large a population: crowding, congestion, excessive pollution, the disappearance of open space—that is why the curve of average well-being eventually turns down at large population sizes. Why does the curve ever climb to a peak in the first place? The generic reason is because of what economists call economies of scale, because it takes a population of a certain size and density to support an efficient chemical industry, or publishing industry, or symphony orchestra, or engineering university, or airline, or computer hardware and software industry, especially if you would like several firms in each, so that they can be partially regulated by their own competition. But after all, it only takes a population of a *certain* size or density to get the benefit of these economies of scale. And I'm prepared to guess that the U.S. economy is already big enough to do so; I find it hard to believe that sheer efficiency would be much served in the United States by having a larger market.

As it happens, recent figures seem to show that the United States is heading for a stationary population: that is to say, the current generation of parents seems to be establishing fertility patterns that will, if continued, cause the population to stabilize some time during the next century. Even so, the absolute size of the population will increase for a while, and level off higher than it is now, because decades of population growth have left us with a bulge of population in the childbearing ages. But I have already argued that a few million more or less hardly make a difference; and a population that has once stabilized might actually decrease, if that came to seem desirable.

At the present moment, at least for the United States, the danger of rapid population growth seems to be the wrong thing to worry about. The main object of public policy in this field ought to be to ensure that the choice of family size is truly a voluntary choice, that access to the best birth-control methods be made universal. That seems to be all that is needed. Of course, we know very little about what governs voluntary fertility, about why the typical notion of a good family size changes from generation to generation. So it is certainly possible that these recent developments will reverse themselves and that population control will again appear on the agenda of public policy. This remains to be seen.

In all this I have said nothing about the Doomsday Models because there is practically nothing that needs to be said. So far as we can tell, they make one very bad mistake: in the face of reason, common sense, and systematic evidence, they seem to assume that at high standards of living, people want more children as they become more affluent (though over most of the observed range, a higher standard of living goes along with smaller families). . . .

There is another analytical error in the models, as Fred Singer has pointed out. Suppose resource exhaustion or increased pollution conspires to bring a reduction in industrial production. The model then says that birth rates will rise because, in the past, low industrial output has been associated with high birth rates. But there is nothing in historical evidence to suggest that a once-rich country will go *back* to high birth rates if (as I doubt will happen) its standard of living falls from an accustomed high level. Common sense suggests that a society in such a position would fight to preserve its standard of living by reducing the desired family size. In any case, this is another example of a poorly founded—or unfounded—assumption introduced to support the likelihood of overshoot-and-collapse.

Paying for Pollution

Resource exhaustion and overpopulation: that leaves pollution as the last of the Doomsday Devils. The subject is worth a whole lecture in itself, because it is one of those problems about which economists actually have something important to say to the world, not just to each other. But I must be brief. I think that what one gets from the Doomsday literature is the notion that air and water and noise pollution are an inescapable accompaniment of economic growth, especially industrial growth. If that is true, then to be against pollution is to be against growth. I realize that in putting the matter so crudely I have been unjust; nevertheless, that is the message that comes across. I think that way of looking at the pollution problem is wrong.

A correct analysis goes something like this. Excessive pollution and degradation of the environment certainly accompany industrial growth and the increasing population density that goes with it. But they are by no means an inescapable byproduct. Excessive pollution happens because of an important flaw in the price system. Factories, power plants, municipal sewers, drivers of cars, strip-miners of coal and deep-miners of coal, and all sorts of generators of waste are allowed to dump that waste into the environment, into the atmosphere and into running water and the oceans, without paying the full cost of what they do. No wonder they do too much. So would you, and so would I. In fact, we actually do—directly as drivers of cars, indirectly as we buy some products at a price which is lower than it ought to be because the producer is not required to pay for using the environment to carry away his wastes, and even more indirectly as we buy things that are made with things that pollute the environment.

This flaw in the price system exists because a scarce resource (the waste-disposal capacity of the environment) goes unpriced; and that happens because it is owned by all of us, as it should be. The flaw can be corrected, either by the simple expedient of regulating the discharge of wastes to the environment by direct control or by the slightly more complicated device of charging special prices—user taxes—to those who dispose of wastes in air or water. These effluent charges do three things: they make pollution-intensive goods expensive, and so reduce the consumption of them; they make pollution-intensive methods of production costly, and so promote abatement of pollution by producers; they generate revenue that can, if desired, be used for the further purification of air or water or for other environmental improvements. Most economists prefer this device of effluent charges to regulation by direct order. This is more than an occupational peculiarity. Use of the price system has certain advantages in efficiency and decentralization. Imposing a physical limit on, say, sulfur dioxide emission is, after all, a little peculiar. It says that you may do so much of a bad thing and pay nothing for the privilege, but after that, the price is infinite. Not surprisingly, one can find a more efficient schedule of pollution abatement through a more sensitive tax schedule.

But this difference of opinion is minor compared with the larger point that needs to be made. The annual cost that would be necessary to meet decent pollution-abatement standards by the end of the century is large, but not staggering. One estimate says that in 1970 we spent about $8.5 billion (in 1967 prices), or 1 percent of GNP, for pollution abatement. An active pollution abatement policy would cost perhaps $50 billion a year by 2000, which would be about 2 percent of GNP by then. That is a small investment of resources: you can see how small it is when you consider that GNP grows by 4 percent or so every year, on the average. Cleaning up air and water would entail a cost that would be a bit like losing one-half of one year's growth, between now and the year 2000. What stands between us and a decent environment is not the curse of industrialization, not an unbearable burden of cost, but just the need to organize ourselves consciously to do some simple and knowable things. Compared with the possibility of an active abatement policy, the policy of stopping economic growth in order to stop pollution would be incredibly inefficient. It would not actually accomplish much, because one really wants to reduce the amount of, say, hydrocarbon emission to a third or a half of *what it is now*. And what no-growth would accomplish, it would do by cutting off your face to spite your nose.

The End of the World—A Matter of Timing

In the end, that is really my complaint about the Doomsday school. It diverts attention from the really important things that can actually be done, step by step, to make things better. The end of the world *is* at hand—the earth, if you take the long view, will fall into the sun in a few billion years anyway, unless some other disaster happens first. In the meantime, I think we'd be better off passing a strong sulfur-emissions tax, or getting some Highway Trust Fund money allocated to mass transit, or building a humane and decent floor under family incomes, or overriding President Nixon's veto of a strong Water Quality Act, or reforming the tax system, or fending off starvation in Bengal—instead of worrying about the generalized "predicament of mankind."

Growth and Antigrowth:
What Are the Issues?

E. J. MISHAN

Professor Mishan holds that once the darker side of economic growth is recognized, one comes to the conclusion that continued economic growth will not bring us closer to the good life.

Debate on the growth-antigrowth theme has become a fashionable pastime over the past five years. And since its continued enjoyment must depend to a large extent on its unconclusiveness, it would be boorish as well as presumptuous to propose that we try to reach a settled conclusion.

But the present enjoyment in the continual conflicts of opinion may become marred by a growing sense of frustration from repeated failure to organize our thoughts and to acquire perspective on the subject. The time has come to steer the debate away from rhetorical appeals and toward more direct confrontation—less bark and more bite are called for. I propose, therefore, that we define the issues more carefully and lay down ground rules for a more searching investigation.

There are two aspects to the debate: first, whether continued economic growth is physically possible and, second, whether such growth is desirable. Both questions are linked together in any policy conclusion, but they can be treated separately.

The Physical Possibility
of Sustained Growth

Let us first consider the physical possibility of growth. To ask whether the world *can* continue to maintain a 2–3 percent growth rate is to pose a question about technological possibilities. It might well be that GNP, as conventionally measured, could grow at this rate *provided* all resources were properly allocated. This means that all productive services would have to be correctly priced. *Uneconomic* pollution of air, water, etc., would have to be prevented. Indeed, an ideal allocation might require that all, or nearly all, productivity gains be utilized to increase leisure, which would imply that "real" goods per capita would not grow, or would grow very little. This "constant-physical product" economic growth obviously would be very much easier to maintain over time than the conventional "increasing-physical product" growth.

But is it realistic to expect such allocative wisdom to prevail under existing economic and political institutions? To ask about the actual prospects of growth, we must also speculate about the changes, if any, in political and economic institutions that are likely to be brought about by changes in public attitudes. At the same time, we must abstract from certain present dangers that threaten human survival itself—the danger of ecological catastrophe from ruthless interference in the biosphere, the danger of genetic calamity from increased radiation or new chemicals, the danger of nuclear Armageddon. Each of these threats has arisen from economic and technological growth, and each will be further aggravated by such growth in the future.

Suppose, however, that we can reasonably anticipate a stable world population in the foreseeable future and that the question we have to face is whether, irrespective of the distribution of future world product, an average rate of growth per capita of *physical* product, comparable to that "enjoyed" in the postwar period, can be maintained for the next few centuries. What should we have to know in order to tackle such a question?

Knowledge of existing reserves of materials used in modern industry is clearly not enough. We already have rough estimates of the remaining reserves of coal, oil, and a large number of metals. And even if they turn out to be underestimates by as much as a factor of two or three, it will make little difference in the number of years required to exhaust them at current rates of depletion. If, for example, world oil consumption continues to increase at a rate of about 10 percent per annum, known reserves (including projected future discoveries) should be exhausted in about two decades. Even if reserves turn out to be as much as 4 times as large as currently estimated, we could keep going only for another 14 years; and if they were 8 times as large (which is hardly possible), we could keep going for another 2 decades. There is, I think, general agreement that we cannot continue to mine a wide range of primary materials *at current rates* for much longer than the end of the century.

Knowledge of economics is not enough either. Economists continue to remind us (unnecessarily perhaps) that as a resource becomes scarce, its price rises and it is used less intensively. True, the rise in the price of a depleting resource is also expected to induce enterprises to switch to substitutes. These substitutes are unfailingly on tap in the textbooks, but in the world we live in we cannot be so sure that our luck will continue to hold. Indeed, it may be an unreasonable expectation. At current rates of usage, all known reserves of silver, gold, copper, lead, platinum, tin, and zinc will be used up within 20 years. There is no historical experience of finding substitutes simultaneously for so large a group of important materials.

We may reasonably conclude, therefore, that *were there to be no techno-logical innovation in the future,* we simply would not be able to continue to grow indefinitely. The earth and its resources are all too finite, and our continued absorption of them on an ever-larger scale must eventually exhaust them. The only question would be when.

The crucial variable in all optimistic forecasts, and in all declarations of faith, is technological innovation. Living in a world that is today being transformed before our eyes by new applications of science, we have an almost irresistible presumption in favor of scientific capability. If it merely sounds possible, the layman is ready to believe it will happen.

Thus we are ready to accept the idea of a vast proliferation of nuclear power plants over the earth, with problems of space solved and with radiation and heat hazards all kept well under control. And we are ready to imagine also that technology will discover increasingly more efficient and inexpensive ways of recycling materials. As for food supplies, the optimistic view is that the problem can be solved by intensive monoculture which utilizes large tracts of land and large amounts of chemical fertilizers and pesticides—the methods of the so-called green revolution. We are to ignore the social consequences of such agrotechnology on the economy of the hundreds of thousands of Asian villages, and the urban problems that follow the disruption of traditional ways of life.

I do not want to sound too cynical. It may all be wonderfully possible—or we may all be wonderfully lucky. I would simply affirm that there is room for legitimate doubt. The advance of technology in the West over the past 200 years might well be attributable to especially favorable circumstances. Up to the present there was no problem of limits to the assimilative capacity of the biosphere, or of the availability of cheap fossil fuels. As for scientific progress, we may be running into diminishing returns to the scale of research—partly because of an incipient breakdown in communications among an expanding array of narrowly focused specialists.

Perhaps there are no solutions to a number of problems that scientists are working on. It may be that what we want to do just cannot, in the nature of things, ever be done—though it may take us decades to realize this. Finally, it is possible—alas, more than possible—that should we succeed in wrestling some of nature's closest secrets from her breast, we shall live to wish we had not.

A sustained per capita growth rate of 3 percent per annum implies that the average income in 150 years will be about 100 times as large as the average income today, and 10,000 times as large in another 150 years. Just contemplate the amounts of energy and materials required to meet such fantastic standards. Just what shape will expenditures of this magnitude take? And how on earth (literally) will a person manage to absorb them?

The Desirability of
Sustained Economic Growth

Assuming that per capita growth could be maintained indefinitely at current rates, we must still ask whether such growth is desirable. Has economic growth promoted social welfare in the recent past, and is it likely to do so in the future? An odd assortment of arguments come up in this debate, a number of which are definitely "nonstarters." We can save time and heat by recognizing some of them before going any farther.

First, there is the frequent statement that technology—the main force behind current economic growth—is itself neutral. One cannot associate it with good or evil attributes and "it all depends on how man uses it." But the *potential* of science and technology is not the issue. Their *actual* effects are. Intelligent conjecture about the future presupposes some knowledge of the reach of modern science and also some idea of the probable scientific developments over the foreseeable future. From this we can speculate about some of the more likely consequences on our lives, bearing in mind the limitations of men and the driving forces of modern institutions, economic and political.

A related response, the invocation of a "challenge" to man to "face the future" or to "be worthy of his destiny," must also go off the board. Otherwise we shall find ourselves with a two-headed penny. For wherever science and technology can be seen to have created problems, the technocrats exclaim "challenge" and perceive an immediate need for more technology. We must be alert to the possibility that some of the problems inflicted upon us by the advance of technology can also be solved by using less of the existing technology.

Nor is it, for similar reasons, legitimate to argue that we should seek the "optimal," or just-right, rate of growth. One can imagine some distillation of economic growth, some essence purified of all harmful external effects, which cannot fail to result in ideal human progress. But such flights of inspiration offer no plausible picture of the future and no guide to action. Economists all know that a narrow range of adverse spillovers—such as air and water pollution, noise, congestion, and tourist blight—can be reduced given some political effort. Yet in judging the quality of life over the last two decades, we obviously cannot abstract from the brute facts of expanding pollution. So, also, in debating the foreseeable future, it is not the potential ideal that is at issue, but the political likelihood of realizing significant reductions in each of the familiar forms of pollution.

The "need" to maintain the momentum of economic growth in order to enable us to do good deeds like helping the poor, promoting high culture, or expanding higher education is also not on the agenda. This argument might win ethical support even if it were agreed that economic growth actually entailed a decline in social welfare for the majority of people. But the fact is that such worthy objectives can all be realized *without* sustained economic growth. In the United States, so much is produced which is trivial, inane, if not inimical, that we already have more than enough to transfer resources for these more meritorious purposes.

It is convenient for the professional economist to interpret people's economic behavior as reflecting their mature judgment about what is most conducive to their happiness. But I hope that he is not such a fool as really to believe it. It is also convenient for the economist to champion the right of the citizen to spend his money as he wishes. For my part, I have no objection if he prefers to sleep on a mattress stuffed with breakfast cereal. For I am not questioning his right to choose; I am questioning the consequences of his choice. We can sharpen the debate by focusing not on motivation, but only on the consequences.

Having, hopefully, cleared away some of the verbal undergrowth that tends to impede the progress of this debate, we are better able to perceive the issues that can be decisive. The issues can be divided, arbitrarily perhaps, into two categories:

1. In the first are the conventional array of adverse spillovers—air pollution, water pollution, solid waste pollution, noise, uglification of town and country—all of which have increased alarmingly since the war. The question is whether they have more than offset the "normal" expectations of welfare gains from economic growth.

2. In the second category are the remaining consequences of economic growth. How much weight is to be given to those pervasive repercussions that are less tangible and more complex than the familiar external diseconomies? Unwittingly, through the process of continually and unquestioningly adapting our style and pace of life to technological and commercial possibilities, we may be losing irrevocably traditional sources of comfort and gratification.

It is difficult to draw a balance sheet summarizing the net welfare effects of the increased output of goods and the concomitant spillovers in the last few years. Even if we had all the physical data—from the hazards of chemical pesticides to rising levels of noise, from oil-fouled beaches the world over, to forest-cropping and earth-stripping—we should, in a closely interdependent economic system, be faced with the almost impossible task of evaluation. My inclination is to describe what has been happening on the advancing pollution front in impressionistic terms, taking it for granted that the balance of the argument will be restored by the unremitting efforts of commercial advertising, establishment politicians, company chairmen, and the spate of articles in our newspapers and magazines that speak loudly of the goodies we have and of goodies yet to come.

The incidence of a single spillover alone—be it foul air, endless traffic bedlam, noise, or fear of criminal violence—can be enough to counter all of the alleged gains of economic prosperity. Let a family have five television sets, four refrigerators, three cars, two yachts, a private plane, a swimming pool, and half a million dollars' worth of securities. What enjoyment is left if it fears to stroll out of an evening, if it must take elaborate precautions against burglary, if it lives in continuous anxiety lest one or another, parent or child, be kidnapped, mutilated, or murdered? A fat bag of consumer goods, an impressive list of technical achievements, can hardly compensate for any one of such perils that have come to blight the lives of millions of Americans.

The old-fashioned notion of diminishing marginal utility of goods and the increasing marginal disutility of "bads" can also bear more emphasis. For one thing, choosing from an increasing variety of goods can be a tense and time-consuming process. For another, as Stefan Linder observes in his admirable and amusing *Harried Leisure Classes*, Americans cannot find time to make use of all the gadgets and sports gear they feel impelled to buy.

In addition, the "relative income hypothesis" (or, more facetiously, the "Jones effect") argues strongly against continued economic growth, if only because it is a predicament for which the economists can propose no remedy consistent with such growth. In an affluent society, people's satisfactions, as Thorstein Veblen observed, depend not only on the innate or perceived utility of the goods they buy but also on the status value of such goods. Thus to a person in a high consumption society, it is not only his absolute income that counts but also his *relative* income, his position in the structure of incomes. In its extreme form—and as affluence rises we draw closer to it—only relative income matters. A man would then prefer a 5 percent reduction in his own income accompanied by a 10 percent reduction in the incomes of others to a 25 percent increase in both his income and the incomes of others.

The more this attitude prevails—and the ethos of our society actively promotes it—the more futile is the objective of economic growth for society as a whole. For it is obvious that over time everybody cannot become relatively better off. The economist can, of course, continue to spin his optimal equations even in these conditions, but he has no means of measuring the loss in terms of utter futility. Since the extent of these wealth-dissipative effects are never measured, estimates over the last few years of increments of "real" income (or "measured economic welfare") must be rejected as wholly misleading.

Reflecting on the unmeasurable consequences of economic growth, Gilbert and Sullivan's dictum "Things are never what they seem" is a proper leitmotif.

Consider first the motive force behind economic growth. Bernard Shaw once remarked that "discontent is the mainspring of progress." The secret of how to keep people running is to widen the gap between their material condition and their material expectations. That gap is a fair measure of their discontent, and it was never wider than it is today. It is institutionalized by the agencies of Madison Avenue and hallowed by our system of higher education.

If continued discontent with what they have is required to keep people buying the increasing output of industry, and continued discontent with their status is necessary to keep them operating the machine, can we really believe that people are nonetheless happier as they absorb more goods? Does not the consequent struggle for status in an increasingly anonymous society become so obsessive as to cut a person off from enjoyment of the largeness of life? Does not this "virtue" of motivation act to shrivel a person's generous impulses, to make him use other people as a means of advancement, corrupting his character and his capacity for friendship?

Next, let us look at the "knowledge industry," whose products fuel the engine of economic growth. In a society that pays ritual homage to our great secular cathedrals of knowledge, the words "scientific research" are holy and scholarship is almost synonymous with saintliness. But the social consequences of the disinterested pursuit of knowledge are not all beyond dispute. The harrowing degree of specialization that results from the attempt to advance the expanding boundary of any discipline can crush the capacity of men for instinctual pleasure and can make communication between scientists, even those working in the same field, increasingly difficult.

The advance of scientific knowledge enhances the secular to the detriment of the sacred. One wonders if the loss of the great myths, the loss of belief in a benevolent deity, in reunion after death, has not contributed to a sense of desolation. One wonders also if a code of morality can be widely accepted in a society without belief in any god or in any hereafter.

As decisions are increasingly influenced by experts, democracy becomes more vulnerable. As historical knowledge grows, and hawk-eyed scholars find a vocation in debunking national heroes and popular legend, the pride of peoples in their common past is eroded and, along with it, their morale as well.

We might also want to ponder briefly some of the unexpected repercussions of a number of much-heralded inventions. Consumer innovations over the recent past and foreseeable future appear to be largely labor-saving—inventions that reduce dependence on others, or, rather, transfer dependence to a machine. Given that the machine is incomparably more efficient, can its efficiency in yielding services compensate for the inevitable loss of authentic human experience? Packaged and precooked foods save time for the busy housewife. Personal contacts necessarily decline with the spread of more efficient labor-saving devices. They have already declined with the spread of supermarkets, cafeterias, and vending machines. And they will continue to decline with the trend toward computerization in offices and factories, toward patient monitoring machines and computer-diagnoses in hospitals, toward closed-circuit television instruction, automated libraries, and teaching machines.

Thus the compulsive search for efficiency, directed in the main toward innovations that save effort and time, must continue to produce for us yet more elegant instruments for our mutual estrangement. We might ask if the things commonly associated with the good life—a more settled way of natural beauty and architectural dignity, a rehabilitation of norms of propriety and taste—can ever be realized by affluent societies straining eternally to woo the consumer with ever more outlandish and expendable gadgetry and seeking eternally for faster economic growth.

If it is conceded that, once subsistence levels have been passed, the sources of man's most enduring satisfactions spring from mutual trust and affection, from sharing joy and sorrow, from giving and accepting love, from open-hearted companionship and laughter; it it is further conceded that in a civilized society the joy of living comes from the sense of wonder inspired by the unfolding of nature, from the perception of beauty inspired by great art, from the renewal of faith and hope inspired by the heroic and the good—if this much is conceded, then is it possible to believe that unremitting attempts to harness the greater part of man's energies and ingenuity to the task of amassing an ever-greater assortment of material possessions can add to people's happiness? Can it add more than it subtracts? Can it add anything?

Recognizing the darker side of economic growth, we must conclude that the game is not worth the candle. And the answer to the question of whether continued economic growth in the West brings us any closer to the good life cannot be other than a resounding No.

What Have We Learned About Inflation?

HENRY C. WALLICH AND MABLE I. WALLICH

Phillips curves, demand-pull, cost-push, and so on are all economic concepts that one encounters in any analysis of inflation. The following analysis suggests some of the complications involved in the application of these concepts.

Over the last three years, the annual rise in prices has come down from a rate of 6 percent to 3–3.5 percent. This progress in reducing the rate of inflation has been accomplished by a sequence of the "orthodox" method of tight budgets and money and, subsequently, an "incomes policy" in the form of controls over wages, prices, and profit margins. It has been a partial success at best, although better than many other countries have been able to do. The standard forecast for 1973 points to a renewed rise in the rate of inflation. We can learn something about our chances of avoiding the inflations of the future by looking at the inflations of the past.

Some Lessons of the Past

Our knowledge, such as it is, has not been derived exclusively from the inflation that began in 1965. The United States has been through other big price movements, down as well as up. An econometric finding that even today sends chills down the backs of portfolio managers was made as early as 1896 by Professor Irving Fisher at Yale. He concluded that prolonged increases in interest rates and declines in the bond market were the results of past inflation, and he interpreted this as an effort on the part of investors to compensate for the erosion of their principal. Fisher's finding remains valid today, but with a vital difference. Whereas in the nineteenth century it took savers and borrowers many years to diagnose inflation and adjust interest rates accordingly, current studies have found that nowadays this reaction happens very quickly. Today one can predict with some assurance that another substantial upsurge of inflation would drive interest rates up and push the bond market, and possibly also the stock market, down sharply with very little lag. This is the natural result of the expected drop in the purchasing power of money, which induces investors to demand compensation in the form of higher interest rates.

Since our biggest inflations have been associated with wars, the lessons of experience in dealing with them focus mainly on wage and price controls. World Wars I and II have shown that, under wartime conditions, these controls have to be very comprehensive if they are to work. Even then they constitute a delaying action at best. Rationing and black markets are inevitable accompaniments, and compliance diminishes as time drags on. This experience was one reason for abstaining so long from direct controls in the present case. Meanwhile it has become obvious, however, that the problems created by a violent demand-pull inflation, such as occurred during two World Wars, cannot serve as a guide to dealing with a cost-push inflation, accompanied by an easy supply situation, such as has characterized the present inflation.

Demand-Pull and Cost-Push

The distinction between demand-pull and cost-push inflation—or, better perhaps, its widespread acceptance—dates back to the inflation of the middle 1950s. That was the first real peacetime inflation of this century. It began with a boom that engendered excess demand in the economy. But when the boom collapsed and was succeeded by rising unemployment, prices nevertheless continued rising. This was contrary to the textbooks, as textbooks were then written. Most economists had firmly believed that prices were governed by demand, not by cost. But the evidence of prices rising as costs went up while demand was falling made numerous converts.

Since that time, a number of econometric studies have shown that manufacturing prices are indeed very importantly governed by costs, which for the economy as a whole are mainly labor costs. The costs that manufacturers use in their pricing, however, usually are not the costs incurred at their current level of operations, which may be high or low relative to their capacity, but costs computed on some "standard volume."

Demand-pull and cost-push are not only economic concepts but belong also to the vocabulary of political economy. Labor, particularly, is sensitive to the allegation of cost-push, since wages represent much the largest part of costs. To refute the view that cost-push really means wage-push, the doctrine of "administered prices" has been developed. This says that price increases are really due to the arbitrary use of market power by large corporations. If these corporations were to hold prices constant or even lower them, as would be appropriate in recessions, wage increases would not raise prices.

There is little doubt that large corporations have market power and can, within reason, set their prices in a way that wheat farmers cannot. Profits, however, are a rather thin layer on top of "compensation of employees," which makes up the bulk of national income. Profit margins, moreover, typically have declined in recessions even when prices were rising. There is merit in the idea of reducing market power. But the contribution that administered pricing makes to inflation is probably too small to allow this to become an effective means of combating inflation. Relatively little has been heard about administered price-push in the current inflation.

The Phillips Curve

As so often happens in scientific work, the most fruitful discovery about inflation was made quite independently of current problems. The Phillips Curve; named after a British economist who described his findings in an article in 1958, hypothesizes that unemployment and inflation are functionally related. Phillips found that, over many decades reaching far back into the nineteenth century, wage increases in Britain had been high when unemployment was low, and vice versa. Given that wages and prices are closely related, this points to a similar relationship between unemployment and prices. Phillips' work has proved to be perhaps the most fruitful piece of economic research since the war. Its policy implications were recognized quickly and have been influential in the thinking of probably the dominant group of economists ever since.

If inflation and unemployment are inversely related, the Phillips Curve theorists argue, unemployment can be reduced by pushing the economy to a higher rate of inflation. This means a gain in output, as well as the benefits of a lower level of unemployment. Among the latter are gains for minority groups, who historically have made breakthroughs against discrimination during periods of very tight labor markets. Minimum unemployment thus becomes the source of some very major gains.

Against these, many Phillips Curve theorists argue, the cost of inflation does not weigh heavily. Output, real goods, determines welfare. Prices, which are tickets attached to the real goods, do not. What difference does it make whether bread costs ten cents or a quarter or a dollar, whether its price is rising at 5 percent or 15 percent, so long as everything else goes up in proportion?

Defenders of price stability were put on the defensive by this doctrine. They seemed to find themselves in the morally untenable position of arguing

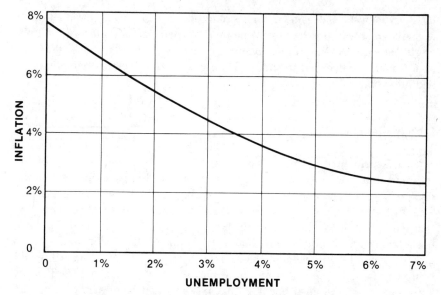

The Phillips Curve shows the supposed relationship between unemployment and inflation. The hypothetical
economy shown here would, for example, have an annual
increase in the price level of about 3 percent along with
a 5 percent unemployment rate. The exact shape and
position of the curve is a subject of current controversy
since the rate of inflation failed to decline significantly
during the 1970 recession.

in favor of more unemployment. They were arguing for the interests of
bankers and bondholders, and against those of debtors and minorities. The
ramparts defending price stability were not crowded.

The defenders of stability could argue, of course, that inflation was
not really costless. Everything did not go up together. In the words of a
Yale student whose father teaches at Yale, "Inflation is when Yale raises
tuition 10 percent every year and freezes Daddy's salary." Some people get
ahead of the game, some fall behind. Debtors gain, creditors lose. Adjustments
to inflation, through bigger wage increases, or higher interest rates, are always
imperfect because the future rate of inflation is itself uncertain. Uncertainty,
moreover, is a cost; and this uncertainty mounts with the rate of inflation.

Even so, it would be difficult to assign a high value to price stability
if the gains from tolerating inflation were at all substantial. The real battle
between the inflationists and the stability advocates has been over the size
and permanence of the gain.

The gain, in the short run, is indicated by the trade-off inherent in
the Phillips Curve. What reduction in unemployment does one additional
percentage point of inflation buy? A reduction by one percentage point would

be a very substantial gain, and almost impossible to reject. A reduction of unemployment by one-tenth of a percentage point could be considered not worth the cost. Numerous econometric estimates have been made, showing, as one might expect, that the trade-off varies with the levels of unemployment and inflation.

Money Illusion

The principal argument has been, however, not over the rate of the trade-off, but over its permanence. Moving from Phillips' empirical finding to a policy prescription involves an assumption that may be illegitimate. The British inflations examined by Phillips were unpredictable. The best that a contemporary observer might have been able to conclude would have been that whenever inflation became pronounced, the Bank of England's credit policy or, in its default, the normal forces of the gold standard would bring it to a halt. The assumption that must be made in turning the Phillips Curve into a policy instrument is that business and labor will behave just the same in an inflation that is the announced policy of the government as in one that is predictable or even likely to disappear. In technical terms, the assumption requires that business and labor have "money illusion," i.e., are unaware of inflation or ignore it, at least in part.

Suppose that at some low level of unemployment, labor demands and business will grant a 5 percent wage increase. Suppose, however, that productivity, i.e., output per man-hour, is rising at only 3 percent, which has been the long-run average rate of gain. In that case, costs will go up 2 percent. If business bases prices on costs, so as to keep profit margins constant, prices will have to go up by 2 percent. This inflation will reduce the 5 percent nominal wage increase to a 3 percent increase in real terms, i.e., in constant purchasing power. Labor cannot get more than that, assuming the share of profits in the national income remains constant, because that is the increment in production available for distribution. The economy has no more to give; and if business promises in excess, inflation takes the excess away. If business and labor have money illusion, things will settle down in this way, with annual wage increases of 5 percent in nominal terms, inflation of 2 percent reducing them to a real 3 percent, and unemployment remaining at its low level as promised by the Phillips Curve analysis.

Suppose, however, that labor becomes aware of the inflation. It is disappointed at getting a real increase of only 3 percent when it had bargained for 5 percent. Expecting a continued inflation of 2 percent, in the next bargaining round labor settles for 7 percent. Costs and prices now go up faster, and labor is again disappointed. In this way, inflation can spiral upward, while real wage gains never exceed 3 percent.

This suggests a very simple conclusion. Inflation will continue to accelerate so long as the level of unemployment is low enough to cause labor to demand, and business to grant, wage increases that labor expects to be larger in real terms, i.e., after deducting the expected inflation, than productivity gains. Inflation will cease to accelerate when unemployment is at a level at which labor's wage demands in real terms are just equal to productivity gains. Inflation will diminish, and eventually prices will begin to fall, if unemployment is larger than the level at which real wage demands equal productivity gains.

The simple notion that price stability depends on wage increases' being equal to productivity gains, these being interpreted as a long-run average for the whole economy, is not particularly controversial. It was the basis of appeals made to labor and business by President Eisenhower; it was spelled out with greater sophistication by President Kennedy's Council of Economic Advisers in the "Guideposts on Prices and Wages"; and it forms the basis for the price and wage standards applied today by the Nixon Administration.

Acceleration

The controversy has been over the tendency of inflation to accelerate, a view which the proponents of the Phillips Curve refer to as the "accelerationist" position. The accelerationists maintain that the Phillips Curve is not stable. If the government tries to reduce unemployment by moving to some particular rate of inflation, the curve will shift upward. The government will find that in order to hold to the chosen level of unemployment, higher and higher rates of inflation must be tolerated. In the long run, these successive points on a curve that is shifting upward will trace out a vertical line. Hence the accelerationists claim that the Phillips Curve in the long run tends toward the vertical.

There is only one set of circumstances in which inflation neither accelerates nor decelerates. That occurs when labor's wage demands in real terms equal productivity gains, as noted before. This equilibrium rate of unemployment has been called by Milton Friedman the "natural rate" of unemployment. Unemployment at this rate does not imply zero inflation. Inflation can be at any level. But whatever it is, it will not change. Labor is getting, in real terms, exactly what it wants. It has no reason to change its demands in nominal terms, which of course include allowance for the expected rate of inflation. Hence inflation stays at whatever level it happens to find itself.

The implication of the accelerationist doctrine, if true, is very damaging to the Phillips Curve philosophy. In the long run, there is no way of reducing unemployment by means of inflation. All rates of inflation produce the same equilibrium unemployment. Only two seemingly minor factors speak for the inflationist case: (1) once a high rate of inflation has been reached, it may be preferable to stick with it rather than go through a period of high unemployment to bring it down to zero, and (2) if the "long run" is very long, it may still pay to work the short-run trade-off between unemployment and inflation, especially from the time perspective of an elected politician.

No Return to Full Stability

The first of these two options confronts the United States at this time. Are we going to make a great effort to get inflation down to zero? It is a fair guess that the decision will be on the side of the Phillips Curve supporters. That is to say, the United States, after making a costly effort to halt an accelerating inflation and then to bring it down from a rate of 6 percent to one of 3.5 percent, is probably not willing to go through the additional agony of bringing inflation down to zero. In order to achieve this, we would have to use wage and price controls in a manner apparently more drastic than the nation is willing to tolerate, or else maintain unemployment above the equilibrium rate in order to obtain deceleration even without controls.

We do not know with precision what the equilibrium rate of unemployment is in the American economy. All we do know is that changes in the composition of the labor force have pushed it higher in recent years. Probably it is now somewhere near 5 percent rather than 4 percent. The widespread expectation that inflation will be rising in 1973 implies that unemployment will be below its equilibrium rate, although the speed of the boom also may push inflation up. In that sense, one may say that we are now practicing the Phillips Curve philosophy.

Lags in Acceleration

There remains the question of how soon and how quickly the Phillips Curve is likely to shift upward. If the lag is long, we could trade low unemployment now against more inflation later. The length of the lag has been much debated, and there is evidence from a number of sources. The kind of explosive inflation that occurred in various European countries after World Wars I and II is not a relevant precedent for the United States. Anyone whose opposition to inflation is based on fear of that kind of development in the United States is not putting up a very strong case. Again, there have been inflations at annual rates of 50 percent and more in various Latin American countries. Obviously, inflation had to accelerate in order to get to those levels. But although some countries, for instance, Chile and Brazil, have long lived with inflations fluctuating over wide ranges, an ultimate explosion has always been avoided. What the Latin American inflations seem to demonstrate is that inflation tends to be unstable and therefore unpredictable, because stabilization efforts, usually associated with high unemployment, tend to be made from time to time.

Why Models Underpredicted

Our own experience of the last few years, however, seems to point in an accelerationist direction. In the late 1960s, the econometric models and equations that are used to predict the course of the economy began to exhibit peculiar miscarriages. Based on the principle of the Phillips Curve, the models predicted a moderate rate of inflation reflecting low but by no means minimal unemployment. Actual inflation increasingly exceeded the forecasts, and the errors became more alarming as unemployment began to rise while inflation also was speeding up. The model builders, their faith in the Phillips Curve unshaken, went to work to revise the models. They built in the fact that, during the early 1960s, the economy had experienced what could be called hidden unemployment—discouraged workers who had withdrawn from the labor force and no longer were counted as unemployed. This hidden unemployment could be made to explain why inflation was so low during the early 1960s, and its disappearance during the subsequent boom then explained the acceleration. The model builders also discovered and built in the fact that the dispersion of unemployment, i.e., the range of unemployment rates in different parts of the economy, had increased. This meant that some labor markets were tight long before average unemployment had come down much, which could also be used to explain high rates of inflation. Finally, it was observed that the structure of the labor force had shifted toward a higher proportion of women and teenagers. Their unemployment, typically above the national average, pulled that average up. The unemployment of the core of the labor force, the heads of households, on the other hand, was lower relative to the national average than before.

With these various adjustments, it remained possible, for a couple of years, to defend the proposition that the Phillips Curve was not shifting upward. But as new data became available year after year, the case became harder and harder to maintain. Increasingly the models and equations began to show that as prices increased by some additional percentage, labor in its wage settlements was not prepared to ignore the increase, nor to settle for some fraction of it, but insisted on raising its demands by the full amount. That, of course, is precisely what the accelerationists had maintained.

Finally, another ingenious piece of econometrics showed that one could do without all the refinements of the unemployment data and explain the course of inflation quite adequately if one were prepared to make one plausible assumption. This was to assume that below some moderate level of inflation, which the equations showed to be about 2.5 percent, people tended to ignore what was happening to prices. Above that flashpoint, however, money illusion vanished and wage demands began to take expected inflation into account fully and quickly. The presumed long lag in the response to inflation, upon which earlier Phillips Curve findings may have rested, had been telescoped.

Changing Responses of Workers and Investors

What had happened to the Phillips Curve theorists was precisely what happened to old Irving Fisher and his finding that interest rates demanded by investors and conceded by borrowers tended to adjust to inflation with a very long lag. This was reasonable so long as governments aimed at price stability and nobody knew whether the long-term trend of prices was up or down. The Phillips Curve theorists could assume the same of the wage demands of labor, which had no grounds for escalating so long as inflation was not expected to continue. Once that premise was changed, investors and workers acted rationally to protect themselves immediately. Inflation began to enter into wages and interest rates fully and with little lag. In other words, it began to escalate.

In real time economics, of course, the last word is never spoken. New facts may appear, new explanations may be devised. Meanwhile, however, the refinements produced by the model builders in their efforts to reconcile the behavior of unemployment with that of prices have supplied some valuable pointers in another direction.

A New Measure of Labor Market Tightness

They have drawn attention to the fact that the overall unemployment rate is a composite of widely divergent rates for particular sectors of the economy and of the labor force. A rate of 5.5 percent, as prevailed in late 1972, is an average of 3.4 percent for heads of households, 5.5 percent for women, 15 percent for teenagers, and 34 percent for black teenagers—in other words, an average of apples and nuts. Simulations with econometric models have shown that even if the average unemployment rate were reduced to some low level, the problems of teenagers and others would remain in large part unsolved. Overheating the economy, aside from the disproportionate costs that it imposes on many people, is an inefficient and inadequate way of curing minority unemployment. Direct action, such as the emergency employment program and training programs, is needed.

The examination of the structure of unemployment has also made clear that the overall unemployment rate, which at 4 percent supposedly signals "full employment," is in fact a poor indicator of inflationary pressure. If the men and women who are strongly unionized, who hold the core jobs in the economy, experience an unemployment rate of 1.8 percent, as they did in 1969, the presence of large numbers of women and teenagers who are only loosely attached to the labor force will not keep wages from rising rapidly. The "heads of households" unemployment rate is a much better signal. To gauge labor market pressure even more accurately, one should eliminate from the unemployment of heads of households that part lasting less than five weeks, which contributes little to labor market balance. In 1969, this would have left 0.9 percent of males in the age bracket 25–64 unemployed for more than five weeks, while the overall unemployment rate was 3.5 percent. Here we have the explanation why inflationary pressures recently have begun to be felt at seemingly high rates of average unemployment.

More evidence keeps coming in, and definitive conclusions are out of place. But the nature of that evidence certainly will be of a sort to tell us that what we call "unemployment" is a very varied and complex phenomenon. The more this is the case, the more we shall be driven to search for varied and complex solutions, and the less we shall probably be able to resolve the problem by the simple method of pushing the economy to the point of inflation.

Curing Inflation
with Unemployment

MICHAEL PIORE

Economists have difficulty explaining current rates of stagflation, argues
Professor Piore, because of the general presumption that prices are set
by supply and demand. He offers a different explanation based on the
concept of fixed-rule pricing.

The current economic situation—the prevailing combination of high
and rising unemployment *and* high and rising rates of price inflation—presents
a special dilemma for economists. This combination simply can't be explained
by accepted economic theory. Unemployment and inflation aren't supposed
to exist together. High unemployment is *the* accepted cure for inflation.
Many economists have maintained that the cure wasn't worth what it cost
the people who are thrown out of work. But virtually no one respected
in the profession has doubted that tolerating joblessness was indeed the way
to curb inflation. Any other policy recommendations have been suspect. They
might be workable but proof was lacking. Thus in the current economic
climate, professionals who dissent from the administration have been objecting
more to the administration's game than to its game plan; they don't have
alternatives to offer.

The reason economists are attached to unemployment as a cure for
inflation is that the relationship derives from the concepts of supply and
demand, concepts that form the foundations of scientific economic theory.
Theoretically prices will rise when demand exceeds the capacity of the economy to produce goods and services, and they will fall when supply exceeds

From Michael Piore, "Curing Inflation with Unemployment," *New Republic* (November 2,
1974), pp. 27–31. Reprinted with the permission of *The New Republic*, © 1974 The New Republic,
Inc.

demands. Unemployment is interpreted as a measure of underutilized productive resources, and hence, of the gap between overall supply and demand. The jobless constitute underutilized resources that can be put to work to expand supply. As everybody knows not all the unemployed really could be conscripted in this way. Some are already on the way to a new job, some are not qualified for the kind of work that's needed, some do not want to work. For this reason, "full employment," in the sense of a balance between aggregate supply and aggregate demand has always been interpreted as involving an unemployment rate higher than zero. *But*, in general, economists have assumed that when unemployment was rising, the gap between demand and supply should be closing and price inflation should be declining.

Given these assumptions economists have been hard pressed to explain the events leading up to the current crisis because the rates of unemployment one would expect to go along with a given rate of price inflation appear to have been increasing. While prices once were thought to stabilize when unemployment reached four or five percent, price stability in the early 1970s seemed to require a rate of unemployment of 5.5 or 6 percent. The only explanation of this that is consistent with the logic of supply and demand is that the number of unemployed who don't really want to work has been increasing. And this has indeed been a major theme in recent writing, even by liberal economists who are not otherwise predisposed to blame the individual for his own economic fate.

To explain the current situation in this way, however, would require a much bolder argument. One cannot argue simply that the percentage of "shirkers" inadvertently thrown into the unemployment figures is rising. One has to argue that the rate of increase has suddenly changed and become so great and so rapid that prices are not stable but rising. If inflation continues to accelerate that argument will be made. But it won't be very convincing.

The idea that prices are determined by supply and demand rests on certain assumptions about the behavior of individual economic agents. These assumptions are plausible, and probably correct in some markets where prices are set by impersonal forces so strong and so compelling that each individual has no choice but to accept the market price or go out of business. The market for most agricultural commodities is of this kind. So is the stock market. In other markets, however, the assumed behavior of prices rests heavily upon certain calculations that people are thought to make in order to maximize their economic welfare. The theory more or less assumes that people estimate the demand and supply curves for their products and use these to set prices and wages.

There have been some studies of the way in which prices and wages actually are set in those markets. The studies do not support the hypotheses of conventional economic theory. People do not appear to make calculations on the basis of anything like estimates of supply and demand. Instead they apply a set of pricing rules. These rules tend to impose a fixed structure of wages and prices. In wage setting, in fact, they seem to do exactly this. Many people are now familiar with this procedure from the arguments about parity among policemen, firemen, and sanitation workers in New York. That was a dispute in which the wage-setting *rule* was explicitly at issue. The significant point for economic analysis is that even in that dispute the discussion did not center on supply and demand. In most of the labor market there is not even a dispute about the rule. Plumbers expect their wages to bear a certain relationship to carpenters; steel workers expect their wages to go up at more or less the same rates as the wages of aluminum and can workers.

Price-setting rules are generally a little more complicated than wage setting, but the basic tendency to impose a fixed structure of relative prices is much the same. Thus, for example, in retailing it is common to use a fixed percentage markup over cost. This guarantees that the relationship between the wholesale and retail prices will be constant whatever the state of supply and demand in the two sectors. Car prices, to give another example, are set as a certain percentage of the median income, and thus they rise automatically with wage increases.

The existence of widespread fixed-rule pricing means that there are essentially two modes of wage and price setting: one governed by supply and demand, in which individual prices rise and fall in response to scarcity or surplus; the second, or rule-determined sector, in which prices and wages are set *relative to each other* in order to maintain a fixed price structure. The two modes of price setting create the possibility of *structural* inflation.

Normally one would expect even in a relatively prosperous economy wide differences in market conditions. Some markets would be in surplus and others would have scarcities. If everybody responded directly to their own market, the prices of scarce commodities would rise; the prices of surplus commodities would fall. Overall these contrary trends should tend to cancel each other out and lead to price stability.

When you have fixed-rule pricing and wage setting in one sector of the economy, however, this balancing will not necessarily occur. It will specifically not occur if the scarcities are concentrated in the market-oriented sectors while the surplus is concentrated in the fixed-rule sectors. Under these circumstances the prices and wages in the market-oriented sectors will rise. Those price increases will feed into the rules of the other sectors, and their prices will *also* rise. This is structural inflation.

It should be noted that structural inflation need not be set off by market forces. It could be triggered by a union political situation that upsets the wages structure, as appeared to be the case in the construction industry in the late 1960s. It might be initiated by the creation of many new plants, without an established place in the existing structure, as tends to happen in an economic boom. It could be triggered by the creation of a new monopoly that seeks to change the position of its product within the national price structure. This in fact occurred in oil after the Arab-Israeli war and is indeed one of the causes of inflation in the United States and abroad. But, in addition, in the last year and a half we have had what appears to be the classic conditions for a structural inflation: major shortages of market-oriented raw materials balanced by surpluses in rule-set prices for manufactured commodities and labor.

How will such structural inflation respond to the conventional remedy of unemployment? Does this characterization suggest alternative economic policies? The answers to these questions depend very much upon how one interprets the commitment to the rules in the fixed-rule sectors. The approach of conventional economists has generally been to dismiss the rules as shorthand or a "rule of thumb" for the more elaborate calculations that are assumed to take place. The people who use these rules, the argument goes, actually are responding to the economic reality described by demand, supply, and profit-maximization procedures of economic theory, and when the gap between the rules and that more fundamental reality becomes important, people will abandon the rules and respond to the market directly. If this interpretation is correct, one can argue that higher unemployment will eventually break up even a structural inflation. The surplus will make it very costly to adhere to the rules and in this way force firms to abandon them in favor of market pricing. The reality of fixed-rule pricing appears, however, to be somewhat more complicated than this conventional interpretation suggests.

In the case of wage rates, the rigidities in the wage structure appear to be a product of a moral commitment on the part of the labor force. Rank-and-file workers tend to view the process of wage determination in moral or ethical terms: they describe their wage rates as *just, fair,* or *equitable.* And they are willing to go on strike to ensure that a *just* wage is received. Workers are not, of course, motivated by concepts of justice alone; they are deterred from striking by high unemployment rates, and they are not above pressuring for a wage that is a little more than "just" in a favorable economic climate. But the just wage is a standard. People are a good deal more willing to strike to preserve it, even in periods of high umemployment, than to better it, and it acts as a restraint upon wage demands even in a tight labor market.

The workers' concept of a just wage involves a fixed relationship with the wage on certain other specific jobs and seems to depend heavily upon past practice and precedent. This means that only wage relationships that are stable over long periods of time come to be regarded as just and equitable, and stable wage relationships that are repeatedly disrupted come to lose their moral compulsion.

A good deal less is known about the process of price determination than about wage rates. The process is more private; academic analysts have never been as intimately involved in its operations as they have in wage setting through collective bargaining; the rules that create rigidities in the price structure seem more complex and more difficult to explain. Still a part of their compulsion also seems to be moral, especially in those situations where buyer and seller have regular, personalized relationships. Both parties come to expect certain pricing patterns to be maintained, and think of any departure from those patterns as unjust and slightly immoral. It is the kind of breach of trust that causes a buyer to look elsewhere for new suppliers, if not immediately then later when the market is slack. And of course the fact that a buyer is likely to see things in this way causes the seller to adhere to the rule, even when he would like to take advantage of a favorable market to boost his margins.

But in the case of pricing, there is a technical as well as moral reason for adherence to conventional rules: there's no really sound alternative. The market forces that economists assume determine relative scarcities are impossible to *know*. The relative scarcities for many commodities, and hence their relative market prices, in fact remain pretty stable over long periods of time. A lot of the changes that do occur are temporary, attributable, for example, to managerial shakeups, the politics of industry, government relations, or just a mistake. They tell nothing about the underlying market conditions but do confuse the picture. Thus the kind of variations in market conditions that might reveal something about the structure of demand and supply is missing. And, as any first-year graduate student will tell you, without that variation it is simply *not possible* to estimate the kind of relationships upon which the calculations assumed in economic theory are predicated.

This last explanation is a little bit like the conventional interpretation of the rules as shorthand calculations but with a critical difference. The conventional interpretation assumes that there is some deeper reality behind the rules, the existence of which economic agents are at least aware, and that the major surpluses created by increasing unemployment will both induce people to seek out that reality and enable them to find it. However the alternative interpretation suggests that neither of these things is the case. For most price and wage setters the structure embodied in their rules *is* reality: nothing in their experience leads them to be aware of the deeper market structure that economists postulate.

If this is the nature of fixed-rule pricing, what is the likely effect of high levels of unemployment? High unemployment will create large surplus in virtually all markets. Such surpluses would confront price and wage makers with a reality lying completely outside the realm of their experience and not encompassed within the constructs through which that experience is understood. Such a confrontation might predispose people to redefine reality. But even if it did, the higher levels of unemployment would not provide the needed information about the underlying structure of supply and demand. And it is not at all clear that high unemployment would in fact predispose people to reconstruct "reality." Psychological studies of people suddenly confronted with situations that do not fit their world view suggest they more often ignore the incongruity than revise their view. Economic agents, of course, cannot easily ignore the situation. Probably they would be forced by the threat of bankruptcy—or bankruptcy itself—simply to abandon established norms of price and wage behavior, and cut prices willy-nilly in some blind effort to shore up demand. They would then be behaving as economic theory says they should, in direct response to market forces, and this would presumably halt the inflationary movement. In this sense unemployment might be a cure.

There is a catch here, inherent in the phrase "abandon the established norms." In any other social setting the kind of wholesale abandonment of established norms of behavior upon which the "unemployment" cure to structural inflation rests would be interpreted as *anarchy*. It would probably be viewed as anarchy in economic activity as well. The orthodox story, in interpreting conventional rules as shorthand expressions of the laws of supply and demand, fails to appreciate this prospect. In that story unemployment merely forces people to recognize that the shorthand is no longer appropriate and to respond *directly* to market forces. From the agent's perspective the traditional rules of price and wage setting represent the *best* construction they can make of economic reality: they don't see any higher, more basic set of forces from which those rules derive. And when the rules are no longer appropriate, they feel that they have lost their grasp on reality. Add to this the vaguely moral flavor surrounding such rules, particularly in wage setting, and one does have anarchy.

What does economic anarchy imply? A panic, perhaps. Probably a prolonged depression. It is extremely unlikely that in the climate of uncertainty that would prevail the private sector would be willing to undertake the kind of investment upon which economic prosperity depends. And the capacity of the government to move fast enough and far enough in increasing its own spending to cover the shortfall in private demand is questionable.

If unemployment won't produce the required adjustments in the wage-price structure, what will? If, as we are arguing, the rules that impose the existing structure are indeed an effort to interpret economic reality, they will probably be revised eventually without a severe deflation. It is difficult to say exactly how this will be accomplished because nobody has taken these rules seriously enough as real economic mechanisms to study the processes of formulation and revision. However one can guess: the attempt of goods in the market-oriented sector to break out of the wage-price structure may be frustrated by existing rules, but it is not without its impact. Relative prices do change at least temporarily, before the rules reassert themselves and other prices catch up. To the extent that prices do not change, shortages occur. All these things are indicators of a change in relative scarcities. They will make it more profitable to reduce the markups in pricing rules. And price makers should eventually find this out, if not by direct calculation, at least by accident. The fact that increases in food and fuel prices are still generating inflationary pressure probably reflects, as much as anything else, a basic skepticism that these crises were generated by permanent changes in the world economic system rather than transitory events—war, famine, and the politics of détente.

In the case of wage determination, the argument is even more straight-forward. There the commitment to a fixed structure rests almost entirely upon past practice and precedent. The leads and lags inherent in the wage setting process mean that a wage or price forced out of line by market pressures will prevail for at least a time. That period becomes a weak prece-dent. If the wage keeps jumping out of line each time efforts are made to restore it, the precedent becomes stronger and stronger. It then becomes something of an independent moral force capable of competing with the traditional wage structure.

It may be possible to facilitate these adjustments in the wage-price structure through public policy. Certain government agencies may, for exam-ple, be in a position to get people to recognize the changes in market condi-tions and revise their decision-making rules accordingly more quickly than people could or would do on their own. The moral authority of governmental institutions, and particularly the presidency, might be brought to bear to excuse people from the moral compulsion inherent in the traditional wage-price structure. In fact this view of the inflationary process points, in many respects, to a program of wage and price *controls*. The conventional distrust of such controls springs from the belief that they would suppress changes in the wage-price structure and, in so doing, forestall adjustments in supply and demand necessary to relieve the inflationary pressure. But if, as we have argued, the structure is rigid and wage-price changes set off an inflationary spiral, the structural changes won't occur anyway, and controls at least pre-vent the spiral from developing. The case for such controls would seem especially strong when combined with other policies designed to convince people directly of changes in economic conditions. Since the price structure has difficulty changing on its own, there is also a case for direct government interventions to expand supply or suppress demand. This is particularly true in sectors of the economy where the price is set by rules, but it is true even in market-oriented sectors, which act to set off the inflationary spiral elsewhere.

All of these interventions constitute an incomes policy of sorts. But it is not a simple matter of announcing—or even enforcing—a single wage-price standard. It is in fact a much more subtle approach to inflation that sees, as the central problem, the revision of a set of decision-making rules, which in turn reflect a particular construction of reality. The specific inter-ventions then must be tailored to the particulars of the rules, which must be revised, and the specific markets in which those revisions occur. Ultimately the policy maker is trying in some sense to get into the heads of the economic agents themselves.

To a very large extent this was John T. Dunlop's approach to incomes policy and the one he tried to implement, first in the construction industry wage-stabilization program and then, as director of the cost-of-living council in the latter phases of the Nixon economic program. As I read that experience, the chief difficulty with the approach is the detailed and intimate knowledge about the specifics of each industry and set of actors that it requires. Indeed, for the actors, it really involves knowing their "mental set." Dunlop himself had this knowledge in the construction industry, and there the stabilization program was an unqualified success. He had, or knew where to get, much of the required knowledge about wage setting elsewhere in the economy, and the general wage-stabilization program, when he controlled it, also had some success. Dunlop, who was a labor mediator, had virtually no experience in price setting and, in controlling price inflation, the program seems to have failed. Given more time Dunlop might have gotten better at the process, and, to this extent, one can conclude from his experience that a policy of the kind he tried to implement could work.

It seems unlikely, however, to work in the present economic and political climate. Dunlop's views about incomes policy are idiosyncratic. His appointment is understandable—politically in terms of the pressures on the President to have an incomes policy and the need for a director with the kind of acceptability to labor that Dunlop had. But the policy itself lacked either the intellectual or political underpinnings that would be required to make it a viable approach to inflation over the long term.

Thus realistically the only alternative is to wait out the current inflation and hope that price and wage setting procedures will eventually be revised without federal intervention. The danger is that the government will try to hasten this revision through increasing unemployment. Both the intellectual and political foundations of that policy are firm. Because the risk of such a policy is panic and depression, the danger is present for all of us. But it is particularly strong for economically disadvantaged and underprivileged groups.

Recession Is Capitalism as Usual

DAVID GORDON

Here is a radical analysis of recession and inflation that views their cause
and function quite differently as compared to conventional analysis. Keeping the Zweig article on paradigms in mind, analize the Wallich and Gordon
pieces as examples of paradigms.

*Capitalism . . . is not intelligent, it is not beautiful, it is not just, it
is not virtuous—and it doesn't deliver the goods.*—JOHN MAYNARD KEYNES,
1933.

I don't know too much about economics. I do know we're in trouble.
—SENATOR MIKE MANSFIELD, 1975.

San Francisco, Christmas, 1974. More than 5,000 of the nation's professional economists had gathered for their annual convention. The atmosphere
was hardly festive. The economy had been unraveling. Economists had neither
predicted its problems nor prescribed their solutions. They had been caught,
as several wits had quipped, "with their parameters down."

Minnesota's Walter Heller, as outgoing president of the American Economic Association, gave the closing address of the convention. Heller
had been a leading public advocate of the "New Economics" in the 1960s,
helping promote the investiture of the secular priests. "We have . . . harnessed
the existing economics . . . to the purpose of prosperity, stability, and growth,"
he wrote in 1966, putting economists "at the President's elbow." Would
he now publicly moderate his claims, perhaps admitting that the priests had
been defrocked?

Undaunted, Heller asked, "What's Right With Economics?" "I intend
to accentuate the positive," he began. "As economists, we have many sins,

From David Gordon, "Recession Is Capitalism as Usual," *The New York Times Magazine* (Sunday,
April 27, 1975), pp. 18, 49–52, 55, 58–60, 63. ©1975 by The New York Times Company. Reprinted
by permission.

none deadly, to confess. But these are far outweighed by the virtues, all quite lively, that we can legitimately profess."

And so it goes. Smiling through the egg on their faces, the established American economists are still keeping the faith. But there is another group of American economists, a smaller, less visible and less prestigious group. We call ourselves "radical political economists." Whatever our forum, we try to make a few basic and different points.

In our view, the current economic crisis flows from corporate and Government efforts to make working people in this country pay the costs of the collapse and reconstruction of the American corporate empire. The crisis is beginning to push the American economic system toward some basic institutional changes. As those changes develop, we shall all be forced to ask whose interests they will serve and whose they will subvert.

I want to try to elaborate that view with some care here. Before we can raise our red flags, we must first weave and dye the cloth. Like the economic problems we analyze, the texture of the fabric is intricate.

Mainstream economists are locked in debate over the date of the downturn and the indicators of continued deterioration or recovery. But the current crisis cannot be measured by any one indicator. Its severity is revealed by a combination of developments, reinforcing one another over the past several years.

Unemployment. The measured rates, while the highest since 1941, provide only a partial count of the jobless. The government officially records more than eight million as "unemployed." At least another five million want and need full-time jobs but cannot find them. The government overlooks those potential workers, either because they have grudgingly accepted part-time jobs or because, as "discouraged workers," they are no longer actively seeking work. Added together, the "official" and "unofficial" jobless now total nearly 15 percent of the labor force.

Inflation. While the rate is slowing, prices still soar by earlier standards. It now costs $1.58 to buy what cost $1.00 in 1967. We have suffered over the past eight years the longest period of sustained inflation in this country since the first tabulated aggregate price statistics in 1820.

Income. Unemployment and inflation have combined to erode workers' purchasing power. By February, 1975, the average American working family could buy less with its weekly earnings than it could in 1964. Workers' real incomes (adjusted for inflation) have declined as rapidly over the past 18 months as they did at the beginning of the Great Depression.

Production. Declining consumer demand and rising wholesale prices have together staged an industrial blood-letting. The index of industrial production fell by almost 10 percent in the first quarter of 1975, the most rapid drop since monthly data were first reported in 1947.

Credit. Both corporations and families have been racing desperately to forestall hard times by borrowing. The credit structure gets shakier and shakier. By 1974, banks had lent a higher percentage of total deposits than before the Great Depression, the highest since before the collapse of 1893.

Trade. Economic events spread like ripples through the world economy. By the middle of 1973, the business cycles of the advanced industrial countries had become synchronized for the first time since World War II. As countries seek protection from the crisis, foreign trade contracts. That only makes the problem worse, for declining exports accelerate the drop in income almost everywhere.

While politics is not "determined" by economics, economic instability is likely to breed political instability. Like marathon dancers stumbling toward their hundredth hour, Western governments have been fainting from exhaustion. There have been major changes of administration during the past three years in the United States, Japan, and 14 of the 16 capitalist countries in western Europe. Only Spain, waiting for Franco to die, and Austria have escaped the trend.

The current crisis caught almost everyone by surprise. With economists as guides, we were apparently traveling the Yellow Brick Road. The primary postulate of the "New Economics," as Yale's James Tobin put it last year, was "that government policy could and should keep the economy close to a path of steady real growth." Instability, like the Wicked Witch of the West, would dissolve.

However appealing, that analysis was superficial. Employment, output, and prices are *derivative* variables in capitalist economies. Capitalism is based on production for *profit*, not for employment. Corporations count their earnings, not the jobs they create. Corporations accumulate profits by getting workers to produce more in value than they earn in wages. Economic growth is conditioned by conflict between the corporate "werewolf hunger" for profits, as Marx called it, and workers' resistance to the relatively lower wages, hierarchical command structures, and degrading working conditions that the hunger requires.

Probing beneath the surface harmonies of full employment, we begin to see that economic stability cannot endure in capitalist economies. The American economy has roller-coastered over at least 16 business cycles in the past 100 years. It turns out that continuous growth, however productive of jobs, is bad for profits. And, as Charles Wilson of General Motors might have put it, what's bad for profits is bad for the country.

Continuous prosperity eventually threatens profits through the market mechanism. Individual capitalists—profit junkies on prosperity highs—invest feverishly during a boom. Sooner or later, they begin to exhaust the reserve supplies of workers. The labor market tightens. This overinvestment has two shattering consequences for corporations. Wages begin to rise rapidly, cutting into profits. And workers take advantage of their scarcity by resisting the "werewolf hunger" more militantly and more effectively; workers' productivity slows, directly undercutting capitalist control of the production process.

In a market economy, corporations have only two recourses. They must restore competition in the labor market in order to ease labor scarcity and undercut labor strength. And they must find new ways to make more efficient use of their workers. When booms persist, they can accomplish neither. Prosperity protects workers from the competition of the unemployed and cushions relatively inefficient enterprises.

In a market economy, therefore, periodic recessions are indispensable for profits. With a rise in unemployment, labor "discipline" improves. As output falls, the razor of market competition trims worker power and pares away inefficient operations. Recessions restore the basis for capital accumulation. "By momentary suspension of labor and annihilation of a great portion of capital," Marx wrote 125 years ago, production for profit can resume.

That analysis helps explain the recent eruption of crisis. A quick review of the past decade through that lens reveals the underlying patterns.

By 1966, the economy had been growing steadily for almost five years and was due for a cooling bath. The government could not afford to admit the costs of the war in Vietnam by raising taxes. The restorative functions of recession were postponed. The boom continued until early 1969.

Corporations began to pay the price of postponement as profits suffered their classic decline. The ratio of profits to wages fell nearly by half between 1965 and 1969. With labor markets tight, worker militancy grew. Productivity growth slowed to one-quarter its rate of increase during the first half of the boom.

Corporations, in classic response, speeded up the pace of production. Industrial accidents increased by more than a quarter in less than six years. Angered by the speedup, workers struck more frequently. By 1970, work-time lost through strikes had risen to three and one-half times its 1963 level. The notorious wildcat strike at the G.M. Vega plant in Lordstown, Ohio, dramatized this resistance. The company had increased the speed of the assembly line the preceding year from 60 cars per hour to more than 100. "The more the company pressured them," a local union leader observed, "the less work they turned out."

By the time President Nixon took office in 1969, the signs of trouble were unmistakable. "Many manufacturing executives [had] openly complained in recent years," The Wall Street Journal observed, "that too much control had passed from management to labor." Nixon knew the remedy. He slammed on the fiscal and monetary brakes. The recession of 1969–70 followed.

But time was short. Because the boom had continued so long, it would take several years for the recession to exercise its fully restorative powers. Nixon was afraid to campaign for president with millions out of work. Corporate profits had fallen to such low levels by 1969 that few businesses could easily countenance the prospect of a sustained recession.

So the administration, in late 1970, stepped on the accelerator again.

Almost immediately, the speedometer indicated that the economy was racing too fast. Prices were climbing. Huge labor contract settlements, as high as 15 percent, chilled corporate spines. Most important, profits fell in 1970 to their lowest share of national income since World War II.

The Administration had few options. It had shrunk from waiting out a sustained recession. Untempered boom could prove disastrous for profits. Continually rising prices would also poison the balance of payments, whose trade deficits were deteriorating every month. "Caught in this trap," as Business Week editorialized at the time, "there is only one thing the Administration can do." Nixon established his New Economic Policy as a compromise. Stimulative measures would continue, but a wage-price freeze, it was hoped, would contain the fires the short-lived recession had failed to cool.

The President assured the public, of course, that controls were designed to protect us all from the ravages of inflation. In fact, their purpose was quite different. Workers had to be disciplined so that profits could recover. Arnold Weber, freeze administrator under Nixon, admitted candidly in a recent interview with Clayton Fritchey that business "had been leaning" on the administration "to do something about wages." "The idea of the freeze and Phase II was to zap labor and we did."

To some extent, the controls worked. Profits recovered momentarily. Workers' militancy was constrained. But the controls did not restore economic stability. Indeed, they largely compounded prevailing distortions by freezing them. When Phase IV guidelines were finally lifted in early 1974, the explosion was felt around the world. Prices skyrocketed. Workers struggled to recover their wage losses and strike activity surged.

By 1974, we were still suffering the consequences of the postponement of recession in the mid-1960s. No substitute had yet been found for the normal functions of recession. The economy was like a car on an icy road. Once the skid began, each steering correction simply seemed to exaggerate it. Now we were careening off the pavement.

This brief history helps explain why some kind of crisis was destined. It does not yet explain why the crunch has been so jarring. There are three additional, equally fundamental reasons why the current crisis is the worst since the Depression.

Concentration. Large corporations have gained increasing control over wealth, markets, and supplies in the United States. The largest 100 corporations now control half of all industrial assets. The effects seem obvious.

When demand is high, prices rise more rapidly in a concentrated than in a competitive economy because powerful corporations can repress the rate of increase in supply. When demand falls, inflation is much less likely to slow down because concentration dampens price-cutting competition. This simple phenomenon helps explain the recent combination of simultaneously rapid inflation and high unemployment. Corporations in protected markets often respond to slack demand by *raising* their prices in order to protect their revenues. The auto companies' recent rebates, for instance, gave back only part of the price increases that had been put into effect at earlier stages of the downturn.

A second effect is just as important. The size of the modern corporation complicates some of the traditional cleansing effects of the recession. When large corporations confront the downturn, they can often afford to keep their inefficient operations afloat. Often they can't tell the inefficient from the productive. Because the postwar prosperity lasted so long, a more than usually stringent recession will be required to restore American corporations, flabby from 20 years on the winter banquet circuit, to something like their normal spring-training trim. Yet their size magnifies the hazards of stringent recession. If a small firm folds, fewer than 100 workers may lose their jobs; if a giant corporation tumbles, as many as 100,000 employes may hit the

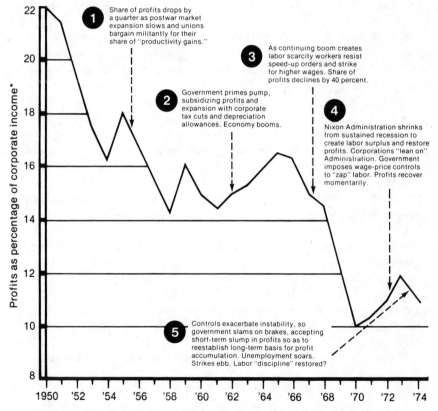

1 Share of profits drops by a quarter as postwar market expansion slows and unions bargain militantly for their share of "productivity gains."

3 As continuing boom creates labor scarcity workers resist speed-up orders and strike for higher wages. Share of profits declines by 40 percent.

2 Government primes pump, subsidizing profits and expansion with corporate tax cuts and depreciation allowances. Economy booms.

4 Nixon Administration shrinks from sustained recession to create labor surplus and restore profits. Corporations "lean on" Administration. Government imposes wage-price controls to "zap" labor. Profits recover momentarily.

5 Controls exacerbate instability, so government slams on brakes, accepting short-term slump in profits so as to reestablish long-term basis for profit accumulation. Unemployment soars. Strikes ebb. Labor "discipline" restored?

Profits as the key to economic crisis. A radical economist's view of how we got into the current recession.

*Share of profits in gross corporate product of nonfinancial corporations. Source: U.S. Commerce Dept. Data from W. Nordhaus, "The Falling Share of Profits," Brookings Papers on Economic Activity, 1974.

streets. "The huge U.S. corporations have become such important centers of jobs and incomes," Business Week concludes, "that [the government must] protect . . . the great corporations instead of letting the economy make deflationary adjustments."

International instability. American corporations emerged from World War II with international hegemony. They rapidly dominated world business, helping stabilize the world economy. The dollar cemented trade relations. Imperialist rivalries moderated. But the age of Pax Americana has come to an end. The world economy will never be the same. Three developments have combined to erode international economic stability.

First, western European and Japanese corporations have begun to flex their muscles. The big kid on the block has some rivals. International economic competition has intensified.

Second, the political dominance that supported American economic supremacy has also eroded. Following the interventions in Greece, Iran, Guatemala, Lebanon, and the Dominican Republic, Vietnam was supposed to have added another victory bead to the imperialist necklace. The American defeat in Vietnam, the fall of Cambodia and the Arab challenge all dramatize the decline of American power.

Third, American corporations, like their European and Japanese rivals, have gone multinational. And growing multinationals begin to escape the government leverage that is necessary for Keynesian anticyclical strategies. With scattered resources, they can quickly shift either real investment or liquid capital to avoid tax increases or government controls. The more rapid these movements, the more quickly the economic ripples spread.

This international instability has contributed to the current crisis in many ways. International competition compounded the profit squeeze on United States corporations in the late 1960s. The collapse of American supremacy exacerbated balance-of-payments deficits; this in turn narrowed the government's options in dealing with the crisis. Multinational growth helped bring business cycles among the advanced countries into a single worldwide cycle; that congruence has been amplifying the recent collapse. Finally, at the highest level, the collapse of American hegemony has contributed to the chaos of the present situation. The "enforcer" has lost its power. "For the world economy to be stabilized," Charles P. Kindleberger of the Massachusetts Institute of Technology has written, "there has to be a stabilizer."

Economic growth under capitalism is like an expanding balloon with a leak. We have to keep blowing to avoid deflation. As we huff and puff, the leak may itself widen. If we blow it up too fast, the balloon may burst. Growth itself may collapse.

Why do capitalist economies have leaks? Profits provide the clue.

On one side, capitalists may seek to earn higher profits by depressing their workers' relative wages. When many act in the same way, they run the risk that workers may not be able to purchase commodities available on the market. Unable to sell those products, producers must eventually cut back on production. *Unless* they can discover new markets with new customers.

On another side, corporations may expand production too rapidly, creating labor shortages, paying overtime, bidding up wages. As wages rise, they may compensate by replacing workers with machines, hoping to reduce their costs. But this response may backfire in the end. Individual employers earn profits only on the basis of "value added" within their own enterprises, profiting from the margin between the value their workers produce and the wages their workers earn. Machines can't add value because the individual producers must pay some other capitalist, the one who made the machine, the full worth of that machine. (If a machine contributed more over its lifetime than it cost, other producers would rush to join the parade, bidding up the machine's price.) The only purchase on which the producers may earn some extra money is the purchase of the workers' labor time. The fewer workers the employers hire, therefore, the narrower the base for profit accumulation. As they replace workers by machines, the rate of profit may fall. *Unless* they can find some ways of increasing the productivity of their declining numbers of workers fast enough.

Unless, unless! Those "ifs" pose continuing risks for individual corporations and, in the aggregate, for the entire economy. The risks seemed remote for a time after World War II. New markets had opened up in Europe and Japan. The Depression and the war had created conditions in which corporations could replace their inefficient operations. But the expansion of those markets slowed. And unions began to struggle for a bigger share of those "productivity gains." On an average, profits as a percentage of national income declined during the nineteen-fifties by more than a quarter. The leaks were beginning to appear. Corporations and the Government began huffing and puffing to keep the balloon inflated.

One source of extra air was the government. The effective tax rate on corporate profits fell from 45.8 percent of corporate net income in 1961 to 26.9 percent in 1970. Oil depletion allowances, accelerated depreciation, investment tax credits—all those provisions amounted to government welfare programs for corporate profits.

Another source of inflation has had potentially more dangerous consequences. Corporations have been borrowing money frenetically, hoping to stay ahead of the profit squeeze. Corporate bank loans as a percentage of corporate product have doubled in just 14 years, rising from 13.8 percent in 1960 to 25.2 percent in 1974. Banks have been straining to meet the demand. Less than one-seventh of total bank deposits are now covered by available bank reserves, down from a reserve ratio of more than one-third in 1960. As banks have raced to lend money, they have had to borrow themselves. Banks' short-term borrowings rose from 4.5 percent of their total loans to customers in 1960 to 48.5 percent in 1974.

All those numbers add up to one simple and frightening picture. American economic growth has been constructed for the past 15 years like a house of credit cards. If the tremors increase, the house of credit cards may collapse.

All this indicates that the current crisis has deep roots. But according to the media, Government officials and mainstream economists, a few accidents are to blame for almost all our problems. Lousy weather cut into food supplies. Greedy Arab oil sheiks hiked petroleum prices. "We've had the food shock, the oil shock, Watergate, and its malaise," moans Harvard's Otto Eckstein, ". . . wholly unforeseen shocks that upset all our economic forecasts in the last couple of years."

Blaming fundamental economic problems on "unforeseen shocks" deflects our attention from the economic system itself. Accidents may have helped trigger some recent complications, but they did not cause the crisis. First and simply, the economy was already in crisis before the weather failures of 1972 and the Arab oil price hikes of 1973. Second, the weather and the Arabs do not explain why the food and energy "shortages" had such a wide impact. That second argument requires elaboration.

Food prices began to rise precipitously in 1972. It appeared that bad weather and Soviet buyers had caused those increases by cutting into supplies. In fact, supplies had been artificially limited since World War II. American grain dealers had been gaining control over world grain production for more than two decades. They sought more and more to tighten supplies in order to increase their leverage over both domestic and world prices. Government policies supported their efforts. Arable acreage was withheld from production in the United States. Export subsidies and the threat that the government would "dump" surplus commodities on the world market kept world prices artificially low; since most developing countries have accrued heavy debts to the rich countries and must pursue foreign earnings relentlessly, low world grain prices have maintained pressures on those countries to garner foreign exchange by specializing in cash crops for export, like cocoa, coffee, tin, or rubber, and have discouraged them from allocating their resources to the expansion of domestic grain production. (During the 1930s, Third World countries exported more grain than North America; now they import roughly four times what they used to export.) World year-end grain reserves had fallen from 25 percent of annual consumption in 1961 to just under 15 percent in 1971. With world supplies down, world grain prices were more than usually vulnerable to the sudden drops in annual production that occurred because of bad weather in late 1972 and 1973.

Similarly, the sheiks have been made the scapegoats for the inflation of fuel prices. Almost everyone except the oil corporations and the government is now willing to admit that there was no real energy shortage during the winter of 1973–74. American oil corporations took advantage of Middle Eastern events to justify domestic price increases. The companies had actually created most of the shortages themselves, holding surplus oil in overseas refineries and offshore tankers long enough to establish the effect. Oil started flowing again a month before the Arabs lifted their own embargo.

This analysis suggests that the current crisis has flowed from the internal character and dynamics of our modern capitalist economy. Capitalism requires periodic recessions to restore profits and discipline labor; we finally got ours—worse because later. Corporate concentration, an inescapable development under capitalism, has accentuated the depth of recession required to fulfill those restorative functions. The dissolution of American hegemony, whose benefits many North Americans enjoyed for 25 years, has thrown the world capitalist economy into a period of intense international instability. Desperate corporate attempts to postpone their days of reckoning are proving counterproductive, as our bloated debt economy stumbles toward an entirely conceivable collapse.

Business leaders and the business press appreciate the magnitude of the crisis. Business Week has recently editorialized: "It is inevitable that the U. S. economy will grow more slowly. . . . Some people will obviously have to do with less. . . . The basic health of the U.S. is based on the basic health of its corporations and banks. . . . Yet it will be a hard pill for many Americans to swallow—the idea of doing with less so that big business can have more. It will be particularly hard to swallow because it is quite obvious that if big businesses are the most visible victims of what ails the Debt Economy, they are also in large measure the cause of it. . . ."

How will business try to ease the pill down our throats? Only two clear options now present themselves. One looks backward. The other augurs a new era.

The Ford Administration only appears to be indecisive. In public, both Nixon and Ford have offered tolerable economic imitations of Herbert Hoover. One notes the litany, in Arthur Schlesinger's words, "of pep talks, slogans, incantations, voluntarism, 'natural forces,' and random measures of manifest inadequacy." But public appearances aside, the Ford Administration has made a clear choice. Dominated by the advice of free marketeers like Alan Greenspan and William Simon, the administration is staging the Invisible Hand's Last Stand. They believe that the basis for corporate profits can only be restored if labor's strength is broken and inefficient operations are eliminated. If the market's razor has been dulled, sharpen it!

The administration made its choice in 1973. Production bottlenecks were about to force the discontinuation of wage-price guidelines. Worse yet, 1974 promised a period of intense collective bargaining, with the contracts of millions of American workers expiring. The time had come for a direct challenge to labor militancy.

The administration moved quickly. Government spending was cut sharply in the middle of 1973. The monetary screws were tightened a little later. The brakes were screeching.

The present plunge began, as a result, as a politically induced recession.

In a fact sheet accompanying Ford's economic address last fall, the White House regretted that "twice within the past decade, in 1967 and in 1971–72, we let an opportunity to regain price stability slip through our grasp." They have vowed not to repeat the mistake.

Many economic observers now acknowledge the administration's private intentions. "If you turn the present recession upside down and read on the bottom," Nobel Prize Laureate Paul Samuelson said, "it will say 'Made in Washington.'" Pierre Rinfret, a leading economic consultant to the business world, calls the program "benign neglect—there is no program and it has been done on purpose. Greenspan wants to let the economy take a deep bath to correct inflation."

From the corporate perspective, of course, the strategy is working. Real wages have fallen sharply. Workers seem subdued, with the incidence of strike activity down. As one American labor official explained, "Layoffs take the steam out of members. . . . They take away the urge to strike." But the administration's "cold bath" strategy is too risky to last long. The economy is teetering closer to the brink than Ford and his free marketeers realized. The administration is in "the position of the sorcerer's apprentice," Harvard's Nobel Prize Laureate Wassily Leontief observes. "They took steps to produce unemployment, and now they can't stop it."

The second risk is that many Americans might be pushed toward open political rebellion. More and more people recognize the recession's political roots. Job marches in Washington have begun and will surely spread. Union anger is mounting. Congress is restless. The "free market" solution can "work" economically if it is applied long enough. It cannot work politically because, as depression approaches, political instability carries radical potential. Even gritty Harry Truman turned squeamish at the thought of deep recessions. As he commented in 1950 about the 1930s, "There was real danger that the American people might turn to some other system. If we are to win the struggle between freedom and Communism, we must be sure that we never let such a depression happen again."

If the "free market" strategy cannot work, only one other option seems to remain: "state planning." What steps might conceivably lead to adoption of that alternative?

The first stage would necessarily involve new governmental fiscal and monetary stimulus to pull out of the recession. If the government gives the economy a big booster shot soon—well beyond the recent $22-billion tax cut—we may be able to avert a major depression and resume economic growth. But, as in 1971, we will continue to experience growth with rapid inflation and unremitting instability.

Anticipating those strains, many now expect relatively permanent wage-price controls. Like ordinary stimulus, however, wage-price controls will be insufficient to restore stability to the economy. Some firms will have their prices frozen at relatively high levels and will find it profitable to produce as much as possible. Others, for whatever reason, will find their prices frozen at lower levels and will cut back on production. However adept the administrators, bottlenecks, shortages, and distortions can quickly emerge.

"Suppress the Invisible Hand for long," as Harvard's Stephen Marglin has put it, "and it must be replaced by the Visible Hand." If we cannot avoid the problems of controls by doing without controls, then we can probably overcome those problems by moving beyond controls—by adding direct government management of allocation and investment. If shortages develop, the government can direct that production be expanded in that sector. (Such directives, aimed at oil refining capacity, would certainly have tempered the energy "shortages.") If some firms are slipping into bankruptcy but are engaged in "essential" production, the government can provide investment and credit for a salvage operation. That kind of government management digs beneath wages and prices to supervision of the physical quantities of commodities produced for and exchanged in the market. And this would mean, in Richard Goodwin's words, "rudimentary government planning for the entire economy."

Free marketeers blanch at such thoughts, of course, and the whole language of "state planning" sounds dissonant to many American ears. Does this prospect smack too much of a "socialist" America to have a chance of adoption?

Perhaps not. Unregenerate capitalists have begun to call for such planning. Their public discussion has focused around a resurrection of the New Deal's Reconstruction Finance Corporation. Advocated by Henry Ford II, Rohatyn, and others, a new RFC would channel investment funds toward sectors and firms whose own funds were too tight to finance necessary expansion. The RFC advocates have no illusions that such reforms will be temporary. "There can be no denying," Rohatyn writes, "that such an organization . . . can be perceived as a first step toward state planning of the economy. . . . What many will call state planning would, to the average family be no more than prudent budgeting."

The corporate community has begun to believe that more intensive state intervention is necessary to protect its very existence. State planning, from this perspective, becomes the mechanism by which business gets the rest of America to "swallow the pill" of material sacrifice. As government capital begins to flow toward shaky corporations, taxpayers will be compelled to support private corporations that cannot make it on their own. (Penn Central, Rolls Royce, and Lockheed writ large!) *Forbes* magazine characterized Rohatyn's proposal candidly: "As a boardroom philosopher once remarked: 'Socialize the losses and keep the profits private!'"

Some labor leaders and liberals have also called for state planning. One group, called the Initiative Committee for National Economic Planning, is co-chaired by the United Automobile Workers' Leonard Woodcock and

Harvard's Wassily Leontief. Its members range from J. K. Galbraith, who has finally declared himself a socialist, to World Bank President Robert Mc-Namara and Robert Roosa of Brown Bros., Harriman, who most certainly have not.

State planning, in fact, seems sure to come. When it arrives, it will politicize all those hard economic choices whose consequences are normally hidden by the Invisible Hand. In a new era of declining American power, planners will continually have to balance the reduction of business profits aginst the reduction of our own living standards. And every time they reach a decision, the rest of us will be asking: Who made that decision in whose interests?

Many radical economists entered graduate school in the 1960s. If our professors ever deigned to mention Marx at all, they typically dismissed him, in Samuelson's words, as a "minor post-Ricardian." Growing more and more critical through our political experiences and our studies of the economy, most of us eventually decided that the Marxian perspective provided a more penetrating view of the world than conventional analyses. While we are still "first fired, last hired" in economics departments around the country, we have begun to claim some professional turf. As the economy continues to deteriorate and mainstream economists have not yet come up with a cure, more and more people have begun to listen to other kinds of explanations.

And many are beginning to ask about different kinds of solutions. It may be that a quick move toward state planning will save us from depression. Many will once again praise the resilience and flexibility of our system. We shall sigh obligatory relief. Such a wonderful "mixed economy"!

But it will still be capitalism. Corporations will still dominate state planning policies, arguing credibly, as Nixon himself put it, that "all Americans will benefit from more profits." As long as profits remain private, the profit addicts will still pursue their prosperity trips, pushing us feverishly toward recurrent instability. As long as profitability dominates corporate decisions about resource allocation, we shall continue to endure the wastefulness of our past and future ecological blight. As long as our livelihoods are tied directly to private property ownership, we shall continue to suffer or avert our gaze from egregious poverty and inequality. As long as corporations claim absolute authority during the working time of their employes, we shall continue to wither from and/or struggle against the boredom, degradation, and submissiveness of our working lives.

For those of us who are seeking to move beyond that economic system, two main issues will emerge in the coming years.

First, the evolution of state planning will provide a central challenge. Most Americans will have to organize defensively at the national level simply to protect our interests against those of the corporations. As that national movement develops, can we move beyond? Can we liberate ourselves from capitalist instabilities by securing an even and balanced growth in output, with income and job security for all? Can we sever our dependence on some of the excrescences of our present economy—energy-wasting, fire-trapping skyscrapers and fuming private cars—and move toward more useful and collective patterns of social living?

Equally important for many radicals, I think, is the issue of greater control over our working and political lives. Capitalism has historically promoted hierarchical and authoritarian working relations. State planning will directly involve the government in the organization of production. Will this involvement, combined with the abolition of private property, provide the basis for the transition toward a society in which everyone is free from the bonds of subsistence and shares equally in his/her material and social relations? Even if meeting the consumption needs of the working majority, a state planning system could tend quickly toward the kind of centralized economy manifest in the Soviet Union, featuring tight discipline over the labor process. Many of us place high priority on reversing historical tendencies toward such hierarchical control of work. As state planning develops in this country, we shall be forced to defend ourselves more and more vigorously against centralized control over the pace and character of our jobs and communities. As we develop local institutions of resistance and collective support, can we forge decentralized planning systems that would combine local autonomy with the requirements of collective planning?

As we grapple with those issues, we begin to perceive the real possibilities of their resolution.

Taking advantage of our technological sophistication, our affluence, and our individual capacities, we could clearly begin to break down hierarchies within enterprises and reduce the specialization of many jobs. Involved in more participatory work relations and more varied jobs, Americans might find more motivation for energetic work in their work's intrinsic satisfactions, requiring fewer material rewards. Becoming more active in decisions about production, many might develop a much more collective consciousness about the needs of their communities and the impact on social life of different kinds of commodities. Investment and allocation decisions could consequently begin to reflect other criteria than their "profitability."

The possibilities proliferate. Emboldened, we dare more and more openly to struggle for a socialist America, a society promoting both rational planning and democratic control of our working and political lives. Arguing the possibility of that transition, none of us can yet provide a "model" of the specific social relations that might eventually unfold, so some call us "utopian" for dreaming about the future. We think it is the mainstream economists who are "utopian" for dreaming that our present economic system could possibly work.

Unemployment and the "Dual Labor Market"

PETER B. DOERINGER AND MICHAEL J. PIORE

Any explanation of unemployment depends significantly on which theory of labor markets operations underlies that analysis. In the following analysis, three different theoretical approaches are contrasted and evaluated.

Since the end of World War II, the United States has experienced persistently high unemployment. There have been 19 postwar years in which the unemployment rate exceeded 4 percent; in 11 of those years it surpassed 5 percent; in only four years did it fall below 3.5 percent. This is a record far worse than that of any of the industrialized nations of western Europe or Japan.

To explain this situation there were, until recent years, two divergent theories, the "structuralist" and the Keynesian. The structuralists argued that its principal causes were technological displacement, shifting patterns of industrial production, foreign competition, and similar features which disrupted the matching of jobs and workers in the labor market. The Keynesians, on the other hand, were less concerned about labor market imbalances. They saw the labor market as a long "queue": If the government's macroeconomic policies stimulated expansion, then eventually almost everybody in the line would be absorbed; where such policies were cautious and failed to keep pace with an increasingly productive labor force or the influx of workers into the market, unemployment would rise.

Both these interpretations saw unemployment as involuntary—i.e., individuals were actively seeking jobs and unable to find them—but their remedial policies differed. The structuralists argued for programs to correct im-

From Peter B. Doeringer and Michael J. Piore, "Unemployment and the 'Dual Labor Market,'" *The Public Interest* (Winter 1975), pp. 67–78. Reprinted with the permission of the publisher and the authors.

balances through training and relocation—an approach that was embodied in manpower legislation in the 1960s. The Keynesians favored increasing demand through more aggressive monetary and fiscal policies.

Now the policy debate has been complicated by a third explanation, which disputes the *chronic* and *involuntary* character of unemployment, and argues that a significant portion of the unemployment in recent decades is both *temporary* and *voluntary*. This is the argument, for example, of Martin Feldstein in *The Public Interest* ("The Economics of the New Unemployment," No. 33, Fall 1973). It holds that the measured level of unemployment exaggerates the degree of underlying imbalances in the labor market. In the case of youth, where the unemployment rates have been double or triple that of older workers, Feldstein argues that many young workers adopt a casual attitude to work, holding many jobs briefly, with spells of unemployment in between, and prefer this as a way of life. More generally, it is said that much of our unemployment does not reflect any Keynesian "shortages" or structural skill imbalances, but results from the fact that many jobs are unattractive because of low pay or other undesirable characteristics; thus individuals choose an in-and-out pattern, combined with unemployment compensation, rather than stick to such jobs as steady work.

There is some evidence to support this view. In periods of both high and low unemployment, the duration of joblessness tends to be surprisingly short. More than half the unemployed are "job searchers," individuals who have just entered the labor market or have quit to change jobs. These "voluntary" movements are especially common among women and young persons, the groups which have composed a growing fraction of the unemployed in recent years. Many of the unemployed, particularly among the relatively low-paid, can find work, but only in dead-end jobs. Much unemployment, therefore, seems to be "voluntary," in that jobs may be available but are undesirable; and this is why the overall rate is high and the turnover of the jobless is so large.

This view of unemployment has gained a variety of adherents. For economists, it has the attraction of newly discovered "facts" that seem to contradict much of the conventional wisdom in the field. For policy makers, particularly those advocating free markets and fiscal conservatism, it challenges the interventionist thinking that guided employment and training policy in the 1960s. From such data, it is but a short step to argue that responsibility for unemployment should be shifted from the public sphere (where it rested in the 1960s) to individuals. The failure of workers to take jobs, not inadequate aggregate demand or ineffective manpower policies, becomes the root of unemployment. Where labor market policy is to be faulted is in its intrusion into the structure of employment incentives through welfare, unemployment compensation, and minimum wages. Given the new interpretation of unemployment, it is argued that the effort to reduce unemployment to a 3 or 4 percent level by Keynesian or structuralist policies is misguided.

In short, the unemployment problem may best be "solved" by accepting more slack in the economy and by reducing some of our social welfare arrangements.

The Nature of Labor Markets

What is clear is that the "conventional" explanations of unemployment, or more specifically, of the nature of labor markets in American society, are inadequate. Even though there is some agreement on the *facts* about "voluntary" unemployment, there is certainly less agreement about the reasons for such unemployment, and still less about the policy consequences that would derive from such facts. Behind all this controversy is a major effort within economics to recast the old theories and find some better explanation for how individuals behave in the labor market. It is only by going to these theories, and the differences among them, that we can seek to understand the "chronic" character of unemployment in the United States.

Within the terms of the current debate, there are three somewhat conflicting approaches to understanding the character of labor markets and the responses of individuals to them. These are: (1) human capital theories; (2) job search theories; and (3) dual labor market theories.

1. *Human capital.* The human capital perspective on the labor market is most commonly associated with economists at the University of Chicago, particularly Gary Becker. It takes as its model the rational economic man who acts to maximize his returns, and extends this to labor market decisions. The theory of human capital treats unemployment as part of a concern with the determinants of earnings. Unemployment, like income, is thought to reflect differences among workers in ability, in levels of training and education, and in types of work experience. The latter two, it is argued, are to be understood in terms of "investment" decisions of time and money, made by *individuals* (workers and sometimes their employers), to acquire skills necessary for different kinds of jobs and levels of pay. The unemployed are those whose abilities, skills, and productive capacities are insufficient to make it worthwhile for employers to hire them *at the prevailing market wages.*

2. *Job search.* This theory grows out of efforts to explain an observed trade-off between unemployment and rates of change in wages. The work done in this area, much of it by Charles Holt and his colleagues at the Urban Institute in Washington, emphasizes that unemployment is the outgrowth of a process of job search where workers have limited information, uncertainty, or faulty expectations about the labor market. It assumes, for example, that people who first begin looking for jobs lack basic information about the labor market, and have higher expectations about pay than can

be realized. As a result, workers may reject the jobs that they first encounter and continue searching. Gradually, this procedure enables them to make a more realistic evaluation of available jobs and to adjust their expectations accordingly. Eventually the search process results in employment, or in withdrawal from the labor market; thus the emphasis is on the job hunt and its outcomes. In its extreme form, this theory would interpret all unemployment as "frictional"—i.e., largely "temporary" and always resolved in one way or another.

3. *Dual labor markets.* The third revision of the traditional views of unemployment—with which the authors of this article are strongly identified—derived from empirical study of the lower-paying labor markets. Much of this experience was gained in the civil rights activities and studies of antipoverty programs in the 1960s, but the theories to which it leads are closely related to an earlier tradition of institutional labor economics associated with names such as John R. Commons, Selig Perlman, and John T. Dunlop.

The dual labor market approach postulates a labor market which is divided into *primary* and *secondary* sectors. The primary sector contains the better-paying, steady, and preferred jobs in the society. Those employed in this sector possess job security and advancement opportunities, established working conditions, and, whether unionized or not, employment relationships governed by a more or less explicit system of industrial jurisprudence. Work in the primary sector is associated with an *established position* in the economy. Workers here tend to identify with institutions: the company for which they work, their union, their craft, or other occupation. One who has lost a primary-sector job is unemployed in the involuntary, Keynesian sense. He has not chosen to go to look for another job, but has been laid off because of contractions in the economy or in his industry. He may accept less attractive work temporarily, but essentially he is waiting to regain the clearly identified position from which he has been displaced. Being "unemployed" really means being out of one's accustomed place of work.

The secondary sector, by contrast, is marked by low-paying, unstable, and dead-end employment, with frequent lay-offs and discharges. Because secondary sector jobs tend to be self-terminating, or are basically unattractive, they provide little incentive for workers to stick with them, and consequently have high voluntary turnover as well. Unemployment in the secondary sector thus is not associated with workers waiting around to regain an accustomed position, but is part of a shuttling process from one low-paying position to another.

What is important to note is that the kind of unemployment which public policy has recently focused upon (and which Feldstein has dealt with) is less the displacement of primary-sector workers than the umemployment concentrated among teenagers, women, and ethnic and racial minorities— those who tend to be employed in the secondary labor market.

Social Patterns and Institutional Forces

The human capital and job search theories both share a common tie to traditional economic theory. They presume the existence of a fluid and competitive labor market shaped by economic motivation. Relative wages are assumed to be flexible, employers are believed willing and able to adjust their employment in response to changes in wages and productivity, and workers are assumed to make training and information investments easily in response to changes in relative wages. For both human capital and search theories, unemployment is the result of personal barriers to job access within this competitive market framework. In human capital theory, the main barrier is thought to stem from insufficient "purchases" of education and training. In search theory, lack of information is the main barrier, and the job hunt of the unemployed is interpreted as an investment process, i.e., gathering further information about the labor market. For both theories, investment by workers of time and money to secure higher future incomes is assumed to be the major way adjustment takes place in the labor market.

Within the economics profession there is a growing uneasiness with these assumptions—particularly the assumption that self-development or human investment decisions are made by individuals acting independently of one another, are motivated largely by economic gain, and are implemented through the market system. Yet economists do not find it easy to dismiss these assumptions, for they do derive from the utilitarian theory of human behavior on which the models of neoclassical economics rest. While few economists have argued that such assumptions characterize the entire range of human behavior, there has been almost no attempt to define the limits within which they are realistic.

One could say that the nature of educational and informational barriers could equally explain the nature of dual labor markets. But the research on which the dual labor market hypothesis is based rejects that interpretation. Put most baldly, it argues that the character of dual labor markets is best explained by institutional and sociological, not economic variables (in the neoclassical sense)—that the problem of unemployment is rooted less in individual behavior than in the character of institutions and the social patterns that derive from them.

Let us take one important instance where the dual labor market theory stands in contrast to human capital theory. This is the argument, based on our empirical observation, that much skill training is not the outgrowth of economic decisions. A considerable portion of the training necessary for the preferred jobs in the primary sector takes place not in schools or in classes, but *on the job,* and is essentially a process of "socialization" as this is understood in sociology. The acquisition of the skills to perform particular tasks— what, in other words, is normally thought of as being acquired through education or formal training—really depends on the new employee's acceptance by the established group of workers, who must show him what to do in order for learning to take place. Without such acceptance, and his conformity to their norms, the employee faces not only the psychological discouragement of being excluded from the group, but the failure to acquire the requisite skills—the "learning of the ropes" of the job.

In effect, a key factor in obtaining "primary-sector" skills and a job in the primary sector is "social acceptability," which cannot be "bought" in the usual sense. This means that jobs and upward mobility in the primary sector are sensitive to such factors as *race, sex, and shared social beliefs,* which determine social acceptability within incumbent work groups.

Institutional factors also account for observed rigidity in the labor market. Wages often seem unresponsive to changes in the supply and demand for labor, not because of trade unions or governmental wage relations, but because the sociological character of the training process and of the demands for equity at the work place discourage the type of competition among workers upon which competitive pay adjustments are predicated. Similarly, the *job structure* within enterprises is relatively unresponsive to changes in wages or productivity, not because employers fail to make rational manning and equipment decisions, but because the economics of job design is dominated by other variables such as the degree of product standardization and the scale of production.

Thus the dual labor market hypothesis suggests that microeconomic theory needs to be recast on the basis of a very different set of assumptions from those which underlie much of contemporary economic thought. If reductions in unemployment are to occur through changes in job structure, through on-the-job training, or through adjustments in relative wage rates, then the *institutional* forces governing these variables must be explicitly considered. In a theoretical sense, it is this conflict about the very assumptions of contemporary economics that lies at the heart of the recurrent controversies over the interpretation of unemployment.

Theory and Public Policy

Controversy over the theory of labor markets is of more than academic interest, for it entails differences about the policies necessary to reduce unemployment. Basically, both human capital and job search theories lead to policies directed at the supply side of the labor market and at the decisions of individual workers. These theories favor solutions that subsidize worker investments in training, that facilitate the realistic assessment of employment prospects, and that permit market forces to express (free of "distortions") the economic incentives that are thought to govern worker investments in training, information, and job search. These theories do not inquire into the social factors affecting worker choice, nor do they concern themselves with understanding the determinants of training opportunities that are presumed to control such investments.

The policies suggested by Martin Feldstein in his article in *The Public Interest* illustrate the job search–human capital approach to reducing unemployment. The most novel of these are proposed changes in the application of minimum wage laws to youth and in the unemployment insurance system. The minimum wage, he argues, prevents youths from "purchasing" training from employers by forbidding wage bargains that would allow youth to get training on the job, and some way must be found to get around this obstacle. Similarly, Feldstein argues that the large cushion of unemployment insurance both encourages an "overinvestment" in job search on the part of workers and reduces incentives for their employers to eliminate cyclical and seasonal fluctuations in jobs. He would correct these "perverse effects" by imposing penalties upon individuals, through reduced compensation, as the frequency and duration of their unemployment increased.

Such proposals are open to question even within the theoretical framework in which they were conceived. The suspension of minimum wages for teenagers might mean simply the supplanting of adult women and minorities in the secondary-sector employment opportunities which these groups now share in common; the price of increased employment for youth, therefore, might be higher unemployment rates for women and minorities. The proposed changes in the unemployment system would penalize all the unemployed—those without control of their employment patterns as well as those with a substantial range of choice.

The dual labor market approach, however, questions these policy proposals on broader analytical grounds. The critique centers on two main issues: the origins of short-term unemployment in the secondary sector, and the importance of the structure of employment and training opportunities as a cause of unemployment.

The first point can be illustrated by the labor market behavior of high-unemployment groups, such as youth and ethnic minorities. It is often argued that young workers are interested only in short-term employment which will interfere minimally with school or leisure-time activities, yet will yield incomes capable of supporting these activities. Thus jobs in the secondary sector, with their tolerance of lateness, absenteeism, and high turnover, are particularly suited to such workers, and it is this combination of casual work attachment and irregular jobs that seems to explain a great deal about youth unemployment.

Yet virtually all young people in our society eventually decide to marry and settle down into permanent employment. The timing of such decisions and the shift to a stable life style is in large part a function of the availability of stable jobs. In periods of full employment, stable job attachment occurs earlier in working life as employers in the primary sector reach into the youth labor pool. And recent studies of youth, especially low-income youth, suggest that if more such primary-sector jobs were available, more youths would settle down, and settle down earlier.

There also seem to be important threshold effects. Most youths, particularly those from lower-class and working-class backgrounds, during their adolescence belong to relatively tight peer groups. Under favorable labor market circumstances, the members of the group marry and obtain permanent jobs at about the same time. The fact that the group makes the move together supports each individual in the transition to stable life styles and work routines. When the labor market is loose, however, and most people cannot find stable jobs, the group continues its adolescent pattern of behavior. The few individuals who do find steady jobs are forced either to abandon their friends, or to face a continual choice between the demands of their new life style and those of their old associates. For many this conflict is resolved by abandoning stable employment.

The conflict is particularly acute for many minority youths, who have difficulty in forming the kinds of social bonds at work which might substitute for the adolescent bonds on the street. That problem, combined with the difficulty of finding a sufficient number of stable jobs to permit the street group as a whole to shift its routine, undoubtedly contributes to the relatively high rates of failure in employment among even those few youths who manage to find stable shelters in the labor market.

Processes of this kind make it difficult to evaluate youth unemployment by a simple economic measure. They also suggest that the historical spread between teenage and adult unemployment rates is not immutable, but is rooted in the sociological character of group life.

Like the employment difficulties of young people, those of ethnic and racial minorities are directly related to the socioeconomic structure. As far back as these markets can be traced, the low-paying job market in general, and that for minorities in particular, has to be understood in terms of migration. Historically there have always been secondary-sector jobs ("dirty work") which the native labor force has refused to accept. Thus migrants from less-affluent rural areas or immigrants from foreign countries have been imported to fill them. These migrants usually conceive of their stay as temporary. Many immigrants intend to, and a great many actually do, return home within months. Or, if they stay, they accept these jobs as the "price" of change and hope that their children will do better. And quite often, such jobs, unstable and dead-end though they may be, are still preferable to the conditions in the place which the migrant has left.

Out of the migration stream, however, there eventually grows a "second generation" raised in the urban areas. This second generation shares the perspective of the native population and no longer accepts the kinds of jobs which originally attracted its parents. But unlike the earlier white migrant groups that were assimilated into the good, primary-sector jobs, today's "new" immigrants—largely black or Spanish-speaking—face continuing discrimination that largely confines them to the secondary sector.

The current black labor force is the offspring of a migratory stream from the rural agricultural South, initiated by the World War II and postwar boom. But the old migration is exhausted, and the changing unemployment and labor force participation rates among blacks in urban areas are a product of a gradual transition from "first"-generation migrants, to a new generation that is unable to move up to the kinds of jobs in the primary sector to which it aspires. The high unemployment rates in the minority labor force are less a result of unwillingness to work than of an inability to obtain jobs in the primary sector.

The Distribution of Jobs

If this diagnosis of youth and minority unemployment is correct, then what is needed are two kinds of responses: (1) Public policies which end the discrimination that has closed primary-sector jobs to various groups of workers, and (2) policies which shift the distribution of jobs away from the secondary and into the primary sector.

The idea of discrimination is not neglected today in orthodox economic theory. But the orthodox view, as expressed in the work of Gary Becker, implies that discrimination operates in the market and is restrained by competitive forces. It can be eliminated by strengthening competition and by raising the cost of discriminatory behavior. This kind of analysis thus calls for "economic," not "political" action. But the dual labor market hypothesis, by viewing hiring, training, and promotion as social processes, suggests that race, sex, and ethnicity are central factors in determining who gains access to the primary sector, and suggests that the necessary corrective action lies in instruments like the Federal Contract Compliance program and Title VII of the Civil Rights Act of 1964. The political opposition to compliance programs such as affirmative action really seeks primarily to preserve the existing social character of job allocations, rather than to protect the efficiency of the market.

The means of shifting the distribution of jobs from the secondary to the primary sector are more difficult to develop. Market dualism is the result of a complex array of decisions that govern recruitment, hiring, training, subcontracting, technological change, and capital investment. These decisions are made by corporations, trade unions, and informal work groups and, when looked at individually, they seem to be dominated by unique circumstances—local labor market conditions, particular personalities and social attitudes, political considerations, and the varied objectives of trade unions. The complexity of these relationships between institutional policies and labor market structures almost defies rational analysis and has been largely ignored by economists in the United States, leaving the economic literature barren of clues to the specific origins of dualism.

But in Japan and Italy, two industrialized countries where dualism is a widespread theme in economic analysis, the labor market structure is seen as closely related both to differences in employment practices between large and small business enterprises and to the relative strength of trade unions. In these countries, the initial emergence of dualism can be traced to rigidities in labor utilization introduced by large firms and to strong work-place union organizations. Because large corporations can smooth out fluctuations in production through marketing efforts, inventory adjustments, and subcontracting, their employment tends to be stable relative to smaller enterprises. Stability of employment and large size also favor union organization at the work-place, and union activity appears to foster further improvements in the employment security and economic advancements associated with the primary sector. The persistence of labor market duality as these countries industrialize can be traced, in part, to the failure of unionization to penetrate the secondary sector and to the tendency of government to subsidize indirectly the secondary sector through the exemption of small businesses from various costs of social welfare legislation.

Some obvious parallels can be found in the United States. Large enterprises dominate the primary sector and, with some notable exceptions such as the garment industry, union activity has historically been concentrated in the primary sector. Until quite recently, the smallest firms have received exemptions from the coverage of social welfare legislation, and in some states and localities government assistance has contributed to keeping secondary employment alive.

These limited examples of the sources of market duality imply that reform of the structure of labor markets must be undertaken in a wider policy context than is ordinarily considered. It must include policies of governing industrial structure, trade unions and collective bargaining, patterns of exemption from social welfare legislation, and the competitive position of small business, as well as manpower training and employment. Such widespread intervention, however, is outside the scope of labor market policy as it has traditionally been conceived and certainly exceeds our present capacity to manage labor market processes through public policy.

Transforming Labor Markets

While major reorganization of the dual market structure through microeconomic policies seems beyond the reach of government action, there do remain important and largely untapped opportunities for inducing structural change through aggregate employment policy. To illustrate this point, consider the effect of expanding the demand for labor uniformly throughout the economy. In principle, adding workers to the primary sector would require employers to reduce hiring standards, to recruit from among previously rejected or excluded sources of labor, and to enlarge their training and upgrading activities—in short, the secondary sector would provide the major supply of new hires in the primary sector. The logic of this scenario would indicate that a policy of full emplyment, if pursued long enough and far enough, would either eliminate the secondary sector or, through competition for scarce labor, cause secondary-sector jobs to conform more closely to those of the primary sector.

Unfortunately, however, full employment policy is too crude an instrument to insure that a tightening of the labor market would expand the primary sector significantly. In fact, employers and unions in the primary sector often seem to favor *temporary* solutions to tight job markets, solutions that do not provide the newly hired with the full career benefits of primary employment. Thus one finds companies in the primary sector relying on subcontracting and the use of temporary workers to avoid the costs and risks associated with giving primary market status to workers from the secondary sector.

As a result, the pressures for structural change that should accompany full employment often leave the dual labor market intact during periods of both high and low unemployment. Much of this preference for temporary solutions can be traced to the historical experience with "stop-and-go" growth. Recessions reduce labor demand in the primary sector, but they do not provide corresponding relief in the costs of commitment to career employment. These costs, combined with aversion to uncertainty, and with race and sex issues that inevitably accompany the expansion of the primary sector, often lead to the avoidance of structural adjustments that might be irreversible.

In general, obligations of steady employment are accepted only when there is an expectation of a stable level of demand. In the factory, these are the jobs associated with relatively permanent production levels. In the craft union, this is the level that yields relatively continuous employment for permanent members. The unstable employment residual is left to the secondary sector. Any use of aggregate policy as an instrument of structural change, therefore, means that one has to establish a credible commitment to stable and continuous full employment.

On the basis of these contrasting theories of the labor market, the efforts to transform labor markets can go in either of two directions. The human capital and search theories would seek either to make the labor market more flexible and competitive by reducing or offsetting the importance of market "distortions" like minimum wages and "transfer payments" that reduce work incentives or, when necessary, to subsidize the employment of those with labor market difficulties.

The alternative, suggested by the dual labor market analysis, is to focus on the importance of market institutions and the behavior of work force groups in the operation of the labor market. The search for policy instruments to redress labor market duality involves improved antidiscrimination activities, the reorganization of the secondary sector to stabilize and rationalize the utilization of manpower, and the exploration of institutional solutions to encourage the growth of primary-like employment in the secondary sector. Above all, the dualist approach stresses the primary role of full employment in encouraging the structural transformations required to reduce inequalities in employment and training opportunities. Full employment is necessary on the demand side to expand the primary labor market and to facilitate the absorption of hard-to-employ groups. And on the supply side of the labor market, this increase in primary opportunities should favorably affect the labor market commitment of many of the young and the disadvantaged.

Standards of Income Redistribution

MARTIN REIN AND S. M. MILLER

What does it mean to say "I am for equality"? Nine different kinds of equality are explored in the following article.

During the 1950s, there were widespread proclamations of an "Income Revolution" in the United States. Optimists of the day pointed to the Simon Kuznets study which concluded that the share of the national income going to the upper 5 percent of the income recipients was declining. Unnoticed was the fact that the share of the bottom fifth had not decreased and that the income lost by the upper 5 percent was picked up by the second highest group. (Some, of course, have contested whether the share of the topmost bracket dropped at all or was simply disguised in various forms.) Since the time of Kuznets's study the groups just below the top have continued to increase their shares, while the proportionate income of the bottom 20 percent has been altered very little. Do these changes indicate greater equality? The Gini coefficient, which measures how much the distribution of income departs as a whole from a standard where everyone's income is the same, might show less concentration, but few people would be satisfied if income redistribution meant only a shift within, say, the top 30 percent bracket. Obviously, then, we need a more precise way of defining a desirable redistribution.

Some critics have gone further than simply declaring the need for more accurate measures of distribution; they have asserted that those who support greater income equality must avoid generalities and should, in Irving Kristol's words, specify "the 'proper' shape of the income distribution curve." For these critics, the American polity should be presented with specific redis-

From Martin Rein and S. M. Miller, "Standards of Income Redistribution," *Challenge* (July-August 1974), pp. 20–26. Copyright © 1973 by International Arts and Sciences Press, Inc. Reprinted with the permission of International Arts and Sciences Press, Inc.

tribution goals for debate and evaluation rather than be confronted with vague utopian ideals which are used to flog the "system."

The question of goals concerns not simply the specific "amount" of redistribution, but rather the *type* of equality that is sought. The income equality goal has many dimensions and, as with the "Income Revolution," it is misleading to think of it in terms of one single indicator. Indeed, a "social-indicators" approach would require many different ways of viewing changes in income distribution if an adequate assessment of progress were to be achieved.

But what is "progress"? We cannot hope to attain an "adequate assessment" without a further clarification of objectives. It is necessary to define what kinds of changes are desired. The first step, then, is to specify the variety of things that people want or prefer when they hold income equality as a goal.

A simple uniformity of income is almost never the goal. Variations by age, family structure and personal needs are so great that even where complete leveling is desired, rules are still necessary to govern departures from that standard to apply to particular circumstances. For example, the apparently simple question of how much income is necessary for children of different age and sex is a matter of value as well as of cost measurement.

Even if the question of need-graduated income is satisfactorily handled, the issue of the ideal standard of income distribution is still not settled. In analyzing explicit or implied standards of a more desirable income distribution, we have identified nine different goals. This list is a start, not an end; once a list of targets is in hand, it is necessary to consider how each goal can be respecified from the general to the concrete, whether the individual targets conflict, which of the goals are attainable, and whether each target can be made to float politically. Our objective in this essay is much more modest—to bring together some current notions of the various goals of greater income equality and to indicate the diversity of views that the concept suggests.

Nine Kinds of Equality

One-Hundred-Percentism.   This objective is concerned with horizontal equity: people in similar situations should be treated similarly. Factors extraneous to quality and level of work should not contribute to pay differentials. The slogan of "equal pay for equal work" epitomizes one situation where people believe in 100 percent equality. Women and blacks should get the same pay when they have the same ability and training and perform the same tasks as men and whites. Sexual and racial *discrimination* should not be permitted; that principle is established in law, though not in practice, and is widely understood. The more troubling issue is that of gaining *access* to well-paying positions for groups which have long been victims of discrimination. Quotas, targets, and preferences for such groups have created considerable discontent.

Discrimination by social class is more difficult to perceive than racial or sexual biases. A study by Torsten Husén shows that individuals in Sweden with working class origins but with the same level of education as those of middle and upper income groups get about one-half their pay. When IQ and scholastic achievement are taken into account, children with middle class upbringing still receive one-third more income. Other studies suggest similar conclusions. The Swedish Low Income Commission has shown that social class accounts for more of the variance in the distribution of income than does education.

Finally, we should note that the recent data showing a greater dispersion of wages within a given occupation than among occupations provoke the disturbing question: Does one-hundred-percentism require that everyone in an occupation be close to the median income in that occupation?

The Social Minimum or the Floor of Protection. The objective here is that no one should fall below some minimum level of income and service. Where to place that floor is the subject of disagreement, but the principle is accepted that *poverty* should be eliminated. Frequently, however, the basic standard, whatever its specifications, remains unachieved. Then, there are reports of "casualties of the welfare state," people living below even the lowest official standard of subsistence; basic services are quantitatively (as well as qualitatively) inadequate, and a *rationing of the minimum* results— some get it, and others do not. The vaunted "floor" of the welfare state turns out to be a net through which individuals plunge (or they are never brought up to it). In practice, then, the issue is not only the level of the minimum but also its actual availability.

"The elimination of poverty" is not, strictly speaking, an exercise in the reduction of inequalities, for it does not formally deal with the position of one group relative to that of another. In practice, however, the "social minimum" is defined in terms of the changing practices or standards of society, so that an element of relativity enters in. Recall that Marx's subsistence definition included the concept of the amount that is "socially necessary" to maintain the proletariat; what is "socially necessary" shifts with the times. In the course of the 1960s, the income standard of poverty (the "poverty line") fell from a level of about one-half the median family income to one-third. When the ability to purchase the same market basket of goods and services is used as a definition of poverty, the amount of measured poverty invariably declines during expansion periods. This pattern helps explain why the extent of poverty is ignored as the economy grows; the level is then periodically redefined and poverty is once again "rediscovered" as we come to recognize that many persons have not kept up with the rising standards of society.

Equalization of Lifetime Income Profiles.   This goal involves inequalities in the growth of income over a lifetime, not the income differences among groups. A sense of improvement is important. Some groups in society can count on the satisfaction of rising incomes; others cannot. Peter Doeringer found that lower-level and women workers reach their peak wage while they are fairly young; higher-level workers have a longer, steadier rise to a higher peak (relative to their earlier salary level).

There are three different aspects to the income-profile goal:

—Everyone should have an upward-sloping age-income profile, that is, his position in real income terms relative to family structure should improve with age, at least until close to retirement. Everyone should have a career ladder rather than a dead-end job where the income ceiling is quickly reached. Another way of stating this goal is that we should wipe out the dual labor market which relegates so many people to low, insecure, fairly horizontal wage prospects.

—Income differentials among different labor groups should not widen with age to any appreciable extent. These differentials are much narrower in first jobs (age 20 or so) than they are in later years. (Both American and Swedish data show this pattern.) What is at issue is not the shape of the lifetime slope but the distance between the slopes.

—People should have greater freedom to distribute lifetime earnings as they choose. Presently, higher-income groups do this through tax-sheltered annuities and heavy employer pension contributions rather than salary increases. While such practices are aimed at reducing current taxes, they do provide considerable flexibility and confidence in governing one's resources. Lower-income persons do not have a similar possibility; some of them might prefer to use their Social Security payments both at a younger age and for a variety of purposes. For example, in Australia children's allowance payments for several future years can be received in a lump sum to aid in the purchase of a home.

In considering equality of lifetime income profiles, there are difficult choices to be made if we take the prevailing distribution as our starting point. For example, do we want an individual's income to rise over time in relation to his own starting point or in relation to the national average? The former would still permit older persons to lag behind the young. If we choose the national average as our standard, on the other hand, the result would be to redistribute income from earners with young children to older people who are at a relatively affluent stage of the family cycle.

Stratum Mobility.   The goal here is the narrowing of income differentials among occupational groups. It is not always clear which comparison is the most significant. Should it be white-collar (nonmanual) to blue-collar (manual)? Skilled manual to unskilled manual? Upper white-collar to lower white-collar? Upper white-collar to lower blue-collar? This is a goal of collective mobility in which people rise with and through their occupational group, rather than one of individual mobility in which successful individuals rise out of and away from their occupational grouping.

Frequently two competing principles are involved in stratum mobility: the first is that occupational groups should advance together so that traditional differences remain unchanged (the equity argument); the second is that the income differences among occupational groupings should decline (the equality argument). In collective bargaining, the first goal calls for similar percentage gains for all occupations; the second, for the same absolute gain.

Recently a new mode of analysis, similar to the income shares standard, has been employed in the analysis of wage differences. In contrast to the classic studies of wage differentials, this type of analysis ignores occupations. Instead, the top fifth of wage earners is compared with the bottom fifth, or the top half with the bottom half. These two methods may not yield the same results.

Economic Inclusion. The objective of economic inclusion is to eliminate, or at least reduce, the contribution of income differences to the feelings of exclusion from society. Exclusion seems to be organized around an implicit conception of where the middle or mainstream of society is. Deprivations are judged by reference to the middle. Concepts of equal opportunity and equal treatment carry with them the ideal of access to what the middle stratum of a society enjoys. Those who fall below the median suffer from a sense of exclusion derived from a perceived experience of lacking membership in the whole of society. Thus, according to Lee Rainwater, "The central measure of how much equalization from the *bottom up* is necessary will involve determination of the extent to which, at different levels of command of resources, individuals are treated as and consider themselves to be full members of their society." Rainwater's studies suggest that this figure can be placed at about 80 percent of median family income. Hence, he supports an income distribution profile which looks much like a triangle, because in such a distribution no one falls below the median income, or at least a narrow income band close to the median.

This target jars many people since at first glance it does not appear to be mathematically possible. But it is. The definitional requirement that half the population must be below the median does not dictate how far below the median they will be. On the other hand, the "bottoms up" approach does not put a lid on the top, so that the spread of incomes between the highest and lowest can widen even though no one has an income that is more than 20 percent below the median.

Income Shares. This is the most commonly used standard. The objective is to influence the share of national income which goes to particular segments of the population, usually defined in terms of deciles or quintiles.

Whether to emphasize one segment or another is an important decision. Central concern with the bottom fifth may block efforts to better the very worst off (the bottom tenth). The social characteristics of the bottom tenth and the next tenth may be very different. Indeed, the characteristics of the entire bottom fifth have changed a great deal over time, and this complicates the analysis of trends. For example, in 1952 about one-quarter of the families in the bottom fifth, ranked by money income, contained no wage earners; in 1972, the figure was over one-third (36 percent). Are we as anxious about the economic position of the bottom quintile when those outside the labor force occupy the most disadvantageous position in society? Clearly, this is not a settled issue.

While in principle the question of income shares involves the entire distribution and not a segment of it, in practice the emphasis is on the lower quintile or quintiles. Most discussions of changing income distribution do not specify how much the share of the bottom should be increased. When this issue is considered, it is usually in terms of short-run possibilities rather than long-term objectives. One rule of thumb might be to double the share of national income going to the bottom quintile (in most industrialized countries, around 5 percent) and to increase by a third the share of the second lowest quintile. The objective of raising the share of the bottom groups does not specify which of the other three quintiles are to be the losers. It is the next goal that deals more centrally with this issue.

Lowering the Ceiling. The objective here is to narrow the spread of incomes by reducing the peakness or concentration of income at the top. Because of the easy transmutation of income and wealth in this income group, wealth must be part of the concern with deconcentration. Lowering the ceiling may be a goal inspired by envy of the rich or by a desire for fairness in the sharing of tax burdens. What is particularly anomalous and offensive is that the tax laws permit some of the very wealthiest to pay low taxes or none at all. Whatever the motive, the aim is not so much to improve the economic position of those at the bottom as to reduce the advantage of those at the very top.

Whether "the top" is regarded as the top twentieth, top decile, top quintile or the two highest quintiles does make a difference. Even more important is whether "lowering the ceiling" is related to a "bottoms up" approach. What can happen—as occurred in the misperceived "Income Revolution" in the United States and the emergence of the welfare state in Britain—is that the next highest income groups gain from the reduced share of the very top group while the bottom quintile's share does not improve at all, or even declines.

The zeal for tax reform aimed at ensuring that the very rich do not escape taxation can reduce interest in the comprehensive reduction of inequalities. The plugging of tax loopholes used by the very rich eliminates one type of inequity but may have little significance for the most disadvantaged groups in society. Their share of national income may not increase even if the share going to the very wealthy declines.

Avoidance of Income and Wealth Crystallization. This ideal would reduce or eliminate the advantage that high income and wealth give in the areas of education, medical services, or even in humane and dignified treatment from and acceptance by others. Advantages tend to feed off one another so that an advantage in one area creates advantages in other areas as well. The converse is to avoid situations where low incomes produce multiple deprivations. Currently, being down in one area of life means being down in many others—"dirty work" at "lousy pay"; low economic status resulting in low social and political status. Lee Rainwater concludes that "American egalitarianism means that everyone be treated the same regardless of what he has." The objective, as British sociologist Ray Pahl has indicated, is to avoid the crystallization and convergence of different types of status rather than to encourage their fusion.

A broad ideal is embedded in this objective: individuals should be judged by a variety of standards and not simply by their economic position. Michael Young, the British sociologist who coined the term *meritocracy,* argues that greater income equality is desirable, for it would reduce the emphasis on materialism and the economic measuring which intrudes into personal interactions.

International Yardsticks. This standard specifies that a nation should have as equal an income distribution as that achieved by similar nations. Countries at the same level of economic development differ in income distribution. The more egalitarian performance should be the goal for the lagging nations. Japan is alleged to have a 4:1 wage spread. Can the United States be content with a much wider one? A particularly important comparison would center on the size and redistributive effects of cash and service transfers within various countries. In this respect, the United States lags behind a number of other high-income nations.

Competing Clusters

Thus far we have outlined the various goals implicit or explicit in discussions of egalitarian income standards. We will now consider how they cluster to form competing choices or ideologies about the specific objectives of income equality. It would be possible to scale each cluster so that it embodied the policies of the preceding choice. We have decided against doing this because it implies a simple and "natural" progression that is belied by the kinkiness of belief systems. Even so, our listing is overly smooth and continuous; it overlooks the considerable variations that exist within a cluster.

It does, however, point to the quite differing orienting principles that emerge from various combinations of these goals.

Equality of Opportunity.   The aim is to eradicate illegitimate barriers to improving incomes and to abolish illegitimate opportunities that are available to some groups but not to others. The *chance* to enjoy unequal position and privilege would thereby be equalized. A more equal distribution of educational services, at least, is intrinsic to the concept. But this income-oriented outlook goes beyond the traditional reliance on access to schools to promote equality of opportunity. Bringing everyone above the poverty line of income and services is important in order to reduce some of the environmental barriers to opportunity. The idea of inherited privileges, unrelated to ability, offends those who hold this conception of equality so that some degree of deconcentration of income and wealth at the top would be a major action. Discrimination violates the principle of equal chances so that one-hundred-percentism is important.

In the main, the equal opportunities approach takes a market-oriented economy as given. The chief emphases are rather on restructuring educational opportunities, utilizing taxes to reduce the role of inherited wealth, and providing transfers to eliminate poverty, usually specified at a relatively low level.

Since the objective is that all people should have an equal chance to alter their income positions, the overall distribution of income is not affected by the freeing of the processes which move individuals into different occupational and income positions.

Lessened Inequalities.   The objective is to constrain inequalities, to have "tolerable or acceptable inequalities" rather than to eliminate them altogether. This cluster incorporates the policies of the opportunitarians but goes beyond them to include placing a firmer lid on top incomes and wealth, bringing up the bottom by improving the situation of the lower quintiles, raising the minimum of basic services, reducing the importance of income in determining access to legal and political institutions and narrowing (some) wage differentials.

The assumption is that market capitalism will continue to operate but that considerable effort will be made to alter or offset its income effects, chiefly through the tax and transfer system.

Normative Egalitarianism.   This cluster of objectives goes beyond the preceding two because it holds equality as the orienting goal, although in practice it does not seek a complete leveling. This cluster establishes a minimum level based on some variation of the Rainwater model of no-one-far-below-the-median and adds to it a ceiling on the upper level so that minima and maxima define the acceptable income band. Lifetime income profiles of all occupations should be upward sloping; everyone should have a "career" and not simply a job. Medical care, education, and recreation should become universal goods, and access to them should not be governed by the command over income. Providing these services is part of the broader concern with reducing status crystallization.

Very sizable tax and transfer changes would be required to bring about the goals of normative egalitarianism. The practices of all enterprises would have to change to some extent. Economic policies concerning the nature of growth and development would probably have to be altered if wage differentials were to be affected.

Some adherents make the frequently unexamined assumption that market capitalism can be regulated so that a high degree of redistribution can be achieved; many of them would not be disturbed if socialism evolved from such efforts. Others believe that only a socialist economy could produce such results. A smaller group sees a political rather than economic need for socialism: in a regulated capitalism, they believe, important business groups would constantly stymie or erode efforts to produce redistribution.

Practicing Egalitarianism.   This principle is stark in its bold simplicity—everyone should have the same income. Adjustments to the principle of full equality are made to take account of special conditions such as age, family size, hardship, and danger of work. But these modifications are not to reward unequal talent unequally but to accommodate differences in individual circumstances. Therefore, the band of income variation would be very narrow indeed. Larger differences would be acceptable only on the basis of the principle formulated by John Rawls that such a temporary difference would add to the well-being of all members of the community. (The Rawls formula is the super-Pareto Optimality principle: for anyone to be allowed to gain, all others must also gain.) A departure from full income equality is not a normal situation and must be defended on specific and community grounds. Market forces, even within a socialist system, would have no play.

One version of practicing egalitarianism is a community of equals existing within a society which may or may not be egalitarian. This model has recently reemerged. In its current form, young dissidents seeking to withdraw from a materially oriented society have established communes, both rural and urban, where everyone gives what he or she can and takes what he or she needs. "Sharing" is the fundamental ideal. There are few rules. The communitarian model is a form of anarchism which assumes that if people truly love and trust each other, if there are no distinctions of quality among people and no artificial hierarchy emerges, then there will be no need to regulate income. When applied to a society as a whole, the practicing egalitarianism model includes an implicit wage system, but that is not true of the communitarian model. This pure communism is the most far-reaching of all the goals and is in the historical tradition of utopianism. Its continual reappearance indicates its attractiveness to many, if not its practicality.

From Philosophy to Politics

This effort to call attention to the variety of objectives that people have in mind when they espouse income equality is not intended as an intellectual exercise in the complexity of ideals nor is it a prescription for inaction until clarity and agreement emerge. Rather, the aim is to discourage worship of the "false god" of limited objectives, where the narrowness of the ideal disappoints us once we have made some progress toward achieving it.

Equality is not a "state in itself," a fixed end; it is, as Daniel Bell says, about relationships. It means many things to many different people. The task we now face is to consider how each goal can be made concrete; whether the individual targets converge or conflict; whether some goals are attainable; and whether each target can be made politically acceptable. The 1972 defeat of George McGovern does not signify the end of the interest in redistribution through tax reform, but it does indicate the need for more careful interpretation of redistribution proposals to the public and for a better understanding of their economic, social and political character.

We consider ourselves normative egalitarians. But summary statements of long-term goals only partially dictate what one's immediate political behavior should be. Since a dominating concern for redistribution does not exist, elaborating the goals of redistribution with philosophical exactness does not provide us with many leads as to what we should do today. Philosophical labels and long-term arithmetical goals of redistribution divide people; the more immediate aim of moving the distribution of income in more egalitarian directions is less likely to do so. This may be the time to seek out that which diverse political agendas have in common rather than to highlight the points that divide them.

A Case for Redistributing Income

KENNETH J. ARROW

A distinguished American economist argues persuasively for redistributing income. Where does he fall in the nine kinds of equality discussed in the previous article?

The use of taxing power to achieve a redistribution of income has been increasing over time in a marked way. Popular support of this doctrine has also tended to increase, though with much ebb and flow. The 1972 presidential campaign represented something of a check, though it was perhaps the first time the issue had been made a major one in that context and the ineptness of the presentation was surely a significant factor in McGovern's defeat.

The philosophical and ethical foundations of redistribution have come under sharp debate in intellectual and academic circles as well. Economists, after much neglect, have revivified their interest in the axioms that underlie the distribution and redistribution of income. Perhaps the most important recent intellectual event in the area of distributive justice has been the publication of John Rawls' *A Theory of Justice,* followed by attacks on Rawls and on the desirability of equality in general by Irving Kristol, Robert Nisbet, and others.

Among other strands of the debate is the old idea of a conflict between liberty and equality. The debate occurs against the background of a presumed common acceptance of the ideals of a democratic society, and democracy clearly includes in its sayings both these ideals. I want to argue here that a commitment to democratic values strongly implies an ideal of redistribution of income and wealth.

I think we may safely agree that the notion of democracy has two components, both indispensable: (1) the securing of the freedom of the indi-

From Kenneth J. Arrow, "Taxation and Democratic Values," *New Republic* (November 2, 1974), pp. 23–25. Reprinted with the permission of *The New Republic,* © 1974, The New Republic, Inc.

vidual so that he may develop his individual potential; (2) a symmetric mutual respect of the individuals in the society for each other. These aims are, as has been frequently remarked, partly competitive; but, it must also be stressed, they are to a very considerable extent complementary. A hierarchical society marked by great inequalities in power and esteem will surely not tolerate the liberties of those most disadvantaged. Conversely a world in which individuals have their liberties tightly confined must be one in which there are large inequalities of power.

I would like to enlarge somewhat on the meaning of the second criterion, the symmetry of respect. Any society, democratic or not, must have as a root element some degree of mutual obligation and some sense of respect for every individual, however low he may wind up in the hierarchy. The strong element of truth in all social contract theories is that the Hobbesian nightmare can be avoided only if the bulk of society feels in fact incorporated and accepted in it.

What is distinctive about the democratic society is that mutual relations are conceived of as symmetric in spirit. Individuals, at least in some initial sense, have to be treated equally by the society, if it is to be worthy of the name "democratic." One can attempt to give deeper philosophical foundations for this symmetry, perhaps Rawls' idea of an "original position," in which society chooses its values at a point where the members do not know what roles they will play. More prosaically, we can think of democratic decision-making procedures as a kind of insurance arrangement, in which individuals do not know what interests they will have in the long future, a view developed by James Buchanan, for example.

An immediate implication of the symmetry assumption is clearly some form of egalitarianism. Classically this has been interpreted in a political sense, that of equality of the right to vote. A long history of struggles has led to an almost universal acceptance of this democratic principle, at least on paper.

It might be objected that political democracy is in fact only nominal, that this ideal is never realized. As we look around we see rather obviously that political power is in practice exercised by a small minority. But the implications of this are perhaps less obvious. There are two reasons for the operation of "the iron law of oligarchy": (1) a straightforward and inescapable need for specialization of function; and (2) the translation into political power of inequalities in other forms of power, especially, in the modern world, economic power. I want to return to the second point later. The first of course is simply the fact that everyone can't do everything; politics is a vocation and you can only expect a limited number of people to engage in it, for obvious economic reasons, just as we have specialization in other occupations. But in principle, the practical importance of the specialization and of the hierarchical political structures needed for efficiency is blunted by the fact of political competition. Like economic competition it implies that the concentrations of power apparent to the eye are less significant than they seem; the politician or the entrepreneur has to satisfy the customers or voters. Of course these checks are imperfect, and perhaps more so for political than for economic competition; but they are real and important.

Assume then a roughly viable democratic system in the political sphere. Let us take the basic structure of decision-making in the economic sphere as it is today. Most economic decisions are made in the private sector, but the government has a considerable hand in the allocation of resources and in regulating the operations of the private sector. The division of responsibility can be argued in terms of both efficiency and ethical considerations and will not be discussed here. The operations of the government require, then, control of resources toward the ends that it is supposed to satisfy. These ends have been mainly the production of public goods but increasingly also redistributive measures, payments to individuals regarded as in some way disadvantaged. The latter amount to negative taxes.

Many among both the intellectual and general publics regard redistribution as a deprivation of liberty, in that property is taken away by coercion. I disagree with this viewpoint most strongly. It ignores the freedom-enhancing value of redistribution to the recipients, and it erects property unwarrantedly into a fundamental institution. Let me develop these arguments a little more fully.

In essence the ideal of redistribution is an extension of the principles of symmetry of respect and obligation from the political sphere to the economic. The symmetric regard for others is a desire to have them treated like oneself. In the absence of good reasons the presumption is always for equality of treatment, and equality of treatment will imply equality of outcome, again in the absence of special reasons to the contrary. One can indeed argue convincingly that complete equality can be achieved only at the cost of other values that we are not prepared to sacrifice. But one cannot start with the idea that a given state of inequality needs no question.

Let us start with elementals. Income and property are certainly the instruments of an individual's freedom. Clearly the domain of choice is enhanced by increases in those dimensions. It is true not merely in the sense of expanded consumer choice but also in broader contexts of career and opportunity to pursue one's own aims and to develop one's own potential. Unequal distribution of property and of income is inherently an unequal distribution of freedom. Thus a redistribution of income, to the extent that it reduces the freedom of the rich, equally increases that of the poor. Their control of their lives is increased.

There is an interesting sidelight on this in one of the outcomes of the experiments on the so-called negative income tax. The one kind of labor that is withdrawn from the markets in significant amounts is that of young adolescents; the income transfers induced them to return to their education rather than take low-paying jobs. This is precisely the kind of increased freedom that the most ardent libertarian should favor. A democratic position that starts from the equal importance of all individuals can only applaud a move to a more egalitarian distribution of autonomy and liberty.

A great deal of intellectual confusion comes, in my view, from thinking of property rights as basic and axiomatic. The forms of private property are indeed capable of mystification. In a world where incomes are derived in the first place from the sale of labor and other assets, the use of resources by the government takes the form of diverting income and wealth out of private hands into public ones. It therefore presents itself as an infringement on freedom. This is only a matter of forms of payment.

One could equally well think of the world's resources as a common pool from which allocations to private and public uses have to be made. We could make some payments in the form of rewards for services rendered and some in the form of grants to meet needs. Then the redistributive payments would not appear on their face to be a deprivation, but the effect in real terms would be the same.

I do not want to be misunderstood. Property, like the government, is an extraordinarily useful institution. Property is a protector of liberty. Equally important, the rights of property afford some guarantee for the efficient use of resources. But the current distribution of income and wealth has no particular claim to priority in itself.

There is some argument in justice and in practical efficiency for predictability, therefore an argument against arbitrary, large redistributions. In fact, however, the present capitalist system by its essence has a strong degree of unpredictability; for example destruction of property through development of someone else's innovation is a frequent occurrence and one that we regard as essential to the interests of progress.

There is one serious objection to relativizing and pragmatizing the rights of property. The most important items of property are personal. They are the skills and talents of individuals. It can certainly be argued that we do not want to put such assets into the common pool, that somehow each individual has the right to development of his own personal attributes. I think one can make a fairly sharp differentiation between the exercise of personal attributes and the enjoyment of unlimited income rights therefrom. I would be tempted to say that an individual with unusual talents, medicine or art, has something of an obligation to the world to use these talents; but even apart from that, I see no argument against saying that if he is highly rewarded for applying his talent, those rewards should in part be devoted to the less fortunately endowed.

There is a very different line of argument for redistribution, also based on the preservation of democratic values. This is the one referred to briefly above, the fact that unequal economic power is bound to be translated into political power. The mechanisms that this transformation takes are no secret. Campaign contributions, the many rewards that can be conveyed by contributions of wealth to complaisant political leaders, the ability to control communication, the greater leisure and the ability to be informed, all of these skew the distribution of political power.

The aim of achieving an equal distribution of political power requires a restriction on the inequalities of wealth and income.

The two arguments presented thus far have somewhat different implications for the nature of the redistribution. The expansion of the freedom of the poorer individuals leads mainly to antipoverty measures, to operations on the lower end of the income distribution. Of course mere arithmetic requires that this have an effect on the upper tail, but it is sometimes argued that the very high incomes (say about $100,000 a year) have such a small fraction of total income in them that they play a minor role in redistribution to the lower end. On the other hand the preservation of political equality may require especially strong redistributive measures against the upper end of the distribution. Of course there is no conflict between these two goals.

There is a third, more technical, argument. It is that a more equal redistribution of income will lead to an improved efficiency in expenditures on public goods. As matters stand now, such expenditures are partly directed toward improving efficiency in the economy but also partly directed toward redistributive aims. If a more or less equal distribution of income were achieved, one could confine the role of public goods to pure efficiency considerations.

There are of course well-known arguments toward limiting the extent of redistribution. The most familiar is that redistribution is bound to be accompanied by strong adverse incentive effects. Developers of new enterprises will be inhibited if their rewards are heavily taxed. Workers will not shift jobs as readily if the wage differentials are taxed away. These considerations are real and important and do set limits on the extent to which the income tax, for example, can be used for redistributive purposes. But one must not be too cautious. It is surely true that a great deal of very high personal incomes are essentially rewards for shifting incomes from one person's hands into another's, as in speculation or competitive practices that have little social product. Furthermore they are in good measure a reward for exercising talents that are in themselves pleasant to exercise and will therefore continue to be used even at considerably lower reward levels. It is also possible to consider taxes other than income taxes as instruments of redistribution. One that has been frequently proposed is a progressive tax on an individual's total consumption, thus providing an incentive for saving. There are severe administrative and conceptual difficulties, but it is possible that these are by no means insuperable.

Another argument against redistribution, which I think is less serious, is that anything that enhances the role of government is bound to increase the concentration of political power. This argument presupposes that the political competition, discussed above, is ineffective or imperfectly effective.

Even to the extent that this is true, a redistribution based on an automatic tax-like law, rather than on the basis of individual applications, should not result in any real increase in the effective power of the state.

I would therefore argue the scope for redistribution, as manifest by progressive taxation extending into the negative area of lower incomes, should be high on the agenda of those desiring the expansion of democratic values.

The Revival of
Political Economy

EDWARD J. NELL

Here is a deep and searching criticism of conventional economics and its theoretical approach to the distribution of income. Note the alternative explanation and the direction of economic reconstruction that is suggested.

I

Since the latter decades of the nineteenth century, orthodox economic theory has made its main business the demonstration that a well-oiled market mechanism will produce the most efficient allocation of scarce resources among competing ends. This preoccupation has in turn dictated a characteristic mode of analysis, in which the economy is conceived in terms of "agencies," or institutions, which, whatever their other differences, find their common denominators in terms of their market functions. Thus Rockefellers and sharecroppers are both "households," GM and the corner grocery are both "firms." Households, rich and poor, all demand "final goods" and supply labor and other "services" (meaning the use of capital and land); firms, big and small, demand labor and other factor services, and in turn supply final goods.

This way of subdividing the economy fits neatly into the framework of "rational choice." Factors supply services and demand goods in the amounts and proportions that will maximize their "utilities," given their "initial endowments," a polite way of referring to property holdings. It can be shown that the amounts finally chosen, the so-called equilibrium supplies and demands, will be simultaneously compatible solutions to all these different individual maximizing problems.

The task of high theory, then, is twofold: first, since the models are complex, *to show that there are, indeed, such simultaneous, mutually compati-*

From Edward J. Nell, "The Revival of Political Economy," *Social Research* (Spring 1972), pp. 32–52. Reprinted with the permission of the publisher.

ble solutions. This is not obvious, and, in fact, not always true. Second, of equal mathematical and of greater ideological importance, are what might be called the Invisible Hand Theorems, which *show that the system of market incentives will direct the economy toward these equilibrium prices, supplies, and demands.* In other words, the Invisible Hand Theorems demonstrate that the system is automatically self-adjusting and self-regulating.

This architecture of thought has many strengths. Market incentives often *do* direct the system in various predictable ways. Maximizing is, under some conditions, an indispensible part of rational behavior, and so must be spelled out. That it is all done at an exceptionally high level of abstraction is not only not an objection, but—it is claimed—may be a positive merit. The analysis is not cluttered with irrelevancies.

But when all is said, the theory of the efficiency of competitive markets has never provided much practical insight into historical reality. Since it presupposes effective market incentives and institutions devoted to maximizing behavior, it cannot easily be applied to the study either of premarket economics or of postmarket ones—i.e., ideal communist (or anarchist) societies. More important, traditional theory fails to provide a good model for studying the working and misworking of present-day capitalism.

There is a simple reason for this very important failure. Basically, orthodox theory is a theory of markets and market interdependence. It is a theory of general equilibrium as applied to *exchange,* extended almost as an afterthought to cover production and distribution. But exchange is a limited aspect of economic, much less social, reality. Therefore, orthodox theory is not a theory of economic power and social class, much less of a social system in its entirety. As we have noted, the initial "endowments," wealth, skills, and property of the populations are taken as *given.* Moreover, since the object of the theory is to demonstrate the tendency toward equilibrium, class and sectoral conflict tend to be ruled out almost by assumption.

As a result, the orthodox approach has comparatively little interesting to say about such important socioeconomic questions as the distribution of wealth and income. It cannot say how these came about originally; nor how different they might be under another kind of economic system. It does, however, have one major claim to social and historical relevance. It offers a definite though limited theory of the division of the value of net output between land, labor, and capital in a market system. This is known as "marginal productivity" theory. Briefly, it states that each agent in the system will tend to be rewarded in proportion to—and as a limiting case, in direct equivalence with—the contribution he makes to output. Thus a man earns what he (literally) makes; a landlord reaps what he (metaphorically) sows.

But with the revival of interest in recent years in the great problems of Political Economy, this central claim has come under increasingly heavy attack. This attack, which began as particular and limited objections to specific orthodox doctrines, has in the past few years developed into an alternative conception of the economic system as a whole. It is no longer simply a rival theory of market dispensations—a "non-Neoclassical" theory; nor can it be regarded merely as a return to the approach of the Classical greats—Smith, Ricardo, and Marx. It is both of these, but it is considerably more. In currently fashionable terminology, it is the emergence of a new paradigm.

II

To see this, let us contrast the view of income distribution given by the new paradigm with that of orthodox marginal productivity theory. At first glance, marginal productivity theory appears eminently sensible. Essentially, it states that factors—land, labor, and capital—will be hired as long as they produce more than they cost to hire. Expanding the employment of any one factor, the others held constant, will (the theory assumes) cause the returns on the extra units of that factor to decline, since it has proportionately less of the others to work with. Thus employment will cease when the declining returns to the factor in question just equal the cost of hiring more of the factor. Competition will cause each factor to be used up to the point where its marginal product equals that of the other factors. The total earnings of any factor will then be equal to the amount of it that is employed, times its marginal product, summed up over all the industries in which it is used. Clearly the relative shares of factors—land, labor, and capital—will then depend on their respective marginal products.

So far so good. To be sure, this story depends on the existence of markets, specifically on markets for land, labor, and capital, so that the theory won't be much use in examining the emergence or evolution of the market system. But note that, in a sleight of hand so deft as to have passed virtually unnoticed for an intellectual generation, the theory attributes responsibility for the distribution of income (under market competition) wholly and solely to the impersonal agency of technology. It is technology, not man, nor God, least of all politics, that has decreed what the shares of labor and capital are to be in the total product. *For it is technology that determines how rapidly returns diminish.* Thus only through technological changes, inventions that alter the engineering possibilities, can relative shares be changed. For if income shares are to change, marginal products must change faster or slower than they will change simply by the slow changes in the relative supplies of factors, e.g., population growth. Thus everything depends on how rapidly marginal returns to the different factors diminish, relative to one another, and this is a matter that depends only on technology.

From this perspective the class struggle is an illusion, and unions are valuable only as mother substitutes—providers of security and a sense of identification. Minimum-wage legislation may or may not raise wages, but in all cases the effect will depend entirely on what the technology permits. Only moves that change the relative marginal products of labor and capital can affect income distribution (though even they might not change if, for example, the movement in the relative amounts of labor and capital employed just offsets the changes in their marginal products). The influence of factor supplies is felt only through marginal productivity. Hence technology is what finally determines income distribution. Aggregate demand, monetary policy, inflation, unions, politics, even revolutions, are, in the end, all alike, irrelevant insofar as Who Gets What.

Socialist and left-wing economists, indeed social critics generally, have always gagged on this. Property and power, they maintain, are the essential elements in class struggles and sectional conflicts; it is ridiculous to say they don't matter—that the outcome, given the competitive market, is predetermined by the accidents of technological inventiveness. From their vantage point, income distribution—the division of society's annual product among the members of society—is *the* central question. For if we put income distribution at the center of the stage, the concern of the orthodox theorists with how factors spend their incomes seems relatively minor. The framework of rational choice looks flimsier and more makeshift; essentially a consumer-oriented theory, it has come to resemble so many consumer products: ingenious, brilliant, but unsuited to human needs.

This is not to say that the Political Economist rejects the theory of rational choice outright: he rejects it merely as an appropriate framework for the analysis of production and distribution *in the aggregate*. The framework he erects in its place is one that reveals the *links* between sectors and classes; shows how the products of one industry or set of industries are used as inputs by other industries (whose products, in turn, are used by still others); and makes clear how the earnings of one class are spent supporting production in some sector or industry. These interindustry and intersectoral relations are crucial to understanding how changes in demand or in technology transmute themselves into prosperity for some, disaster for others. Links between revenue from sales, social classes, and spending are crucial for understanding how the distribution of income is established and maintained in the face of considerable changes in the composition of output and in government policy.

The difference may seem one more of emphasis than of substance, but putting income distribution at the center and relating it to different patterns of linkages, of payment streams, and of technological dependencies between industries, sectors, and classes, leads to an altogether different vision of how the economy works.

III

The new vision can be called a "general equilibrium" approach, if one likes. But it immediately departs from the orthodox meaning of that phrase by emphasizing the interdependence of *production*, rather than of markets; technical and institutional "interlocks"—or their absence—rather than purely market relationships.

A second difference between the new approach and the old lies in the treatment of "substitution." In the old picture, substitution is the law of life on both the supply and demand sides. In response to price changes, different patterns of goods and/or factors will be chosen; when prices change, cheaper things will be substituted for more expensive ones in household budgets and industrial processes. The problem is that this conventional picture assumes that households and firms have *given* ends—the maximization of "utility" or output respectively. Hence, it does not deal with the more important questions of introducing altogether new products and processes, changes that often alter the parameters of the system or perhaps even the consciousness of society. Even within the narrow focus of the Neoclassical lens, however, many alleged cases of "substitution" involve something quite different—technological progress, changes in the nature of the product, external effects on parameters of the system, and so on. Indeed, in this wider sense, Neoclassical substitution is only a *special* case, and that is how the matter is treated in the new vision.

Third, the old vision treats the consumer as sovereign, and the effects of his choices enter into the determination of all major variables. This, of course, does not render the old vision incapable of discussing market power, producer sovereignty, or the "new industrial state." But, inevitably, such phenomena appear as special cases, limitations on the *general* principle of consumer sovereignty. In the new vision the consumer is cut down to size from the start. His preferences have little or no effect on prices or income distribution.

As a consequence, markets and the "price mechanism" are not seen in the new vision as a stable method of bringing about social optimality. On the contrary, prices are seen as determined largely from the supply side, and so depend on income distribution, which in turn may be influenced by many nonmarket and even noneconomic considerations. Ideologically, this means that the "market" should not be seen as some sort of alternative to bureaucracy, or as a method of allocating resources. Allocation depends on distribution, which depends at least in part on property and class.

A further fundamental difference can be seen when we consider the *purposes* of the two visions. The basic constituents of the old vision are consumers and firms' agents whose optimizing behavior, individually or in the aggregate, the equations of the models describe. In particular, maximizing behavior is what the theory is all about, and the *object of the theory, by and large, is to predict the consequences of such behavior.* But the circumstances in which this behavior takes place are taken for granted.

By contrast—and oversimplifying—the new vision is primarily interested in structure, in the patterns of dependency between established institutions, in how the system hangs together, and how it works or fails to work.

The job of economic theory is to delineate the *blueprint* of the economic system, of the environment in which economic behavior takes place. The basic constituents of theory are industries, sectors, processes, or activities, defined in technological terms; so defined, the new vision's basic constituents normally will not coincide with decision-making "agencies." Neither the word *household* nor the word *firm*, nor any synonym for either, appears in Sraffa's *Production of Commodities by Means of Commodities*, the basic work laying the foundation of the new paradigm. For decision making, the prediction of behavior or of what *will* happen, is not the goal. The new vision is concerned with seeing how an economy keeps going, what is *supposed* to happen; from that to discover what makes it break down and what makes it develop into an economy of a different kind. These are seen as questions addressed primarily to the analysis of the system of production, and of the social relations surrounding production.

The central distinction between the two visions, then, lies in the treatment of production and distribution. For the traditional Neoclassical economist, production is a one-way street, running from primary "factors" to "final products." Among the primary factors are land, labor, and, above all, *capital*, each receiving in competition a reward proportional, in some sense (depending on market circumstances), to its "contribution."

But not so in the new paradigm. The notion that the three traditional factors are on the same footing is discarded altogether. The great achievement of the Marginalist Revolution, as seen by its nineteenth-century proponents—namely, the development of a unified theory applying to all three factors—is dismissed. This can be seen nowhere so clearly as in the new conception of "capital," in reality a revival of a point well understood before the Marginalists confused things. "Capital" has two meanings. On the one hand, it is property in the means of production, enabling owners of equal amounts of claim in these means to receive equal returns (given competitive conditions). In this sense it is a homogeneous fund of value, capable of being embodied in different forms. On the other hand, "capital" also means produced means of production—that is, specific materials, tools, instruments, machines, plant, and equipment, on which, with which, and by means of which labor works. In this sense it is a set of heterogeneous, disparate products. *Capital goods are not the same thing as capital.* "Capital" is relevant to the analysis of the division of income among the members of society, but a nonspecific fund has no bearing on production. "Capital goods" are relevant to the study of production, but have no bearing on the distribution of income, since profit is earned and interest is paid on the *fund* (value) of capital invested, regardless of its specific form. "Capital goods," specific instruments, can only be converted into a fund of "capital" on the basis of a given set of prices for those instruments; but to know these prices we must already know the general rate of profit (in a reasonably competitive capitalist economy). Hence the amount of "capital" cannot be among the factors that set the level of the rate of profit. But in the orthodox, or Neoclassical, theory the "contribution" of "capital" to *production* supposedly determines the demand for capital, which together with the supply determines the rate of profit. This must be rejected. No sense can be given to the "contribution" to production of a *fund* of capital.

This is not to say that *saving and investment*, and their long-run consequences, are irrelevant to determining the rate of profits and relative shares. Quite the reverse; by eliminating the alleged "contribution of capital" in production as an influence or determinant of distribution, we open the way for a theory of distribution based on the relation between the growth of spending, of capacity, and of the labor force, on the one hand; and on the market power available to the various parties, on the other. Unequal rates of inflation of money wages and prices necessarily imply changes in the relative shares going to capital and labor, as Keynes pointed out in the *Treatise on Money*, his earlier major and now neglected work. Inflation is partly a consequence of the ratio of demand to supply, but it also reflects relative market power. And here is where the rules of the game—the rules of property—come in. For property confers advantages, though not absolute ones, in the setting of prices and in bargaining for money wages. Exactly what these advantages are, how they work, and by what kinds of forces, are among the questions that a theory of distribution should be able to answer.

In short, the new vision adopts a picture of the relation between production and distribution altogether distinct from that which has ruled the economist's roost since the Marginalist Revolution. This, in turn, entails rejecting some widely used techniques of empirical analysis, in favor with both radical and orthodox economists. In particular, "production function" studies, e.g., of technical progress, the contribution of education, the effects of discrimination, and of shares during growth, all involve a fatal flaw. For insofar as they proceed by assuming that a factor's *income share* indicates in any way its *productive power* at the margin, they are based on precisely the relationship that the new vision rejects.

It thus seems that conventional theory, although it contains much of value and importance, contains serious deficiencies. The Neoclassical theory of the general equilibrium of production, distribution, and exchange holds that the payments in the *factor markets* are *exchanges* in the same sense as payments in the *product markets*. "Distribution is the species of exchange," wrote Edgeworth, "by which produce is divided between the parties who have contributed to its production." Distribution, say the proponents of the new vision, is *not* a species of exchange; and capital *goods*, rather than capital, contribute to production. The ideological teeth begin to bite; an exchange, in equilibrium, means that *value equivalent is traded for value equivalent*. No exploitation there. But if distribution is *not* a form of exchange, then we must ask Who Whom?

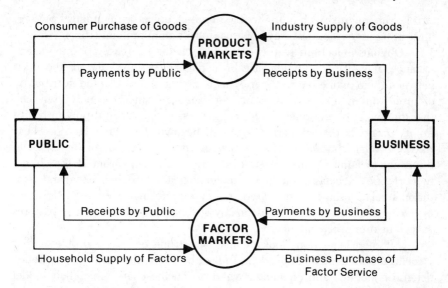

Consumer Purchase of Goods   Industry Supply of Goods

PRODUCT MARKETS

Payments by Public   Receipts by Business

PUBLIC

BUSINESS

Receipts by Public   Payments by Business

FACTOR MARKETS

Household Supply of Factors   Business Purchase of Factor Service

This catalogue of differences, and especially the last point, can be nicely illustrated by comparing two simple diagrams that visually summarize the two paradigms. The first, adapted from Samuelson and echoed in all major textbooks, presents what might be called a same-level division of society: business and the public (producers and consumers) confront each other more or less as equals in the markets for both products and factors. (The equality is an overall one; there are some large or allied firms, some collective consumers.) Households demand final goods and services and supply the services of productive factors, in both cases in accord with what economists rather pompously call "their given relative preference schedules," meaning, what they like best. Businesses supply final goods and services according to their cost schedules in relation to the prices that consumers are prepared to pay, and demand the services of productive factors according to their technical opportunities and needs in relation to consumer demand for products.

So goods and services flow counterclockwise, while money flows clockwise. In each set of markets, *equivalents are traded for equivalents*, the value of goods and services flowing in one direction being just matched by the stream of revenue in the other. No exploitation is possible in competitive equilibrium. The value of household factor supplies just matches aggregate household demand, and the output of goods and services matches business demands. This may seem to ignore the fact that households save and businesses invest, meaning that some final demand flows not from the Public but from Business. But that is easily allowed for. To finance this demand, Business must borrow Household savings, by supplying bonds that the public demands. Bonds are treated as a kind of good, flowing counterclockwise. These points enable the microflow picture to be summed up as a macroflow picture, illustrating in the simplest way how macro rest on microfoundations.

Obvious objections to this economic schema can easily be raised. For instance, not all "households" are on a par, since some *own* all the firms between them, while the rest merely *work* for the firms. Also the distribution of profit and similar income is not an exchange, since the only "service" that the owner of a business (in his capacity as owner) need supply in return for its profits is that of permitting it to be owned by him. He does bear risks, of course, but so do the employees who will be out of their jobs in the event of failure. Other objections were mentioned earlier in the charge that orthodox Neoclassicism ignores technological interdependences and institutional relationships, as the circular flow picture makes evident. Nowhere in it can one find social classes or any specific information about patterns of technical interdependence.

All these objections look at first like strong empirical problems that Neoclassicists should meet head on. In fact, however, the customary orthodox defense is oblique and of dubious validity. To the charge that their model rests on unrealistic assumptions, they reply that the *only* test of a model is the success of its predictions. So there is no *a priori* error in making unrealistic assumptions. Moreover, "simplifying assumptions" and "theoretical constructs" are bound to be, in some sense, "unrealistic," and there is no predicting without them. Unrealistic assumptions may therefore be warranted, and the warrant is philosophical, positivism itself.

We will return to these defenses. But first consider quite a different picture of capitalist society. The following diagram epitomizes the new approach, which, if the old is "Neoclassical," could be dubbed "Classical-Marxian." It cannot be claimed that this is the only, or necessarily the best, distillation of an alternative picture from that tradition, but it will serve to illustrate the contrasts.

To keep the diagram comparable to the first, we retain the circle for the final goods market and the box standing for industry, though we shall interpret both quite differently. "Households" and the "factor market" disappear altogether. Instead we have a pyramid, representing the social hierarchy, divided into two parts: a small upper class of owners and a large lower class of workers. Owners own industry and receive profits; workers work for industry and receive wages. Workers consume, but do not, in this simplified model, save; owners both consume and save, in order to invest.

Now consider the flows of services and money payments. Labor is the only "factor input"; other inputs are produced by industry itself, which is assumed to have access to land, mines, etc. (We are lumping landlords and capitalists together.) Hence we might expect to be able to value the total product in terms of labor, and though the mathematics is complicated, this can indeed be done, though not in all cases. The arrows running back and

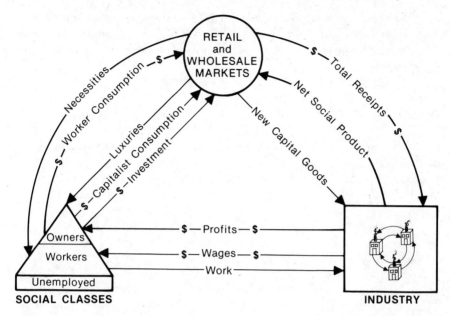

forth between factories represent interindustry transactions, the exchanges between industries necessary to replace used-up means of production. The Net Social Product is sold for Total Receipts, and consists of all goods over and above those needed for replacement. These can be divided (for convenience) into Necessities, Luxuries, and New Capital Goods. Necessities go for Worker Consumption, Luxuries for Capitalist Consumption, and New Capital Goods are installed in the factories in return for Investment payments. Hence, the national accounts work out:

Total Receipts = Net Social Product = Wages + Profits = Wage Consumption + Capitalist Consumption + Investment Demand = Necessities + Luxuries + New Capital Goods.

From the point of view of Political Economy, however, the most important fact is that while wages are paid for work, and one can (and in some circumstances should) think of the wage bill, equal here to Worker Consumption, as reproducing the power to work, *profits are not paid for anything at all.* The flow of profit income is not an exchange in any sense. The Samuelson diagram is fundamentally misleading; there is no "flow" from "household supply" to the factor market for capital. The *only* flow is the flow of profit income in the other direction. And this, of course, leads straight to that hoary but substantial claim that the payment of wages is not an exchange either, or at any rate, not a fair one. For Wages plus Profits adds up to the Net Income Product; yet Profits are not paid for anything, while wages are paid for work. Hence the work of labor (using the tools, equipment, etc., replacement and depreciation of which is already counted in) has produced the entire product. Is labor not therefore exploited? Does it not deserve the whole product?

IV

The latter question opens Pandora's box; as for the former, it all depends on what you mean. What does certainly follow, however, is that distribution is *not* an exchange, profits are not paid *for* anything and serve no function which cannot be met in other ways. This may not be exploitation but it shows clearly that the traditional economic justification—the "reward" for services—cannot be applied to profits, interest, dividends, and the like. Moreover, since the payment of profit is no exchange, there can be no equilibrium in the usual sense. A century-old school of thought, holding that our troubles come from the *excessive* profits sucked in by giant monopolies, and idolizing small competitive enterprise earning "normal profits," is thereby undercut. There is no merit in "normal profit"; indeed there is no such thing. The issue for Political Economy is the profit system itself, not its alleged abuse.

But surely, under both capitalism and market socialism, do not profits serve the essential function of indicating where investment can most advantageously be directed? Does not the *rate* of profit, similarly, serve to allocate productive resources between producing for current consumption and expansion for the future?

There are two things wrong with this common claim. First (as sophisticated Neoclassical economists will quickly admit), the function of profits and the rate of profit as indicators require merely that they be *calculated*, *not that they be actually paid out.* Calculated profit indicators are compatible with many different incentive schemes (e.g., salary bonuses to managers of state-owned enterprises, moral incentives, etc.). Second, profit-based indicators are only one set among several. In a stationary economy, for example, the correct indicators to achieve maximum output would be based not on profits but on *labor values*! Indeed, profit indicators alone are likely to be misleading; the rate and pattern of growth must also be considered in trying to identify the best investment plans. Thus, from the strict economic point of view, forgetting social complications, the best choices for maximizing consumption may differ from the best choices for maximizing growth. Once we allow for quality, the effect on the environment, and so on, the variety of possible indicators becomes considerable.

To return to the diagram: the new model helps us to understand how the division of income comes about. Remember that the orthodox doctrines held that the distribution of income was determined in the factor market, by the marginal "contribution" of factors in conjunction with their relative scarcity. The diagram makes it clear that income distribution interacts with all aspects of the economy, not just with the "factor market." This point can be made quite simply, though its consequences are far-reaching. Labor's share is given by the real wage times the amount of work. But the *real* wage is the *money* wage divided by an index of consumer goods prices. The money wage is set in the labor market, but prices are set in the final goods market. Labor's share, then, depends on *both* markets. Thus the system is interdependent in ways no hint of which can be found in orthodox teaching.

This puts inflation in a new and clearer light. The standard approach is to distinguish "demand-pull" inflation (originating in the final goods market) from "cost-push" inflation (originating in the factor market). Very few actual cases seem to fit either category. On the new approach this should come as no surprise, for the question has been wrongly posed. This issue is not where inflation originates, but how fast it proceeds in different markets. In the orthodox diagram it is natural to suppose that a price increase in the product market will be transmitted directly to the factor market, and vice versa. Unless costs and prices rise together the circular flow cannot continue unimpeded. In the new diagram it is evident that this is not so—costs and prices rising in the same proportion will be the special, limiting case. In all other cases the effect will be to raise or lower Profits. When wages rise faster than prices, there will be Profit Deflation; when prices rise faster than wages, Profit Inflation, to use the terminology suggested by Keynes in the *Treatise on Money*. In all cases except the limiting one, then, inflation will affect income distribution and so aggregate demand and employment.

What determines the relative rate of price and wage increases? The first answer, of course, must be "supply and demand," and this is surely right. For example, large numbers of unemployed will tend to act as a drag on money wages. But the same balance of supply and demand may have a very different total impact on price in different circumstances, depending on market power; on the financial position of companies and unions; on the ability to make use of the law, or state agencies, to manipulate the press and the media; and so on. These considerations are preeminently ones of Political Economy, but they play an essential role in theory, for they determine the relative responsiveness of markets, and hence the relative speed of wage and price inflation.

V

We have now presented and contrasted the two paradigms. The Neoclassical one is far better known, and most contemporary work is conceived in its terms. But if the preceding argument is sound, it is significantly misleading. The new paradigm, by contrast, is clearly more realistic sociologically, and is capable of handling questions, such as those concerning property income and social class, that the other tends to submerge.

These two claims, that the old paradigm is misleading and the new more realistic, suggest that there is a strong *prima facie* case for adopting the new. This conclusion, however, is widely resisted, and the reasons, already mentioned, are interesting. Those who defend the old approach often contend that a paradigm cannot be "misleading" in its representation of institutions *if it leads to models that predict well.* "Realism" is not important; abstraction must take place, and a model can abstract from anything, so long as it performs well.

Such a defense must be seen for what it is. It is a methodological claim, and one based on a particular, and today rather questionable, philosophy of science. One straightforward retort might be that Neoclassical models have not done very well on their chosen ground. Prediction has not been the greatest success of modern economics. But a more fundamental response would be to challenge the methodology itself. There is no time to argue the case now, but there is an intuitive appeal to the idea that a model of social institutions must be a good representation of things as they are at a given moment of time, regardless of how they work out over time. To demand of economics that it predict what *will* happen may be asking too much. In modern industrial societies the economic system is too closely interlocked with other aspects of society; it cannot be isolated enough for effective tests to be run. But to add a long string of *ceteri paribus* clauses simply tends to reduce predictions to vacuity. Instead, we must examine the definitions and assumptions of our models for their realism, and for the extent to which they incorporate the essentials. If they are realistic, then the working of the model should mirror the working of the economic system in relatively simple and abstract form. To argue this further would take us far afield. It should be clear, though, that the case we have presented can be defended from the methodological objections of the Positivists.

In short, the new approach presents a coherent picture of the economy, perfectly adapted to modern empirical methods and capable of providing technical analysis of a sophisticated nature. But it has not been developed for its own sake, or simply because it presents a better, more accurate picture of capitalism. The new picture is intended precisely as *Political* Economics, as a guide to the criticism of the capitalist socioeconomic system. Its basic challenge to orthodox thinking is that, in treating the distribution of income as a form of exchange, it misrepresents the way the system works. But if it is not an exchange then someone is getting something for which he is not giving a value equivalent. The step to social criticism is then short.

Orthodox economics tries to show that the markets allocate scarce resources according to relative efficiency; Political Economics tries to show that markets distribute income according to relative power. It is good to know about efficiency, but in the world we live in, it tends to be subservient to power. By failing to appreciate this, and consequently failing also to accord the distribution of income between labor and capital a properly central role, orthodox economics has become cut off from the central economic issues of our time, drifting further into ever more abstract and mathematically sophisticated reformulations of essentially the same propositions. The heart of the matter is the concept of "capital" and its relation to social class and economic power. When this is put right, as in the new paradigm, economic theory can once again speak to the critical issues of the day.

PART III

ECONOMIC PHILOSOPHIES

At this point one might say, "Ok I see the argument, now who's right?" We suggest that as important as that question is, it is not answerable by simply appealing to the facts in the matter. Economics has always been more than an "engineering" tool kit. Economists have consistently been involved either with advocating particular economic systems or advocation how particular economic systems ought to be run. For example, the consistent framing of theories in terms of capitalistic institutional structure points to the substantial amount of ideology and value judgment implicit in economic theory. To recognize this is to see only half the problem. Another crucial task confronting economic analysts of social systems lies in determining what goal or goals economic systems should be directed toward. One frequently stated objective is economic freedom. Notice that freedom is a term subject to many different meanings. Conservatives frequently oppose government regulation because it reduces *freedom to* . . . ; and liberals support government regulation because it increases *freedom from*. . . . Again one can see the intrusion of values into economic analysis in terms of giving meaning to the concept of economic freedom. One can see this quite clearly in this section by contrasting the readings by Friedman and Simon to those of Heilbroner and Baran and Sweezy.

Another question that need be kept in mind when one reads this section is whether or not modern economic orthodoxy has transposed ends and means through time. When looking at Classical economists, one sees that they all held in common the belief that economic systems were the means to the end objective of human development. They were all concerned with the creation of humane societies in which women and men could fully achieve their potential. A major disagreement was whether capitalism (reformed or otherwise) was the best system to provide this. With the coming of modern economics there was a movement away from growth and distribution toward allocative efficiency and stability problems. Increasingly through time economic analysis has addressed itself to issues of system maintenance to the point where one wonders if we have not transposed ends and means. Whereas formerly man was the end and systems were the means, have we now inverted the economic problem to regard systems as the end and man the means?

A.F.

Worldly Philosophies

SMITH, MILL, MARX, MARSHALL, AND KEYNES

Adam Smith is the intellectual father of what is now labelled Classical economics. In the later works of Mill, Marshall, and Keynes we see not only the evolution of "western economics," but a concern for areas of inadequate performance. For example, Mill raised the problem of distribution; Keynes the problem of full employment. In addition, they disagreed as to whether the system was tending upward in a progressive spiral or toward a stationary state. The common ground among Mill, Marshall, and Keynes was the belief that these problems could be resolved within the capitalistic system. Some modifications may be necessary, but the system was basically sound. The works of Karl Marx stand as a direct challenge to the soundness of the capitalistic system. His distinction lies in a theoretical analysis which concluded that capitalism could not resolve its problems within its own system. A word of caution. These excerpts only hint at the richness of thought of our "founding fathers" and again we urge the student to dip into the originals.

Wealth of Nations, Adam Smith

The greatest improvement in the productive powers of labor, and the greater part of the skill, dexterity, and judgment with which it is anywhere directed, or applied, seem to have been the effects of the division of labor.

The effects of the division of labor, in the general business of society, will be more easily understood by considering in what manner it operates in some particular manufactures. It is commonly supposed to be carried furthest in some very trifling ones; not perhaps that it really is carried further in them than in others of more importance: but in those trifling manufactures which are destined to supply the small wants of but a small number of people, the whole number of workmen must necessarily be small; and those employed in every different branch of the work can often be collected into the same workhouse, and placed at once under the view of the spectator. In those great manufactures, on the contrary, which are destined to supply the great wants of the great body of the people, every different branch of the work employs so great a number of workmen that

From the books *The Wealth of Nations* by Adam Smith. Introduction by Professor Edwin R. A. Seligman. Vols. I and II. Everyman's Library Edition. Published by E. P. Dutton & Co., Inc., and reprinted with their permission.

it is impossible to collect them all into the same workhouse. We can seldom see more, at one time, than those employed in one single branch. Though in such manufactures, therefore, the work may really be divided into a much greater number of parts than in those of a more trifling nature, the division is not near so obvious, and has accordingly been much less observed.

To take an example, therefore, from a very trifling manufacture; but one in which the division of labor has been very often taken notice of, the trade of the pin-maker; a workman not educated to this business (which the division of labor has rendered a distinct trade), nor acquainted with the use of the machinery employed in it (to the invention of which the same division of labor has probably given occasion), could scarce, perhaps, with his utmost industry, make one pin in a day, and certainly could not make 20. But in the way in which this business is now carried on, not only the whole work is a peculiar trade, but it is divided into a number of branches, of which the greater part are likewise peculiar trades. One man draws out the wire, another straightens it, a third cuts it, a fourth points it, a fifth grinds it at the top for receiving the head; to make the head requires two or three distinct operations; to put it on is a peculiar business, to whiten the pins is another; it is even a trade by itself to put them into the paper; and the important business of making a pin is, in this manner, divided into about 18 distinct operations, which, in some manufactories, are all performed by distinct hands, though in others the same man will sometimes perform two or three of them. I have seen a small manufactory of this kind where ten men only were employed, and where some of them consequently performed two or three distinct operations. But though they were very poor, and therefore but indifferently accommodated with the necessary machinery, they could, when they exerted themselves, make among them about 12 pounds of pins in a day. There are in a pound upwards of 4,000 pins of a middling size. Those ten persons, therefore, could make among them upwards of 48,000 pins in a day. Each person, therefore, making a tenth part of 48,000 pins, might be considered as making 4,800 pins in a day. But if they had all wrought separately and independently, and without any of them having been educated to this peculiar business, they certainly could not each of them have made 20, perhaps not one pin in a day; that is, certainly, not the 240th, perhaps not the 4,800th part of what they are at present capable of performing, in consequence of a proper division and combination of their different operations.

In every other art and manufacture, the effects of the division of labor are similar to what they are in this very trifling one; though, in many of them, the labor can neither be so much subdivided, nor reduced to so great a simplicity of operation. The division of labor, however, so far as it can be introduced, occasions, in every art, a proportionable increase of the

productive powers of labor. The separation of different trades and employments from one another seems to have taken place in consequence of this
advantage. This separation, too, is generally carried furthest in those countries which enjoy the highest degree of industry and improvement; what
is the work of one man in a rude state of society being generally that of
several in an improved one. In every improved society, the farmer is generally nothing but a farmer; the manufacturer, nothing but a manufacturer. The labor, too, which is necessary to produce any one complete
manufacture is almost always divided among a great number of hands.

This great increase of the quantity of work which, in consequence
of the division of labor, the same number of people are capable of performing, is owing to three different circumstances; first, to the increase of
dexterity in every particular workman; second, to the saving of the time
which is commonly lost in passing from one species of work to another;
and last, to the invention of a great number of machines which facilitate
and abridge labor, and enable one man to do the work of many.

This division of labor, from which so many advantages are derived,
is not originally the effect of any human wisdom, which foresees and intends that general opulence to which it gives occasion. It is the necessary
though very slow and gradual consequence of a certain propensity in
human nature which has in view no such extensive utility; the propensity
to truck, barter, and exchange one thing for another.

Whether this propensity be one of those original principles in human
nature of which no further account can be given; or whether, as seems
more probable, it be the necessary consequence of the faculties of reason
and speech, it belongs not to our present subject to inquire. It is common
to all men, and to be found in no other race of animals, which seem to
know neither this nor any other species of contracts. Two greyhounds, in
running down the same hare, have sometimes the appearance of acting
in some sort of concert. Each turns her towards his companion, or endeavors to intercept her when his companion turns her towards himself. This,
however, is not the effect of any contract, but of the accidental concur-
rence of their passions in the same object at that particular time. Nobody
ever saw a dog make a fair and deliberate exchange of one bone for another
with another dog. Nobody ever saw one animal by its gestures and natural
cries signify to another, this is mine, that yours; I am willing to give this
for that. When an animal wants to obtain something either of a man or of
another animal, it has no other means of persuasion but to gain the favor
of those whose service it requires. A puppy fawns upon its dam, and a
spaniel endeavors by a thousand attractions to engage the attention of its
master who is at dinner, when it wants to be fed by him. Man sometimes
uses the same arts with his brethren, and when he has no other means of
engaging them to act according to his inclinations, endeavors by every

servile and fawning attention to obtain their good will. He has not time, however, to do this upon every occasion. In civilized society he stands at all times in need of the cooperation and assistance of great multitudes, while his whole life is scarce sufficient to gain the friendship of a few persons. In almost every other race of animals each individual, when it is grown up to maturity, is entirely independent, and its natural state has occasion for the assistance of no other living creature. But man has almost constant occasion for the help of his brethren, and it is in vain for him to expect it from their benevolence only. He will be more likely to prevail if he can interest their self-love in his favor, and show them that it is for their own advantage to do for him what he requires of them. Whoever offers to another a bargain of any kind, proposes to do this. Give me that which I want, and you shall have this which you want, is the meaning of every such offer; and it is in this manner that we obtain from one another the far greater part of those good offices which we stand in need of. It is not from the benevolence of the butcher, the brewer, or the baker that we expect our dinner, but from their regard to their own interest. We address ourselves, not to their humanity but to their self-love, and never talk to them of our own necessities but of their advantages.

What are the common wages of labor, depends everywhere upon the contract usually made between those two parties, whose interests are by no means the same. The workmen desire to get as much, the masters to give as little as possible. The former are disposed to combine in order to raise, the latter in order to lower the wages of labor.

It is not, however, difficult to foresee which of the two parties must, upon all ordinary occasions, have the advantage in the dispute, and force the other into a compliance with their terms. The masters, being fewer in number, can combine much more easily; and the law, besides, authorizes, or at least does not prohibit their combinations, while it prohibits those of the workmen. We have no acts of parliament against combining to lower the price of work; but many against combining to raise it. In all such disputes the masters can hold out much longer. A landlord, a farmer, a master manufacturer, a merchant, though they did not employ a single workman, could generally live a year or two upon the stocks which they have already acquired. Many workmen could not subsist a week, few could subsist a month, and scarce any a year without employment. In the long run the workman may be as necessary to his master as his master is to him; but the necessity is not so immediate.

We rarely hear, it has been said, of the combinations of masters, though frequently of those of workmen. But whoever imagines, upon this account, that masters rarely combine, is as ignorant of the world as of the subject. Masters are always and everywhere in a sort of tacit, but constant and uniform combination, not to raise the wages of labor above their actual rate. To violate this combination is everywhere a most unpopular action, and a sort of reproach to a master among his neighbors and equals. We seldom, indeed, hear of this combination, because it is the usual, and one may say, the natural state of things, which nobody ever hears of. Masters, too, sometimes enter into particular combinations to sink the wages of labor even below this rate. These are always conducted with the utmost silence and secrecy, till the moment of execution, and when the workmen yield, as they sometimes do, without resistance, though severely felt by them, they are never heard of by other people. Every individual who employs his capital in the support of domestic industry, necessarily endeavors so to direct that industry that its produce may be of the greatest possible value.

The produce of industry is what it adds to the subject or materials upon which it is employed. In proportion as the value of this produce is great or small, so will likewise be the profits of the employer. But it is only for the sake of profit that any man employs a capital in the support of industry; and he will always, therefore, endeavor to employ it in the support of that industry of which the produce is likely to be of the greatest value, or to exchange for the greatest quantity either of money or of other goods.

But the annual revenue of every society is always precisely equal to the exchangeable value of the whole annual produce of its industry or rather is precisely the same thing with that exchangeable value. As every individual, therefore, endeavors as much as he can both to employ his capital in the support of domestic industry . . . every individual necessarily labors to render the annual revenue of the society as great as he can. He generally, indeed neither intends to promote the public interest, nor knows how much he is promoting it . . . he intends only his own gain, and he is in this, as in many other cases, led by an invisible hand to promote an end which was no part of his intention.

Theses on Feuerbach and Das Kapital, Karl Marx

The philosophers have only interpreted the world, in various ways; the point, however, is to change it.

Historical Tendency of Capitalist Accumulation. What does the primitive accumulation of capital, i.e., its historical genesis, resolve itself into? In so far as it is not immediate transformation of slaves and serfs into wage laborers, and therefore a mere change of form, it only means the expropriation of the immediate producers, i.e., the dissolution of

From *Selected Works of Karl Marx and Frederick Engles,* pp. 30, 235–37. Reprinted by permission of International Publisher's Co., Inc. Copyright © 1968.

private property based on the labor of its owner. Private property, as the antithesis to social, collective property, exists only where the means of labor and the external conditions of labor belong to private individuals. But according as these private individuals are laborers or not laborers, private property has a different character. The numberless shades that it at first sight presents, correspond to the intermediate stages lying between these two extremes. The private property of the laborer in his means of production is the foundation of petty industry, whether agricultural, manufacturing, or both; petty industry, again, is an essential condition for the development of social production and of the free individuality of the laborer himself. Of course, this petty mode of production exists also under slavery, serfdom, and other states of dependence. But it flourishes, it lets loose its whole energy, it attains its adequate classical form, only where the laborer is the private owner of his own means of labor set in action by himself; the peasant of the land which he cultivates, the artisan of the tool which he handles as a virtuoso.

This mode of production presupposes parceling of the soil, and scattering of the other means of production. As it excludes the concentration of these means of production, so also it excludes cooperation, division of labor within each separate process of production, the control over, and the productive application of, the forces of nature by society, and the free development of the social productive powers. It is compatible only with a system of production, and a society, moving within narrow and more or less primitive bounds. To perpetuate it would be, as Pecqueur rightly says, "to decree universal mediocrity." At a certain stage of development, it brings forth the material agencies for its own dissolution. From that moment, new forces and new passions spring up in the bosom of society; but the old social organization fetters them and keeps them down. It must be annihilated; it is annihilated. Its annihilation, the transformation of the individualized and scattered means of production into socially concentrated ones, of the pygmy property of the many into the huge property of the few, the expropriation of the great mass of the people from the soil, from the means of subsistence, and from the means of labor, this fearful and painful expropriation of the mass of the people forms the prelude to the history of capital. It comprises a series of forcible methods, of which we have passed in review only those that have been epoch-making as methods of the primitive accumulation of capital. The expropriation of the immediate producers was accomplished with merciless vandalism, and under the stimulus of passions the most infamous, the most sordid, the pettiest, the most meanly odious. Self-earned private property, that is based, so to say, on the fusing together of the isolated, independent laboring individual with the conditions of his labor, is supplanted by capitalistic private property, which rests on exploitation of the nominally free labor of others, i.e., on wage-labor.

As soon as this process of transformation has sufficiently decomposed the old society from top to bottom, as soon as the laborers are turned into proletarians, their means of labor into capital, as soon as the capitalist mode of production stands on its own feet, then the further socialization of labor and further transformation of the land and other means of production into socially exploited and, therefore, common means of production, as well as the further expropriation of private proprietors, takes a new form. That which is now to be expropriated is no longer the laborer working for himself, but the capitalist exploiting many laborers.- This expropriation is accomplished by the action of the immanent laws of capitalistic production itself, by the centralization of capital. One capitalist always kills many. Hand in hand with this centralization, or this expropriation of many capitalists by few, develop, on an ever-extending scale, the cooperative form of the labor process, the conscious technical application of science, the methodical cultivation of the soil, the transformation of the instruments of labor into instruments of labor only usable in common, the economizing of all means of production by their use as the means of production of combined, socialized labor, the entanglement of all peoples in the net of the world market, and with this, the international character of the capitalistic regime. Along with the constantly diminishing number of the magnates of capital, who usurp and monopolize all advantages of this process of transformation, grows the mass of misery, oppression, slavery, degradation, exploitation; but with this too grows the revolt of the working class, a class always increasing in numbers, and disciplined, united, organized by the very mechanism of the process of capitalist production itself. The monopoly of capital becomes a fetter upon the mode of production, which has sprung up and flourished along with, and under, it. Centralization of the means of production and socialization of labor at last reach a point where they become incompatible with their capitalist integument. This integument is burst asunder. The knell of capitalist private property sounds. The expropriators are expropriated.

The capitalist mode of appropriation, the result of the capitalist mode of production, produces capitalist private property. This is the first negation of individual private property, as founded on the labor of the proprietor. But capitalist production begets, with the inexorability of a law of nature, its own negation. It is the negation of negation. This does not reestablish private property for the producer, but gives him individual property based on the acquisitions of the capitalist era, i.e., on cooperation and the possession in common of the land and of the means of production.

The transformation of scattered private property, arising from individual labor, into capitalist private property is, naturally, a process incomparably more protracted, violent, and difficult, than the transformation of capitalistic private property, already practically resting on socialized production, into socialized property. In the former case, we had the expropriation of the mass of the people by a few usurpers; in the latter, we have the expropriation of a few usurpers by the mass of the people.

Principles of Political Economy, J. S. Mill

It must always have been seen, more or less distinctly, by political economists, that the increase of wealth is not boundless: that at the end of what they term the progressive state lies the stationary state, that all progress in wealth is but a postponement of this, and that each step in advance is an approach to it. We have now been led to recognize that this ultimate goal is at all times near enough to be fully in view; that we are always on the verge of it, and that if we have not reached it long ago, it is because the goal itself flies before us. The richest and most prosperous countries would very soon attain the stationary state, if no further improvements were made in the productive arts, and if there were a suspension of the overflow of capital from those countries into the uncultivated or ill-cultivated regions of the earth.

This impossibility of ultimately avoiding the stationary state—this irresistible necessity that the stream of human industry should finally spread itself out into an apparently stagnant sea—must have been, to the political economists of the last two generations, an unpleasing and discouraging prospect; for the tone and tendency of their speculations goes completely to identify all that is economically desirable with the progressive state, and with that alone. With Mr. [James Ramsay] McCulloch, for example, prosperity does not mean a large production and a good distribution of wealth, but a rapid increase of it; his test of prosperity is high profits; and as the tendency of that very increase of wealth, which he calls prosperity, is towards low profits, economical progress, according to him, must tend to the extinction of prosperity. Adam Smith always assumes that the condition of the mass of the people, though it may not be positively distressed, must be pinched and stinted in a stationary condition of wealth, and can only be satisfactory in a progressive state. The doctrine that, to however distant a time incessant struggling may put off our doom, the progress of society must "end in shallows and in miseries," far from being, as many people still believe, a wicked invention of Mr. Malthus, was either expressly or tacitly affirmed by his most distinguished predecessors, and can only be successfully combated on his principles. Before attention had been directed to the principle of population as the active force in determining the remuneration of labor, the increase of mankind was virtually treated as a constant quantity: it was, at all events, assumed that in the natural and normal state of human affairs population must

From "Principles of Political Economy," Vol. 2 (New York: D. Appleton & Co., 1889), pp. 334–39.

constantly increase, from which it followed that a constant increase of
the means of support was essential to the physical comfort of the mass
of mankind. The publication of Mr. Malthus's *Essay* is the era from which
better views of this subject must be dated; and notwithstanding the
acknowledged errors of his first edition, few writers have done more
than himself, in the subsequent editions, to promote these juster and more
hopeful anticipations.

Even in a progressive state of capital, in old countries, a conscientious
or prudential restraint on population is indispensable, to prevent the
increase of numbers from outstripping the increase of capital, and the
condition of the classes who are at the bottom of society from being
deteriorated. Where there is not, in the people, or in some very large
proportion of them, a resolute resistance to this deterioration—a determination to preserve an established standard of comfort—the condition
of the poorest class sinks, even in a progressive state, to the lowest point
which they will consent to endure. The same determination would be
equally effectual to keep up their condition in the stationary state, and
would be quite as likely to exist. Indeed, even now, the countries in
which the greatest prudence is manifested in the regulating of population,
are often those in which capital increases least rapidly. Where there is an
indefinite prospect of employment for increased numbers, there is apt
to appear less necessity for prudential restraint. If it were evident that a
new hand could not obtain employment but by displacing, or succeeding
to, one already employed, the combined influences of prudence and public
opinion might in some measure be relied on for restricting the coming
generation within the numbers necessary for replacing the present.

I cannot, therefore, regard the stationary state of capital and wealth
with the unaffected aversion so generally manifested towards it by political
economists of the old school. I am inclined to believe that it would be,
on the whole, a very considerable improvement on our present condition.
I confess I am not charmed with the ideal of life held out by those who
think that the normal state of human beings is that of struggling to get
on; that the trampling, crushing, elbowing, and treading on each other's
heels, which form the existing type of social life, are the most desirable
lot of human kind, or anything but the disagreeable symptoms of one
of the phases of industrial progress. The northern and middle states of
America are a specimen of this stage of civilization in very favorable
circumstances; having, apparently, got rid of all social injustices and
inequalities that affect persons of Caucasian race and of the male sex,
while the proportion of population to capital and land is such as to ensure
abundance to every able-bodied member of the community who does not
forfeit it by misconduct. They have the six points of Chartism, and they
have no poverty: and all that these advantages seem to have yet done
for them (notwithstanding some incipient signs of a better tendency) is

that the life of the whole of one sex is devoted to dollar-hunting, and of the other to breeding dollar-hunters. This is not a kind of social perfection which philanthropists to come will feel any very eager desire to assist in realizing. Most fitting, indeed, is it, that while riches are power, and to grow as rich as possible the universal object of ambition, the path to its attainment should be open to all, without favor or partiality. But the best state for human nature is that in which, while no one is poor, no one desires to be richer, nor has any reason to fear being thrust back, by the efforts of others to push themselves forward.

That the energies of mankind should be kept in employment by the struggle for riches, as they were formerly by the struggle of war, until the better minds succeed in educating the others into better things, is undoubtedly more desirable than that they should rust and stagnate. While minds are coarse they require coarse stimuli, and let them have them. In the meantime, those who do not accept the present very early stage of human improvement as its ultimate type, may be excused for being comparatively indifferent to the kind of economical progress which excites the congratulations of ordinary politicians; the mere increase of production and accumulation. For the safety of national independence it is essential that a country should not fall much behind its neighbors in these things. But in themselves they are of little importance, so long as either the increase of population or anything else prevents the mass of the people from reaping any part of the benefit of them. I know not why it should be matter of congratulation that persons who are already richer than anyone needs to be, should have doubled their means of consuming things which give little or no pleasure except as representative of wealth; or that numbers of individuals should pass over, every year, from the middle classes into a richer class, or from the class of the occupied rich to that of the unoccupied. It is only in the backward countries of the world that increased production is still an important object: in those most advanced, what is economically needed is a better distribution, of which one indispensable means is a stricter restraint on population. Leveling institutions, either of a just or of an unjust kind, cannot alone accomplish it; they may lower the heights of society, but they cannot, of themselves, permanently raise the depths.

On the other hand, we may suppose this better distribution of property attained, by the joint effect of the prudence and frugality of individuals, and of a system of legislation favoring equality of fortunes, so far as is consistent with the just claim of the individual to the fruits, whether great or small, of his or her own industry. We may suppose, for instance, a limitation of the sum which any one person may acquire by gift or inheritance, to the amount sufficient to constitute a moderate independence. Under this twofold influence, society would exhibit these leading features: a well-paid and affluent body of laborers; no enormous fortunes, except what were earned and accumulated during a single life-time; but a much larger body of persons than at present, not only exempt from the coarser toils, but with sufficient leisure, both physical and mental, from mechanical details, to cultivate freely the graces of life, and afford examples of them to the classes less favorably circumstanced for their growth. This condition of society, so greatly preferable to the present, is not only perfectly compatible with the stationary state, but, it would seem, more naturally allied with the state than with any other.

Principles of Economics, Alfred Marshall

Economics is a study of men as they live and move and think in the ordinary business of life. But it concerns itself chiefly with those motives which affect, most powerfully and most steadily, man's conduct in the business part of his life. Everyone who is worth anything carries his higher nature with him into business; and, there as elsewhere, he is influenced by his personal affections, by his conceptions of duty and his reverence for high ideals.

The advantage which economics has over other branches of social science appears then to arise from the fact that its special field of work gives rather larger opportunities for exact methods than any other branch. It concerns itself chiefly with those desires, aspirations and other affections of human nature, the outward manifestations of which appear as incentives to action in such a form that the force or quantity of the incentives can be estimated and measured with some approach to accuracy; and which therefore are in some degree amenable to treatment by scientific machinery. An opening is made for the methods and the tests of science as soon as the force of a person's motives—not the motives themselves—can be approximately measured by the sum of money, which he will just give up in order to secure a desired satisfaction; or again by the sum which is just required to induce him to undergo a certain fatigue.

Economists study the actions of individuals, but study them in relation to social rather than individual life; and therefore concern themselves but little with personal peculiarities of temper and character. They watch carefully the conduct of a whole class of people, sometimes the whole of a nation, sometimes only those living in a certain district, more often those engaged in some particular trade at some time and place: and by the aid of statistics, or in other ways then ascertain how much money on the average the members of the particular group, they are watching, are just willing to pay as the price of a certain thing which they desire, or how

From Alfred Marshall, *Principles of Economics*, pp. 14–15, 25–26, 33, 36–37. Reprinted by permission of St. Martin's Press, Inc., New York, The Macmillan Company of Canada, and The Macmillan Company of Houndmills Basingstoke Hampshire.

much must be offered to them to induce them to undergo a certain effort or abstinence that they dislike. The measurement of motive thus obtained is not indeed perfectly accurate; for if it were, economics would rank with the most advanced of the physical science; and not, as it actually does, with the least advanced.

The term *law* means then nothing more than a general proposition or statement of tendencies, more or less certain, more or less definite. Many such statements are made in every science. . . . Thus a law of social science, or a Social Law, is a statement of social tendencies; that is, a statement that a certain course of action may be expected under certain conditions from the members of a social group.

Economic laws, or statements of economic tendencies, are those social laws which relate to branches of conduct in which the strength of the motives chiefly concerned can be measured by a money price.

It is sometimes said that the laws of economics are "hypothetical." Of course, like every other science, it undertakes to study the effects which will be produced by certain causes, not absolutely, but subject to the condition that other things are equal, and that the causes are able to work out their effects undisturbed. Almost every scientific doctrine, when carefully and formally stated, will be found to contain some proviso to the effect that other things are equal; the action of the causes in question is supposed to be isolated, certain effects are attributed to them, but on the hypothesis that no cause is permitted to enter except those distinctly allowed for. It is true however that the condition that time must be allowed for causes to produce their effects is a source of great difficulty in economics. For meanwhile the material on which they work, and perhaps even the causes themselves, may have changed; and the tendencies which are being described will not have sufficiently "long run" in which to work themselves out fully.

Though economic analysis and general reasoning are of wide application, yet every age and every country has its own problems; and every change in social conditions is likely to require a new development of economic doctrines.

The General Theory of Employment, Interest, and Money, John Maynard Keynes

The outstanding faults of the economic society in which we live are its failure to provide for full employment and its arbitrary and inequitable distribution of wealth and incomes.

From *The General Theory of Employment, Interest, and Money*, by John Maynard Keynes. Reprinted by permission of Harcourt Brace Jovanovich, Inc., and The Royal Economic Society. (Royal Economic Society Edition of Keynes' Writings, Volume VII.)

Since the end of the 19th century significant progress towards the removal of very great disparities of wealth and income has been achieved through the instruments of direct taxation—income tax and surtax and death duties—especially in Great Britain. Many people would wish to see this process carried much further, but they are deterred by two considerations; partly by the fear of making skilful evasions too much worthwhile and also of diminishing unduly the motives towards risk-taking, but mainly, I think, by the belief that the growth of capital depends upon the strength of the motive towards individual saving and that for a large proportion of this growth we are dependent on the savings of the rich out of their superfluity. . . . We have seen that, up to the point where full employment prevails, the growth of capital depends not at all on a low propensity to consume but is, on the contrary, held back by it; and only in conditions of full employment is a low propensity to consume conducive to the growth of capital. Moreover, experience suggests that in existing conditions saving by institutions and through sinking funds is more than adequate, and that measures for the redistribution of incomes in a way likely to raise the propensity to consume may prove positively favorable to the growth of capital.

Thus our argument leads towards the conclusion that in contemporary conditions the growth of wealth, so far from being dependent on the abstinence of the rich, as is commonly supposed, is more likely to be impeded by it. One of the chief social justifications of great inequality of wealth is, therefore, removed. I am not saying that there are no other reasons, unaffected by our theory, capable of justifying some measure of inequality in some circumstances. But it does dispose of the most important of the reasons why hitherto we have thought it prudent to move carefully.

For my own part, I believe that there is social and psychological justification for significant inequalities of incomes and wealth, but not for such large disparities as exist today. There are valuable human activities which require the motive of money-making and the environment of private wealth-ownership for their full fruition. Moreover, dangerous human proclivities can be canalized into comparatively harmless channels by the existence of opportunities for money-making and private wealth, which, if they cannot be satisfied in this way, may find their outlet in cruelty, the reckless pursuit of personal power and authority, and other forms of self-aggrandizement. It is better that a man should tyrannize over his bank balance than over his fellow citizens; and whilst the former is sometimes denounced as being but a means to the latter, sometimes at least it is an alternative. But it is not necessary for the stimulation of these activities and the satisfaction of these proclivities that the game should be played for such high stakes as at present. Much lower stakes will serve the purpose equally well, as soon as the players are accustomed to them.

The task of transmuting human nature must not be confused with the task of managing it. Though in the ideal commonwealth men may have been taught or inspired or bred to take no interest in the stakes, it may still be wise and prudent statesmanship to allow the game to be played, subject to rules and limitations, so long as the average man, or even a significant section of the community, is in fact strongly addicted to the money-making passion.

The State will have to exercise a guiding influence on the propensity to consume partly through its scheme of taxation, partly by fixing the rate of interest, and partly, perhaps, in other ways. Furthermore, it seems unlikely that the influence of banking policy on the rate of interest will be sufficient by itself to determine an optimum rate of investment. I conceive, therefore, that a somewhat comprehensive socialization of investment will prove the only means of securing an approximation to full employment; though this need not exclude all manner of compromises and of devices by which public authority will cooperate with private initiative. But beyond this no obvious case is made out for a system of State Socialism which would embrace most of the economic life of the community. It is not the ownership of the instruments of production which it is important for the State to assume. If the State is able to determine the aggregate amount of resources devoted to augmenting the instruments and the basic rate of reward to those who own them, it will have accomplished all that is necessary.

Excerpts from
Capitalism and Freedom

MILTON FRIEDMAN

Here, in capsule form, are sections from the best-known statement of the "libertarian" view. The interested reader may want to compare this economic philosophy with its critique in the next essay.

In a much quoted passage in his inaugural address, President Kennedy said, "Ask not what your country can do for you—ask what you can do for your country." It is a striking sign of the temper of our times that the controversy about this passage centered on its origin and not on its content. Neither half of the statement expresses a relation between the citizen and his government that is worthy of the ideals of free men in a free society. The paternalistic "what your country can do for you" implies that government is the patron, the citizen the ward, a view that is at odds with the free man's belief in his own responsibility for his own destiny. The organismic, "what you can do for your country" implies that government is the master or the deity, the citizen, the servant or the votary. To the free man, the country is the collection of individuals who compose it, not something over and above them. He is proud of a common heritage and loyal to common traditions. But he regards government as a means, an instrumentality, neither a grantor of favors and gifts, nor a master or god to be blindly worshipped and served. He recognizes no national goal except as it is the consensus of the goals that the citizens severally serve. He recognizes no national purpose except as it is the consensus of the purposes for which the citizens severally strive.

The free man will ask neither what his country can do for him nor what he can do for his country. He will ask rather "What can I and my compatriots do through government" to help us discharge our individual

From *Capitalism and Freedom,* by Milton Friedman (Chicago: University of Chicago Press, 1962), pp. 1–21, 196–202. © 1962 by the University of Chicago. Reprinted by permission.

responsibilities, to achieve our several goals and purposes, and above all, to protect our freedom? And he will accompany this question with another: How can we keep the government we create from becoming a Franken- stein that will destroy the very freedom we establish it to protect? Freedom is a rare and delicate plant. Our minds tell us, and history confirms, that the great threat to freedom is the concentration of power. Government is necessary to preserve our freedom, it is an instrument through which we can exercise our freedom; yet by concentrating power in political hands, it is also a threat to freedom. Even though the men who wield this power initially be of good will and even though they be not corrupted by the power they exercise, the power will both attract and form men of a different stamp.

How can we benefit from the promise of government while avoiding the threat to freedom? Two broad principles embodied in our Constitution give an answer that has preserved our freedom so far, though they have been violated repeatedly in practice while proclaimed as precept.

First, the scope of government must be limited. Its major function must be to protect our freedom both from the enemies outside our gates and from our fellow-citizens: to preserve law and order, to enforce private contracts, to foster competitive markets. Beyond this major function, government may enable us at times to accomplish jointly what we would find it more difficult or expensive to accomplish severally. However, any such use of government is fraught with danger. We should not and cannot avoid using government in this way. But there should be a clear and large balance of advantages before we do. By relying primarily on voluntary cooperation and private enterprise, in both economic and other activities, we can insure that the private sector is a check on the powers of the governmental sector and an effective protection of freedom of speech, of religion, and of thought.

The second broad principle is that government power must be dispersed. If government is to exercise power, better in the county than in the state, better in the state than in Washington. If I do not like what my local community does, be it in sewage disposal, or zoning, or schools, I can move to another local community, and though few may take this step, the mere possibility acts as a check. If I do not like what my state does, I can move to another. If I do not like what Washington imposes, I have few alternatives in this world of jealous nations.

The very difficulty of avoiding the enactments of the federal govern- ment is of course the great attraction of centralization to many of its proponents. It will enable them more effectively, they believe, to legis- late programs that—as they see it—are in the interest of the public, whether it be the transfer of income from the rich to the poor or from private to governmental purposes. They are in a sense right. But this coin has two sides. The power to do good is also the power to do harm; those who control the power today may not tomorrow; and, more important, what one man regards as good, another may regard as harm. The great tragedy of the drive to centralization, as of the drive to extend the scope of government in general, is that it is mostly led by men of good will who will be the first to rue its consequences.

The preservation of freedom is the protective reason for limiting and decentralizing governmental power. But there is also a constructive reason. The great advances of civilization, whether in architecture or painting, in science or literature, in industry or agriculture, have never come from centralized government. Columbus did not set out to seek a new route to China in response to a majority directive of a parliament, though he was partly financed by an absolute monarch. Newton and Leibnitz; Einstein and Bohr; Shakespeare, Milton, and Pasternak; Whitney, McCormick, Edison, and Ford; Jane Addams, Florence Nightingale, and Albert Schweitzer; no one of these opened new frontiers in human knowledge and understanding, in literature, in technical possibilities, or in the relief of human misery in response to governmental directives. Their achievements were the product of individual genius, of strongly held minority views, of a social climate permitting variety and diversity.

Government can never duplicate the variety and diversity of individual action. At any moment in time, by imposing uniform standards in housing, or nutrition, or clothing, government could undoubtedly improve the level of living of many individuals; by imposing uniform standards in schooling, road construction, or sanitation, central government could undoubtedly improve the level of performance in many local areas and perhaps even on the average of all communities. But in the process, government would replace progress by stagnation, it would substitute uniform mediocrity for the variety essential for that experimentation which can bring tomorrow's laggards above today's mean. . . .

It is widely believed that politics and economics are separate and largely unconnected; that individual freedom is a political problem and material welfare an economic problem; and that any kind of political arrangements can be combined with any kind of economic arrangements. The chief contemporary manifestation of this idea is the advocacy of "democratic socialism" by many who condemn out of hand the restrictions on individual freedom imposed by "totalitarian socialism" in Russia, and who are persuaded that it is possible for a country to adopt the essential features of Russian economic arrangements and yet to ensure individual freedom through political arrangements. The thesis of this chapter is that such a view is a delusion, that there is an intimate connection between economics and politics, that only certain combinations of political and economic arrangements are possible and that in particular, a society which is socialist cannot also be democratic, in the sense of guaranteeing individual freedom.

Economic arrangements play a dual role in the promotion of a free society. On the one hand, freedom in economic arrangements is itself a component of freedom broadly understood, so economic freedom is an end in itself. In the second place, economic freedom is also an indispensable means toward the achievement of political freedom.

The first of these roles of economic freedom needs special emphasis because intellectuals in particular have a strong bias against regarding this aspect of freedom as important. They tend to express contempt for what they regard as material aspects of life, and to regard their own pursuit of allegedly higher values as on a different plane of significance and as deserving of special attention. For most citizens of the country, however, if not for the intellectual, the direct importance of economic freedom is at least comparable in significance to the indirect importance of economic freedom as a means to political freedom.

The citizen of Great Britain, who after World War II was not permitted to spend his vacation in the United States because of exchange control, was being deprived of an essential freedom no less than the citizen of the United States, who was denied the opportunity to spend his vacation in Russia because of his political views. The one was ostensibly an economic limitation on freedom and the other a politicial limitation, yet there is no essential difference between the two.

The citizen of the United States who is compelled by law to devote something like 10 percent of his income to the purchase of a particular kind of retirement contract, administered by the government, is being deprived of a corresponding part of his personal freedom. How strongly this deprivation may be felt and its closeness to the deprivation of religious freedom, which all would regard as "civil" or "political" rather than "economic," were dramatized by an episode involving a group of farmers of the Amish sect. On grounds of principle, this group regarded compulsory federal old-age programs as an infringement of their personal individual freedom and refused to pay taxes or accept benefits. As a result, some of their livestock were sold by auction in order to satisfy claims for social security levies. True, the number of citizens who regard compulsory old-age insurance as a deprivation of freedom may be few, but the believer in freedom has never counted noses.

A citizen of the United States who under the laws of various states is not free to follow the occupation of his own choosing unless he can get a license for it, is likewise being deprived of an essential part of his freedom. So is the man who would like to exchange some of his goods with, say, a Swiss for a watch but is prevented from doing so by a quota. So also is the Californian who was thrown into jail for selling Alka-Seltzer at a price below that set by the manufacturer under so-called fair trade laws. So also is the farmer who cannot grow the amount of wheat he wants. And so on. Clearly, economic freedom, in and of itself, is an extremely important part of total freedom.

Viewed as a means to the end of political freedom, economic arrangements are important because of their effect on the concentration or dispersion of power. The kind of economic organization that provides economic freedom directly, namely, competitive capitalism, also promotes political freedom because it separates economic power from political power and in this way enables the one to offset the other.

Historical evidence speaks with a single voice on the relation between political freedom and a free market. I know of no example in time or place of a society that has been marked by a large measure of political freedom, and that has not also used something comparable to a free market to organize the bulk of economic activity.

Because we live in a largely free society, we tend to forget how limited is the span of time and the part of the globe for which there has ever been anything like political freedom: the typical state of mankind is tyranny, servitude, and misery. The 19th century and early 20th century in the Western world stand out as striking exceptions to the general trend of historical development. Political freedom in this instance clearly came along with the free market and the development of capitalist institutions. So also did political freedom in the golden age of Greece and in the early days of the Roman era.

History suggests only that capitalism is a necessary condition for political freedom. Clearly it is not a sufficient condition. Fascist Italy and Fascist Spain, Germany at various times in the last 70 years, Japan before World Wars I and II, tzarist Russia in the decades before World War I— are all societies that cannot conceivably be described as politically free. Yet, in each, private enterprise was the dominant form of economic organization. It is therefore clearly possible to have economic arrangements that are fundamentally capitalist and political arrangements that are not free.

Even in those societies, the citizenry had a good deal more freedom than citizens of a modern totalitarian state like Russia or Nazi Germany, in which economic totalitarianism is combined with political totalitarianism. Even in Russia under the Tzars, it was possible for some citizens, under some circumstances, to change their jobs without getting permission from political authority, because capitalism and the existence of private property provided some check to the centralized power of the state.

The relation between political and economic freedom is complex and by no means unilateral. In the early 19th century, Bentham and the Philosophical Radicals were inclined to regard political freedom as a means to economic freedom. They believed that the masses were being hampered by the restrictions that were being imposed upon them, and that if political reform gave the bulk of the people the vote, they would do what was good for them, which was to vote for laissez faire. In retrospect, one cannot say that they were wrong. There was a large measure of political reform that was accompanied by economic reform in the direction of a great deal of laissez faire. An enormous increase in the well-being of the masses followed this change in economic arrangements.

The triumph of Benthamic liberalism in 19th-century England was followed by a reaction toward increasing intervention by government in economic affairs. This tendency to collectivism was greatly accelerated, both in England and elsewhere, by the two World Wars. Welfare rather than freedom became the dominant note in democratic countries. Recognizing the implicit threat to individualism, the intellectual descendants of the Philosophical Radicals—Dicey, Mises, Hayek, and Simons, to mention only a few—feared that a continued movement toward centralized control of economic activity would prove *The Road to Serfdom,* as Hayek entitled his penetrating analysis of the process. Their emphasis was on economic freedom as a means toward political freedom.

Events since the end of World War II display still a different relation between economic and political freedom. Collectivist economic planning has indeed interfered with individual freedom. At least in some countries, however, the result has not been the suppression of freedom, but the reversal of economic policy. England again provides the most striking example. The turning point was perhaps the "control of engagements" order which, despite great misgivings, the Labour party found it necessary to impose in order to carry out its economic policy. Fully enforced and carried through, the law would have involved centralized allocation of individuals to occupations. This conflicted so sharply with personal liberty that it was enforced in a negligible number of cases, and then repealed after the law had been in effect for only a short period. Its repeal ushered in a decided shift in economic policy, marked by reduced reliance on centralized "plans" and "programs," by the dismantling of many controls, and by increased emphasis on the private market. A similar shift in policy occurred in most other democratic countries.

The proximate explanation of these shifts in policy is the limited success of central planning or its outright failure to achieve stated objectives. However, this failure is itself to be attributed, at least in some measure, to the political implications of central planning and to an unwillingness to follow out its logic when doing so requires trampling rough-shod on treasured private rights. It may well be that the shift is only a temporary interruption in the collectivist trend of this century. Even so, it illustrates the close relation between political freedom and economic arrangements.

The basic problem of social organization is how to coordinate the economic activities of large numbers of people. Even in relatively backward societies, extensive division of labor and specialization of function is required to make effective use of available resources. In advanced societies, the scale on which coordination is needed, to take full advantage of the opportunities offered by modern science and technology, is enormously greater. Literally millions of people are involved in providing one another with their daily bread, let alone with their yearly automobiles. The challenge to the believer in liberty is to reconcile this widespread interdependence with individual freedom.

Fundamentally, there are only two ways of coordinating the economic activities of millions. One is central direction involving the use of coercion —the technique of the army and of the modern totalitarian state. The other is voluntary cooperation of individuals—the technique of the market place.

The possibility of coordination through voluntary cooperation rests on the elementary—yet frequently denied—proposition that both parties to an economic transaction benefit from it, *provided the transaction is bilaterally voluntary and informed.*

Exchange can therefore bring about coordination without coercion. A working model of a society organized through voluntary exchange is a *free private enterprise exchange economy*—what we have been calling competitive capitalism.

In its simplest form, such a society consists of a number of independent households—a collection of Robinson Crusoes, as it were. Each household uses the resources it controls to produce goods and services that it exchanges for goods and services produced by other households, on terms mutually acceptable to the two parties to the bargain. It is thereby enabled to satisfy its wants indirectly by producing goods and services for others, rather than directly by producing goods for its own immediate use. The incentive for adopting this indirect route is, of course, the increased product made possible by division of labor and specialization of function. Since the household always has the alternative of producing directly for itself, it need not enter into any exchange unless it benefits from it. Hence, no exchange will take place unless both parties do benefit from it. Cooperation is thereby achieved without coercion.

Specialization of function and division of labor would not go far if the ultimate productive unit were the household. In a modern society, we have gone much farther. We have introduced enterprises which are intermediaries between individuals in their capacities as suppliers of service and as purchasers of goods. And similarly, specialization of function and division of labor could not go very far if we had to continue to rely on the barter of product for product. In consequence, money has been introduced as a means of facilitating exchange, and of enabling the acts of purchase and of sale to be separated into two parts.

Despite the important role of enterprises and of money in our actual economy, and despite the numerous and complex problems they raise, the central characteristic of the market technique of achieving coordination is fully displayed in the simple exchange economy that contains neither enterprises nor money. As in that simple model, so in the complex enterprise and money-exchange economy, cooperation is strictly individual and voluntary *provided*: (1) that enterprises are private, so that the ultimate contracting parties are individuals and (2) that individuals are effectively free to enter or not to enter into any particular exchange, so that every transaction is strictly voluntary.

It is far easier to state these provisos in general terms than to spell them out in detail, or to specify precisely the institutional arrangements most conducive to their maintenance. Indeed, much of technical economic literature is concerned with precisely these questions. The basic requisite is the maintenance of law and order to prevent physical coercion of one individual by another and to enforce contracts voluntarily entered into, thus giving substance to "private." Aside from this, perhaps the most difficult problems arise from monopoly—which inhibits effective freedom by denying individuals alternatives to the particular exchange—and from "neighborhood effects"—effects on third parties for which it is not feasible to charge or recompense them. . . .

So long as effective freedom of exchange is maintained, the central feature of the market organization of economic activity is that it prevents one person from interfering with another in respect of most of his activities. The consumer is protected from coercion by the seller because of the presence of other sellers with whom he can deal. The seller is protected from coercion by the consumer because of other consumers to whom he can sell. The employee is protected from coercion by the employer because of other employers for whom he can work, and so on. And the market does this impersonally and without centralized authority.

Indeed, a major source of objection to a free economy is precisely that it does this task so well. It gives people what they want instead of what a particular group thinks they ought to want. Underlying most arguments against the free market is a lack of belief in freedom itself.

The existence of a free market does not of course eliminate the need for government. On the contrary, government is essential both as a forum for determining the "rules of the game" and as an umpire to interpret and enforce the rules decided on. What the market does is to reduce greatly the range of issues that must be decided through political means, and thereby to minimize the extent to which government need participate directly in the game. The characteristic feature of action through political channels is that it tends to require or enforce substantial conformity. The great advantage of the market, on the other hand, is that it permits wide diversity. It is, in political terms, a system of proportional representation. Each man can vote, as it were, for the color of tie he wants and get it; he does not have to see what color the majority wants and then, if he is in the minority, submit.

It is this feature of the market that we refer to when we say that the market provides economic freedom. But this characteristic also has implications that go far beyond the narrowly economic. Political freedom means the absence of coercion of a man by his fellow men. The fundamental threat to freedom is power to coerce, be it in the hands of a monarch, a dictator, an oligarchy, or a momentary majority. The preservation of freedom requires the elimination of such concentration of power to the fullest possible extent and the dispersal and distribution of whatever power cannot be eliminated—a system of checks and balances. By removing the organization of economic activity from the control of political authority, the market eliminates this source of coercive power. It enables economic strength to be a check to political power rather than a reinforcement.

Economic power can be widely dispersed. There is no law of conservation which forces the growth of new centers of economic strength to be at the expense of existing centers. Political power, on the other hand, is more difficult to decentralize. There can be numerous small independent governments. But it is far more difficult to maintain numerous equipotent small centers of political power in a single large government than it is to have numerous centers of economic strength in a single large economy. There can be many millionaires in one large economy. But can there be more than one really outstanding leader, one person on whom the energies and enthusiasms of his countrymen are centered? If the central government gains power, it is likely to be at the expense of local governments. There seems to be something like a fixed total of political power to be distributed. Consequently, if economic power is joined to political power, concentration seems almost inevitable. On the other hand, if economic power is kept in separate hands from political power, it can serve as a check and a counter to political power.

The force of this abstract argument can perhaps best be demonstrated by example. Let us consider first, a hypothetical example that may help to bring out the principles involved, and then some actual examples from recent experience that illustrate the way in which the market works to preserve political freedom.

One feature of a free society is surely the freedom of individuals to advocate and propagandize openly for a radical change in the structure of the society—so long as the advocacy is restricted to persuasion and does not include force or other forms of coercion. It is a mark of the political freedom of a capitalist society that men can openly advocate and work for socialism. Equally, political freedom in a socialist society would require that men be free to advocate the introduction of capitalism. How could the freedom to advocate capitalism be preserved and protected in a socialist society?

In order for men to advocate anything, they must in the first place be able to earn a living. This already raises a problem in a socialist society, since all jobs are under the direct control of political authorities. It would take an act of self-denial whose difficulty is underlined by experience in the United States after World War II with the problem of "security" among federal employees, for a socialist government to permit its employees to advocate policies directly contrary to official doctrine.

But let us suppose this act of self-denial to be achieved. For advocacy of capitalism to mean anything, the proponents must be able to finance their cause—to hold public meetings, publish pamphlets, buy radio time, issue newspapers and magazines, and so on. How could they raise the funds? There might and probably would be men in the socialist society with large incomes, perhaps even large capital sums in the form of government bonds and the like, but these would of necessity be high public officials. It is possible to conceive of a minor socialist official retaining his job although openly advocating capitalism. It strains credulity to imagine the socalist top brass financing such "subversive" activities.

The only recourse for funds would be to raise small amounts from a large number of minor officials. But this is no real answer. To tap these sources, many people would already have to be persuaded, and our whole problem is how to initiate and finance a campaign to do so. Radical movements in capitalist societies have never been financed this way. They have typically been supported by a few wealthy individuals who have become persuaded—by a Frederick Vanderbilt Field, or an Anita McCormick Blaine, or a Corliss Lamont, or by a Friedrich Engels. This is a role of inequality of wealth in preserving political freedom that is seldom noted—the role of the patron.

In a capitalist society, it is only necessary to convince a few wealthy people to get funds to launch any idea, however strange, and there are many such persons, many independent foci of support. And, indeed, it is not even necessary to persuade people or financial institutions with available funds of the soundness of the ideas to be propagated. It is only necessary to persuade them that the propagation can be financially successful; that the newspaper or magizine or book or other venture will be profitable. The competitive publisher, for example, cannot afford to publish only writing with which he personally agrees; his touchstone must be the likelihood that the market will be large enough to yield a satisfactory return on his investment.

In this way, the market breaks the vicious circle and makes it possible ultimately to finance such ventures by small amounts from many people without first persuading them. There are no such possibilities in the socialist society; there is only the all-powerful state.

Let us stretch our imagination and suppose that a socialist government is aware of this problem and is composed of people anxious to preserve freedom. Could it provide the funds? Perhaps, but it is difficult to see how. It could establish a bureau for subsidizing subversive propaganda. But how could it choose whom to support? If it gave to all who asked, it would shortly find itself out of funds, for socialism cannot repeal the elementary economic law that a sufficiently high price will call forth a large supply. Make the advocacy of radical causes sufficiently remunerative, and the supply of advocates will be unlimited.

Moreover, freedom to advocate unpopular causes does not require that such advocacy be without cost. On the contrary, no society could be stable if advocacy of radical change were costless, much less subsidized. It is entirely appropriate that men make sacrifices to advocate causes in which they deeply believe. Indeed, it is important to preserve freedom only for people who are willing to practice self-denial, for otherwise freedom degenerates into license and irresponsibility. What is essential is that the cost of advocating unpopular causes be tolerable and not prohibitive.

But we are not yet through. In a free market society, it is enough to have the funds. The suppliers of paper are as willing to sell it to the *Daily Worker* as to the *Wall Street Journal*. In a socialist society, it would not be enough to have the funds. The hypothetical supporter of capitalism would have to persuade a government factory making paper to sell to him, the government printing press to print his pamphlets, a government post office to distribute them among the people, a government agency to rent him a hall in which to talk, and so on.

Perhaps there is some way in which one could overcome these difficulties and preserve freedom in a socialist society. One cannot say it is utterly impossible. What is clear, however, is that there are very real difficulties in establishing institutions that will effectively preserve the possibility of dissent. So far as I know, none of the people who have been in favor of socialism and also in favor of freedom have really faced up to this issue, or made even a respectable start at developing the institutional arrangements that would permit freedom under socialism. By constrast, it is clear how a free market capitalist society fosters freedom.

A striking practical example of these abstract principles is the experience of Winston Churchill. From 1933 to the outbreak of World War II, Churchill was not permitted to talk over the British radio, which was, of course, a government monopoly administered by the British Broadcasting Corporation. Here was a leading citizen of his country, a Member of Parliament, a former cabinet minister, a man who was desperately trying by every device possible to persuade his countrymen to take steps to ward

off the menace of Hitler's Germany. He was not permitted to talk over the
radio to the British people because the BBC was a government monopoly
and his position was too "controversial."

Another striking example, reported in the January 26, 1959 issue of
Time, has to do with the "Blacklist Fadeout." Says the *Time* story:

> The Oscar-awarding ritual is Hollywood's biggest pitch for dignity,
> but two years ago dignity suffered. When one Robert Rich was
> announced as top writer for the *The Brave One*, he never stepped
> forward. Robert Rich was a pseudonym, masking one of about 150
> writers . . . blacklisted by the industry since 1947 as suspected Com-
> munists or fellow travelers. The case was particularly embarrassing
> because the Motion Picture Academy had barred any Communist or
> Fifth Amendment pleader from Oscar competition. Last week both
> the Communist rule and the mystery of Rich's identity were sud-
> denly rescripted.
>
> Rich turned out to be Dalton (*Johnny Got His Gun*) Trumbo, one of
> the original "Hollywood Ten" writers who refused to testify at the
> 1947 hearings on Communism in the movie industry. Said producer
> Frank King, who had stoutly insisted that Robert Rich was "a young
> guy in Spain with a beard": "We have an obligation to our stock-
> holders to buy the best script we can. Trumbo brought us *The Brave
> One* and we bought it". . . .
>
> In effect is was the formal end of the Hollywood blacklist. For
> barred writers, the informal end came long ago. At least 15 percent
> of current Hollywood films are reportedly written by blacklist mem-
> bers. Said Producer King, "There are more ghosts in Hollywood
> than in Forest Lawn. Every company in town has used the work of
> blacklisted people. We're just the first to confirm what everybody
> knows."

One may believe, as I do, that communism would destroy all of our
freedoms, one may be opposed to it as firmly and as strongly as possible,
and yet, at the same time, also believe that in a free society it is intolerable
for a man to be prevented from making voluntary arrangements with
others that are mutually attractive because be believes in or is trying to
promote communism. His freedom includes his freedom to promote communism. Freedom also, of course, includes the freedom of others not to deal
with him under those circumstances. The Hollywood blacklist was an
unfree act that destroys freedom because it was a collusive arrangement
that used coercive means to prevent voluntary exchanges. It didn't work
precisely because the market made it costly for people to preserve the
blacklist. The commercial emphasis, the fact that people who are running
enterprises have an incentive to make as much money as they can, protected the freedom of the individuals who were blacklisted by providing

them with an alternative form of employment, and by giving people an incentive to employ them.

If Hollywood and the movie industry had been government enterprises or if in England it had been a question of employment by the British Broadcasting Corporation it is difficult to believe that the "Hollywood Ten" or their equivalent would have found employment. Equally, it is difficult to believe that under those circumstances, strong proponents of individualism and private enterprise—or indeed strong proponents of any view other than the status quo—would be able to get employment.

Another example of the role of the market in preserving political freedom, was revealed in our experience with McCarthyism. Entirely aside from the substantive issues involved, and the merits of the charges made, what protection did individuals, and in particular government employees, have against irresponsible accusations and probings into matters that it went against their conscience to reveal? Their appeal to the Fifth Amendment would have been a hollow mockery without an alternative to government employment.

Their fundamental protection was the existence of a private market economy in which they could earn a living. Here again, the protection was not absolute. Many potential private employers were, rightly or wrongly, averse to hiring those pilloried. It may well be that there was far less justification for the costs imposed on many of the people involved than for the costs generally imposed on people who advocate unpopular causes. But the important point is that the costs were limited and not prohibitive, as they would have been if government employment had been the only possibility.

It is of interest to note that a disproportionately large fraction of people involved apparently went into the most competitive sectors of the economy—small business, trade, farming—where the market approaches most closely the ideal free market. No one who buys bread knows whether the wheat from which it is made was grown by a Communist or a Republican, by a constitutionalist or a Facist, or, for that matter, by a Negro or a white. This illustrates how an impersonal market separates economic activities from political views and protects men from being discriminated against in their economic activities for reasons that are irrevelant to their productivity—whether these reasons are associated with their views or their color.

As this example suggests, the groups in our society that have the most at stake in the preservation and strengthening of competitive capitalism are those minority groups which can most easily become the object of the distrust and enmity of the majority—the Negroes, the Jews, the foreign-born, to mention only the most obvious. Yet, paradoxically enough, the enemies of the free market—the Socialists and Communists—have been recruited in disproportionate measure from these groups. Instead of recognizing that the existence of the market has protected them from the attitudes of their fellow countrymen, they mistakenly attribute the residual discrimination to the market.

In the 1920s and the 1930s, intellectuals in the United States were overwhelmingly persuaded that capitalism was a defective system inhibiting economic well-being and thereby freedom, and that the hope for the future lay in a greater measure of deliberate control by political authorities over economic affairs. The conversion of the intellectuals was not achieved by the example of any actual collectivist society, though it undoubtedly was much hastened by the establishment of a communist society in Russia and the glowing hopes placed in it. The conversion of the intellectuals was achieved by a comparison between the existing state of affairs, with all its injustices and defects, and a hypothetical state of affairs as it might be. The actual was compared with the ideal.

The attitudes of that time are still with us. There is still a tendency to regard any existing government intervention as desirable, to attribute all evils to the market, and to evaluate new proposals for government control in their ideal form, as they might work if run by able, disinterested men, free from the pressure of special interest groups. The proponents of limited government and free enterprise are still on the defensive.

Yet, conditions have changed. We now have several decades of experience with governmental intervention. It is no longer necessary to compare the market as it actually operates and government intervention as it ideally might operate. We can compare the actual with the actual. Which if any of the great "reforms" of past decades has achieved its objectives? Have the good intentions of the proponents of these reforms been realized?

Regulation of the railroads to protect the consumer quickly became an instrument whereby the railroads could protect themselves from the competition of newly emerging rivals—at the expense, of course, of the consumer.

An income tax initially enacted at low rates and later seized upon as a means to redistribute income in favor of the lower classes has become a facade, covering loopholes and special provisions that render rates that are highly graduated on paper largely ineffective. A flat rate of 23.5 percent on presently taxable income would yield as much revenue as the present rates graduated from 20 to 91 percent. An income tax intended to reduce inequality and promote the diffusion of wealth has in practice fostered reinvestment of corporate earnings, thereby favoring the growth of large corporations, inhibiting the operation of the capital market, and discouraging the establishment of new enterprises.

Monetary reforms, intended to promote stability in economic activity and prices, exacerbated inflation during and after World War I and fostered a higher degree of instability thereafter than had ever been experienced before. The monetary authorities they established bear primary responsibility for converting a serious economic contraction into the catastrophe of the Great Depression from 1929 to 1933. A system established largely to prevent bank panics produced the most severe banking panic in American history.

An agricultural program intended to help impecunious farmers and to remove what were alleged to be basic dislocations in the organization of agriculture has become a national scandal that has wasted public funds, distorted the use of resources, riveted increasingly heavy and detailed controls on farmers, interfered seriously with United States foreign policy, and withal has done little to help the impecunious farmer.

A housing program intended to improve the housing conditions of the poor, to reduce juvenile delinquency, and to contribute to the removal of urban slums, has worsened the housing conditions of the poor, contributed to juvenile delinquency, and spread urban blight.

In the 1930s, "labor" was synonymous with "labor union" to the intellectual community; faith in the purity and virtue of labor unions was on a par with faith in home and motherhood. Extensive legislation was enacted to favor labor unions and to foster "fair" labor relation. Labor unions waxed in strength. By the 1950s, "labor union" was almost a dirty word; it was no longer synonymous with "labor," no longer automatically to be taken for granted as on the side of the angels.

Social security measures were enacted to make receipt of assistance a matter of right, to eliminate the need for direct relief and assistance. Millions now receive social security benefits. Yet the relief rolls grow and the sums spent on direct assistance mount.

The list can easily be lengthened: the silver purchase program of the 1930s, public power projects, foreign aid programs of the postwar years, F.C.C., urban redevelopment programs, the stockpiling program—these and many more have had effects very different and generally quite opposite from those intended.

There have been some exceptions. The expressways crisscrossing the country, magnificent dams spanning great rivers, orbiting satellites are all tributes to the capacity of government to command great resources. The school system, with all its defects and problems, with all the possibility of improvement through bringing into more effective play the forces of the market, has widened the opportunities available to American youth and contributed to the extension of freedom. It is a testament to the public-spirited efforts of the many tens of thousands who have served on local school boards and to the willingness of the public to bear heavy taxes for what they regarded as a public purpose. The Sherman antitrust laws, with all their problems of detailed administration, have by their very existence fostered competition. Public health measures have contributed to the reduction of infectious disease. Assistance measures have relieved suffering and distress. Local authorities have often provided facilities essential to the life of communities. Law and order have been maintained, though in many a large city the performance of even this elementary function of government has been far from satisfactory. As a citizen of Chicago, I speak feelingly.

If a balance be struck, there can be little doubt that the record is dismal. The greater part of the new ventures undertaken by government in the past few decades have failed to achieve their objectives. The United States has continued to progress; its citizens have become better fed, better clothed, better housed, and better transported; class and social distinctions have narrowed; minority groups have become less disadvantaged; popular culture has advanced by leaps and bounds. All this has been the product of the initiative and drive of individuals cooperating through the free market. Government measures have hampered not helped this development. We have been able to afford and surmount these measures only because of the extraordinary fecundity of the market. The invisible hand has been more potent for progress than the visible hand for retrogression.

Is it an accident that so many of the governmental reforms of recent decades have gone awry, that the bright hopes have turned to ashes? Is it simply because the programs are faulty in detail?

I believe the answer is clearly in the negative. The central defect of these measures is that they seek through government to force people to act against their own immediate interests in order to promote a supposedly general interest. They seek to resolve what is supposedly a conflict of interest, or a difference in view about interests, not by establishing a framework that will eliminate the conflict, or by persuading people to have different interests, but by forcing people to act against their own interest. They substitute the values of outsiders for the values of participants; either some telling others what is good for them, or the government taking from some to benefit others. These measures are therefore countered by one of the strongest and most creative forces known to man—the attempt by millions of individuals to promote their own interests, to live their lives by their own values. This is the major reason why the measures have so often had the opposite of the effects intended. It is also one of the major strengths of a free society and explains why governmental regulation does not strangle it.

The interests of which I speak are not simply narrow self-regarding interests. On the contrary, they include the whole range of values that men hold dear and for which they are willing to spend their fortunes and sacrifice their lives. The Germans who lost their lives opposing Adolf Hitler were pursuing their interests as they saw them. So also are the men and women who devote great effort and time to charitable, educational, and religious activities. Naturally, such interests are the major ones for few men. It is the virtue of a free society that it nonetheless permits these interests full scope and does not subordinate them to the narrow materialistic interests that dominate the bulk of mankind. That is why capitalist societies are less materialistic than collectivist societies.

Why is it, in light of the record, that the burden of proof still seems to rest on those of us who oppose new government programs and who seek to reduce the already unduly large role of government? Let Dicey answer: "The beneficial effect of State intervention, especially in the form of legislation, is direct, immediate, and, so to speak, visible, whilst its evil effects are gradual and indirect, and lie out of sight.... Nor ... do most people keep in mind that State inspectors may be incompetent, careless, or even occasionally corrupt...; few are those who realize the undeniable truth that State help kills self-help. Hence the majority of mankind must almost of necessity look with undue favor upon governmental intervention. This natural bias can be counteracted only by the existence, in a given society,... of a presumption or prejudice in favor of individual liberty, that is, of laissez faire. The mere decline, therefore, of faith in self-help— and that such a decline has taken place is certain—is of itself sufficient to account for the growth of legislation tending towards socialism."

The preservation and expansion of freedom are today threatened from two directions. The one threat is obvious and clear. It is the external threat coming from the evil men in the Kremlin who promise to bury us. The other threat is far more subtle. It is the internal threat coming from men of good intentions and good will who wish to reform us. Impatient with the slowness of persuasion and example to achieve the great social changes they envision, they are anxious to use the power of the state to achieve their ends and confident of their own ability to do so. Yet if they gained the power, they would fail to achieve their immediate aims and, in addition, would produce a collective state from which they would recoil in horror and of which they would be among the first victims. Concentrated power is not rendered harmless by the good intentions of those who create it.

The two threats unfortunately reinforce one another. Even if we avoid a nuclear holocaust, the threat from the Kremlin requires us to devote a sizable fraction of our resources to our military defense. The importance of government as a buyer of so much of our output, and the sole buyer of the output of many firms and industries, already concentrates a dangerous amount of economic power in the hands of the political authorities, changes the environment in which business operates and the criteria relevant for business success, and in these and other ways endangers a free market. This danger we cannot avoid. But we needlessly intensify it by continuing the present widespread governmental intervention in areas unrelated to the military defense of the nation and by undertaking ever new governmental programs—from medical care for the aged to lunar exploration.

As Adam Smith once said, "There is much ruin in a nation." Our basic structure of values and the interwoven network of free institutions will withstand much. I believe that we shall be able to preserve and extend freedom despite the size of the military programs and despite the economic powers already concentrated in Washington. But we shall be able to do so only if we awake to the threat that we face, only if we persuade our fellow men that free institutions offer a surer, if perhaps at times a slower, route to the ends they seek than the coercive power of the state. The glimmerings of change that are already apparent in the intellectual climate are a hopeful augury.

Elegant Tombstones:
A Note on Friedman's Freedom

C. B. MACPHERSON

Although it is not in itself a statement of economic "philosophy,"
Macpherson's reply to Friedman is germane to the problem of using
economics to achieve an historical perspective.

Academic political scientists who want their students to think about
the problem of liberty in the modern state are properly anxious to have
them confront at first-hand various contemporary theoretical positions on
the relation between freedom and capitalism. The range of positions is
wide: at one extreme freedom is held to be incompatible with capitalism;
at the other freedom is held to be impossible except in a capitalist society;
in between, all sorts of necessary or possible relations are asserted. Different concepts of freedom are involved in some of these positions, similar
concepts in others; and different models of capitalism (and of socialism)
are sometimes being used. It is clearly important to sort them out. But
there is some difficulty in finding adequate theoretical expositions of the
second extreme position, which might be called the pure market theory
of liberalism. These are very few of them. Probably the most effective, and
the one most often cast in the role, is Milton Friedman's *Capitalism and
Freedom* which is now apt to be treated by political scientists as the
classic defense of free-market liberalism. As such it deserves more notice
from the political theorists' standpoint than it got on publication, when
its technical arguments about the possibility of returning to laissez faire
attracted most attention. Whether or not *Capitalism and Freedom* is now
properly treated as the classic defense of the pure market theory of liberalism, it is at least a classic example of the difficulty of moving from the level

From *Canadian Journal of Political Science* (March 1968), pp. 95–106. Reprinted by permission
of the Canadian Political Science Association, Kingston, Ontario, and the author.

of controversy about laissez faire to the level of fundamental concepts of freedom and the market.

This note deals with (1) an error which vitiates Friedman's demonstration that competitive capitalism coordinates men's economic activities without coercion; (2) the inadequacy of his arguments that capitalism is a necessary condition of political freedom and that socialism is inconsistent with political freedom; and (3) the fallacy of his case for the ethical adequacy of the capitalist principle of distribution.

Professor Friedman's demonstration that the capitalist market economy can coordinate economic activities without coercion rests on an elementary conceptual error. His argument runs as follows. He shows first that in a simple market model, where each individual or household controls resources enabling it to produce goods and services either directly for itself or for exchange, there will be production for exchange because of the increased product made possible by specialization. But "since the household always has the alternative of producing directly for itself, it need not enter into any exchange unless it benefits from it. Hence no exchange will take place unless both parties do benefit from it. Cooperation is thereby achieved without coercion" (p. 13). So far, so good. It is indeed clear that in this simple exchange model, assuming rational maximizing behavior by all hands, every exchange will benefit both parties, and hence that no coercion is involved in the decision to produce for exchange or in any act of exchange.

Professor Friedman then moves on to our actual complex economy, or rather to his own curious model of it:

> As in [the] simple model, so in the complex enterprise and money-exchange economy, cooperation is strictly individual and voluntary *provided*: (a) that enterprises are private, so that the ultimate contracting parties are individuals and (b) that individuals are effectively free to enter or not to enter into any particular exchange, so that every transaction is strictly voluntary (p. 14).

One cannot take exception to proviso (a): it is clearly required in the model to produce a cooperation that is "strictly individual." One might, of course, suggest that a model containing this stipulation is far from corresponding to our actual complex economy, since in the latter the ultimate contracting parties who have the most effect on the market are not individuals but corporations, and moreover, corporations which in one way or another manage to opt out of the fully competitive market. This criticism, however, would not be accepted by all economists as self-evident: some would say that the question who has most effect on the market is still an open question (or is a wrongly-posed question). More investigation and analysis of this aspect of the economy would be valuable. But political scientists need not await its results before passing judgment on Friedman's position, nor should they be tempted to concentrate their attention on proviso (*a*). If they do so they are apt to miss the fault in proviso (*b*), which is more fundamental, and of a different kind. It is not a question of the correspondence of the model to the actual: it is a matter of the inadequacy of the proviso to produce the model.

Proviso (*b*) is "that individuals are effectively free to enter or not to enter into any particular exchange," and it is held that with this proviso "every transaction is strictly voluntary." A moment's thought will show that this is not so. The proviso that is required to make every transaction strictly voluntary is not freedom not to enter into any *particular* exchange, but freedom not to enter into any exchange *at all*. This, and only this, was the proviso that proved the simple model to be voluntary and non-coercive; and nothing less than this would prove the complex model to be voluntary and noncoercive. But Professor Friedman is clearly claiming that freedom not to enter into any *particular* exchange is enough: "The consumer is protected from coercion by the seller because of the presence of other sellers with whom he can deal. . . . The employee is protected from coercion by the employer because of other employers for whom he can work . . ." (pp. 14–15).

One almost despairs of logic, and of the use of models. It is easy to see what Professor Friedman has done, but it is less easy to excuse it. He has moved from the simple economy of exchange between independent producers, to the capitalist economy, without mentioning the most important thing that distinguishes them. He mentions money instead of barter, and "enterprises which are intermediaries between individuals in their capacities as suppliers of services and as purchasers of goods" (pp. 13–14), as if money and merchants were what distinguished a capitalist economy from an economy of independent producers. What distinguishes the capitalist economy from the simple exchange economy is the separation of labor and capital, that is, the existence of a labor force without its own sufficient capital and therefore without a choice as to whether to put its labor in the market or not. Professor Friedman would agree that where there is no choice there is coercion. His attempted demonstration that capitalism coordinates without coercion therefore fails.

Since all his specific arguments against the welfare and regulatory state depend on his case that the market economy is not coercive, the reader may spare himself the pains (or, if an economist, the pleasure) of attending to the careful and persuasive reasoning by which he seeks to establish the minimum to which coercion could be reduced by reducing or discarding each of the main regulatory and welfare activities of the state. None of this takes into account the coercion involved in the separation of capital from labor, or the possible mitigation of this coercion by the regulatory and welfare state. Yet it is because this coercion can in principle be reduced by the regulatory and welfare state, and thereby the amount of effective individual liberty be increased, that liberals have been justified in pressing, in the name of liberty, for infringements on the pure operation of competitive capitalism.

While the bulk of *Capitalism and Freedom* is concerned with the regulatory and welfare state, Friedman's deepest concern is with socialism. He undertakes to demonstrate that socialism is inconsistent with political freedom. He argues this in two ways: (1) that competitive capitalism, which is of course negated by socialism, is a necessary (although not a sufficient) condition of political freedom; (2) that a socialist society is so constructed that it cannot guarantee political freedom. Let us look at the two arguments in turn.

The argument that competitive capitalism is necessary to political freedom is itself conducted on two levels, neither of which shows a necessary relation.

(a) The first, on which Friedman properly does not place very much weight, is a historical correlation. No society that has had a large measure of political freedom "has not also used something comparable to a free market to organize the bulk of economic activity" (p. 9). Professor Friedman rightly emphasizes "how limited is the span of time and the part of the globe for which there has ever been anything like political freedom" (p. 9); he believes that the exceptions to the general rule of "tyranny, servitude and misery" are so few that the relation between them and certain economic arrangements can easily be spotted. "The 19th century and early 20th century in the Western world stand out as striking exceptions to the general trend of historical development. Political freedom in this instance clearly came along with the free market and the development of capitalist institutions" (pp. 9–10). Thus, for Professor Friedman, "history suggests . . . that capitalism is a necessary condition for political freedom" (p. 10).

The broad historical correlation is fairly clear, though in cutting off the period of substantial political freedom in the West at the "early 20th century" Friedman seems to be slipping into thinking of economic freedom and begging the question of the relation of political freedom to economic freedom. But granting the correlation between the emergence of capitalism and the emergence of political freedom, what it may suggest to the student of history is the converse of what it suggests to Professor Friedman: i.e., it may suggest that political freedom was a necessary condition for the development of capitalism. Capitalist institutions could not be fully established until political freedom (ensured by a competitive party system with effective civil liberties) had been won by those who wanted capitalism to have a clear run: a liberal state (political freedom) was needed to permit and facilitate a capitalist market society.

If this is the direction in which the causal relation runs, what follows (assuming the same relation to continue to hold) is that freedom, or rather specific kinds and degrees of freedom, will be or not be maintained according as those who have a stake in the maintenance of capitalism think them useful or necessary. In fact, there has been a complication in this relation. The liberal state which had, by the mid-19th century in England, established the political freedoms needed to facilitate capitalism, was not democratic: that is, it had not extended political freedom to the bulk of the people. When, later, it did so, it began to abridge market freedom. The more extensive the political freedom, the less extensive the economic freedom became. At any rate, the historical correlation scarcely suggests that capitalism is a necessary condition for political freedom.

(b) Passing from historical correlation, which "by itself can never be convincing," Professor Friedman looks for "logical links between economic and political freedom" (pp. 11–12). The link he finds is that "the kind of economic organization that provides economic freedom directly, namely, competitive capitalism, also promotes political freedom because it separates economic power from political power and in this way enables the one to offset the other" (p. 9). The point is developed a few pages later. The greater the concentration of coercive power in the same hands, the greater the threat to political freedom (defined as "the absence of coercion of a man by his fellow men"). The market removes the organization of economic activity from the control of the political authority. It thus reduces the concentration of power and "enables economic strength to be a check to political power rather than a reinforcement" (p. 15).

Granted the validity of these generalizations, they tell us only that the market *enables* economic power to offset rather than reinforce political power. They do not show any necessity or inherent probability that the market *leads* to the offsetting of political power by economic power. We may doubt that there is any such inherent probability. What can be shown is an inherent probability in the other direction, i.e., that the market leads to political power being used not to offset but to reinforce economic power. For the more completely the market takes over the organization of economic activity, that is, the more nearly the society approximates Friedman's ideal of a competitive capitalist market society, where the state establishes and enforces the individual right of appropriation and the rules of the market but does not interfere in the operation of the market, the more completely is political power being used to reinforce economic power.

Professor Friedman does not see this as any threat to political freedom because he does not see that the capitalist market necessarily gives coercive power to those who succeed in amassing capital. He knows that the coercion whose absence he equates with political freedom is not just the physical coercion of police and prisons, but extends to many forms of economic coercion, e.g., the power some men may have over others' terms of employment. He sees the coercion possible (he thinks probable) in a socialist society where the political authority can enforce certain terms of employment. He does not see the coercion in a capitalist society where the holders of capital can enforce certain terms of employment. He does not see this because of his error about freedom not to enter into any particular exchange being enough to prove the uncoercive nature of entering into exchange at all.

The placing of economic coercive power and political coercive power in the hands of different sets of people, as in the fully competitive capitalist economy does not lead to the first checking the second but to the second reinforcing the first. It is only in the welfare-state variety of capitalism, which Friedman would like to have dismantled, that there is a certain amount of checking of economic power by political power.

The logical link between competitive capitalism and political freedom has not been established.

Professor Friedman argues also that a socialist society is so constructed that it cannot guarantee political freedom. He takes as the test of political freedom the freedom of individuals to propagandize openly for a radical change in the structure of society: in a socialist society the test is freedom to advocate the introduction of capitalism. He might have seemed to be on more realistic ground had he taken the test to be freedom to advocate different policies within the framework of socialism, e.g., a faster or slower rate of socialization, of industrialization, etc.: it is on these matters that the record of actual socialist states has been conspicuously unfree. However, since the denial of freedom of such advocacy has generally been on the ground that such courses would lead to or encourage the reintroduction of capitalism, such advocacy may all be subsumed under his test.

We may grant at once that in the present socialist states (by which is meant those dominated by communist parties) such freedom is not only not guaranteed but is actively denied. Professor Friedman does not ask us to grant this, since he is talking not about particular socialist states but about any possible socialist state, about the socialist state as such; nevertheless the actual ones are not far from his mind, and we shall have to refer to them again. His case that a socialist state as such cannot guarantee political freedom depends on what he puts in his model of the socialist state. He uses in fact two models. In one, the government is the sole employer and the sole source from which necessary instruments of effective political advocacy (paper, use of printing presses, halls) can be had. In the other, the second stipulation is dropped.

It is obvious that in either model a government which wished to prevent political advocacy could use its economic monopoly position to do so. But what Professor Friedman is trying to establish is something different, namely, that its economic monopoly position would render any socialist government, whatever its intentions, incapable of guaranteeing this political freedom. It may be granted that in the first model this would be so. It would be virtually impossible, for a government which desired to guarantee freedom of political advocacy, to provide paper, presses, halls, etc., to all comers in the quantities they thought necessary.

But in the second model this would not apply. The second model appears when Professor Friedman is urging a further argument, namely, that a government which desired to guarantee free political advocacy could not effectively make it possible because, in the absence of capitalism and hence of many and widely dispersed private fortunes, there would be no sufficient source of private funds with which to finance propaganda activities, and the government itself could not feasibly provide such funds. Here there is assumed to be a market in paper, presses, and halls: the trouble is merely shortage of funds which advocates can use in these markets.

This second argument need not detain us, resting as it does on the unhistorical assumption that radical minority movements are necessarily unable to operate without millionaire angels or comparably few sources of large funds. Nor, since the second argument assumes that paper, presses and halls can be purchased or hired, need we challenge the assumption put in the first model, that these means of advocacy are unobtainable in the socialist state except by asking the government for them.

We have still to consider the effect of the other stipulation, which is made in both models: that the government is the sole employer. Accepting this as a proper stipulation for a socialist model, the question to be answered is: does the monopoly of employment itself render the government incapable (or even less capable than it otherwise would be) of safeguarding political freedom? Friedman expects us to answer yes, but the answer is surely no. A socialist government which wished to guarantee political freedom would not be prevented from doing so by its having a monopoly of employment. Nor need it even be tempted to curtail political freedom by virtue of that monopoly. A government monopoly of employment can only mean (as Friedman allows) that the government and all its agencies are, together, the only employers. A socialist government can, by devolution of the management of industries, provide effective alternative employment opportunities. True, a government which wished to curtail or deny the freedom of radical political advocacy could use its monopoly of employment to do so. But such a government has so many other ways of doing it that the presence or absence of this way is not decisive.

It is not the absence of a fully competitive labor market that may disable a socialist government from guaranteeing political freedom; it is the absence of a firm will to do so. Where there's a will there's a way, and for all that Friedman has argued to the contrary, the way need have nothing to do with a fully competitive labor market. The real problem of political freedom in socialism has to do with the will, not the way. The real problem is whether a socialist state could ever have the will to guarantee political freedom. This depends on factors Friedman does not consider, and until they have been assessed, questions about means have an air of unreality, as has his complaint that Western socialists have not faced up to the question of means. We shall return to both of these matters after looking briefly at the factors which are likely to affect such a will to political freedom.

On the question of the will, we cannot say (nor indeed does Professor Friedman suggest) that a will to guarantee political freedom is impossible, or even improbable, in a socialist state. True, if one were to judge by existing socialist states controlled by communist parties, the improbability would be high. (We are speaking here of day-to-day political freedom, which is the question Friedman has set, and not with the will to achieve some higher level of freedom in an ultimately transformed society.) But if we are to consider, as Professor Friedman is doing, socialist states that might emerge in the West, we should notice the differences between the forces in the existing ones and those inherent in possible future Western ones.

There are some notable differences. First, the existing socialist states were virtually all established in underdeveloped societies, in which the bulk of the people did not have the work habits and other cultural attributes needed by a modern industrial state. They have had to change an illiterate, largely unpolitical, peasant population into a literate, politicized, industrially oriented people. While doing this they have had to raise productivity to levels which would afford a decent human minimum, and even meet a rising level of material expectations. The pressures against political freedom that are set up by these factors are obvious. In the few instances, e.g., Czechoslovakia, where socialism did not start from such an underdeveloped base, it started under an external domination that produced equal though different pressures against political freedom. None of these pressures would be present in a socialist state which emerged independently in an already highly developed Western society.

Second, in the existing socialist states the effort to establish socialism has been made in the face of the hostility of the Western powers, whether manifested in their support of counter-revolution or in "encirclement" or "cold war." The ways in which this fact has compounded the pressures against political freedom due to the underdeveloped base are obvious.

Presumably the force of this hostility would be less in the case of future socialist takeovers in Western countries.

Third, the existing socialist states were all born in revolution or civil war, with the inevitable aftermath that "deviations" from the line established from time to time by the leadership (after however much or little consultation) tend to be treated as treason against the socialist revolution and the socialist state. We may at least entertain the possibility of a socialist takeover in an advanced Western nation without revolution or civil war (as Professor Friedman presumably does, else he would not be so concerned about the "creeping socialism" of the welfare state). A socialist state established without civil war would not be subject to this third kind of pressure against political freedom.

Thus of the three forces that have made the pressures against political freedom generally predominate in socialist states so far, the first will be absent, the second reduced or absent, and the third possibly absent, in a future Western socialist state that emerged without external domination.

When these projections are borne in mind, Professor Friedman's complaint about Western socialists appears somewhat impertinent. He complains that "none of the people who have been in favor of socialism and also in favor of freedom have really faced up to this issue [of means], or made even a respectable start at developing the institutional arrangements that would permit freedom under socialism" (p. 19). Perhaps the reason is that they think it more important, in the interests of freedom, to examine and even try to influence the circumstances in which socialism might arrive, than to begin planning institutional arrangements. Western socialists who believe in political freedom are, or should be, more concerned with seeking ways to minimize the cold war (so as to minimize the chances that the second of the projected forces against political freedom will be present in the socialist transformation they hope to achieve in their country), and seeking ways to minimize the likelihood of civil war (so as to minimize the third of the forces against political freedom), than with developing "institutional arrangements that would permit freedom under socialism."

But although, in a socialist state, the existence of a predominant will for political freedom may be more important than institutional arrangements, the latter should not be neglected. For even where there is, on the whole, a will to guarantee political freedom, there are likely always to be some pressures against it, so that it is desirable to have institutions which will make infringements difficult rather than easy. What institutional arrangements, beyond the obvious ones of constitutional guarantees of civil liberties and a legal system able to enforce them, are required? Let us accept Professor Friedman's statement of additional minimum institutional requirements. Advocates of radical change opposed to the government's

policies must be able to obtain the indispensable means of advocacy—
paper, presses, halls, etc. And they must be able to propagandize without
endangering their means of livelihood.

As we have already seen, there is no difficulty inherent in socialism
in meeting the first of these requirements, once it is granted (as Professor
Friedman's second model grants) that the absence of a complete capitalist
market economy does not entail the absence of markets in paper, presses,
and halls.

The second requirement seems more difficult to meet. If the government (including all its agencies) is the sole employer, the standing danger
that the monopoly of employment would be used to inhibit or prevent certain uses of political freedom is obvious. The difficulty is not entirely met
by pointing out that a socialist state can have any amount of devolution
of industry or management, so that there can be any number of employers,
or by stipulating as an institutional arrangement that this devolution be
practiced. For it is evident that if there is a ubiquitous single or dominant
political party operating in all industries and all plants (and all trade
unions), it can make this multiplicity of employment opportunities wholly
ineffective, if or in so far as it wishes to do so. The problem is not the absence of a labor market but the possible presence of another institution, a
ubiquitous party which puts other things ahead of political freedom.

The stipulation that would be required to safeguard political freedom from the dangers of employment monopoly is not merely that there
be devolution of management, and hence employment alternatives (which
could be considered an institutional arrangement), but also that there be
no ubiquitous party or that, if there is, such a party should consistently
put a very high value on political freedom (which stipulation can scarcely
be set out as an institutional arrangement). We are back at the question
of will rather than way, and of the circumstantial forces which are going
to shape that will, for the presence or absence of such a party is clearly
going to depend largely on the circumstances in which a socialist state
is established.

There is, however, one factor (which might be institutionalized)
which may, in any socialist state established in the West, reduce even the
possibility of such intimidation through employment monopoly. This is
the decreasing necessity, in highly developed societies whose economic
systems are undergoing still further and rapid technological development,
of relating income to employment. One need not be as sanguine as some
exponents of the guaranteed income to think it possible, even probable,
that before any advanced Western nation chooses socialism it will have
seen the logic of using its affluence and averting difficulties both political
and economic by introducing a guaranteed minimum annual income to
everyone regardless of employment. In this event, the technical problem

that worries Professor Friedman—how to ensure that a threat to employment and hence to livelihood could not be used to deny political freedom—
would no longer be a problem. A threat to employment would no longer
be a threat to livelihood. It would indeed be a cost, but as Professor Friedman says, "what is essential is that the cost of advocating unpopular causes
be tolerable and not prohibitive" (p. 18).

But even without such a separation of employment from income, the
technical problem of securing political freedom from being denied by the
withholding of employment can be met by such devolution of management as would constitute a set of alternative employments *provided* that
this is not offset by a ubiquitous party hostile to political freedom. If there
is such a party, no institutional arrangements for safeguarding political
freedom are reliable; if there is not, the institutional arrangements do not
seem to be difficult.

We noticed that Professor Friedman, in arguing that freedom would
be increased if most of the regulatory and welfare activities of contemporary Western states were abandoned, did not take into account the
coercion involved in the separation of capital from labor or the possible
mitigation of this coercion by the regulatory and welfare state. But in
Chapter 10, on the distribution of income, he does deal with a closely
related problem. Here he sets out the ethical case for distribution according to product, as compared with "another [principle] that seems ethically
appealing, namely, equality of treatment" (p. 162). Distribution according
to product he describes, accurately enough, as the principle "To each
according to what he and the instruments he owns produces" (pp. 161–
162): to be strictly accurate this should read "resources" or "capital and
land" instead of "instruments," but the sense is clear. This is offered as
"the ethical principle that would directly justify the distribution of income
in a free market society" (p. 161). We can agree that this is the only principle that can be offered to justify it. We may also observe that this principle is not only different from the principle "to each according to his
work," but is also inconsistent with it (except on the fanciful assumption
that ownership of resources is always directly proportional to work). Professor Friedman does not seem to see this. His case for the ethical principle
of payment according to product is that it is unthinkingly accepted as a
basic value-judgment by almost everybody in our society; and his demonstration of this is that the severest internal critics of capitalism, i.e. the
Marxists, have implicitly accepted it.

Of course they have not. There is a double confusion here, even if
we accept Friedman's paraphrase of Marx. Marx did not argue quite, as
Friedman puts it (p. 167), "that labor was exploited . . . because labor produced the whole of the product but got only part of it"—the argument was
rather that labor is exploited because labor produces the whole of the value

that is added in any process of production but gets only part of it—but Friedman's paraphrase is close enough for his purpose. Certainly the implication of Marx's position is that labor (though not necessarily each individual laborer) is entitled to the whole of the value it creates. But in the first place, this is, at most, the principle "to each according to his work," not "to each according to what he and the instruments he owns produces" or "to each according to his product." In the second place, Marx accepted "to each according to his work" only as a transitionally valid principle, to be replaced by the ultimately desirable principle "to each according to his need." Professor Friedman, unaccountably, only refers to this latter principle as "Ruskinian" (p. 167).

Having so far misread Marx, Professor Friedman gives him a final fling.

> Of course, the Marxist argument is invalid on other grounds as well . . . [most] striking, there is an unstated change in the meaning of "labor" in passing from the premise to the conclusion. Marx recognized the role of capital in producing the product but regarded capital as embodied labor. Hence, written out in full, the premises of the Marxist syllogism would run: "Present and past labor produce the whole of the product." The logical conclusion is presumably "Past labor is exploited," and the inference for action is that past labor should get more of the product, though it is by no means clear how, unless it be in elegant tombstones [pp. 167–168].

This nonsense is unworthy of Professor Friedman's talents. The Marxist premises are: Present labor, and the accumulation of surplus value created by past labor and extracted from the past laborers, produce the whole value of the product. Present labor gets only a part of that part of the value which it creates, and gets no part of that part of the value which is transferred to the product from the accumulated surplus value created by past labor. The logical conclusion is presumably that present labor is exploited and past labor was exploited, and the inference for action is that a system which requires constant exploitation should be abandoned.

Ignorance of Marxism is no sin in an economist, though cleverness in scoring off a travesty of it may be thought a scholarly lapse. What is more disturbing is that Professor Friedman seems to be satisfied that this treatment of the ethical justification of different principles of distribution is sufficient. Given his own first postulate, perhaps it is. For in asserting at the beginning of the book that freedom of the individual, or perhaps of the family, is the liberal's "ultimate goal in judging social arrangements," he has said in effect that the liberal is not required seriously to weigh the ethical claims of equality (or any other principle of distribution), let alone the claims of any principle of individual human development such as was given first place by liberals like Mill and Green, against the claims of freedom (which to Friedman of course means market freedom). The humanist liberal in the tradition of Mill and Green will quite properly reject Friedman's postulate. The logical liberal will reject his fallacious proof that the freedom of the capitalist market is individual economic freedom, his undemonstrated case that political freedom requires capitalism, and his fallacious defense of the ethical adequacy of capitalism. The logical humanist liberal will regret that the postulate and the fallacies make *Capitalism and Freedom* not a defense but an elegant tombstone of liberalism.

Getting Government Out of the Marketplace

WILLIAM E. SIMON

The following is an excellent example of a conservative strategy for future development of capitalism. You might try to determine, in this article and those that follow, the set of subjective values that underlie their analysis.

For more than 40 years, we have turned increasingly to the government to solve our economic and social problems, because it presumably represents the single most effective and accountable source of power within our society. Yet, as the government has enlarged its dominion over our affairs, it has become apparent that concentrating power in Washington can be inefficient, wasteful, and ultimately destructive to our freedoms. Indeed, I believe that the forces of big government—however well intentioned—bear a significant responsibility for creating the mess we have in the economy today, and until we wake up to that fact, we may well sink deeper and deeper into the morass.

The Threat of Big Government

Before we succumb to temptation and wander still farther down the path of centralization, it is urgent that we take a hard look at where we're going:

Item. In 1930, just before the New Deal, total government spending—local, state, and federal—accounted for 12 percent of our gross national product. Today it has grown to over 33 percent of our gross national product,

From William E. Simon, "A Strategy For Prosperity," *Saturday Review* (July 12, 1975), pp. 10–13, 16, 20. Reprinted with the permission of the publisher.

and if present trends continue, it will constitute nearly 60 percent of GNP by the year 2000. Any government that taxes away more than half of what people earn and produce is utterly certain to dominate their personal lives.

Item. It took 186 years for our federal budget to reach the $100 billion figure, a line it crossed in 1962. Only nine more years were required for the budget to reach the $200 billion mark and then only four more years—this year—for it to top $300 billion.

The sum of $300 billion is beyond comprehension for many people. If, on the day that Christ was born, someone had been given all of that money and was told to spend $400,000 a day until the money ran out, he would still have cash on hand today.

Item. Excluding the war years, the federal budget ran a surplus about four out of every five years until the thirties. When we close the books on the current fiscal year, we will have had 14 deficits in the past 15 years.

Item. One out of every five working people is now employed by the government at the federal, state, or local level. The government has become the nation's biggest boss, employing more people than do the auto industry, the steel industry, and all other durable-goods manufacturers combined.

Item. In 1963 the federal government sponsored 160 different grant programs. Then along came the Great Society, and today we have more than 900 different grant programs, a hodgepodge so immense that the government has been compelled to print a catalog of programs to keep track—and the catalog is thicker than the Manhattan telephone directory.

The spending and employment figures tell only part of the story, for hidden from the glare of normal reports on the government has been its increasing dominance of the private capital markets. Traditionally, those markets have provided money that industry has needed to borrow in order to expand and to employ new workers. In recent years, however, more and more of the money available in the private markets has been siphoned off to finance deficits and other borrowing needs of the government. During the coming fiscal year, total government borrowing will soak up more than 80 percent of the net new funds available in the private capital markets. Less than 20 percent will be left for private enterprise. This is an alarming situation, reflecting the even more alarming growth of government in this country.

It's not that big government *per se* is undesirable, just as bigness in any organization is not undesirable *per se.* Big Government becomes Bad Government because of what it does to our economy and what it does to our personal freedoms. To an extent far greater than it is commonly realized, the practices and policies of American government are at the root of many of the difficulties we are experiencing today:

Impact of Big Government on Inflation and Growth. Much of today's inflation, for instance, can be directly traced to the patterns of large government spending and to the ever larger deficits accumulated during the past decade. Lord Keynes is often cited for the proposition that when the economy is weak, deficit spending by the government helps to pump it up; the corollary to his theory, of course, is that when the economy is strong and inflationary, the government should discipline itself to achieve budgetary surpluses and stabilize prices. Instead, in our incessant desire to buy more than we can afford as a nation, we have slipped into a pattern of loose deficit spending every year, good and bad. And because the economy was booming during much of the past decade, federal budget deficits have become a major source of economic and financial instability.

Monetary policy has been another inflationary element in this witches' brew. Between 1955 and 1965 the money supply grew at a rate of about 2.5 percent a year, and we enjoyed a period of reasonable price stability. Since 1965, however, the annual rate of increase in the money supply has more than doubled, to nearly 6 percent. When monetary stimulus goes far beyond the sustainable growth level that is needed for stable economic growth, as it has over most of the past decade, the only way that extra money can be absorbed is through higher prices. Although monetary policy was more restrictive during most of 1974, the long-term trend has been in the direction of too much money for our own good.

The inflationary momentum generated by fiscal and monetary policies was sharply accelerated in the past few years by the explosion in food prices, the quadrupling of oil prices, the ill effects of wage and price controls, and other factors. And as inflation hit record peacetime levels, it had a secondary effect: it tipped the economy into a downward spiral toward recession. As prices went up, consumer confidence declined, bringing the biggest drop in consumer purchases since World War II. As inflation drove up interest rates, the housing market also fell and housing—one of our largest industries—went into a deep slump. In short, inflation has been a major factor in creating the recession and remains our most fundamental underlying problem.

Impact on Production.   Closely related to the inflationary pressures created by the government are the impediments that restrictive government policies place on production. Government interventions in the free marketplace, even when done for the most laudable of purposes, frequently result in less competition, less incentive for production, higher costs, higher prices, and ultimately fewer goods and services than we need.

Federal regulation of natural gas is a classic example of government intervention that has backfired. For more than two decades, despite repeated warnings by experts, the Federal Power Commission has controlled the wellhead price of natural gas at an abnormally low level in order to hold down prices for consumers. In the process, however, the FPC has also discouraged producers from developing new supplies, and today we have a shortage of natural-gas supplies. An increasing number of consumers, especially in New England, are unable to obtain natural gas and must substitute oil or foreign liquefied natural gas at a considerably higher price. Government regulation has, in effect, created a national shortage of natural gas and has driven many consumers to higher-priced fuels.

The most realistic solution is to deregulate the price of new natural gas, a move strongly supported by both the Nixon and the Ford administrations. In Congress, where such legislation has lain dormant for over three years, critics argue that deregulation would allow the price of natural gas to skyrocket. It is true that prices would rise, but the objection is misleading. For consumers now forced to rely upon oil instead of on natural gas, our estimates show that the higher price of deregulated natural gas should still be only two-thirds as much as the oil equivalent. Moreover, we must soon come to realize that if we want to maintain a growing economy, we will inevitably have to offer greater production incentives to the energy industry as well as to other businesses in this country.

I could go on at length about the perversities of governmental intervention in the marketplace, and even then I would want to set aside a special volume for another particularly vexing problem: the practices of the eight independent regulatory agencies of the federal government and other regulatory bodies at the national and state level. The regulatory agencies of the federal government now exercise direct control over air, rail, and truck transportation, the securities markets, power generation, television, and radio—industries that account for 10 percent of everything made and sold here. Although the agencies were initially set up for good reasons and may still be needed for some purposes, the regulatory process is in dire need of reform. Over the years, regulation of industry has become complex, cumbersome, inefficient, and overly protective—all at the expense of the consumer. The Interstate Commerce Commission, for instance, now has on its books some 40 trillion rates and 400,000 new tariff schedules telling the transportation industry what they can charge customers. With the help of Ralph Nader and others, including one of the agencies' most thoughtful chairmen, the Federal Trade Commission's Lew Engman, egregious regulatory practices are finally attracting greater attention.

Impact On Economic Growth. Of even greater concern should be the general downward trends in business profits, in capital growth, and in productivity—all contributing to a slowing of the economy in recent months. I often wonder whether we have forgotten the economic facts of life. To put it simply, companies have traditionally depended upon profits to upgrade and expand their operations. As the companies have grown and become more efficient, workers have increased their productivity and have thus been able to earn higher incomes without raising the cost of living. New workers could also be added to the payrolls. In turn, as the general standard of living has increased, the public has increased its demands for goods and services and thereby generated still further profits—continuing the benefit cycle. This cycle is the essence of free enterprise, the system that has provided the United States with the highest standard of living the world has ever known.

Clearly, that system is no longer working as well as it should. It has developed problems of its own, and we have abused it and let many of its parts become rusted and worn. To pay for the rising costs of government, we have transferred more and more of our wealth from the most productive part of our economy, the private sector, to the least productive part, the public sector. We have shackled the free-enterprise system with many different forms of controls, and we have erected a tax system that exacts heavy penalties, especially during periods of extreme inflation. To put people back to work, not only must we provide public service jobs but also, more importantly, we must return to economic fundamentals.

Profits have suffered a perilous decline since the mid-sixties. Indeed, when they are measured realistically, it is not unfair to say that the country has entered a "profits depression." Declining profits? How can that be, you may ask, when "reported profits" by non-financial corporations were almost twice as high in 1974 as in 1965? The answer is that the apparent rise since 1965 is an optical illusion caused by inflation and outmoded accounting methods.

The effect of declining profits reverberates throughout the economy. This is perhaps most easily seen in figures for retained earnings—the money that business has available to finance *new* plant and equipment, as distinguished from the replacement of existing capacity. In 1965 our best measurements showed that retained earnings amounted to $20 billion. By 1973, after eight years in which real GNP had increased by 36 percent, retained earnings had *dropped* 70 percent, to $6 billion. And for 1974, our preliminary estimate for retained earnings is a *minus* figure of $16 billion. We have moved into the position of hardly having enough profits to replace existing capacity and nothing to finance investment in additional plant and equipment.

Another simple but compelling fundamental is that increases in productive performance are needed in order to sustain a higher standard of living. Yet, as a nation, we are rapidly expanding public payments to individuals but neglecting to provide adequate incentives for new investment. Since the early sixties, the United States has had the worst record of capital investment of all major industrialized nations. As a result, our rate of productivity growth has also been one of the lowest. It bears repeating that increased productivity is the only way to increase our standard of living.

Unless we are willing to accept a lower standard of living, it is imperative that we make better provision for the future. The capital requirements of a growing American economy over the next decade will be enormous—at least *three times* those of the past decade. We will need up to a trillion dollars for energy alone, and we will need extremely large sums for urban transportation, control of pollution, and the rebuilding of some of our basic industries in which new investment has languished. In addition, we face the more conventional, but still mammoth, capital requirements of replacing and adding to the present stock of housing, factories, and machinery. All this means that we must begin placing much greater emphasis upon saving and investment and much less upon consumption and government spending.

Three Roads to Nowhere

In concluding his famous essay *On Liberty,* John Stuart Mill made the following observation:

> A state which dwarfs its men, in order that they may be more docile instruments in its hands even for beneficial purposes, will find that with small men no great things can be accomplished; and that the perfection of machinery to which it has sacrificed everything will in the end avail it nothing, for want of the vital power which, in order that the machine might work more smoothly, it has preferred to banish.

When we survey the full sweep of governmental powers in the United States today—from the enormous influence that federal spending now has over our economy to the penetration of governmental authority into every facet of daily commerce—it is apparent that the modern state could eventually dwarf our private-enterprise system. Before the vital power of free enterprise is further weakened by the state, I believe it is time to say no to those who argue that the answer to current challenges in the economy and in energy lies in further governmental control over our affairs.

There are three "solutions" in particular to which the present administration objects and which I would like to explore:

Greater Federal Spending. It is tempting to think that we can speed up the process of economic recovery by spending our way back to prosperity. The drumbeat for bigger spending programs can be heard daily through the corridors of the Capitol. Because of the continuing threat of inflation, however, this recession must be treated quite differently from those of the past. Unbridled spending would only create new pressures on prices and could set off a new cycle of inflation and recession that would be far more severe than anything we have experienced in recent times.

One danger we would face during the recovery, as I have emphasized many times, would arise in our private capital markets, where a rising tide of private borrowing demands may be forced to compete with large levels of federal demands for money to finance our deficits. It is urgent that the federal government not elbow these private borrowers out of the credit markets through excessive borrowing. Otherwise, the government could easily force up interest rates again, abort a recovery in housing, and bankrupt companies whose financial conditions are already marginal. In the name of spending our way out of the recession, we would only be driving ourselves farther into it.

The immediate impact of huge federal demand during a period of recovery would depend upon the monetary policy of the Federal Reserve. Monetary policy is going to be a critical element in shaping our economic prospects, both now and in the future. If, as the recovery takes hold, oversized federal deficits create strong competition for funds and the Federal Reserve pursues a moderate policy, there is a possibility that we would drive up interest rates and abort the process of recovery. The other alternative is that the Federal Reserve might seek to accommodate the enormous borrowing requirements of the federal government, as well as those of the private sector, by creating a more rapid growth in money and credit. That action might postpone the adverse impact on the recovery for perhaps a year or two, but its consequences would soon catch up with us in the form of a reaccelerated inflation. The only way to avoid such dire choices is to follow a course of prudence in our fiscal affairs.

Wage And Price Controls.   Since 1946, when we passed legislation enshrining full employment as a major national goal, the dilemma of trying to maintain full employment without creating inflation has bedeviled each of our presidents. And each of them has been advised that wage and price controls are the easiest and quickest way to resolve the issue. Controls are waiting in the wings again now, and if inflation flairs up again during the process of economic recovery, we are likely to enter another debate on their merits.

Public opinion polls show that a majority of our people think that controls are effective in controlling inflation. That's discouraging, for it means that we have learned little from history. Controls have been tried over and over again—stretching all the way back to the Roman emperor Diocletian—and never once have they worked. They may yield short-term gains, but within a matter of months they begin to create shortages, distortions, and inequities within the economy. Instead of eliminating inflation, they only bottle it up so that prices ultimately explode. We are still living with the ill effects of our last fling with controls.

Advocates of a planned economy argue that controls failed in the early seventies because they were administered by "nonbelievers." By contrast, they say, controls were carried out during World War II by members of the faith, and, as a result, prices remained relatively stable. What the advocates fail to point out is that when those controls were phased out after the war, wholesale prices shot up 30 percent in only 12 months.

If we are seduced once again by the siren song of controls, it is safe to predict that shortly afterward we will face a cruel choice: whether to lift the controls and uncork horrendous problems of inflation and unemployment or stay with the controls and gradually stifle the free-enterprise system. That is not a choice we should have to make, and we can avoid it if we avoid the controls themselves.

Rationing. Still a third solution pressed upon us by those who incline toward a planned economy is a system of rationing as a means of saving energy. Even though public polls several months ago indicated an interest in rationing, I cannot imagine that the American people would be willing to put up with rationing for very long. It would quickly become the most unpopular program in the country—a fact that is not lost on Congress.

The basic problem with rationing is that it can't be done fairly and practically. Every family, every car and motorcycle, every store, school, church, and business—everything and everybody—would have to obtain a permit for gasoline, electricity, and natural gas. Those allocations would have to be changed every time someone was born or died or moved or got married or divorced, and every time a business was started, merged, or sold, and even when a room was added to the church or school. When we consider the problems involved in just getting the mail delivered, are we really ready to trust an army of civil servants—however able and well intentioned—to decide who gets what?

Make no mistake: a small army would be required. We once considered gasoline rationing at the Federal Energy Office and learned that it would take from four to six months for it to be set up, that it would incur $2 billion a year in federal costs, and that it would employ as many as 20,000 people and would require 3,000 state and local boards to handle exceptions. By simple arithmetic, one can also determine that in order to reduce our oil imports by a million barrels a day by rationing only gasoline, the average driver would be limited to 9 gallons a week—a reduction of 25 percent under present consumption levels. Further conservation would require further limitations. Inevitably, we would be forced into rationing all petroleum products, and because the energy crisis is likely to be a prolonged affair, rationing might be needed for as long as 10 years.

People should ask themselves which they prefer: the small price increase on petroleum products that the president is proposing—and which would be returned to them—or a system that allows the government to tell them how to live their daily lives for the indefinite future. Does anyone honestly believe that the American public is willing to trade its basic freedoms—practically in perpetuity—for a few pennies a gallon?

An Approach That Will Work

There are other ways for us to solve our long-range problems—ways that will work—but they are radically different from those that would concentrate still greater power and influence in Washington. They would require instead that the government play a more neutral role in the economy, no longer trying to regulate and ordain the way that the economy grows but providing an environment which is *conducive* to competition and orderly growth. Let me single out five areas where the Ford administration is trying to follow a different course:

Fiscal and Monetary Discipline.   With revenues off sharply and expenditures rising inexorably, large federal deficits will be inescapable until at least the end of fiscal year 1976. Thereafter, however, as the economy regains its health, we must begin to restore a much greater degree of moderation to our fiscal and monetary policies. Deficits may be unavoidable and even desirable as a stimulant during economic declines, but they should not be countenanced during years of boom. In fact, it would be far more helpful during good years if the government were to run surpluses, thereby checking excessive demand and upward price pressures and freeing more capital for investment purposes.

Assisting The Casualties.   Millions of Americans are suffering the hardships of unemployment, and there will be more before the economy fully recovers. There can be little doubt that the best way to help the jobless is not to create vast numbers of temporary jobs on the public payroll but to bring the economy back to good health. After all, the private sector accounts for more than 80 percent of total employment. And as President Kennedy once remarked, "A rising tide lifts all ships."

Nevertheless, we do have responsibility to provide generous assistance to the victims of recession and inflation, not only for humanitarian reasons but also because the only way to win broad public support for the long-term fight for sound economic policies is to ensure that the recession's burdens are borne equitably. To that end, federal unemployment compensation will be expanded during the coming fiscal year to some $20 billion—almost three times as much as two years ago—and this aid should reach some 14 million workers.

"Sacred Cows."   It will be extremely difficult to achieve meaningful reform of federal regulatory practices because the special interests benefiting from regulation are much more powerful and united than the proponents of change. But we can no longer afford the waste and inefficiencies that these "sacred cows" create. President Ford has made it clear that regulating abuses is one of the primary targets of this administration. Several reform

proposals are already before the Congress, and more will be forthcoming. It is urgent that this matter be seriously addressed by the Congress.

Tax Reform. In the process of overhauling our tax structure, we should examine its impact upon both individuals and businesses and the future course we want to follow as a nation. Both major segments can rightly claim that inflation increases their effective tax rate even though they are no better off. We should also recognize that our system of business taxation bears more heavily on corporations than does the tax system of almost any other major industrialized nation. In recent years most of our major trading partners have eliminated the traditional two-tier system of business taxation, in which income is taxed once at the corporate level and again when dividends are received by stockholders. The administration is now studying a series of tax-reform proposals that would create an economic environment more conductive to economic growth and job creation. We intend to submit a package of such reforms to the Congress before the end of the year.

Energy Self-Sufficiency. The country faces essentially three alternatives in the field of energy. First, we could continue along our present course of doing practically nothing about conservation or production. If we do, the OPEC nations will hold a knife to our throat for years to come. Our foreign oil bills this year will probably hit $30 billion and could rise even more down the road. By 1985 we could be dependent on OPEC for more than half of our oil needs. Meanwhile, the economies of many other oil-importing nations will continue to deteriorate, jeopardizing the economic future of the entire Free World. Clearly, this is not an acceptable alternative. A second choice is to ration fuels, but this approach also presents intolerable objections, as noted earlier.

The third choice is to employ the pricing system as a mechanism for both discouraging consumption and encouraging production. This is the alternative that the President has chosen. He did so with the full recognition that energy prices would increase and that we would suffer a small, one-time rise in the rate of inflation. But he also coupled the price increases with proposed changes in the tax structure that should compensate most energy users, especially low- and moderate-income families, and should also prevent energy producers from realizing windfall profits. This is a sound, thoughtful approach, and it *will* work if only we are willing to try it.

Strengthening The Free-Enterprise System. The most critical economic decision we face today is whether we want to let Washington run the economy or whether we want to leave basic decisions in the hands of private citizens. If we truly want to preserve the private enterprise system, then not only must we take the steps that I have noted here, but we also must seek some fundamental changes in public attitudes toward business and capi-

talism. Ironically, in producing affluence, we have spawned a whole generation of young people who misunderstand and distrust the way our system
works. Too many who enter the business world after school think that they
have been compromised; to them, profits are obscene and competition is
vulgar. In our desire for conspicuous prosperity, we have also come to value
the present over the future, over-consuming and over-borrowing in the vain
hope that the bills will never catch up. The ethics of thrift and savings
has been replaced by the ethics of instant pleasure, and we have turned
to the modern state to satisfy our hunger.

In a very basic sense, the nation has now reached a crossroads where
we must choose between the restoration of a more competitive, more open
society or commit ourselves—perhaps irrevocably—to a society in which
the large decisions about our economic and personal welfare are made by
a central government.

History surely teaches us that the system of free enterprise, despite
its many flaws, is the most compatible with the protection of rights and
liberties as well as the most productive of material goods. Equally so, recent
history shows that the government, despite its splendid intentions, is incapable
of matching the vitality, the wisdom, and the ingenuity of free men.

"In the end," Gibbon is reported to have written in an epitaph on
ancient Greece, "more than they wanted freedom, they wanted security.
They wanted a comfortable life and they lost it all—security, comfort, and
freedom. When the Athenians finally wanted not to give to society but for
society to give to them, when the freedom they wished for most was freedom
from responsibility, then Athens ceased to be free."

Whether the same will one day be said of America is the basic decision
now before us.

The Coming Corporatism

R. E. PAHL and J. T. WINKLER

It is asserted here that the danger facing modern capitalism is not creeping socialism, rather it is creeping fascism. Although the analysis is based on recent development in England, to what extent does the analysis apply to recent events in the United States?

The Four Goals of Corporatism

"Corporatism" is a comprehensive economic system under which the state intensively channels predominantly privately owned business towards four goals, which have become increasingly explicit during the current economic crisis: Order, Unity, Nationalism, and "Success." Let us first look at these four values in turn:

1. Order. Elimination of the "anarchy" of the market in all its forms (including extreme success or failure for capital or for labor). This desire for stability emanates from a revulsion against the market processes that lead, on the one hand, to the collapse of major companies in important industries and, on the other, to "excessive" speculative and windfall profits (by property developers, asset strippers, and, most recently, by clearing banks and oil and sugar oligopolies).

Similarly, there is a growing intolerance toward the "anarchy" of the labor market—as seen, on the one hand, in the threat of 1 million unemployed and, on the other, in the disruptions to production caused by frequent unofficial strikes or very successful wage bargaining by unions (now pejoratively

Excerpted from R. E. Pahl and J. T. Winkler, "The Coming Corporatism," *Challenge* (March-April 1975), pp. 28–35. Reprinted with the permission of International Arts and Sciences Press, Inc.

called "holding the nation to ransom"). Indeed, our first inkling of the corporatist trend came at the businessmen's fete, the annual Institute of Directors
conference. Edward Heath preached the philosophy of expansion and growth
through competition. He was tepidly received. Vic Feather, then Secretary
of the Trades Union Congress, offered the prospect of a deal for labor peace.
He was cheered. The assembled business leaders knew what they wanted:
order.

Principally, a corporatist government will attempt to create order by
the final, overt killing off of the various still-existing markets (land, labor,
money, shares, raw materials, for example), which some Neoclassical and
socialist economists alike have been prematurely assuring us were long since
dead. It will be done through imposing intensive state control in all major
areas of private economic activity.

2. Unity.   Substitution of cooperation for competition. This desire for
collaborative effort arises from a revulsion against the perceived wastefulness
of competitive struggles on all fronts: the inflationary pursuit of sectional
economic interests, class divisiveness, party gamesmanship, sectarian bomb-
ings, Celtic fissiparousness, the Arab-European oil confrontation, the financial
institutions bidding up interest rates, home buyers gazumping up house prices,
or "extremism" of any complexion.

The theme of the election in October was not the virtues of slow but
steady progress through successive compromises by numerous interest groups.
Support for the beneficent "Invisible Hand" of liberal economics and pluralist
politics has been conspicuous by its absence. In its stead, there has been
a harmonious chorus from all three parties on the need for national unity.
Of course, there are quibbles about the means—a social contract, "tripar-
tism," a work-together movement, a new manipulated consensus, a coercive
framework of law, or a coalition government. But the emphasis has been
unanimously on the need for the nation to *cooperate* in overcoming the current
crisis. We suspect that the strategy of the current government (or any other)
to create this unity on a voluntary basis will meet rank and file workers'
opposition, leading within a year or so to a corporatist intervention and
state regulation of labor markets and some attempt to control strikes, probably not initially by legal prohibitions, but perhaps through union discipline
or, ultimately, coercion.

The attempt to create a *spirit* of unity will then shift to the already
strong theme of nationalism.

3. Nationalism.   The elevation of "general welfare" to complete priority over self-interest or sectional advantage. The index of economic success
is no longer personal affluence or opportunities for individual mobility, but
Britain's national performance—whether measured by growth, balance of
payments, per capita income, inflation rates, productive investment or any

other criterion. These standards are comparative. They measure the country's collective well-being against that of other advanced industrial nations. These indicators have, of course, been in heavy use since at least the early 1960s; but comparisons have grown more neurotic in the 1970s. Thus, Labour's election manifesto justified its interventionist economic program in order to stop Britain's "slipping behind other nations." The Tory slogan expressed the essence of the current value: "Putting Britain First."

Whatever government rules for the next few years, we may thus expect a strong dose of economic nationalism. In other words, the specific and aggressive protection and furtherance of British economic interests, at the expense of the development of the Common Market, or the liberalization of world trade, or the integration of the world monetary system. There is certain to be a backlash (and not just in Britain) against multinational companies. There will be government intervention to prevent foreign takeovers of "vital industries" (not only a current Third World tactic, but one used by Italy in the 1920s). There will be industrial reorganization to create national companies in important sectors.

Business leaders will hardly object to this kind of interventionism. Indeed, it is precisely what those in larger companies want—a protected environment while they get on with the job. For our research we asked 135 directors of firms their views of their job, and got from them a diary of their week. But, most importantly in the present context, we also followed each of the executive directors of 19 companies—82 in all—through one complete working day, as unobtrusive observers. Directors were reluctant to give personal reprimands to their subordinates in our presence. But they had no similar inhibitions about discussing price fixing and cartelization.

Again we spent one complete day with the managing director of a very large, heavy industrial company. He was planning a series of takeovers of medium-sized competitors in order to establish his company's market dominance within Britain. This was a prelude to reaching argeement with larger European firms to stabilize prices and divide up sales areas. This was the only way he could see to achieve a steady growth in profits. What he wanted was a government willing to tolerate his planned monopoly and protect him from the Americans while he built it up.

4. Success. Attainment of national objectives established by the state. For corporatists, this involves more than simply controlling the country's collective economic activity in order to prevent the dissipation of effort and to become more successful. It means giving conscious direction to the economy by establishing priorities and targets and by restricting work done towards alternative objectives. First and foremost, this means the control and concentration of investment and of the allocation of resources. The goal of the moment is clearly to reduce inflation. Thereafter, the most common definition of national economic "success" among politicians of all parties seems to be that of moving Britain up the odd notch or two in the International Growth League Table.

Fascism with a Human Face

Those, then, are the four aims. Let us not mince words. Corporatism is fascism with a human face. What all the major parties have done is to take over the core elements of the *economic* strategy which the Italian fascists, Salazar in Portugal, the Falange in Spain, and the Nazis adopted to deal with the interwar crisis. Vichy France carried this on. The pattern reappeared after the war in such odd guises as Peronism in Argentina—and Nkrumah-style "African socialism." What the parties are putting forward now is an acceptable face of fascism; indeed a masked version of it, because so far the more repugnant *political and social* aspects of the German and Italian regimes are absent or only present in diluted form.

For example, antiparliamentarianism has been present here, so far, only in the advocacy of a temporary suspension of party politics in favor of a national or coalition government. Racialism has appeared on the political agenda here only in vague proposals for immigrant repatriation. Totalitarian mass involvement is only limply reflected in current calls for participation in local government or in management. The moral fervor of regeneration has flourished here only sporadically in exhortations to consider "the national interest." How the economic corporatism, which we foresee, will develop socially is too open and distant a question to do more than speculate upon at the moment.

Given the implications of the economic policies they are now advocating, it is understandable that politicians are reluctant to proclaim corporatism openly, if indeed they even recognize that that is what they are proposing. Labour boasts that it is really "building socialism" this time. The Conservatives demur that they are helping free enterprise through a bad patch. The Liberals claim the middle ground, though they are the most committed of all parties to statutory wage and price controls.

Corporatism is a distinct form of economic structure. It was recognized as such in the 1930s by people of diverse political backgrounds, before Hitler extinguished the enthusiasm which greeted Mussolini's variant. The fact that our blinkered political economic vocabulary now sees the alternative pure forms of economy as simply "capitalism" or "socialism" is a consequence of the fact that the Axis powers lost the Second World War. The essence of corporatism as an economic system is *private* ownership and *state* control. It contrasts with Soviet socialism's state ownership and state control, and pure capitalism's private ownership and private control. Corporatism is also distinguished from postwar Western economic systems by the nature and extent of the state control exercised.

Going beyond Keynesian aggregate demand management and counter-cyclical intervention ("fine tuning"), corporatism attempts detailed control of economic activity and conscious direction of resources. In contrast to the "mixed economy"—partly nationalized and state regulated, partly unregulated private enterprise—a corporatist system attempts total control across the whole spectrum of national economic life, at least over larger companies. Unlike the "technocracy" of Galbraith's *New Industrial State*, where experts rule in the name of science and efficiency, corporatism openly acknowledges political control directed towards ends determined by the state itself.

It is also more than French-type "indicative planning," which relied on a small, unbureaucratic exercise in mutual target-setting by officials and businessmen, backed up by state financial support. Corporatism is more than just a somewhat more thorough-going form of government intervention. It is an attempt to establish state control over all the major aspects of business decision making.

If we combine the two principal variables we have discussed so far—*ownership* and *control*—we can classify the major types of economic systems as shown in the chart below.

		OWNERSHIP	
		Private	**Public**
CONTROL	**Private**	Capitalism	Syndicalism
	Public	Corporation	Socialism

When Corporatism Began

When, in the mid-1960s, economist Andrew Shonfield surveyed the affluent Western capitalist countries, with their various degrees of welfare provision and indicative planning, and contrasted them with the depressed capitalist world in which his generation had grown up, he directly faced the question whether "the economic order under which we now live, and the social structure that goes with it, are so different from what preceded them that it is misleading . . . to use the word 'capitalism' to describe them." He opted for the label "modern capitalism," because the elements of continuity seemed greater than the changes and, besides, not even its severest critics had proposed a better word. No sooner had he published his analysis than interventionism—certainly in Britain—began to escalate, fundamentally restricting the discretion of British owners and managers of capital to use their resources as they saw fit. Capitalism, in this country at least, has changed. The symbolic moment came when the Conservative government of 1970–74 accepted the need for peacetime controls on prices and wages. It is time for a new name. The name, as we have suggested, is corporatism.

Beginning under Labour in the late 1960s, the traditional areas of freedom in business decision making under capitalism have been progressively chipped away. First, the freedoms to set prices and wages were restricted. Then the 1970–74 Heath government established additional controls on dividends, profit margins, capital movements and office rents. It legislated powers to bail out failing firms and to acquire compulsorily almost any corporate information it wished.

These forms of Conservative interventionism were recognized at the time by Anthony Wedgwood Benn, now Minister of Industry, for what they were—not the latest strategy for the strengthening of capitalism, but as "the most comprehensive armoury of government control that has ever been assembled for use over private industry . . . exceeding all the powers thought to be necessary by the last Labour government." Indeed, he went so far as to congratulate the Conservative Prime Minister: "Heath has performed a very important historical role *in preparing for* the fundamental and irreversible transfer in the balance of power." We agree. However, the transfer will not be from capitalism to socialism, but to corporatism.

The ultimate corporatist institution, emphasizing the strategy of state control without nationalization, is Labour's proposed Planning Agreements System. These plans would be comprehensive annual agreements "to align the company's plans with national needs," and covering investment, prices, productivity, employment, exports, imports, savings, product development, industrial relations, and consumer and environmental protection. In short, a comprehensive set of targets governing all major aspects of corporate activity. This is not just Labour. Immediately before the February 1974 election in which Labour replaced the Conservative government, Peter Walker, the departing Conservative Secretary of State for Industry, was advocating "a new kind of interventionism" and was also suggesting that "in the coming quarter of a century the role of government in capitalist economics must go wider still."

One of the fundamentals of any future corporatist regime will be *compulsory investment*. This will include not only state dictation of the level, purpose and location of capital investment for national ends, but a set of enforceable priorities, quotas, and regulation for private lenders. Most crucially, it will involve state control over a determined level of investment funds. This may take many forms—for example, an investment tax, a tax-free diversion for a proportion of corporate profits into an investment fund, or regulated purchase of investment certificates, as well as, of course, direct public-sector spending.

Capitalism without Competition

Why is such a fundamental change in our economic system taking place at this particular time? The obvious (and partly correct) answer is the current economic crisis. Traditionally and historically, businessmen have turned to the government for legal support, subsidization, and protection from outside competitors during hard times. The Conservative Party has always been responsive to these appeals, believing that it should play a more interventionist role in times of crisis. As that nascent interwar corporatist, Harold Macmillan, put it: "our view about the position of government in industry [is that] it is not a principle, it is an expedient."

Certainly the current crisis, coming on top of a long-term decline in corporate profitability, is the precipitating cause. But if it were only the imminence of Latin American inflation rates which induced corporatism, we might expect a reversion to liberal managerial capitalism when the crisis was past. There is, however, an underlying cause, which is a fundamental change in the structure of the British economy. This time, we would argue, there can be no going back.

In recent years, the pace of corporate concentration has accelerated to the point where most of Britain's basic production industries are (or soon will be) controlled by a *very* small number of firms (some may be public or semipublic; but most still are not). With such a structure, the concept of open-market competition is meaningless. So the notion that profit is a sufficient justification for corporate activity is undermined. For a government to tolerate (and, indeed, in some industries, to sponsor) industrial concentration to the point of oligopoly or monopoly, yet still allow the now giant companies to go on pursuing maximum profit, would be to institutionalize exploitation in the most blatant manner possible. As two economists, who are certainly not sympathetic to left-wing tendencies, have concluded: "the relevance of the profit ethic to today's large companies may be debatable; but the very large companies of the near future will represent the final proof of the inappropriateness of the profit ethic and the market ideal" (G. D. Newbould and A. S. Jackson, *The Receding Ideal*). The new structure requires not only controls on the abuse of corporate power, but a new purpose and justification for business activity. Two candidates are emerging: a revised concept of "social responsibility" and "national economic performance." Both can be readily transmuted into the underlying ideology of corporatism.

Will business leaders tolerate state controls on their decision-making freedom once the crisis has passed? The directors we studied had no objection to a type of increased state intervention which they thought they could control—the government shielding them from the vicissitudes of competition and the trade cycle, but leaving them managerial discretion. One company we studied, which had experienced frequent government intervention in its

African subsidiaries, even welcomed it. The state disciplined the workforce, helped out with finance, and the firm still repatriated the profits. Another large firm even saw state economic planning as an opportunity. It willingly acted as an unofficial planning department for the government in drawing up long-term investment and development plans for its industry, because it saw this as a way of manipulating policy decisions in the direction it favored.

What the directors of large companies do *not* want is laissez-faire competition. What they do want is capitalism without competition, a combination of state support and private control. What they will have to accept is corporatism. They may extract a *quid pro quo*. Economic systems are distinguished not only by their patterns of ownership and control, but by the aims or goals toward which they are directed (this is in addition to some sense of "success"). Capitalism itself is divisible into the classic High Tory version, aiming at a defense of property rights, and a liberal managerial version, intent on the meritocratic mobility of the fittest through competitive selection. So there are variants of corporatism.

The main difference between Conservative and Labour-led corporatist regimes may be in the extent of their commitment to a goal of egalitarian redistribution of incomes. The Labour form ought to produce less inequality—perhaps something like the current economic order in Norway or Sweden. But the maintenance of present levels of privilege may be the price the existing business leaders will demand. They may be supported in this by those sections of the labor movement which have traditionally been more concerned with differentials than with equality. When we add egalitarianism/inegalitarianism to our previous diagram, each of the four types of economy splits into two types, as can be seen in the following chart.

		OWNERSHIP	
		Private	**Public**
CONTROL — Private	Inegalitarian	High Toryism (defense of property)	Workers' self-management (Yugoslavia)
	Egalitarian	Meritocracy (equality of opportunity)	Utopian communities (kibbutzim)
CONTROL — Public	Inegalitarian	Conservative-led corporatism (Mussolini model)	Market and revisionist socialism (Hungary and USSR)
	Egalitarian	Labor-led corporatism (Scandinavia)	Pure communism (from each to each)

Who Will Be Affected?

What difference will a corporatist system make for various sectors of the population? How directive will it be in practice?

For *organization men*, the managers of large companies at all levels, the outcome will be neither total dictation from the civil service bureaucracy which turns management into a mere transmission mechanism between Whitehall and the shop floor: nor a once-a-year reconciliation of corporate and national plans, which is Wedgwood Benn's disguise for the reality of his Planning Agreements System. The experience of centrally planned economies, both communist and fascist, suggests rather a continuous bargaining relationship between officials and managers, involving considerable horse trading, collusion, covert evasions, threats, bluster, pique, pleading, bribery, and the manipulation of old-boy nets. A system of "fiddle," rather than totalitarian direction.

There is perpetual negotiation between counterparts, extending quite far down both hierarchies—over revisions to plans; allocation of materials, capital and labor; the surmounting of bottlenecks; contingencies; and all the other problems that need to be solved if any organization is to perform approximately up to its planned level. In a corporatist system, a manager will not have a slow, quiet or easy life (the business caricature of the civil service). The pressure to meet targets is relentless. Every request becomes a demand, which is "urgent" and "essential," or "impossible" and "irresponsible," depending on one's position. Authority in such a system must always appear to reside with the nominal superiors, the officials. But, in fact, the balance of power between bureaucrats and managers shifts with the personalities and roles of the individuals involved. In short, it is something like what goes on in most large corporate bureaucracies already. We saw a miniversion of the process in one of the large conglomerates we studied—a hectic scramble over the fixing of the annual capital investment budget, where the heads of operating companies used every possible device to manipulate their nominal sponsors, the directors, and get their pet projects approved.

For managers in the British subsidiaries of large foreign companies—the so-called *multinationals*—life may be a good deal harder. The nationalist backlash we mentioned earlier will almost certainly take the form of three specific interventions: (*a*) stopping tax avoidance through the manipulation of transfer prices; (*b*) controls on short-term capital movements, to prevent multinationals' destroying monetary policy by swishing their liquid funds about in the bathtub of the European money market; (*c*) compulsory investment programs, to escape the international blackmail whereby companies play one country off against another for the location of future projects.

Some multinationals are particularly vulnerable. Those which have proceeded so far as an international division of labor (making some parts in one country, others in a second, and assembling final products elsewhere) are open to disruption from a corporatist government with nationalist zeal, in much the way that scattered domestic operations can be halted by local shop stewards today.

Small capitalists, by contrast, may escape relatively lightly. A government primarily concerned with national economic performance may only attempt to control those companies big enough to have an impact on aggregate statistics. However, if an industry is not concentrated enough to allow simplified planning through a few giant companies, a corporatist regime might force amalgamations of small business, and might do so in a more energetic manner than the Industrial Reorganization Corporation in the late 1960s.

For *consumers,* there is bound to be a noticeable drop in living standards during the tenure of the current government, and perhaps considerably beyond. By common consent, Britain's chronic economic problem is underinvestment certainly from the 1950s on, if not indeed since the 1870s. The whole point of any corporatist government will be to engineer a forceful shift of resources away from consumption into production. This will mean simultaneously fewer and less varied goods in the shops and less discretionary cash-in-the-pocket with which to buy them. Import controls may limit the availability of foreign designs and luxuries. Investment controls will certainly eliminate some of the trivia, gimmicks, baubles and paraphernalia of contemporary life; and probably a number of the joys as well.

For *investors,* both private and institutional, the prospects are severe, notwithstanding the fact that a corporatist system does not involve any further massive incursions on private ownership. If Labour is in charge of the new corporatist order, the life expectancy of institutional investors is short. Pension funds already anticipate a serious, perhaps fatal, financial squeeze from the latest pension plan proposed by Barbara Castle, Secretary of State for Health and Social Security. Investment trusts would become anachronisms. Banks and insurance companies, if not nationalized out of residual socialist principle, will be very closely controlled out of corporatist concern for directing investment. In the longer term, *any* corporatist government (Labour, Conservative, or coalition-run), once it has brought markets within Britain under its control and has recognized the inapplicability of profit as a corporate goal, will increasingly see shareholders as even more a liability—a simple cost—than they were under managerial capitalism.

A corporatist regime would almost certainly limit dividends, perhaps transmute them into fixed-interest returns, and restrict or limit capital appreciation in shares. Those pessimists in the City who are already predicting the long-term decline of the equity market in Britain are almost certainly right. Ultimately, having assumed responsibility for, and got control of, the investment process, a corporatist government may begin to wonder why it needs private investors at all. Thus, we believe, corporatism will prove a transitory phase, though the transition need not be a short one.

The end of private ownership may not come in a burst of public appropriation. Unless they decide to draw on personal savings as an extra source for investment, government may simply squeeze down returns on private capital until no one invests any more—the corporatist road to socialism.

For *workers,* corporatism has a certain short-term appeal. It offers a softer option for the cure of inflation than the "short, sharp burst of unemployment," prescribed by Neoclassical economics. A corporatist government would certainly guarantee full employment (both out of concern for the value of order and a desire for full production). The price of the guarantee would, of course, be wage control and restraints on the freedom of industrial action. The recent Trades Union Congress conference suggests that much of union officialdom would be willing to make such a deal, if it were suitably disguised or wrapped up softly enough. Whether the rank and file would acquiesce depends on (*a*) the exact terms on which the bargain is offered (not just wage levels, but fringe benefits, social security supports, and the tightness of controls on other groups, as well); and (*b*) the willingness of the government—despite the failure of the previous conservative Industrial Relations Act—to coerce.

We have been arguing that corporatism is the response politicians of all parties are most likely to make to the current crisis. Businessmen and an inflation-burdened middle class are likely to accept it. If resistance is to emerge, and our prediction to prove inaccurate, it will be within the working class (probably *not* the official union movement). Conditions in Britain, 1975, are not so desperate, nor unemployment so high that workers will accept any system which guarantees their jobs. But, for the medium term, no matter which party is in power, the result will be the same.

The Irrational System

PAUL BARAN AND PAUL SWEEZY

A radical view of the failure of capitalism, not only from an economic,
but from a moral point of view.

The paycheck is the key to whatever gratifications are allowed to
working people in this society; such self-respect, status, and recognition
by one's fellows as can be achieved depend primarily on the possession
of material objects. The worker's house, the model of his automobile, his
wife's clothes—all assume major significance as indexes of success or failure. And yet within the existing social framework these objects of consumption increasingly lose their capacity to satisfy. Forces similar to those
which destroy the worker's identification with his work lead to the erosion
of his self-identification as a consumer. With goods being sought for their
status-bearing qualities, the drive to substitute the newer and more expensive for the older and cheaper ceases to be related to the serviceability
of the goods and becomes a means of climbing up a rung on the social
ladder.

In this way consumption becomes a sort of extension and continuation of the process of earning a livelihood. Just as the worker is always
under pressure to get ahead at the expense of his fellows at the shop or
office, so the consumer pursues the same goals at the expense of his neighbors after work. Neither worker nor consumer is ever really satisfied;
they are always on the lookout for a new job, always wanting to move
to a better neighborhood. Work and consumption thus share the same
ambiguity: while fulfilling the basic needs of survival, they increasingly
lose their inner content and meaning.

From "The Irrational System," by Paul Baran and Paul Sweezy, in *Monopoly Capital*,
Monthly Review Press, 1968, pp. 345–49, 351–53, 362–67. Reprinted by permission of
Monthly Review Press. Copyright © 1966 by Paul M. Sweezy.

Nor are matters any better when it comes to another aspect of the worker's nonwork life—the expenditure of leisure time. Leisure has traditionally been thought of as serving the purpose of "recreation," that is to say the revival and refocusing of mental and psychic energies from their compulsory commitment to work to genuinely interesting pursuits. Now, however, the function of leisure undergoes a change. As Erich Fromm has observed, leisure becomes a synonym of time spent in passivity, of idleness. It no longer signifies doing what a person *wants* to do, as distinct from doing, at work, what he *must* do; to an ever-increasing extent it means simply doing nothing. And the reason for doing nothing is partly that there is so little that is humanly interesting to do, but perhaps even more because the emptiness and purposelessness of life in capitalist society stifles the desire to do anything.

This propensity to do nothing has had a decisive part in determining the kinds of entertainment which are supplied to fill the leisure hours— in the evenings, on weekends and holidays, during vacations. The basic principle is that whatever is presented—reading matter, movies, radio and TV programs—must not make undue demands on the intellectual and emotional resources of the recipients; the purpose is to provide "fun," "relaxation," a "good time"—in short, passively absorbable amusement. Even the form and organization of the material is affected. The show is continuous, the movie theater can be entered at any time; the book can be read from front to back or from back to front; skipping a few installments of a serial does not matter; the TV can be switched from channel to channel without loss of coherence or comprehension.

Other forms of "killing time"—what a revealing expression!—are hardly more exacting. Being a sports fan does not involve participation in any activity or acquiring any skill. Events are provided for all seasons, and it is not even necessary to attend in person since giant corporations find it a profitable form of advertising to sponsor radio and TV broadcasts of games and matches. Elaborate statistical records are compiled and regularly published in specialized books and periodicals, enabling even fans who have never played a game in their lives to discuss the various teams and players with all the assurance of experts. Being interested at different times of the year in the sports appropriate to the season turns into something people have in common. Like the largely imaginary good and bad points of different makes and models of automobiles, the strengths and weaknesses of teams and players become topics of conversation which the inherent triviality of the theme transforms into mere chatter.

Perhaps nothing is more symptomatic of the part played by leisure in daily life than this degeneration of conversation into chatter. Like friendship, conversation presupposes the existence of some common purposes, interests, and activities. Friendship implies an emotional commit-

ment; conversation demands an intellectual effort. When these precon-
ditions do not exist—when people exist together but do not relate to one
another in any fundamental way—both friendship and conversation are
bound to atrophy. When people have nothing to say, "small talk" becomes
the order of the day. As the word friend fades and comes to designate
someone whom one happens to have met, it applies to a multitude of
acquaintances and to no one in particular. Social gatherings are motivated
less by a desire to be with other people than by fear of being alone. People's unrelatedness at these gatherings is often and characteristically dis-
solved in alcohol.

The satisfaction derived from this kind of conviviality is fleeting;
the hangover is inevitable. Although suffocating in his solitude, the individual does not overcome it, as David Riesman has observed, by becoming
a particle in a crowd. The misery of loneliness and the horror of together-
ness produce an attitude of ambivalence between involvement and withdrawal. Leaving one party with the thought that he might as well have
stayed at home, he goes to another thinking that he might as well be there.
Thus he is drawn into an uninterrupted whirl of socializing—on different
levels and scales of course, depending on class, status, and income—or
concluding, as Arthur Miller has put it, that if one has to be alone one
may as well stay by oneself, he turns into a recluse, spending hours on
end "working around the house," mowing the lawn, pottering in the back-
yard. Brooding and muttering to himself, he turns on the radio, listens to
a scrap of news or a singing commercial, switches over to the TV to see
the end of a Western, leaves both and looks absent-mindedly at the newspaper filled with accounts of crime and scandal—in short, shifts restlessly
from one way of doing nothing to another way of doing nothing, all the
while longing for and dreading the beginning of the work week when he
will start longing for and dreading the coming of the weekend.

In these conditions the sensation produced by leisure is closely related to that experienced at work—grinding, debilitating boredom. Only
it must be added that the boredom lived through in the hours and days
of free time can be even more oppressive than that endured during the
work week. In the case of work it appears to be natural, an aspect of
the grim necessity to earn one's bread in the sweat of one's brow. All of
human history has taught people to take it for granted that physical suffering and psychic distress are the price of survival. And as long as scarcity
dominated the human condition, this calculus, cruel as it undoubtedly
was in the light of the idleness and luxury enjoyed by the privileged few,
appeared cogent and convincing to the have-nots. For them every shortening of the work day, every reduction in the work week were precious
steps in the direction of freedom.

Today we must ask what remains of that cogency, of that progress toward freedom when the torture of work buys a longer span of nonwork which is itself robbed of all joy, which turns into an extension of work itself, into the emptiness, tedium, and torpor of modern leisure? What rationality is left in bearing the self-denial, the repression, the compulsion of work when what follows at the end of the working day and the working week is the barren desert of boredom that is free time in this society?

Repression has always marked the exploitation of man by man. Curbing the striving for freedom, subduing the aversion to toil and self-denial, destroying the sense of compassion and solidarity with fellow men, repression has forced man into molds making him fit to exploit and be exploited. As Freud put it, "it is impossible to ignore the extent to which civilization is built up on renunciation of instinctual gratifications, the degree to which the existence of civilization presupposes the non-gratification (suppression, repression, or something else?) of powerful instinctual urgencies."

For many centuries the forces of repression derived much of their formidable power from two sources which remained relatively invariant. One was the state of constricting scarcity which was—in the conditions of the time, rightly—considered to be an inescapable fact of nature. The incidence of burdens imposed by that scarcity was of course open to question and criticism: the injustices associated with it gave rise to almost continuous popular protest; convincing arguments could be and were advanced to show that in a different social order the dire effects of scarcity could be mitigated. But the existence of scarcity could not be denied. And the recognition of its existence necessarily implied the recognition of the inevitability of life-long labor and bare subsistence standards of living for the vast majority of mankind.

The other source of fuel for the engine of repression is closely related to the first: the people's unquestioning belief in the basic principles underlying the taboos and prohibitions, the rules and regulations governing the behavior of men in society. These principles, elaborated by society's cultural and religious apparatus, transmitted from one generation to the next, internalized and appearing as an immutable aspect of "human nature," coagulated into a conscience, a superego, ever watchful and sternly punishing violators of its precepts with bitter feelings of guilt. Society thus acquired what might be called a psychic police force effectively upholding spiritual "law and order."

What distinguishes our time from all earlier epochs is that by now in the advanced capitalist countries the mechanism of repression has accomplished its historical mission. The work discipline and self-denial which it imposed made possible the massive accumulation of capital and with it the building up of an enormously productive industrial apparatus. The development of automation and cybernation in the last two decades

signals the end of the long, long era in which the inevitability of scarcity
constituted the central fact of human existence. There can be no doubt
that the continued acceptance of that inevitability under conditions such
as prevail in the United States today is false consciousness par excellence.
It now serves only to maintain and support an oppressive social order, and
its sway over the minds of people reflects nothing but the anachronistic
prevalence of an outlived ideology.

This state of affairs cannot be changed by wishing or incantation.
Declarations that what the United States needs is a "spiritual revival"
or a clarification of "national goals" are as symptomatic of the pathological
condition they are directed against as of a profound inability to comprehend its nature and origins. When a writer as sensitive and observant
as Paul Goodman truthfully states that "our society cannot have it both
ways: to maintain a conformist and ignoble system *and* to have skilled
and spirited men to man the system with," only to conclude that "if 10,000
people in all walks of life will stand up on their two feet and talk out
and insist, we shall get our country back," one gets the full measure of
the failure of even our best social critics to face up to the real character
and dimensions of the crisis of our time.

For behind the emptiness, the degradation, and the suffering which
poison human existence in this society lies the profound irrationality and
moral bankruptcy of monopoly capitalism itself. No outraged protests,
no reforms within the monopoly capitalist framework can arrest the decay
of the whole. And as becomes clearer every day, this decay makes increasingly problematical the rationality of even the most spectacular advances
in scientific knowledge and technical and organizational skills. Improvements in the means of mass communication merely hasten the degeneration of popular culture. The utmost perfection in the manufacture of
weapons of destruction does not make their production rational. The
irrationality of the end negates all improvements of the means. Rationality
itself becomes irrational. We have reached a point where the only true
rationality lies in action to overthrow what has become a hopelessly
irrational system.

Will such action be forthcoming in sufficient volume and intensity
to accomplish its purpose? The future of the United States and of monopoly capitalism obviously depends on the answer. So also, though more
indirectly, does the future of mankind itself for a long time to come.

The answer of traditional Marxian orthodoxy—that the industrial
proletariat must eventually rise in revolution against its capitalist oppres-
sors—no longer carries conviction. Industrial workers are a diminishing
minority of the American working class, and their organized cores in the
basic industries have to a large extent been integrated into the system as
consumers and ideologically conditioned members of the society. They
are not, as the industrial workers were in Marx's day, the system's special

victims, though they suffer from its elementality and irrationality along with all other classes and strata—more than some, less than others.

The system of course has its special victims. They are the unemployed and the unemployable, the migrant farm workers, the inhabitants of the big city ghettos, the school dropouts, the aged subsisting on meager pensions—in a word, the outsiders, those who because of their limited command over purchasing power are unable to avail themselves of the gratifications, such as they are, of consumption. But these groups, despite their impressive numbers, are too heterogeneous, too scattered and fragmented, to constitute a coherent force in society. And the oligarchy knows how, through doles and handouts, to keep them divided and to prevent their becoming a lumpen-proletariat of desperate starvelings.

If we confine attention to the inner dynamics of advanced monopoly capitalism, it is hard to avoid the conclusion that the prospect of effective revolutionary action to overthrow the system is slim. Viewed from this angle, the more likely course of development would seem to be a continuation of the present process of decay, with the contradiction between the compulsions of the system and the elementary needs of human nature becoming ever more insupportable. The logical outcome would be the spread of increasingly severe psychic disorders leading to the impairment and eventual breakdown of the system's ability to function even on its own terms.

But as we emphasized, advanced monopoly capitalism does not exist in isolation, and any speculation about its future which takes account only of its inner laws and tendencies is certain to be misleading. The United States dominates and exploits to one extent or another all the countries and territories of the so-called free world and correspondingly meets with varying degrees of resistance. The highest form of resistance is revolutionary war aimed at withdrawal from the world capitalist system and the initiation of social and economic reconstruction on a socialist basis. Such warfare has never been absent since the Second World War, and the revolutionary peoples have achieved a series of historic victories in Vietnam, China, Korea, Cuba, and Algeria. These victories, taken together with the increasingly obvious inability of the underdeveloped countries to solve their problems within the framework of the world capitalist system, have sown the seeds of revolution throughout the continents of Asia, Africa, and Latin America. Some of these seeds will sprout and ripen rapidly, others slowly, still others perhaps not until after a long period of germination. What seems in any case clear is that they are now implanted beyond any prospect of exterpation. It is no longer mere rhetoric to speak of the world revolution: the term describes what is already a reality and is certain to become increasingly the dominant characteristic of the historical epoch in which we live.

The implications of this fact for the future of monopoly capitalism are only beginning to become apparent. The ruling class of the United States understands, instinctively and through experience, that every advance of the world revolution is a defeat—economic, political, and moral—for itself. It is determined to resist such advances wherever they may threaten, by whatever means may be available; and it counts on its enormous superiority in the technology of warfare to bring it victory. But the truth is that in this struggle there can be no real victories for the counter-revolutionary side. Underlying the revolutionary upsurge are real economic, social, and demographic problems; and is the very nature of counter-revolution to prevent these problems from being rationally attacked, let alone solved. Counter-revolution may win, indeed already has won, many battles, but the war goes on and inexorably spreads to new peoples and new regions. And as it spreads so does the involvement of the United States.

No one can now foresee all the consequences for the United States of this increasing commitment to the cause of world counter-revolution, but equally no one can doubt that it will profoundly affect the inner as well as the outer course of events. In the long run its main impact may well be on the youth of the nation. The need for military manpower seems certain to rise sharply; it may soon be normal for young Americans to spend several years of their lives, if they are lucky enough to survive, fighting in the jungles and mountains of Asia, Africa, and Latin America. The psychic stress and physical suffering experienced by them and their families will add a new dimension to the agony inflicted by an anti-human social order. Will the effect be merely to hasten the process of decay already so far advanced? Will the shock perhaps awaken more and more people to the urgent need for basic change? Or will, as some believe, the increasingly evident hopelessness of its cause lead the American ruling class to the ultimate irrationality of unleashing nuclear holocaust?

That no one can now answer these questions means that all the options are not foreclosed, that action aimed at altering the course of events has a chance to succeed. There are even indications, especially in the Negro freedom movement in the South, in the uprisings of the urban ghettos, and in the academic community's mounting protest against the war in Vietnam, that significant segments of the American people are ready to join an active struggle against what is being cumulatively revealed as an intolerable social order. If this is so, who can set limits to the numbers who may join them in the future?

But even if the present protest movements should suffer defeat or prove abortive, that would be no reason to write off permanently the possibilty of a real revolutionary movement in the United States. As the world revolution spreads and as the socialist countries show by their example that it is possible to use man's mastery over the forces of nature to build a rational society satisfying the human needs of human beings, more and more Americans are bound to question the necessity of what they now take for granted. And once that happens on a mass scale, the most powerful supports of the present irrational system will crumble and the problem of creating anew will impose itself as a sheer necessity. This will not happen in five years or ten, perhaps not in the present century: few great historical dramas run their course in so short a time. But perhaps even fewer, once they are fairly started, change their nature or reverse their direction until all their potentialities have been revealed. The drama of our time is the world revolution; it can never come to an end until it has encompassed the whole world.

In the meantime, what we in the United States need is historical perspective, courage to face the facts, and faith in mankind and its future. Having these, we can recognize our moral obligation to devote ourselves to fighting against an evil and destructive system which maims, oppresses, and dishonors those who live under it, and which threatens devastation and death to millions of others around the globe.

The Limits of American Capitalism

ROBERT L. HEILBRONER

Is capitalism static or dynamic; changeless or in flux? Here is a view that asserts that a deep-seated "revolution" is in process in our very midst.

The definition of "capitalism" seemed of primary importance in establishing the boundaries of change, and for this reason the slow left-ward movement of the business ideology assumed a putative central role in enlarging the perimeter of social action.

Assuming that the ideology of business would continue along its gradual path of liberalization, how far did this mean that capitalism could change? What limits, we asked, were inherent in the system, rather than in any particularly ideology of the day?

The answer at which we have arrived is necessarily imprecise, but it does not seem entirely indeterminate. In the dynamic process of social change, the economic relationships that give rise to privilege are those that fix the degree of social resistance, and these relationships give us a general indication of what is possible and what is not.

It is not difficult to recapitulate this difference. What seems possible is to bring about social change—in the distribution of wealth or in the control over output or in the imaginative destination of society or its relations with the noncapitalist world—that stops short of an intolerable curtailment of those privileges that all elites within American capitalism— and indeed, the general public as well—are eager to protect. What is impossible, within the time period in which we are interested, is to effect changes that would involve the virtual destruction of the central institutions of the system itself. This means, for example, that the distribution

From Robert L. Heilbroner, *The Limits of American Capitalism,* pp. 111–34. Reprinted with the permission of Harper & Row, Publishers. Copyright © 1965, 1966 by Robert L. Heilbroner.

of wealth can be corrected at the bottom but not at the top. It means that the control over output can be improved very greatly, but that the essential commercial character of a market system is beyond alteration. It means that a considerable accommodation can be made with the noncapitalist world, but that the imagination of that world (or of the American mind) is not likely to be captured by the capitalist rhetoric. There are, in a word, deep-seated attributes to the quality of American life that constitute an impregnable inner keep of the system of American capitalism as we know it.

And yet, if we now recall our earlier concern with feudalism, we will recall that, despite the seeming impregnability of its institutions in the 13th century, by the 18th century somehow the system had nonetheless changed out of all recognition. Hence we must ask whether the inner keep of capitalism, although out of range of bombardment today, may not also be ultimately vulnerable to the kind of penetration that finally invested the feudal citadels of privilege.

The question asks us to reflect on how feudalism expired. The answer is not by revolution. However important for other reasons, the revolutions of the 18th and 19th centuries merely ripped off the tattered covers of feudalism to reveal new economic societies, already full-formed and operative, beneath them. Rather, feudalism gave way to capitalism as part of a subversive process of historic change in which a newly emerging attribute of daily life proved to be as irresistibly attractive to the privileged orders of feudalism as it was ultimately destructive of them.

This subversive influence was the gradual infiltration of commercial relationships and cash exchanges into the everyday round of feudal existence, each act of marketing binding men more fully into the cash nexus and weakening by that degree the traditional duties and relationships on which feudalism was based. Against this progressive monetization the old order struggled in vain, for the temptations and pleasures of the cash economy were greater than the erosion of privileges that went with it: "It is the costliness of clothes that is destroying the nobles of our German lands," wrote one chronicler, telling of a widow who sold a village to raise the price of a blue velvet gown to wear to a tournament.

Could there be an equivalent of that powerfully disintegrative and yet constitutive force in our day—a force sufficiently overwhelming to render impotent the citadel of capitalism and yet as irresistibly attractive to its masters as the earlier current of change was to feudalism? I think there is such a force, and that it already bulks very large within our world, where it is cumulatively and irreversibly altering the social system even more rapidly than did the process of monetization during the medieval era. This revolutionary power is the veritable explosion of organized knowledge and its applied counterpart, scientific technology, in modern times.

The extraordinary rate of expansion of this explosion is sufficiently familiar to require only a word of exposition. There is, for instance, the often-quoted but still astonishing statement that of all the scientists who have ever lived in all of history, half are alive today. There is the equally startling calculation that the volume of scientific publication during the past ten to fifteen years is as large as or larger than that of all previous ages. Such examples are no doubt more impressionistic than exact, but they serve accurately enough to convey the notion of the exponential growth of scientific inquiry in our day. As to the equally phenomenal growth of the powers of the technology, if that needs any demonstration, there is the contrast cited by Kenneth Boulding between the decades needed to reconstruct Germany after the Thirty Years' War or the centuries needed to recuperate from the physical destruction that accompanied the collapse of the Roman Empire and the scant 20 years in which the shattered and burned cities of modern Europe and Japan were rebuilt after the Second World War.

This explosion of science and scientifically based technology is often thought of as a product *of* capitalism, insofar as it arose within a capitalist milieu and in an age dominated by capitalism. Yet the association was far more one of coexistence than of causal interrelation. Science, as we know it, began well before capitalism existed and did not experience its full growth until well after capitalism was solidly entrenched. At best we can say that the secular air of bourgeois culture was compatible with, perhaps even conducive to, scientific investigation, but we can hardly credit the acceleration of scientific activities after the middle of the 19th century—the work of Darwin, Maxwell, Rutherford, Freud, Mendel, not to mention the great contemporary mathematicians—to the direct stimulus or patronage of capitalism itself.

Perhaps more surprising, even scientific technology exhibits but little debt to the existence of capitalism. The technology on which capitalism began its long course of growth in the 18th and early 19th centuries was mainly of a pragmatic, intuitive, prescientific kind. The Second Law of Thermodynamics was not formulated by Kelvin until 1851, and its immense practical significance was only slowly realized thereafter. The English textile, iron and steel, or chemical industries were founded and prospered with no "scientific" underpinnings at all. The same is true for the young railroad industry, for canal building, or road laying. Even as late as the mid-19th century, a proposal by the famous Siemens brothers of Berlin that cable be scientifically tested before being laid was dismissed by British engineers as "humbug."

There was, of course, a certain amount of systematic industrial experimentation in the mid-1800s, and a burst of important inventions, many of which depended on some application of scientific knowledge, in the second half of the century. Yet the deliberate employment of scientific investigation to create or refine the technology of production was considerably delayed in arriving. In this country the first private industrial laboratory was not built until 1900 by the General Electric Company, and organized research and development on a large scale did not really get under way until 1913.

Thus we find the flowering of science and the application of science to technology—the very hallmarks of the modern era—to be currents that arose *within* capitalism, but that do not owe their existence directly to capitalism. Rather, like the first manifestations of the market in the medieval era, science and its technology emerge as a great underground river whose tortuous course has finally reached the surface during the age of capitalism, but which springs from far distant sources. But that is not where the resemblance ends. As with the emergent market forces, the river of scientific change, having now surfaced, must cut its own channel through the existing social landscape—a channel that will, as in the case with the money orientation in medieval life, profoundly alter the nature of the existing terrain. Indeed, if we ask what force in our day might in time be strong enough to undercut the bastions of privilege and function of capitalism and to create its own institutions and social structures in their place, the answer must surely be the one force that dominates our age—the power of science and of scientific technology.

There is, I suspect, little to argue about as to the commanding presence of science in modern times. What is likely to be a good deal less readily accepted, however, is the contention that this force will cause drastic modifications in, or even the eventual supersession of, capitalism. For at first glance the new current of history seems to have imparted an immense momentum to capitalism by providing it with the very thing it most required—a virtually inexhaustible source of invention and innovation to ensure its economic growth. Merely to review in our minds the broad areas of investment and economic output that owe their existence entirely to the laboratory work of the past three decades—the nuclear and space establishments, electronics, the computerization of industry, the wonder drugs, the creation of new materials such as plastics—is to reveal the breadth of this new gulf stream of economic nourishment.

Yet, like the attractions of the cash market for the feudal lord, the near-term advantages of science and technology conceal long-term conflicts and incompatibilities between this new force of history and its host society. Just as the insertion of cash exchanges into the fine structure of feudalism ultimately made obsolete the functional mechanism of a manorial society, so the insinuation of science and technology into the interstices of business enterprise promises to outmode the fundamental working arrangements of capitalism.

At least one of these disruptive manifestations is already familiar to us. This is the tendency of technology to create social problems that require *nonmarket controls* to correct or forestall. In part these agencies of control are contained and concealed within the centers of production themselves, where they show up as the rising echelons of corporate administration and supervision that are needed to regulate the underlying traffic of production. In part the controls show up in the familiar bureaus of government that directly oversee the operation of the new technology—the bureaus that cope, with greater or lesser success, with the social repercussions of transportation, nuclear energy, drugs, air pollution, etc. In still a different aspect, the controls invade areas of social life rather than production, as in the astonishing network of government required solely to manage the automobile (an effort that requires the labor of one out of every ten persons employed by all state and local governments) or in the multiplying administrative requirements of the mega-city, itself so much a product of modern technology. Meanwhile, in the background of the social system the controls are manifest as the growing apparatus of regulation over wages and prices, and over the total flow of economic activity all ultimately traceable to the need to intervene more closely into an economy of increasing technological complexity.

Not that the disruptive effect of technology is itself a new phenomenon. The dislocations of the technology of the prescientific age—say the spinning jenny—were quite as great as those of the modern age, such as the computer. The difference is that in an earlier age the repair of technological disturbances was largely consigned to the adaptive powers of the individual, to the ameliorative efforts of small-scale local government, and to the annealing powers of the market itself. Today, however, these traditional agencies of social recovery can no longer cope effectively with the entrance of technology. The individual, now typically a member of a small urban family rather than of a large extended rural family, is much less capable of withstanding economic displacement without external assistance. The local community, faced with large-scale problems of unemployment or ecological maladjustment brought about by technical change, has no recourse but to turn to the financial help and expertise available only from larger government units. The market, which no longer "clears" when the marketers are enormous firms rather than atomistic business units, also discovers that the only antidote to grave economic disjunction is the countervailing influence or *force majeur* of central governing authority. In a word, technology in the modern era seems to be exerting a steady push from many levels and areas of the economy in the direction of a society of *organization*.

This well-known effect of technical progress is, however, only the most obvious, and perhaps not the most fundamental, way in which the scientific current works against the enveloping economic order. A deeper cutting edge of technology lies in another attribute of its impact on society—its capacity to render redundant the physical energies of man, at least as these energies are mainly harnessed in a market setting. That is, machines do man's work for him, thereby freeing him from the bonds of toil and, not less important in the context of our inquiry, from the hegemony of the market process.

We can see this disemployment effect most dramatically in the case of agriculture. A century ago farming, as the basic activity of society, absorbed the working energies of 60 to 70 percent of the population. Today, although no less essential to the provisioning of the human community, agriculture requires only the effort of some 8 percent of the population (working only two-thirds as long as its forebears in the 1860s) and even this small fraction will probably be further reduced to about 4 to 5 percent within a decade.

But equally startling is the labor-displacing effect of modern technology in that congeries of activities associated with the extraction of basic materials from nature and their fabrication, assembly, conversion, or transport to point of sale. If we look back to 1900 we find that about 38 of every 100 working Americans were then employed in mining, manufacturing, the generation of power, transport, or construction. Since then science and technology have given us a stupendous array of new products, each requiring large amounts of human effort—the automobile and truck, the whole range of consumer durables, the communications industry, office machinery, new metals, fabrics, and materials of all kinds to name but a few. Yet at the end of that period the total requirements for labor in all the goods-centered industries had risen by only *two percentage points*, to 40 out of every 100 workers. As fast as demand grew for these myriad products, that fast did technology and science permit labor to be economized. During the era of the greatest increase in factory production ever known, virtually no increase in labor was needed—indeed, since the hours of work fell, there was actually a relatively *decreased* need for human effort in the output of goods.

The point is important enough to warrant another word of exposition. What technology has done over a 50-year span is to enable relatively fewer workers in the "goods sector" to supply the needs of a richer population. As the table below shows, this is due to a deep penetration of technology into mining, construction, transportation, and utilities. In manufacturing proper there was a 12 percent increase in labor needs in terms of relative *numbers* of men, although in terms of *hours*, there was a reduction of labor requirements here, too. By way of contrast, there has been an increase in the proportion of workers required to provide services —retail and wholesale trade, finance, government, domestic service, etc.

This secular shift takes on new significance in the light of the technology of automation. We do not yet know whether the new devices that count, sort, remember, check, and respond to stimuli will intensify the labor displacement process in those industries where technology has already long been at work. But there is reason to believe that technology has begun to invade what has heretofore been a sanctuary of relatively unmechanized work—the vast numbers of jobs in the office, administrative, and service occupations. In 1900 less than one-fourth of the total working population was employed in these nonfarm, nonfactory kinds of work—as lawyers, teachers, government officials, stenographers, bookkeepers, clerks, servants. By 1960 more than half the labor force was in these jobs. And now, into this varied group of occupations, technology is starting to penetrate in the form of machines as complex as those that can read and sort checks or as relatively simple as those that dispense coffee and sandwiches.

Table 1. Workers Per 1,000 Population, United States

	1900	1965
Mining	10	3
Manufacturing	82	92
Construction	22	16
Transportation and utilities	27	21
All "goods sector" (above)	141	132
All service sector	93	178

Source: For 1900, *Historical Statistics of the United States* Bureau of the Census, Washington, 1960, Series D 57–71; for 1965, *Economic Indicators.*

This is not to maintain that no new areas of employment exist to take the place of those occupied by machinery. Certainly there remain very large and still untapped possibilities for work in the repair and reconstruction of the cities; the provision of education, public safety, and conveyance; in the improvement of health and recreation facilities; in the counseling of the young and the care of the aged; in the beautification of the environment. Provided only that demand can be marshaled for these activities, there will surely be no dearth of job prospects for the coming generation.

But that is precisely the point. The incursion of technology has pushed the frontiers of work from the farm to the factory, then from the factory to the store and the office, and now from store and office into a spectrum of jobs whose common denominator is that they require *public action and public funds* for their initiation and support. The employment-upsetting characteristics of technology thus act to speed capitalism along the general path of planning and control down which it is simultaneously impelled by the direct environment-upsetting impact of technological change.

If we look further ahead, the necessity for planning is apt to become still more pressing. Given the trajectory of present scientific capabilities, the day of a "fully automated" society is by no means a fantasy, although its realization may well require another century, or possibly more. But in the long evolutionary perspective in which we are now interested, one can surely look to the time when all or nearly all of the paid labor of our present society outside the categories of professional or managerial work (and a good deal within those echelons) could be accomplished by machinery with but little human supervision. That is to say, we can, without too much difficulty, imagine a time when as small a proportion of the labor force as now suffices to overprovide us with food will serve to turn out the manufactured staples, the houses, the transportation, the retail services, even the governmental supervision that will be required.

What the leisured—not to use the word "unemployed"—fraction of the population will then do with itself is an interesting and important question. If it is not to starve, it must be given the chance to share in society's output. Should there exist sufficient modes of activity resistive to mechanization, this may be accomplished through the market mechanism: instead of taking in one another's wash, we will buy one another's paintings. But even in this best outcome, the underlying processes of production, now enormously mechanized and intricately interconnected, would almost certainly require some form of coordination other than the play of market forces. And then, of course, if the leisured population does not find adequate opportunities for unmechanizable employments, it will simply have to be *given* a right to share in society's output—an even more basic infringement on the hegemony of the market.

Thus, in a manner not entirely dissimilar from the way in which the steady monetization of feudal life weakened the relevance and effectiveness of manorial ties, the incorporation of technology into the working mechanism of the capitalist system also renders less relevant and effective the market ties on which that system is ultimately founded. Partly because of the social disturbances it creates in an urban industrial environment, partly because of the progressive compression of the need for human effort in the provisioning of society, the steady entrance of technology into capitalism forces new social structures of control and supervision to rise within and over the marketplace.

But the erosion of the market goes deeper yet. For the introduction of technology has one last effect whose ultimate implications for the metamorphosis of capitalism are perhaps greatest of all. This is the effect of technology in steadily raising the average level of well-being, thereby gradually bringing to an end the condition of material need as an effective stimulus for human behavior.

This is by all odds the most generally hailed attribute of science and technology, for everyone recognizes that the end to want would represent the passage over an historic watershed. But it must be equally clear that such a passage will also represent a basic revision of the existential situation that has hitherto provided the main impetus for work. As the level of average enjoyments increases, as needs diminish and wants become of such relative unimportance that they can be easily foregone, the traditional stimuli of capitalism begin to lose their force. Occupations now become valued for their intrinsic pleasures rather than for their extrinsic rewards. The very decision to work or not becomes a matter of personal preference rather than of economic necessity. More telling, the drive for profit—the nuclear core of capitalist energy—becomes blunted as the purchasable distinctions of wealth decline. In a society of the imaginable wealth implicit in another hundred years of technical progress, who will wish to be the rich man's servant at any price? In such a society the services that have always been the prerogative of the rich will have to be performed by machine or dispensed with altogether—a state of affairs already visible in many areas if we compare the life of the wealthy today with that of the past.

All this is no doubt a gain in human dignity, as the bowers and scrapers, the waiters and flunkeys—not to mention the performers of menial tasks everywhere—escape from work hitherto performed only under the lash of necessity. But that is not an end to it. As a result of this inestimable gain in personal freedom, a fundamental assurance for social viability also vanishes, for the market stimuli that bring about social provisioning are no longer met with obedient responses. One has but to imagine employees in an industry of central importance going on strike, not with the slim backing of unemployment insurance and a small union supplement, as today, but with liquid assets sufficient to maintain them, if need be, for a year or more, to envisage the potential for social disorder inherent in the attainment of a genuinely widespread and substantial affluence.

Yet it is precisely such an affluence that is within clear sight provided that the impetus of science and technology continues to propel the economy for another century. In this impasse there is but one possible solution. *Some authority other than the market must be entrusted with the allocation of men to the essential posts of society should they lack for applicants.*

We have concerned ourselves so far only with the curious two-edged effect of science and technology on the functional aspects of capitalism, both sustaining and hurrying along its growth, and by that very fact pressing it into a more organized social form. Now we must pay heed to a second and perhaps even more critical effect. This is the conquest of the capitalist imagination by science and scientific technology.

I think it is fair to say that capitalism as an *idea* has never garnered much enthusiasm. The acquisitive behavior on which it is perforce based has suffered all through history from the moral ambivalence in which it has been held; all efforts to raise money-making to the level of a positive virtue have failed. The self-interest of the butcher and the baker to whom Adam Smith appealed in lieu of their benevolence may serve as powerful sources of social energy, but not as powerful avatars of social imagination.

By way of contrast, I think it is also fair to say that science and its technical application *is* the burning idea of the 20th century, comparable in its impact on men's minds to the flush of the democratic enthusiasm of the late 18th century or to the political commitment won by communism in the early 20th. The altruism of science, its "purity," the awesome vistas it opens, and the venerable path it has followed, have won from all groups, and especially from the young, exactly that passionate interest and conviction that is so egregiously lacking to capitalism as a way of life.

And it is not only within capitalism that the charismatic powers of science reveal their extraordinary appeal. Within the citadel of economic commitment itself, inside Russia, we hear that science, and science alone, has the capacity to penetrate and to overrule the orthodoxies of Marxist philosophy. A. J. Ayer, after lecturing at the Faculty of Philosophy in Moscow University in 1962 reports: "The prestige of science is so great that it is now becoming a question of (the philosophers) having to adapt their philosophical principles to current scientific theory than the other way round."

It is not alone that science carries a near-religious ethos of conviction and even sacrifice. In Russia as well as in America the new elites arising within the framework of the old society—and as a social order focused on economics, contemporary communism is, like capitalism, an "old" society— owe their ascendancy and their allegiance in large part of science. The scientific cadres proper, the social scientists, the government administrative personnel, even the military, all look to science not merely as the vehicle of their expertise but as the magnetic north of their compass of values. These new elites, as we have indicated, have not as yet divorced their social goals from those of the society to which they are still glad to pay allegiance, and no more than the 13th-century merchants huddled under the walls of a castle do they see themselves as the potential architects and lords of a society built around their own functions. But, as with the merchants, we can expect that such notions will in time emerge and assert their primacy over the aims of the existing order.

What sorts of notions are these apt to be?

One general direction of thought will surely be the primacy of scientific discovery as a central purpose of society, a *raison d'être* for its existence, perhaps even a vehicle for its religious impulses. To partake in the adventure of the scientific mission or its technological realization should accordingly become as dominating a motivation for the future as the wish to participate in economic adventure is at present, and no doubt the distribution of social resources and of privileges will reflect this basic orientation toward scientific exploration and application.

Not less characteristic will be an emphasis on rational solutions to social problems that are today not yet subject to human direction. Not alone economic affairs (which should become of secondary importance), but the numbers and location of the population, its genetic quality, the manner of social domestication of children, the choice of life-work—even the very duration of life itself—are all apt to become subjects for scientific investigation and control. Indeed, the key word of the new society is apt to be *control*.

It is tempting but idle to venture beyond these few suggestions. What manner of life, what institutions, what ideologies may serve the purposes of a society dedicated to the accumulation of scientific knowledge and power we cannot foretell; the variations may well be as great as those observable in societies dedicated to the accumulation of material wealth. Nor does there seem to be much point in attempting to foresee by what precise strategems the elites and ideas of the future may finally assert their claims. Who, for instance, could have foreseen that the long evolution into capitalism would require not merely the diffusion of market relations but the indispensable way station of mercantilism, the "mixed economy" of the 18th century? Or who could have predicted that the nobility of England, traditionally one of the haughtiest in Europe, would learn to protect its social privileges by intermarrying with the despised mercantile families, so that English feudalism could melt imperceptibly into a capitalist aristocracy, whereas in France the nobility would widen the social distance from the bourgeoisie until, as de Tocqueville says, "the two classes were not merely rivals, they were foes"?

Such twists of the historic route warn us that historic projection is rarely, if ever, a matter of simple extrapolation from the present and recent past. Neither routes nor time-tables are laid out in history with an eye to regularity or a concern for Euclidean simplicities. Should there arise radical parties in America, broadly based and aimed at a rational reorganization of economic affairs, the pace of transition would be quicker. Should there not—the perhaps pessimistic premise on which this analysis is based, for I do not believe that such parties are a likely phenomenon if capitalism achieves the degree of change that is within its compass—change will still occur, but more slowly. Veblen was too impatient for his engineers to take over; Schumpeter more realistic when he advised the intelligentsia to be prepared to wait in the wings for possibly a century, a "short run" in affairs of this kind, he said.

So, too, the examples of the past discourage us from attempting to prophesy the manner of demise of the social order to be superseded. The new institutions of social and economic control will appear only slowly and sporadically amid the older forms, and will lack for some time an articulate conception of a purposively constituted and consciously directed social system. The old ideas of the proper primacy of economic aims will linger together with newer ideas of the priority of scientific interests. And no doubt the privileges of the older order will endure side by side with those of the new, just as titles of nobility exist to this very day, some assimilated to the realities of capitalism, some adorning doormen or taxi drivers. It is conceivable that violence may attend the displacement of power and responsibility from one elite to another, but more probably the transfer will be imperceptible; managed as in the case of the English aristocracy, by the sons of the old elite entering the professions of the new.

All these are the merest speculations, difficult to avoid entirely, not to be taken too literally. What is certain is only one thing. It is the profound incompatibility between the new idea of the active use of science within society and the idea of capitalism as a social system.

The conflict does not lie on the surface, in any clash between the immediate needs of science and those of capitalism. It lies in the ideas that ultimately inform both worlds. The world of science, as it is applied by society, is committed to the idea of man as a being who shapes his collective destiny; the world of capitalism to an idea of man as one who permits his common social destination to take care of itself. The essential idea of a society built on scientific engineering is to impose human will on the social universe; that of capitalism to allow the social universe to unfold as if it were beyond human interference.

Before the activist philosophy of science as a social instrument, this inherent social passivity of capitalism becomes archaic and eventually intolerable. The "self-regulating" economy that is its highest social achievement stands condemned by its absence of a directing intelligence, and each small step taken to correct its deficiencies only advertises the inhibitions placed on the potential exercise of purposeful thought and action by its remaining barriers of ideology and privilege. In the end capitalism is weighed in the scale of science and found wanting, not alone as a system but as a philosophy.

That an ascendant science, impatient to substitute reason for blind obedience, inquiry for ideology, represents a great step forward for mankind I do not doubt. Yet it seems necessary to end on a cautionary note. Just as the prescient medievalist might have foreseen in capitalism the possibilities for the deformation of human life as well as for its immense improvement, so the approaching world of scientific predominance has its darker as well as its more luminous side. Needless to say, there lurks a dangerous collectivist tinge in the prospect of controls designed for the enlargement of man but inherently capable of his confinement as well. But beyond that there is, in the vista of a scientific quest grimly pursued for its own sake, a chilling reminder of a world where economic gains are relentlessly pursued for their own sake. Science is a majestic driving force from which to draw social energy and inspiration, but its very impersonality, its "value-free" criteria, may make its tutelary elites as remote and unconcerned as the principles in whose name they govern.

Against these cold and depersonalizing possibilities of a scientifically organized world, humanity will have to struggle in the future, as it has had to contend against not dissimilar excesses of economic involvement in this painful—but also liberating—stage of human development. Thus if the dawn of an age of science opens larger possibilities for mankind than it has enjoyed heretofore, it does not yet promise a society whose overriding aim will be the cultivation and enrichment of all human beings, in all their diversity, complexity, and profundity. That is the struggle for the very distant future, which must be begun, nonetheless, today.

Socialist Economy

ERNEST MANDEL

A long-term view of the economic possibilities of socialism.

The socialization of the major means of production and exchange brings into existence a new mode of production, no longer based on *private appropriation of the social surplus product*. During the period of transition from capitalism to socialism, however, socialization of the means of production is still linked with *private appropriation of the necessary product in the form of wages,* of exchange, of selling of labor-power for a money wage. Furthermore, part of the social surplus product is still appropriated in the form of individual consumer privileges, and under a bureaucratically deformed regime of the transitional society these privileges may assume very considerable dimensions. Private interest thus remains the basic stimulant of individual economic effort. The economy continues to be a money economy.

From the economic standpoint, the contradiction between a mode of production based on collective ownership of the major means of production and collective appropriation of the social surplus product, on the one hand, and on the other, the private interest which continues to operate as chief driving-force of individual economic activity, is a constant source of friction and contradiction under planned economy. But even more important than this economic contradiction is the *social* contradiction that follows from it. "Labor," regarded as the full development of all the potentialities of each individual, and at the same time as conscious service by

From *Marxist Economic Theory, Vol. 2,* by Ernest Mandel, pp. 654–86. Reprinted by permission of Monthly Review Press. Copyright © 1962, 1968 by Ernest Mandel. Translation Copyright © The Merlin Press, London, 1968.

the individual to society, is a concept which in the long run is incompatible with the concept of "labor" as the way of "earning one's living," of ensuring one's means of subsistence, or appropriating, so far as possible, all the goods and services that enable an individual to satisfy his needs.

So long as the economy continues to be fundamentally a money economy, with the satisfaction of the bulk of people's needs depending on the number of currency tokens a person possesses, and so long as, under conditions of relative shortage, rationing by the purse governs distribution, the struggle of all against all to appropriate a bigger proportion of these currency tokens will inevitably persist. So long as the exercise of certain social functions makes it easier to appropriate comparatively scarce goods and services, it is inevitable that the phenomena of careerism, nepotism, corruption, servility towards "superiors" and an autocratic attitude to "inferiors" will remain widespread. The absence of a genuine democracy of producers, consumers and citizens, of strict and untrammeled supervision by them of the activity of administrators and leaders, of the possibility of replacing the latter without coming up against a jointly organized resistance and without having to go beyond legal methods: all these gaps cannot but accentuate the corrupting influence of money in all spheres of social life. The continued existence of money and commodity economy in itself implies the survival of the phenomenon of *universal "mercenariness" of life* which their original appearance give rise to in primitive communities based upon the production of use-values. If, in the economy of the transitional period, access to comfort were institutionalized instead of remaining directly negotiable by means of money, the influence of this "mercenariness" would be indirect rather than direct—which does not mean that it would be any the less. The public discussions which have taken place in the U.S.S.R. about the abuses entailed by the stampede to get university places have told us a great deal on this point.

The authorities and the influential writers who continually declare, in the U.S.S.R. and elsewhere, that it is necessary first and foremost to "create a new outlook," that labor must first become "an individual necessity felt to be such by the individual," before material incentives can be abolished, and the transition made to distribution according to need, reveal a "voluntarist deviation" and reverse a relationship of cause and effect which is nevertheless quite obvious. It is necessary *first* to see the withering away of money economy through the production of an abundance of goods and services, before the psychological and cultural revolution can fully manifest itself, and a new socialist consciousness bloom in place of the egoistic mentality of the "old Adam." In the era of the transitional society, and *afortiori* in the U.S.S.R. or China, it is not "capitalist survivals" that give rise to a desire for individual enrichment, but *the everyday reality of distribution rationed by money.* To hope to create, under these conditions, a "communist consciousness" by means of a "struggle against the survivals from the capitalist past" is to undertake a real labor of Sisyphus.

Before the acquisitive outlook of individuals can disappear as the essential driving force of economic behavior, these individuals must have acquired experience that society has ceased to treat them as Cinderellas and become a generous and understanding mother, automatically satisfying all the basic needs of her children. This experience must have penetrated into the unconscious of individuals, there to encounter the echoes from the primitive-communist past which have never been completely buried by the effects of 7,000 years of exploitation of man by man. This experience must have produced a conscious awareness of the new situation, and, more than that, *new habits and customs,* for the psychological revolution to occur and for the "old Adam" to die and give place to the socialist or communist man of the future.

If Marxists consider that plenty is a necessary condition for the coming of a fully developed socialist society, it is in this sense and for this reason. The new way of life cannot be born otherwise than from the *integration* of a new mode of production and a new mode of distribution. It is not a matter of preaching socialist morality, but of creating the material social and psychological conditions for this morality to be applied by the great majority as a matter of course.

Since the beginning of the monopoly capitalist era and the rise of a powerful labor movement in the advanced industrial countries, individual wages are no longer the *only* way in which individual labor is paid for. Alongside them has appeared the *social dividend or social wage.* This means the totality of the payments which are made to the individual by society, regardless of what the former has or has not given in exchange, as an individual: free elementary (and, later, secondary) education; free school meals; free health services, free hospital care and even free prescriptions; free parks, museums and sports-grounds; free, or almost free, municipal services, such as public lighting; etc.

One must, of course, be clear about the meaning of the expression "free education" or "free health service." The freedom from payment applies only *to the individual; society,* must, of course, "pay" for these services, that is, devote part of its resources (of its total available labor-time) to the satisfaction of these needs. The "social wage" is thus the *socialization of the cost* of satisfying a certain number of needs for all citizens.

This "social wage" foreshadows, at least potentially, the mode of distribution of the future, that is, of an economy directed towards satisfying the needs of all individuals. An economy based on the satisfaction of needs differs from a commodity economy in so far as it satisfies these needs *a priori,* distributing goods and services *regardless of any exactly-measured counter-payment* (exchange) supplied by the individual.

Even in capitalist society, elementary education is free whether or not a child's parents pay their taxes, perform useful work for society, are "good citizens" or are hardened criminals.

But this "social wage" merely *foreshadows* the mode of distribution according to need; it does not offer a true image of it, even in societies which are in transition from capitalism to socialism (except, perhaps, where this transition takes place in the richest countries). It is only the commodity, money *form* of wages that has been given up; the *content,* poor and measured out with miserly care, is still the same.

Since we are still in an economy of semi-shortage, the social services are usually treated like poor relations. The way they are distributed is more akin to *rationing* than to *plenty;* sometimes it is even accompanied by an *obligation* (elementary education, vaccination, etc.). Excessively large classes; "mass-production" medical treatment ("doctoring on the cheap"); neglect of "nonpaying" clients in favor of "paying" ones—these features link the embryonic forms of the "social wage" which much more closely to the commodity society which has given rise to them than to the socialist society whose task will be to open the way to plenty. Only in a few special cases can the infinitely richer, freer and more varied content of the socialization of costs reveal itself; free libraries which offer practically *all* kinds of books which may be asked for (and here it is necessary that room in such libraries be not strictly rationed!); museums and parks, open free of charge, which enable all citizens to enjoy the pleasures formerly reserved to a few narrow strata of rich or highly educated people.

The prodigious development of the productive forces in the era of transition from capitalism to socialism makes it possible to set in motion two processes which radically alter the mode of distribution: on the one hand, the "social wage" must draw closer and closer to its "ideal" norm, that of plenty; on the other, more and more goods and services must pass out of the category of those distributed through exchange (purchase) and into that of goods and services distributed according to need.

The conditions governing this transformation of the mode of distribution are still linked to the requirements of a society based on semi-shortage. Before freeing itself from the heavy, age-old burden of economic calculation, society needs to calculate more exactly and precisely than ever before. The first goods and services to which the new norms of distribution can be applied are thus those

1. which are very homogeneous;
2. for which demand has become inelastic, in relation to a fall in prices and a rise in incomes;

3. which it is hard to use as products or services replacing those
   which are still distributed according to the norms of exchange
   of a commodity economy;
4. or the distribution of which in return for payment in money involves obvious injustices (actually reducing the national income),
   whereas free distribution would considerably enhance social welfare (providing a potential source of increase of the national
   income).

In short, society first socializes the costs of satisfying needs under
conditions such that this socialization does not involve a considerable
increase in these costs. When demand for a product has become inelastic,
however much prices fall or incomes rise, the socialization of the costs of
production of this product entails no extra charge for society as a whole.
This is the position, for instance, with *salt* in every industrially advanced
country, where consumption of it does not vary, in normal times, either
with its price or with people's incomes.

The economic law which governs the withering-away of commodity
economy can be formulated like this: as society gets richer, and as planned
economy ensures a mighty expansion of the productive forces, it acquires
the resources needed to socialize the costs of satisfying an increasing number of needs for all citizens. And as the standard of living of the citizens
rises, the elasticity of demand for more and more goods and services declines to zero, or even becomes negative, in relation to price reductions
and increases in income. In other words, for these two reasons, the advances of planned economy make it possible to transfer more and more
goods and services into the category of those which can be distributed in
accordance with needs.

A number of writers admit that such a *partial* transformation of the
mode of distribution is feasible. But they do this, usually, only in order to
deny at once that it could become universal in its application. Are there
not constantly new needs arising, as fast as the "classical" needs are satisfied? Is it possible to bring *all* products, one after another, into the category of those which are distributed according to need, without at the same
time giving rise to all-round wastage of society's resources, and thus seeing
the reappearance of shortage in new spheres? Do not the products which
satisfy even such basic needs as food, clothing and shelter vary *ad infini-
tum* in diversity and quality? Will not an attempt to do away with exchange and money in these spheres result in a dreary uniformity and lack
of freedom?

Let us take first the question of the alleged variety of needs. Any
moderately serious study of anthropology and history will show, on the
contrary, how remarkably stable they are: food, clothing, shelter (and in

certain climatic conditions, warmth), protection against wild animals and the inclemency of the seasons, the desire to decorate, the desire to exercise the body's muscles, the satisfaction of sexual needs, the maintenance of the species—there are half a dozen basic needs which do not seem to have changed since the beginning of *homo sapiens,* and which still account for the bulk of consumer expenditure.

To these we may add needs for hygiene and health-care (simple expressions of the instinct of self-preservation at a certain level of consciousness) and needs to enrich one's leisure (simple extensions of the needs to decorate, to exercise one's muscles, and to increase one's knowledge, which are as old as the human race), and we have almost exhausted the list of consumer expenses even in the richest countries of the world, on the basis of a small number of basic needs which are anthropological characteristics to a much greater extent than products of special historical conditions.

Since these needs have remained basically unchanged since the appearance of man on earth, and since even the richest classes of past ages have not extended their consumer expenditure beyond this remarkably short list of satisfactions, there is no reason to suppose that the coming of a socialist society, of abundance of products, and of individual and social consciousness at a much more mature level than ever before, will give rise to any revolutions in this sphere. Nowhere does the law of "diminishing returns" apply more than in regard to the intensity of needs. Thus the first objection is disposed of.

Let us now look at the apparently infinite variety of means to satisfy these few basic needs. There is, first, the problem of the *quantity* of the products required to meet these needs. On this point, history has already provided an answer, on the part of the possessing classes of our era. Between the stout country squire of the early 19th century stuffing himself with roast beef and swilling port wine, or the big bourgeois of the "Belle Epoque" with his 20-course dinners, on the one hand, and, on the other, the rich capitalist of today, slim, devoted to sport, and constantly watching his weight, the change is undeniable. With the increase in income, *the increasing consumption of food has given way to a more rational kind of consumption;* the criterion of health has superseded that of blind or showy self-indulgence. This change does not so much reflect and ethical progress as it reflects the demands of self-preservation, the self-interest of the individual himself.

The same applies where dress is concerned. True, in this sphere, especially among women, the amount of clothing "consumable" without damage to health and the possibilities of waste (clothes worn only once or twice) are much greater than in the sphere of food. Nevertheless, if the restraints of health do not apply here, those of *comfort* and *taste* soon come into play. Without the help of lackeys and servants it is not very comfortable to change one's clothes too often or even to possess too many. Indeed, though excesses in this sphere are constantly committed by the "new rich," several sociologists have observed that in the richest families of Britain and the United States a real reversal of this trend has occurred; clothes which are worn but comfortable, or simply clothes one likes, are preferred to clothes glowing with freshness or which are continually being replaced. Others even speak of a stylistic evolution in clothing, which they describe like this: "first, a steady trend toward uniformity, with the clothing worn by people of moderate income coming to approximate the appearance and materials of the clothing worn by people of high income; second, a decline in the number of frills, reflecting a movement in the direction of greater simplicity; third, and most recent, an 'accent on youth.'

The same situation exists in respect of housing and furnishing. When domestic servants and even housekeepers have vanished—and the new level of wages, together with social disapproval, will certainly make them vanish in the transitional society between capitalism and socialism!—there is a limit to the number of rooms one can *wish* to have (and can get) for one's accommodation, a limit dictated precisely by individual comfort. Already, today, except for a handful of millionaires, the luxury flat is preferred by most bourgeois to the 19th-century country house. Sweeping away the old-time rooms crowded with furniture and knick-knacks, the evolution of comfort and taste has dictated a mode of furnishing the sobriety and functional nature of which set a relatively narrow limit to quantitative accumulation. This tendency even goes so far as to impose a voluntary restriction on the number of gadgets.

There is no reason to suppose that these tendencies, which are already manifest in the last phase of capitalist society, *despite* a striking degree of social inequality and unlimited chances for waste on the part of the possessing classes, will be reversed in the era of transition from capitalism to socialism, or in socialist society itself. On the contrary, it is infinitely more probable that *rational consumption* will develop further, at the expense of consumption inspired by mere caprice, desire to show off, and lack of taste or sense of proportion, forms of consumption which, in capitalist society, are not so much "innate in the consumer" as dictated and conditioned by the general social climate and the efforts of advertisers.

It remains to consider the problem of the diversity and quality of products which, instead of their quantity, delay the coming of the times when demand for them becomes inelastic both to price changes and to income changes. The phenomena of diversity and quality are nowadays dictated by fashion, by the compartmentalizing of society, and by technical progress ("new products"). All these phenomena are, in the last analysis, *independent* of individual whims; even in capitalist society they are *social phenomena,* guided if not consciously determined by social forces.

Fashion is a typically social phenomenon, with the impetus coming from the side of the producers (the designers), not from that of the consumers. It is a few important *couturiers* in Paris who "make" fashion, not the "public." Already today, for the huge majority of consumers, the range of variety is remarkably *narrow*, and not at all limitless. At any given moment there are not an infinite number of styles "coexisting," but only a few. Even in the *haute couture* of our time, based on craft methods and the individual client, there are not "thousands" of different models; the number is more limited than is supposed. And alongside these specially-made models, intended for a few rich women, there is a small range of models which are mass-produced and intended for the masses. A socialist economy would probably be able to *expand* much more widely this range of varieties at present available, rather than have to restrict it, so as to be able to go over to distribution according to need. To do this it would rely on the law of large numbers, on the permanence of physical requirements, on the educative effect of "socialist advertising," on public opinion polls, on public competitions and other techniques which would make it possible really to proceed from the tastes and wishes of consumers in order to determine the variety of goods produced. For this reason we cannot go along with Oskar Lange and H. D. Dickinson when they propose to retain commodity economy in a socialist economy so far as all high-quality products are concerned.

As for new products, their mass production and their "launching" on the market, that is, their large-scale distribution among consumers, is already determined by the firms which produce them and not by the whims of the consumers. It is thus well and truly "planned"—but planned by a handful of capitalist firms, in accordance with criteria of private profit alone, and not in accordance with the objective and rational needs of the community and of the individuals composing it. How indeed can one talk of the consumer's "urgent need" for products which he does not know exist, "urgent needs" which do not reveal themselves until, as though by chance, the producer launches his new product on to the market?

A socialist society would of course not hand over this planning to the "masters" of production and of promotion. It would avoid duplication of work and obvious waste. But it would take into account much more fully than is done today the real wishes of consumers, through the use of all available techniques of sampling opinion, direct questioning and meetings of citizens. It would extend the range of choice much further than today. And as in the sphere of consumer durables the measurement of needs is much easier and more precise, and waste can be easily checked, it is also much easier to determine the quantity of products needed to be accumulated in store in order to produce inelasticity of demand in relation to prices and incomes.

A certain margin of uncertainty may, of course, continue to exist. It will long, if not always, remain possible that there will be a conflict between the socialization of certain household tasks and their carrying out on an individual basis with the help of improved mechanical means. The washing-machine and the dish-washing-machine will go on being sought for, even when a very extensive and convenient network of restaurants and laundries has put high-quality services, free, at the disposal of all citizens. A socialist society will never *dictate* to its members the obligatory use of communal services by refusing to make available to them the means of securing these same services on an individual basis. Because such a society will aim to satisfy *all* the rational needs of man, it will respect the need for periodical isolation and solitude, which is the dialectical and permanent corollary of man's social nature. Similarly, while the individual motor-car is obviously irrational as a means of transport in towns, it remains by far the most flexible means of transport for leisure trips over a short or medium distance, and even when travel by air, rail and bus are free, men will go on wanting a private motor-car in order to follow their own itineraries, stopping where trains and buses do not stop, or merely in order to be alone. A socialist society will respect these wishes and, far from condemning them as "petty-bourgeois survivals" will endeavor to meet these needs, the rational nature of which will be obvious to anyone of good faith.

There is thus no substantial obstacle to the progressive universalization of the new mode of distribution, according to need, without any counterpart in the form of an exactly measured amount of labor being required. On the contrary, present-day evolution, though distorted by all the consequences of a social setting dominated by money, exploitation, inequality and the desire to "succeed" at the expense of one's neighbor, already clearly shows the main lines of the future evolution of consumption. Consumption on a basis of plenty and freedom, far from developing without any limit towards irrational caprice and waste, will increasingly assume the form of *rational consumption.* The requirements of *physical health and mental and nervous equilibrium* will more and more take precedence over the other motives of human behavior. They will logically be the chief concerns of men whose basic needs have been met. Arrival at this conclusion requires no "idealization" of man. As we see from the example of food-consumption by the capitalists of today, this corresponds to the very nature of the vertical animal, to his most obvious physical interests.

While the "social wage" affects only a very small part of total consumption, its profound psychological and social implications remain limited or even quite hidden. The social climate of capitalism corrupts everything it touches, even those buds of the future society which are slowly opening within it.

But when the "social wage" extends to the bulk of individual consumption its economic, social and psychological implications are sharply manifest. Until then, economic growth, the rise in the standard of living, always implied an *extension of money and commodity economy,* in the era

of transition from capitalism to socialism as in earlier periods. Now, however, they imply, on the contrary, a more and more marked *shrinkage* of
measured exchanges and of the use of money.

This happens in the first place, for obvious economic reasons. If an
increasing proportion of needs are satisfied without expenditure of money
by the consumers, this expenditure must relate to an increasingly restricted
sphere of economic life. And if *increasing* money income is spent on acquiring a steadily *decreasing* number of commodities and services, then useless
tensions are caused. There would have to be either a frantic increase in
prices in this sector, or else the artificial stimulation of a continual emergence of "new" products, and the appearance of "new needs," or else the
soaking-up of an increasing proportion of this money income by means
of taxation. The circulation of money would appear as more and more
futile and pointless. In practice, the producers would receive ever-higher
"wages," an increasing proportion of which would, however, be kept back
at source, the remainder being spent on more and more casual and minor
requirements. Money would thus in any case be excluded from the essential economic circuits, concerned with meeting basic and ordinary needs,
and driven into the periphery of economic life (conspicuous consumption,
gambling, forms of expenditure which socialist society would increasingly
subject to more disapproval and penal taxation).

The most logical solution would be to *reduce*, and not increase, the
amount of individual money wages and salaries, to reduce the circulation
of money, in proportion as the new mode of distribution according to need
spread and became general. "Individual wages" would become increasingly a small supplementary bonus to ensure the distribution of the last
"scarce" goods and services, the last vestiges of "status" inherited from
the age of social inequality. It would increasingly lose its function of
preserving the consumer's freedom of choice, from the moment when
plenty embraced an increasing range of goods and services. "Choice" will
be restricted to spending one's time in shifting from one point of distribution to another, dividing one's time between one form of consumption and
another, instead of substituting one form of expenditure for another. Commodity economy, money economy, the economy of semi-shortage, will
have begun to wither away.

It is not only the logic of the new mode of production that will bring
about this withering away of commodity production. *Automation* entails
the same logical necessity in the sphere of production. The production of
an abundance of goods and services is in fact accompanied by the more
and more rapid elimination of all living, direct, human labor from the production process, and even from the distribution process (automatic power
stations; goods trains driven by remote control; self-service distribution
centers; automatic vending machines; mechanized and automatized offices,
etc.). But the elimination of living human labor from production means the

elimination of wages from the cost of production! The latter is increasingly reduced to the "costs" of operations between enterprises (purchase of raw materials and depreciation of fixed plant). Once these enterprises have been socialized, this involves much less transfers of real money than simply accounting in monetary units.

As services will continue nonautomatized for a longer period than goods, money economy will retreat more and more into the spheres of exchange of services for services, purchase of services by consumers, and purchase of services by the public sector. But in proportion as the principal services become automatized in their turn (e.g., public services, automatic machines for providing drinks and standardized articles of current use, laundries, etc.), money economy will become restricted more and more to "personal services" only, the most important of which (medicine and education) will, however, be the first to undergo a radical abolition of money relations for reasons of social priority. In the end, automation will leave to money economy only the periphery of social life: domestic servants and valets, gambling, prostitution, etc. But in a socialist society which ensures a very high standard of living and security to all its citizens, and an all-round revaluation of "labor," which will increasingly become intellectual labor, creative labor, who will want to undertake such forms of work? Socialist automation thus brings commodity economy to the brink of absurdity and will cause it to wither away.

This withering-away, begun in the sphere of distribution, will spread gradually into the sphere of production. Already in the era of transition from capitalism to socialism, socialization of the major means of production and planning imply a more and more general substitution of money of account for fiduciary money in the circulation of means of production.

So far we have considered only the economic consequences of the new mode of production, the withering-away of commodity economy and of money to which it will lead. We must now consider the social and psychological results, that is, the complete upheaval in relations between men, between individuals and society, as these have developed out of thousands of years of social experience derived from antagonism between classes of exploitation of man by man.

Free distribution of bread, milk and all other basic foodstuffs will bring about a psychological revolution without precedent in the history of mankind. Every human being will henceforth be ensured his subsistence and that of his children, merely by virtue of being a member of human society. For the first time since man's appearance on earth, *the insecurity and instability of material existence will vanish,* and along with it the *fear* and frustration that this insecurity causes in all individuals, including, indirectly, those who belong to the ruling classes.

It is this uncertainty about the morrow, this need to "assert oneself" in order to ensure one's survival in a frenzied struggle of all against all, that is at the basis of egoism and the desire for individual enrichment, ever since the beginning of capitalist society and even, to a certain extent, since the development of commodity economy. All the material and moral conditions for the withering away of egoism as a driving force in economic conduct will have vanished. True, individual ownership of consumer goods will doubtless expand to an unheard-of degree. But in face of the abundance of these goods, and the freedom of access to them, the *attachment* of men to ownership will likewise wither away. It is the adaptation of man to these new conditions of life that will create the basis for the "new man," socialist man, for whom human solidarity and cooperation will be as "natural" as is today the effort to succeed individually, at the expense of others. The brotherhood of man will cease to be a pious hope or a hypocritical slogan, to become a natural and everyday reality, upon which all social relations will increasingly be based.

Will an evolution along these lines be "contrary to human nature"? This is the argument invoked as a last resort against Marxism, against the prospect of a classless society. It is regularly put forward by those who do not know this human nature, who base themselves on crude prejudices or suspicions in order to identify morals and customs *derived from a certain socioeconomic context* with biological or anthropological characteristics alleged to be "unchangeable" in man. It is also invoked by those who endeavor to preserve at all costs a conception of man which is based on the idea of original sin and the impossibility of "redemption" on this earth.

But anthropology starts from the idea that that which is distinctive of man is precisely his *capacity for adaptation,* his capacity to create a second nature in the culture which forms the only framework in which he can live, as Professor A. Gehlen puts it.

These practically unlimited possibilities of adaptation and apprenticeship are the essential anthropological feature. Human "nature" is what precisely enables man continually to rise above what is merely biological, to continually surpass himself.

The tendency to competition, to the struggle of all against all, to the assertion of the individual by crushing other individuals, is not at all something innate in man; it is itself the product of an "acculturization," of an inheritance which is not biological but social, the product of particular social conditions. Competition is a tendency which is not "innate" but socially acquired. Similarly, cooperation and solidarity can be systematically acquired and transmitted as a social heritage, as soon as the social milieu has been radically changed in this direction.

More than that—a disposition to cooperation, to solidarity, to love of one's neighbor corresponds far better to specific biological needs and basic anthropological features than a tendency to competition, conflict or oppression of others.

The withering away of commodity and money economy is, however, only one of the factors bringing about the disappearance of social inequality, classes and the state. The other factor is the considerable extension and creative use of leisure.

The ruling class or stratum of society has always possessed the privilege of leisure. This is the section which, freed from the burden of having to work for its living, from the burden of physically exhausting labor, from mechanical work, has been able to devote itself more or less completely to the accumulation of knowledge and the management of the economy and of society. The extension of such leisure will make it possible for an increasing number of citizens to undertake and carry out these functions. This is the *technical* means to ensuring the progressive withering away of the state.

For nearly a century now the shortening of the working day has been a tremendous civilizing factor, as Karl Marx pointed out when the ten-hour day was introduced. It has provided the basis for everything worthwhile in present-day bourgeois democracy. Nevertheless, it is a contradictory phenomenon. The advantages gained by shortening the working day are largely offset by the lengthening of working life, the lengthening of the time spent in traveling to and from work, the intensification of physical effort (first for manual workers, then later, to an increasing extent, for office workers), and by the commercialization of leisure.

Furthermore, the big step forward essentially remains the change from the ten- or twelve-hour day to the eight-hour day. The latter became general in modern-type industry in the advanced capitalist countries around 1920. Since then, there has been only a relatively slight shortening in the manual worker's working day, the forty-hour week existing only in a few countries, where, moreover, it is accompanied by the five-day week, the week of 45, 44 or 42 hours spread over five days implying even a lengthening of the working day.

We must take into account the considerably intensified pace of work since 1918, the nervous tension involved in operating equipment which is increasingly expensive and often dangerous, the often even greater tension experienced on the way to work, especially if the journey is made by mechanical transport, and also air pollution and insufficiently sound-proofed housing, if we are to draw up *a comprehensive balance-sheet of the physical, mental and nervous fatigue* suffered by the worker of today, as compared with that of the worker of 50 years ago. Much evidence from doctors confirms that this fatigue is greater than it was, in spite of free weekends and two or three weeks' annual holiday.

What follows from this is that a large part of "free time" is not "leisure time" at all but "time spent in getting rid of physical and nervous fatigue." The effect of holidays is largely neutralized because the worker takes his holiday when his organism is in such a state of fatigue that he is at first incapable of real, normal relaxation.

The commercialization of leisure is adapted to this condition of things. It starts from a recognition that after an ordinary working day the average contemporary proletarian is incapable of an intellectual or physical effort. But on the pretext of providing him with "relaxation" or "diversion," commercialized leisure causes either an atrophy of critical capacity or a morbid and lasting excitement which ends by degrading and disintegrating his personality to some degree. All the condemnations of "leisure civilization" nevertheless avoid the question: the ultimate cause of the degradation of leisure lies in the degradation of *work* and of *society*.

What is needed therefore, is a new and radical shortening of the time spent at work, in order to bring about the essential aim of socialism, which is that of the *self-management of producers and citizens.* Taking into account the present intensity of productive effort, the threshold at which the producer becomes materially capable of concerning himself currently, "habitually," with the management of the enterprise where he works, and with the state, is, apparently, *the half-day of work,* or a week of 20 or 24 hours, depending on whether working hours are fixed at five or at six hours a day. At the present rate of progress in productivity (an average of 5 percent per year in the highly-industrialized countries), within the framework of a rationally planned economy freed from all military or parasitic burdens, and consciously directly towards the priority purpose of saving human labor, this objective could be attained before the end of the 20th century. Even within the framework of capitalism, in the United States, the average length of the working week has fallen from 70 hours in 1850 and 60 in 1900 to 44 in 1940, 40 in 1950 and 37.5 in 1960, or a reduction of nearly 40 percent in half a century, nearly four hours per decade. On the basis of this same rate of decline the 24-hour week could be attained around 1990 to 2000 in a socialist society. The American economist George Soule comes to the same conclusion without leaving the framework of capitalist society—but without realizing all the contradictions implicit in such a forecast.

A more rapid reduction in the working day would undoubtedly be possible in a fully developed socialist society, but it would be held back by the raising of the school-leaving age (advancing from universal compulsory secondary education to universal compulsory higher education), and also by the lowering of the age of retirement. These changes would mean a more rational reduction in working hours *per human life* than a more rapid reduction in the working day—while productive life would continue to extend from 16 to 65.

A thoroughgoing reduction in the time spent at work would set the problem of leisure in an entirely different social context. Ultimately, of course, the "useful employment of leisure" is closely linked with the problem of *socializing the cost* of satisfying human needs, with the new mode of distribution. It is infinitely "cheaper" to satisfy the needs of 20 million workers with standardized television programs made up of mass-produced films, or newspapers published in millions of copies, than to satisfy them with high-quality theatrical performances, a wide variety of books or the means of *producing* culture instead of merely *consuming* it. It costs much less to make a film for a million spectators than to enable a million amateurs to make their own films. Galbraith attributes the increase in juvenile delinquency amid affluence to the inadequacy of public expenditure as compared with the excessive amount of private consumption of commercialized leisure. But with the raising of citizens' standards of living, and the general development of social wealth, the useful employment of leisure will become increasingly a transformation of the citizen from being a passive object to being a conscious creative participant in a variety of cultural activities (sport, art, science, literature, technique, education, exploration, etc.). At the same time, participation in the management of the economy and the leadership of social life, which today involves only a tiny fraction of the leisure of the workers as a whole (except in the case of the active members of the workers' organizations), will become more and more important as a way of using "free time." It also will tend to become active and creative rather than passive, as at present ("attendance at meetings" through a feeling of duty, of obligation to others, because one must, or out of personal interest which is often of a very dubious kind).

It is often objected that the workers "do not want to manage their enterprises." Usually, this refers either to attempts at "joint management" within a capitalist economy or to certain "marginal" experiments in the Eastern countries, that is, in both cases, to enterprises whose real fate is felt by the workers concerned to be settled elsewhere, and in socioeconomic context in which exhaustion and alienation on the part of the labor-force have not been reduced. If the worker declines to lose his precious hours of rest attending meetings on which *nothing decisive for his own fate* depends, that should not surprise us. It has been enough, however, in Yugoslavia, for the experience of self-management of enterprises to give the workers concerned the feeling that their activity in the sphere of management has a real and positive, effective influence on their standard of life, for an increasing proportion of the working masses to participate actively in the work of the workers' councils. The latter now control nearly a third of the financial resources of the enterprises.

Automation makes a big contribution to this process. It logically implies a tendency towards the elimination of the laborer, or even the skilled worker, from the production process. It tends to increase the labor-force employed before and after actual production (research and investigation work, administration and distribution), but to the extent that it takes place in a socialized, or already socialist, economy, *it does away with unskilled manual labor, reproducing only more and more highly skilled and "intellectual" labor.* It thus appears as the great force working to abolish the difference between manual work and mental work, leaving only the latter in existence.

The industrialization of agriculture, which has already gone very far in the United States and which is spreading in Western Europe, will be the last tendency of economic evolution connected with the withering-away of classes and of the state. It will cut down to a minimum the number of "countryfolk" engaged in "farm and field" work, and those who remain will be transformed more and more into agronomists, geotechnicians, and engineers in charge of automatic or semi-automatic agricultural machinery. The break-up of the big cities into homogeneous "new towns," each one self-sufficient, will do away with even the outward signs of the difference between "town" and "country" and create integrated areas embracing greenery, cultivation, housing, recreation and social life, and zones of industrial production.

Radical reduction in the size of these areas will make it possible to abolish to an ever-increasing extent those *delegations of power* which continue to predominate in the first phases of the withering away of classes and the state. They will replace self-management by citizens on a rota basis, in ad hoc social organizations, by self-management of *free communes of producers and consumers*, in which everybody will take it in turn to carry out administrative work, in which the difference between "directors" and "directed" will be abolished, and a federation of which will eventually cover the whole world.

Is this a Utopia? What is essential is to see that these possibilities are all contained in an advance of productivity made the most of by an economic system based partly on the socialization of the means of production and the creation of plenty in goods and services, and partly on the replacement of commodity economy by a mode of distribution which eliminates money and the desire for personal enrichment from the life of mankind.

Will the productive forces go on increasing indefinitely in a socialist society? It will be for the citizens of socialist society alone to answer this question, that is, it will really be a matter of free choice for them, and not of any "economic necessity." Under capitalism, and even in the transition period from capitalism to socialism, the idea of exercising "preference" as between the "marginal utility of net investment" and the "marginal utility of increased leisure" is basically absurd. Current consumption by producers, even when it is increasing, always falls short of felt needs; the length of the working day, even when it is being cut down, continues to be limited only by the state of physical and nervous fatigue beyond which output falls precipitously.

As against this, in a socialist society which ensures plenty in goods and services to its citizens, the possibility of a genuine choice between increased wealth and increased leisure will be given for the first time. This will be a real choice, in the sense that it will no longer depend on an economic need to meet pressing needs. The only economic demands which still exist will be that of renewing the stock of machinery (gross investment, depreciation) and that of ensuring an increase in the social product corresponding to the increase in population. As, however, it is to be hoped that socialist mankind will plan its population increase just as it will plan the economy, freedom of choice for the citizens will remain unimpaired.

In any case, economic growth is not an end in itself. The aim is to satisfy the needs of society, of the consumers, within the framework of optimum rational development of all human potentialities. Just as the *optimum* of consumption does not at all imply unlimited increase, the satisfaction of human needs does not in itself imply a continuous and unlimited expansion of the productive forces. When society possesses a stock of automatic machinery which is adequate to cover all current needs, including a reserve of multi-purpose machine-tools sufficient to cope with any emergency, it is probable that "economic growth" will be slowed down or even halted for a time. A man who is completely free from all material and economic worries will have been born; political economy will have had its day, because economic calculation will be finished. The question of "profitability" or of "economy of labor-time" will have vanished as a criterion of wealth, and will be replaced by the mere criterion of leisure and its best use, as Marx foresaw in a prophecy of genius:

> The theft of other people's labor, which is the basis of present-day wealth, is a wretched basis when compared with this new basis of wealth created by large-scale industry itself. As soon as labor in its direct form ceases to be the principal source of wealth, labor-time ceases, and must cease to be the measure of wealth, and therefore exchange-value must cease to be the measure of use-value. The surplus labor of the masses ceases to be the condition for the development of general wealth, just as the leisure of a minority ceases to be the condition for the development of the general capacities of the human mind. Thus there collapses production based on exchange-value, and the immediate process of material production loses its sordid and contradictory form. The free development of individuals, not the shortening of necessary labor-time in order to create surplus labor [becomes the aim of production]; it is thus now a matter of reducing to the minimum the necessary labor of all society, so as to make possible the artistic, scientific, etc. education of individuals through the leisure and resources thus created . . .
>
> . . . If the working masses themselves appropriate their surplus labor

—and if the disposable time thereby ceases to have a contradictory existence—necessary labor time will be limited by the needs of the social individual, and the development of society's productive forces will, on the other hand, increase so rapidly that the leisure of all will increase despite the fact that production will be directed towards increasing the wealth of all. For real wealth is the developed productive power of all the individuals. Thus it will no longer be labor-time that will be the standard of wealth, but leisure."[1]

Or, more precisely: the criterion of wealth will become men's free, rational, creative use of free time, directed towards their own development as complete and harmonious personalities.

But will this creative human activity, integrating theory and practice, leaving all mechanical and routine work to machines, passing from research to production and from the painter's studio to the site where a new town is being built amid the words—will it still be "labor"? This basic category of Maxist sociology and economics must in its turn be subjected to a critical analysis.

Labor is the fundamental characteristic of man. It is through labor that the human race appropriates its necessary means of life; it is labor which is at once the primary reason for, the product of and the cement of social relationships. Man does not become a social being in the anthropological sense of the word, does not acquire his normal physiological equipment, without a phase of "active socialization" which extends from his birth until puberty, if not until his physical and intellectual maturity.

But when the *need* to work in order to produce the means of life has gone, because machines by themselves carry out this work, what remains of labor as man's fundamental characteristic? Anthropology defines the concept of labor. What is, in fact, characteristic of man is *praxis*, action: "Man is a creature so constituted physically that he can survive only by acting."

Labor in the historical sense of the word, labor as it has been practiced up to now by suffering and miserable mankind, condemned to earn their bread in the sweat of their brows, is only the most wretched, the most "inhuman," the most "animal" form of human *praxis*. Just as for Frederick Engels the entire history of class-divided humanity is only the prehistory of mankind, so labor in its traditional form is only the prehistoric form of *creative, all-sided human praxis, which no longer produces things but harmoniously developed human personalities.* After the withering away of the commodity, of value, money, classes, the state and the social division of labor, fully developed socialist society will bring about the *withering away of labor* in the traditional sense of the word.

[1]K. Marx, *Grundrisse . . .* , Vol. 1, pp. 593, 6.

The final purpose of socialism cannot be the humanization of labor, any more than it can be the improvement of wages or of the wage relationship; there are only transitional stages, expedients and palliatives. A modern factory will never constitute a "normal" or "human" setting for human life, no matter how much the working day is shortened or the place and its machinery are adapted to man's needs. The process of the humanization of man will not be completed until labor has withered away and given place to creative *praxis* which is solely directed to the creation of human beings of all-round development.

For a long time, *homo faber*, man as producer of the instruments of labor, has been put before us as the real creator of civilization and of human culture. Recently, writers have tried to show that science, and even philosophy itself, has emerged progressively from productive labor in the strict sense, constantly nourishing itself from practice. The Dutch historian Huizinga has, however, sharply opposed this tradition, with his contrary conception, of *homo ludens*, "man at play," as the real creator of culture.

Marxism, brilliantly confirmed by all present-day anthropology, and to a large extent even by Freudian psychology, enables us to integrate these two currents of thought, each of which reflects a fundamental aspect of human history. At the start, man was both *faber* and *ludens*. Scientific and artistic techniques progressively separated off from production techniques; but, with their specialization, a social division of labor became indispensable for an initial phase of further progress. *Homo faber*, banished to outer darkness, has neither the resources nor the leisure for play, free creation, the spontaneous and disinterested exercise of his faculties, which is the specific aspect of human *praxis*. *Homo Ludens* has become, more and more, man of the privileged classes, that is, of the possessing classes and those dependent on them.

But thereby he has in turn suffered a special kind of alienation: his play becomes increasing *sad play*, and continues so even during the great centuries of social optimism (for instance, the 16th and 19th centuries). Freed from the constraint of routine work, reintegrated in the collective community, socialist man will once again become both *faber* and *ludens*, increasingly *ludens* and at the same time *faber*. Already today, attempts are being made to introduce more and more "play" into certain forms of work, and more and more "serious work" into play. The abolition of labor in the traditional sense of the word implies at the same time a new flowering of the chief productive force, the creative energy of man himself. Material disinterestedness is crowned by the creative spontaneity which brings together in the same eternal youth the playfulness of children, the enthusiasm of the artist, and the *eureka* of the scientist.

For the bourgeoisie, property means freedom. In an "atomized" society of commodity owners, this definition is broadly true; only a sufficient amount of property releases a man from the slavery of selling his labor-power to get the means of existence, from this condemnation to forced labor. This is why bourgeois philanthropists, no less than demagogues, ceaselessly call for the impossible "deproletarisation" of the proletariat through the "diffusion of property."

Vulgar Marxists have taken out of its context a famous phrase of Hegel's, quoted by Engels, according to which freedom is merely "the recognition of necessity." They interpret it in the sense that socialist man will be the subject to the same "iron economic laws" as capitalist man with the sole difference that, having become conscious of these laws, he will endeavor to "use them to his advantage."

This positivist variant of Marxism has nothing in common with the real humanist tradition of Marxist and Engels, with the boldness of their analysis and the profoundity of their vision of the future. Marx and Engels both repeated more than once that the realm of freedom begins *where necessity ends.* Even in a socialist society, factory work would continue to be a *sad necessity*, which was felt as such; it is in one's leisure hours that real freedom unfolds itself. The more that labor in the traditional sense of the word withers away, the more it is replaced by a creative *praxis* of all-round-developed and socially integrated personalities. The more man frees himself from his needs by satisfying them, the more does "the realm of necessity give place to the realm of freedom."

Human freedom is not a "freely accepted" constraint, nor is it a mass of instinctive and disorderly activities such as would degrade the individual. It is a self-realization of man which is an eternal becoming and an eternal surpassing, a continual enrichment of everything human, an all-round development of all facets of humanity. It is neither absolute rest nor "perfect happiness," but, after thousands of years of conflicts unworthy of man, the beginning of the real "human drama." It is a hymn sung to the glory of man by men aware of their limitations who draw from this awareness the courage to overcome them. To the man of today it seems impossible to be both doctor and architect, machine-builder and atom-smasher. But who can speak of limitations that man will *never* be able to break through, man who is stretching out his arms towards the stars, who is on the brink of producing life in test-tubes, and who tomorrow will embrace the entire family of mankind in a spirit of universal brotherhood?